MW01278165

DEMARGINALIZING VOICES

DEMARGINALIZING

Commitment, Emotion, and Action in Qualitative Research

VOICES

Edited by Jennifer M. Kilty,
Maritza Felices-Luna, and Sheryl C. Fabian

UBCPress · Vancouver · Toronto

22 21 20 19 18 17 16 15 14   5 4 3 2 1

Printed in Canada on FSC-certified ancient-forest-free paper (100% post-consumer recycled) that is processed chlorine- and acid-free.

Library and Archives Canada Cataloguing in Publication

Demarginalizing voices : commitment, emotion, and action in qualitative research / edited by Jennifer M. Kilty, Maritza Felices-Luna, and Sheryl C. Fabian.

Includes bibliographical references and index.
Issued in print and electronic formats.
ISBN 978-0-7748-2796-6 (bound). – ISBN 978-0-7748-2798-0 (pdf). – ISBN 978-0-7748-2799-7 (epub)

1. Marginality, Social – Research – Methodology. 2. Qualitative research – Methodology. 3. Social sciences – Research – Methodology. 4. Social groups – Research – Methodology. I. Kilty, Jennifer M., 1978-, author, editor II. Felices-Luna, Maritza, 1975-, author, editor III. Fabian, Sheryl C., 1962-, author, editor

| HM1136.D44 2014 | 305.5'6072 | C2014-904553-0 |
| | | C2014-904554-9 |

Canadä

UBC Press gratefully acknowledges the financial support for our publishing program of the Government of Canada (through the Canada Book Fund), the Canada Council for the Arts, and the British Columbia Arts Council.

This book has been published with the help of a grant from the Canadian Federation for the Humanities and Social Sciences, through the Awards to Scholarly Publications Program, using funds provided by the Social Sciences and Humanities Research Council of Canada.

UBC Press
The University of British Columbia
2029 West Mall
Vancouver, BC V6T 1Z2
www.ubcpress.ca

Contents

Acknowledgments

EDITING A BOOK ENTAILS embarking upon a tremendous and lengthy journey. It has been an incredible experience that would not have been possible without the patience and collaboration of the contributing authors who agreed to partake in this adventure with us. We are incredibly grateful to the authors for their honesty and candour in a process that required that they turn the research eye upon themselves to examine their own practices, emotions, and experiences in doing critical social research. It is certainly not an easy task to expose your work, your personal experiences and, at times, your identities in such a public way, especially given the likelihood of critique in academia. Thank you for your careful reflection and thoughtful consideration of our comments and suggestions, particularly those offered by the anonymous reviewers.

Evaluating scholarly works is a difficult, time-consuming, and oftentimes thankless job. That said, we would like to express our immense gratitude to the two reviewers, those anonymous scholars who took the time to read the full manuscript twice, offering thorough and insightful comments and engaging with the authors and the texts in order to stimulate discussion and debate. Their careful review of the manuscript greatly enhanced the quality of the book, and we thank them for their steadfast support of its publication.

We would also like to thank the team at UBC Press for their hard work. To the editorial board, thank you for ensuring that critical academic work, particularly that which deals with research methods, continues to be published, especially in light of the unfavourable conditions the book industry is currently facing. To the production department, thank you for your careful review and assemblage of the manuscript. Extra special thanks to Randy

Schmidt: thank you for your encouragement, valuable advice, accessibility, and for the incredible diligence you have shown in helping to see this book through to publication.

Finally, we would like to express our collective thanks to our families. To Matthieu, Sandy and Lorenzo, and Dave and Rebecca: you have provided us with unwavering love and emotional support throughout this process, enabling us to continue working through those moments when we were exhausted or discouraged. We could not have done this without you.

DEMARGINALIZING VOICES

Introduction

Jennifer M. Kilty, Maritza Felices-Luna, and Sheryl C. Fabian

CONTEMPORARY SOCIAL SCIENCE research continues to be shaped by awareness of the ethically questionable and deceptive medical and psychological
research that characterized the postwar world. Several examples come to mind,
including, of course, Nazi experimentation, Milgram's classic obedience study,
the Stanford Prison experiment, and Laud Humphreys's tearoom trade study.[1]
At the same time that universities began to develop research ethics review
boards as a way to avoid ethical quagmires in research practice, the new welfare era was also being marked by significant social and political shifts that
emerged as a result of a number of progressive social movements, including
the movements for women's and civil rights, environmental/green concerns,
labour rights, and human rights and social justice. Meshing well with new
ethical concerns for participant-informed consent and well-being, the radical
politics behind these movements helped to shape a more flexible and dynamic research environment, one in which scholars could consider the intersecting roles and influences of their own voices as well as those of their
research subjects or participants on both research methods and findings.
Consequently, since the 1960s, researchers in the humanities and social sciences have consistently brought to the fore concerns about how we conduct
research and the underlying suppositions (usually unconscious) and consequences (usually unintended) of the knowledge produced by it. These researchers continue to identify areas that remain un- or under-researched and
often problematize the normative discourses and measures used to conduct
and evaluate research so as to suggest ways to improve interpretations and
explanations of social phenomena.

Marxist researchers, for instance, pushed us to examine class distinctions (Garland 1990) and participate in the transformation of the living and working conditions of the populations being studied. Early feminism critiqued the lack of gender analysis in most social research (Harding 1987; Smith 1987, 1990) and identified the need to fight for equality. Critical race, black, and Latina feminism criticized early feminism for its failure to account for racial disparity among women as well as between men and women (Hill Collins 2000) and therefore highlighted the need to take positionality into account. Postcolonial researchers opened our eyes to the ownership of research and data (Smith 1999) and to the ethnocentrism of Western science and Western research(ers), and community-based participatory action research has encouraged us to rectify the issues of data ownership and social exclusion by including the communities and groups we study throughout the evolution and analysis of our work (Kirby and McKenna 1989; Kirby, Greaves, and Reid 2006; Ristock and Pennell 1996; Smith 1999).

These critiques made researchers cognizant of the intrinsic power dynamics in research; the inherent political nature of research; and the need for an ethical commitment to the individual participants and the larger population being studied. As a result, researchers began to revise some of their research practices. They aimed to become more reflexive, for example, because they believed that reflexivity would produce "better" and more nuanced knowledge. Some researchers have encouraged the use of qualitative methodologies influenced by critical epistemological paradigms (distinct from qualitative data gathering or analysis techniques) to this effect. Others endorse what some term *committed scholarship* (Bellot, Sylvestre, and St-Jacques, this volume) and the researcher's responsibility to directly and positively affect the lives of the population being studied (also see Dell, Fillmore, and Kilty, this volume).

Although there was some academic and broader institutional acceptance of critical qualitative and ethnographic methods throughout the 1960s and 1970s, methodological developments since then indicate a resurgence of the institutionalization of positivist language, methods, and approaches to conducting research, all of which have been increasingly used by the state, granting councils, ethics review boards, and the academy to determine the types of work recognized as legitimate or valuable (Martel 2004; Martel, Hogeveen, and Woolford 2006; Menzies and Chunn 1999; Chunn and Menzies 2006). To be clear, positivist research – characterized by a realist ontology; a dualist and objectivist epistemology in which findings are considered to be true; and an experimental, manipulative verification of hypothesis methodology drawing chiefly from quantitative methods (Lincoln and Guba 2003, Table 6.1, 256) – has always maintained a privileged space in academia. Lincoln and

Guba (2003) refer to it as the "received view." As a result, conducting critical scholarship, especially qualitative and ethnographic work that draws on innovative or "alternative" methods and practices, requires that researchers tackle a number of diverse challenges to their work, some of which include obtaining grants and access (to sites, material, and people), responding to unfitting ethics demands, and finding suitable publication avenues (Arrigo 1999; Martel 2004; Martel, Hogeveen, and Woolford 2006). These challenges speak to the ways in which the academy, the state, and the public shape the context in which research is conducted, produced, understood, and (de)valued.

Debates about legitimacy and value in research tend to centre on determining what constitutes the legitimate objects, theories, and methods of the discipline. Given the received view's perception that research can and should be objective, neutral, unbiased, and apolitical (Lincoln and Guba 2003), critical social researchers – who work from constructivist, critical, participatory, feminist, postmodern, or postcolonial paradigms – often find themselves confronted by an academic community and a social science audience that dismisses and even scorns critical research for being political and researchers for their activism and subjective biases. Even the growing trend to reflexively examine and document these influences on the research process and findings has not satisfactorily addressed such characterizations (Harvey 1990; Menzies and Chunn 1999; Chunn and Menzies 2006). This critique works both ways, however, as critical social researchers frequently problematize research agendas that claim to be value-neutral. For example, some critical criminologists challenge administrative criminology, which is typically positivist in language and method, for legitimizing conventional crime control measures that can have negative material consequences on the rights, liberties, and freedoms of those who are the object of that knowledge (Hudson 2011). In this light, the discipline of criminology may be seen as an appendage of the state, serving its interests and producing and legitimizing mechanisms of social control. In other words, critical social researchers prioritize efforts to question the state's normalizing projects (Foucault 1975; Harvey 1990; Hudson 2011).

Many scholars suggest thinking beyond established methodological techniques to develop new ways of producing scientific knowledge. One way to do this involves efforts to "experience" method, which is one of the primary objectives of this book. Our notion of experiencing methods means that the chapters, albeit to varying degrees, are written from a personal or reflexive position. The contributing authors aim to showcase different experiences they have had in conducting critical social research and how those experiences have shaped future research endeavours and their understanding of different aspects of research methodology. Whether working with quantitative or qualitative methodologies, researchers who adopt constructivist, critical, feminist, postmodern, participatory, or postcolonial paradigms often see research and the production of knowledge differently from those doing research from positivist or postpositivist paradigms.[2] Yet these scholars are far from homogeneous. All of the contributors in this book are criminologists, sociolegal scholars, sociologists of deviance, or nurses who conduct research on sensitive issues and on marginalized populations using innovative methodological and theoretical perspectives and strategies. The book plays host to the works of new and established scholars from anglophone and francophone Canadian universities in six different provinces who conduct research nationally and internationally. Bringing together such a diverse group of researchers has generated a number of important discussions.

We asked the authors to reflect on the varied and multilevel issues and challenges they face when they embark on research paths seldom taken, adopt unconventional objects and subjects of study, or conceptualize conventional ones in alternative ways. In other words, we asked the contributors to consider what they do, why they do it, and how they conduct their research when they examine marginalized voices or populations and use less traditional methodological tools or perspectives. We also asked contributors to explore what it means to conduct ethical research and to reflect on their experiences with ethics review boards. In addition, we invited them to outline their responses to the ethical quandaries they faced in the field or in the reporting of their research. The authors contextualize the resistance and hurdles they experienced throughout their research journeys, including when those in authority positions attempted to influence, limit, obstruct, and place boundaries on their research.

The purpose of this book is not to rehash the disputes between quantitative and qualitative methodology or between alternative and traditional methodologies, although these debates are part of the context in which the contributors are working and thus shape their perspectives to varying degrees. Rather, the motive for this book is to generate dialogue among critical social researchers who are doing qualitative work and to provide space for discussions that are often sidelined in methodological debates. In part, contributors illustrate with concrete substantive examples that there is no one or right way to do research, and thus they demonstrate the importance of innovation in qualitative research. Our hope is that by describing how they developed innovative methodological approaches, drawn from original and creative theoretical perspectives, and by reflecting upon their research experiences, contributors to this volume will generate an engaging and healthy discussion of a number of issues relevant to doing research on sensitive topics and/or with marginalized groups.

Structure and Content

The volume is divided into three parts. The first, "Alternative Pathways: Opting for the Road Seldom Taken," showcases the use of the diverse methodologies that the contributors have mobilized in their work (e.g., non-participant observation, community-based and participatory action research, dance as an embodied research method, and the importance of feminism in research). Collectively, these chapters examine some of the challenges of conducting critical qualitative social research and speak to the impact they can have on the researcher and the populations being studied. Chapter 1 presents Russel Ogden's original research on self-chosen death and nonparticipant observation. He reflects on his career-long experiences and challenges in studying this controversial topic and provides a kind of autoethnographic account of this research journey, particularly the challenges presented by law enforcement agencies and university administrations, even after having obtained approval from the institutional research ethics review board.

Ogden's chapter is followed by two chapters that endorse community-based and participatory action research. Chapter 2, by Colleen Dell, Catherine Fillmore, and Jennifer Kilty, describes the process of engaging in successful and collaborative research using the principles of ownership, control, access, and possession as a mechanism to create more egalitarian research relationships in which participants act as collaborators and share access and ownership of the data. It is also an example of how this type of research may produce helpful tools, beyond traditional academic research publication venues, that positively affect the lives of participants. Chapter 3, by Céline Bellot, Marie-Ève Sylvestre, and Bernard St-Jacques, showcases how participatory action research can be used as a means to create change at the policy level and simultaneously facilitate and recognize spaces of resistance that directly affect participants' lives. Grounding their research in community needs, Bellot, Sylvestre, and St-Jacques not only produce committed scholarship; they also demonstrate how the transformative agenda and possibilities of critical social research can work to combat the institutional forms of censorship that silence and render invisible marginalized groups such as the homeless. Both the work of Dell, Fillmore, and Kilty and the work of Bellot, Sylvestre, and St-Jacques open the door for a critical discussion on how scholars can endeavour to put research into praxis through community-based mobilization and alternative forms of knowledge exchange and research dissemination.

Chapter 4, by Sylvie Frigon and Laura Shantz, presents dance as a new way of exploring the carceral by looking at the body, space, and movement as sources of knowledge and resistance. Their use of poststructural discussions of the body as a criminological trope situates their use of dance as a way to examine the criminalized body and, through their own bodies, engage with their corporeal experiences of incarceration. In Chapter 5, Dorothy Chunn and Robert Menzies discuss some of the key epistemological debates within feminism and point to the importance of feminist and profeminist research in the production of critical and alternative methodologies aimed at hearing "voices from below." They argue that reflexivity is a central component of feminist and other critical social research because it forces us to consider our own sociopolitical and moral identities, which invariably affect the generation of our research interests and questions and thus the methods we use, as well as the production of knowledge. In Chapter 6, which closes the section, Jennifer Kilty presents voice, politics, praxis, and positionality as the principles of feminist and other critical research. She reflects on her personal experiences in trying to produce feminist research within the carceral environment, which allows her to effectively question and challenge the existing barriers to accessing this research site and marginalized populations through institutional blockage precisely because critical research is viewed as a potential risk or "threat" to the institution. There is little formal documentation and thus limited academic discussion of the effects of barring critical social researchers from conducting ethnographic-inspired research in the prison setting – especially in the Canadian context. Kilty's chapter acts as a starting point from which to begin this avenue of debate and discussion.

The second part of the book, "Ethical Quagmires: Regulating Qualitative Research," focuses on ethics and the role of institutions and administrations in the practice of research. Contributors provide personal and reflexive accounts of their experiences negotiating and navigating ethical questions that arise in the field. These chapters invite the reader to consider whether ethics in research can actually be obtained through predetermined and bureaucratic mechanisms and whether ethical research is facilitated or limited by institutions – including universities and institutional research sites such as correctional and forensic hospital settings – and their administrations, including research ethics review boards. In Chapter 7, Amélie Perron, Dave Holmes, and Jean Daniel Jacob examine the political nature of doing research in correctional and forensic settings. They discuss the challenges of conducting research that maintains a commitment to social justice in a prison and point to a number of ethical issues, including institutional barriers and power relations that shape the production of critical social research in these sites. As in Kilty's chapter, the authors note that critical scholars can be constructed as disruptive and threatening to institutional order, especially when the research challenges institutional norms and practices. Arguably, despite these negative characterizations, in certain circumstances, researchers are obligated to "make waves" and advocate for participants and other vulnerable populations in order to remain ethical.

In Chapter 8, Will van den Hoonaard depicts qualitative research as being colonized by positivism through what he terms *vertical ethics,* which include institutional research ethics review boards in particular. He describes how qualitative researchers participate in and subsequently partially endorse the process of ethics colonization by adopting the cultural signals and the symbols of positivism. In Chapter 9, Maritza Felices-Luna suggests that thinking of ethics as an object that needs to be controlled, predicted, and achieved in a predetermined and bureaucratic fashion leads institutional research ethics review boards and university administrators to focus on procedural ethics as a means of ensuring ethical research and avoiding liability. She shows the inadequacies of such a model for research that uses qualitative methodologies drawing from constructivist, critical, participatory, postmodern, and post-colonial epistemologies. She proposes ethics as a fluid process and ongoing negotiation that may be seen as a form of moral responsibility and commitment toward participants, the population being researched, and the wider research community. In Chapter 10, the final chapter of the section, John Lowman and Ted Palys expose the political nature of university administrations by examining how they challenge and marginalize ethnographic fieldwork on sensitive topics. The authors identify the paradox of how university and other bureaucratic administrations have established distinct oversight mechanisms for individual researchers, while there remains little to no external oversight of administrative practices and the complications this may present for some researchers.

The third and final part of the book, "Emotion Work and Identity: Self-Examination and Self-Awareness," examines the role of emotion and identity in research. Contributors highlight debates about research and data ownership and the sometimes conflicting roles of voice and positionality. In Chapter 11, Sheryl Fabian uses her work for the Canadian federal government, which, in part, determines the outcomes of Aboriginal claims of residential school abuse, to demonstrate how researchers reconcile the emotions they face both in the field and at home. In particular, she considers how the research conducted to determine the legitimacy of claims of residential school abuse plays a role in silencing the voices of Aboriginal applicants. This work does not require "participation" of the communities but rather treats Aboriginal claimants as applicants, which inherently reconstructs researchers as arbiters for the government. In Chapter 12, Stacey Hannem also discusses the emotionality involved in conducting research. However, unlike Fabian, who connects the emotions evoked during research to sympathy for those she researches, Hannem connects them to conducting research on sexual offenders whose actions and discourses she condemns. Both Hannem and Fabian contend that emotionality in research is unavoidable and that, depending on the nature of the work, it can be problematic and debilitating at times.

The final two chapters of the book present the difficulties that arise when negotiating the dual identities of the academic and the activist. In Chapter 13, Melissa Munn identifies the multiple sources and moments of angst that she experienced while conducting her doctoral research. In particular, Munn discusses the evolution of her identity as a researcher throughout this academic process and the tensions that emerged in relation to voice and the potential for voice appropriation and misinterpretation that often plagues the qualitative researcher. Chapter 14, the last chapter of the book, offers an original autoethnographic piece written by Chris Bruckert, a researcher and activist. Her careful and highly reflexive analysis presents the difficulties associated with wearing different hats and the impact these identities have on one's ability to conduct research. Bruckert deftly illustrates how the ways in which researchers' self-identity, in conjunction with how they are identified by others, demonstrably affects their ability to build rapport and trust and to develop the necessary credibility for a group to accept them and allow them entrance into their culture. She candidly discusses how the identity of the researcher impacts both traditional academic pursuits, such as job security and tenure, and research pursuits, such as building a community-based research project – and how self-censorship is a tool that many researchers utilize to protect themselves and their work.

Overall, we hope that this volume is a think piece for critical scholars. Our goal is to problematize the increasing construction and treatment of research as linear and as something that can be methodologically and ethically predetermined. We hope that this text encourages increased methodological reflection among researchers and acts as a discussion point for funding evaluators and ethics protocol officers who review qualitative and methodologically alternative research proposals. This book invites criminologists, sociolegal scholars, and sociologists of deviance in particular to reflect on the diverse and multilevel issues and challenges they face in the production of academic scholarship. As you read the contributors' reflections on their research experiences; the strategies they developed to confront different research challenges; their understanding of the resistance their work faces; and the process of creating or developing a novel, radical, or otherwise alternative research project, we encourage you to consider the following questions. How does the corporate university play a role in our choices regarding who and what to research and how to do so? Given that current research ethics boards appear to focus more on issues of liability than on the hallmark of ethical research (that which "does no harm"), in what ways do they presume researchers to be inherently unethical? How can we use reflexivity to increase the credibility of our work, especially when it involves a considerable emotional response to participant experiences? And finally, what is the relationship between censorship, silencing, and our research decisions? These questions reflect broader threads that run throughout the chapters and structure much of the discussion offered in the concluding chapter.

Notes

1   In 1961, Stanley Milgram (1974) used deception to study obedience to authority figures; he had a control group administer, unknowingly, fake electric shocks to others with increasing voltage to see how far they would go to follow instructions. In 1971, Philip Zimbardo created a prison environment in the Psychology Department at Stanford University; students acted as prison guards and prisoners to study the psychological effects of carceral settings on these relationships. When the guards began to act sadistically, Zimbardo ended the experiment a week early (Zimbardo and Musen 2004). Laud Humphreys (1970) conducted an ethnography of men who have sex with men in public washrooms; he is widely criticized for failing to get his subjects' consent, tracking down names and addresses through licence plate numbers, and interviewing the men in their homes in disguise and under false pretenses.

2   Postpositivism is characterized by critical realism (reality does exist but only imperfectly; it is probabilistically apprehendable) as the ontological position; a modified dualist/objectivist epistemology where findings are probably true; and a modified experimental/manipulative methodology aiming to falsify hypotheses through quantitative and, in some instances, qualitative methods (Lincoln and Guba 2003, 256).

References

Arrigo, B.A. (1999). Critical Criminology's Discontent: The Perils of Publishing and the Call to Action. *Critical Criminologist 19*(1), 10-15.

Chunn, D.E., and Menzies, R. (2006). So What Does All of This Have to Do with Criminology? Surviving the Restructuring of the Discipline in the Twenty-First Century. *Canadian Journal of Criminology and Criminal Justice 48*(5), 663-80.

Foucault, M. (1975). *Discipline and Punish: The Birth of the Prison.* New York: Random House.

Garland, D. (1990). *Punishment and Modern Society: A Study in Social Theory.* Chicago: University of Chicago Press.

Harding, S. (1987). *The Science Question in Feminism.* Ithaca, NY: Cornell University Press.

Harvey, L. (1990). *Critical Social Research.* London: Unwin Hyman.

Hill Collins, P. (2000). *Black Feminist Thought.* New York: Routledge.

Hudson, B. (2011). Critical Reflection as Research Methodology. In P. Davies, P. Francis, and V. Jupp (Eds.), *Doing Criminological Research* (175-93). London: Sage.

Humphreys, L. (1970). *Tearoom Trade: Impersonal Sex in Public Places.* Chicago: Aldine Publishing Company.

Kirby, S., Greaves, L., and Reid, C. (2006). *Experience Research Social Change: Methods beyond the Mainstream* (2nd ed.). New York: Broadview Press.

Kirby, S., and McKenna, K. (1989). *Experience Research Social Change: Methods from the Margins.* Toronto: Garamond Press.

Lincoln, Y.S., and Guba, E.G. (2003). Paradigmatic Controversies, Contradictions, and Emerging Confluences. In N.K. Denzin and Y.S. Lincoln (Eds.), *The Landscape of Qualitative Research: Theories and Issues* (2nd ed.) (253-91). London: Sage.

Martel, J. (2004). Policing Criminological Knowledge: The Hazards of Qualitative Research on Women in Prison. *Theoretical Criminology 8*(2), 157-89.

Martel, J., Hogeveen, B., and Woolford, A. (2006). The State of Critical Scholarship in Criminology and Socio-Legal Studies in Canada. *Canadian Journal of Criminology and Criminal Justice* (September), 633-46.

Menzies, R., and Chunn, D.E. (1999). (1999). Discipline in Dissent: Canadian Academic Criminology at the Millennium. *Canadian Journal of Criminology 41*(2), 285-97.

Milgram, S. (1974). *Obedience to Authority: An Experimental View.* New York: Harper and Row.

Ristock, J.L., and Pennell, J. (1996). *Community Research as Empowerment: Feminist Links, Postmodern Interruptions.* Toronto: Oxford University Press.

Smith, D.E. (1987). *The Everyday World as Problematic.* Boston: Northeastern University Press.

–. (1990). *The Conceptual Practices of Power: A Feminist Sociology of Knowledge.* Boston: Northeastern University Press.

–. (1999). *Writing the Social: Critique, Theory, and Investigations.* Toronto: University of Toronto Press.

Zimbardo, P., and Musen, K.G. (2004). *Quiet Rage: The Stanford Prison Study.* Palo Alto, CA: Stanford University Instructional Television Network.

part 1   Alternative Pathways:
Opting for the Road Seldom Taken

chapter 1

Observing a Self-Chosen Death

Russel D. Ogden

"CALL CAR 10 AND HAVE HIM arrested right away!" The command came through the mobile phone held by the female on-scene coroner. Standing next to me, she had called her boss, the Vancouver regional coroner, to ask if I could remove the plastic hood covering the face of the deceased woman in the next room.

"I heard that," I said, sitting down with resignation. This was serious. "Car 10" is the inspector on duty for the entire Vancouver Police Department (VPD) street patrol.

"You heard that?" said the coroner, looking concerned.

"I heard that," I repeated. I stood and readied myself to leave. There was nothing to gain by waiting for the police. The coroner had already taken my statement and examined the body. "You've got my information," I said. "The police can call me at home if they have questions." Leaving would defuse the situation. If I stayed, the police would focus on me, a "suspect," rather than on the scene evidence. Nothing I could say would reduce suspicion. If I were to leave, they could examine the scene and reach the proper conclusions.

"I can't keep you here," said the coroner in an understanding tone. She had been professional from the moment she had arrived about thirty minutes earlier. She had an open mind, but her boss was challenging her professionalism and ordering her to urge the police to put me in handcuffs. I would later learn that the coroner's boss was a former RCMP officer. Coroner policy requires neutrality in suicide investigations, but policy is not always practice: "Coroners are precluded from finding fault, and must remain neutral, unbiased, factual and objective, not allowing his/her personal bias to cloud the findings of fact in the complex legal/ethical implications of such situations."[1] The deceased woman in the bedroom across the hall was a participant in my research. I will call her Marcie. Ninety minutes earlier, Marcie had purposefully ended her life in her bed while I sat on a chair nearby and took notes. Marcie made her peace. Woody Allen once said that he was not afraid of dying but he didn't want to be there when it happened. I could agree. I was changed. There is no pleasure witnessing a self-chosen death, but it is work that must be done if Science is to help answer Hamlet's enduring question of the human condition, "To be, or not to be?"

Marcie died from oxygen deprivation with helium. This is a technique described in the right-to-die literature as simple, quick, and painless (Humphry 2002; Nitschke and Stewart 2009). Self-chosen death by oxygen deprivation with helium was developed by right-to-die activists seeking nonviolent and effective do-it-yourself solutions for ending life (Martin 2010). For years, I had been researching the right-to-die movement's efforts to develop practical applications for self-chosen death. In 2002, I coauthored, with the scene coroner in South Carolina, the first case report of suicide by oxygen deprivation (Ogden and Wooten 2002). But our report was based on scene evidence, not direct observation, and there were no witnesses to interview. I had, of course, interviewed activists who had seen deaths by oxygen deprivation with helium, but interviews about past events and direct observation are two different things.

It was Marcie's request that I remove the hood from her head, which she had made with adhesive tape, a turkey-roasting bag, and an athletic headband that served as a neck collar. The turkey bag did not repulse Marcie, it amused her. "Please take it off," she said, "so I don't go to the morgue wrapped like a chicken." I wanted to remove the hood with the coroner present, since the Coroners Act prohibits interference with a body. The act also requires reporting of unnatural deaths – including suicides – to a coroner, hence my telephone call to report Marcie's death.

This was the first time I saw someone die; yet my research had been on that trajectory for years. Even so, nothing prepared me for it. I had grown very fond of Marcie. That morning, Marcie greeted me on her porch steps with a brilliant smile and a warm hug. She commented on the fine weather and said she was happy because "Today, I can be free." How could someone smiling so beautifully want to die? The answer for Marcie was simple. She loved life, but progressive physical and mental deterioration and loss of independence were unacceptable to her.

This chapter is not about whether Marcie was right or wrong to end her life, and it is not an analysis of her psychology or motivations. My purpose is to explain the nonprescriptive process by which I came to research Marcie's self-chosen death and describe how institutional resistance paradoxically facilitated the research process and maximized my careful conduct. I describe the experience of doing extremely difficult research under extremely difficult conditions, legal and ethical issues encountered, and some lessons learned.

1991 to 2007: The Path to Meeting Marcie

Becoming a Suicide Researcher

Marcie ended her life in 2007. My research into self-chosen death began sixteen years earlier when I enrolled in a master's program in criminology at Simon Fraser University (SFU). My MA thesis was an exploratory study of assisted suicide and euthanasia among persons with HIV or AIDS (Ogden 1994). It is generally accepted that protecting participant privacy is a foundation stone in criminological research, and on that footing I promised confidentiality to informants who told me about more than thirty assisted deaths that they knew about or had assisted. The SFU Research Ethics Board (REB) authorized me to promise confidentiality even under threat of legal pressure.

Most of the assisted deaths that I documented in my master's study took place without medical supervision. They were clandestine and camouflaged from law enforcers. Some informants described horrific and prolonged suffering during the process of trying to end suffering. Some people vomited while trying to end their lives with mixed drugs, sometimes taking many hours to die what appeared to be a miserable death. In a few cases, individuals resorted to asphyxiation, "pillow talk," and even violence to bring an end to botched attempts.

In 1994, my promise of confidentiality and SFU's ethics policy were tested when the Vancouver regional coroner, Larry Campbell,[2] issued a subpoena and tried to compel me to reveal names and information about two confidential participants who knew about a woman who was suffocated with a plastic bag after she vomited an overdose of pills.[3] On ethical grounds, I refused to disclose the information demanded by Coroner Campbell's inquest. At the same time, SFU's administration abandoned me and declined to support its own policy, believing that there was no privilege to protect the identities of informants and fearing negative publicity for the university (Lowman and Palys 2000).

Coroner Campbell declared that he had no choice but to find me in contempt of court for refusing to name sources. At a subsequent appearance, my lawyers gave submissions and called expert witnesses to argue that I had a legal privilege to protect my informants. A key issue was that confidentiality is critical to gathering the research information in sensitive topics. Commitments to participant privacy enhance the ability to access information that otherwise would not be disclosed, and the public may benefit from this knowledge through improved understanding of the behaviour in question and better development of policies to respond to social problems.

The contempt finding was eventually reversed, and Coroner Campbell ruled that I had a common law privilege to protect the identities of my informants (Lowman and Palys 2000; Palys and Lowman 2002, 2010). It was a personal victory and a step forward for researchers who need strategies for protecting confidential information (Palys and Lowman 2002). The lesson learned was that if research protocols are designed in accordance with the common law principles of Wigmore's test for privileged communications, then the privacy of research participants could be protected from court-ordered disclosure.[4] Four years after the coroner's ruling, SFU's president recognized the importance of upholding ethical principles, and he wrote an apology letter for the university's failure to defend academic freedom:

> The University was wrong to deny you its support during your efforts to protect the integrity of your undertakings to those who provided confidential information for your M.A. thesis. Your actions were in the tradition of defending freedom for academic inquiry while the University's were motivated by narrower legal and procedural concerns ...
>
> Please accept the University's sincere apologies for our earlier decision and its effects on you. (Jack P. Blaney, SFU president, personal communication, 20 October 1998)

The SFU apology and release from contempt after the subpoena by the Vancouver regional coroner was not the end of it for me. In 2003 and again in 2004, British Columbia's Crown Counsel subpoenaed me to the criminal trial of Evelyn Martens, who was charged with aiding two suicides. In a "fishing expedition," Crown Counsel hoped that I might provide information to help convict Martens (Palys and Lowman 2010).

In my view, the subpoenas were threats to free inquiry. Researchers should not act as law enforcement officers and they should not compromise the integrity of confidentially obtained information. Each subpoena was met with a blunt letter that I would be an uncooperative witness. The Crown Counsel withdrew the subpoenas, and I was not required to appear in court to defend participant privacy.

The three subpoenas are strong reminders that researchers must anticipate risks to research-participant privacy. But threats to privacy do not come only from law enforcers. Sometimes the risk comes from the university. For example, the SFU REB chair spent years trying to implement a policy that would force researchers to capitulate to subpoenas for confidential data (Palys and Lowman 2010). In England, the ethics committee at University of Exeter initially felt duty-bound to support me in protecting confidential information in my postgraduate euthanasia research. The ethics committee gave a written pledge to "support and sustain" the confidentiality in my research. Just five days after approving the research, however, the pledge was secretly removed, and a different ethics approval was written (and kept secret from me for the next two years while I carried out more than one hundred face-to-face interviews in Canada, England, United States, and the Netherlands).

The research data, tragically, could not be used. The secret volte-face by the ethics committee meant that I unknowingly misinformed my participants about the conditions for their consent to participate. I had informed them that in accordance with the ethics committee's written commitment to "support and sustain" my promises of confidentiality, both I and the university would protect their privacy. But, since the university had quietly countermanded its written commitment and did not tell me, participants were misinformed and it was not possible to locate them to try to negotiate a new consent agreement.

I filed a formal complaint in 1997 and in 2003 England's lord chancellor settled the ethical breaches by the research ethics committee and awarded me damages for Exeter's misconduct (Farrar and Baty 2003; Ogden 2003).

Botched Assisted Deaths and the Search for a Better Way Out

My study of assisted death and AIDS revealed the difficulties that laypersons often have in trying to find information about effective and nonviolent means for assisted dying. In a similar study in Australia and the United States, Magnusson (2002) found that assisted deaths are often "botched" because of a lack of information about drugs and suicide techniques.

Guidebooks about suicide techniques have been around for decades. One of the earliest was Dr. George B. Mair's *How to Die with Dignity* (1980), a booklet produced by Scottish Exit (later called Voluntary Euthanasia Society of Scotland). It described how to acquire and ingest lethal barbiturates, as well as other techniques. The first how-to guide with mass-market appeal was *Final Exit: The Practicalities of Self-Deliverance and Assisted Suicide for the Dying* (Humphry 1991). It was on the *New York Times* bestseller list for eighteen weeks and has since been released in several revised editions and languages (Humphry 2008). After *Final Exit,* other publications combined scientific research with anecdotal accounts of suicides (e.g., Docker and Smith 1993; Last

Rights Publications 1995-2000, 2000; Smith et al. 1995; Stone 1999). In the mid-1990s, networks of people, particularly in Canada, the United States, and Australia, committed themselves to the promotion of autonomy and self-empowerment by developing and refining suicide techniques (Ogden 2001).

Because I defended the privacy of research informants, right-to-die activists trusted me with confidential information. In 1999, NuTech – New Technologies for Self-Deliverance – was formed, and I was soon invited to research its activities (Ogden 2001). This international group of activists was funded primarily through Derek Humphry, founder of the Hemlock Society in the United States, and promoted by John Hofsess from the Right to Die Society of Canada.

NuTech had a research agenda. "Fieldworkers" delivered covert assistance to individuals who needed help to die, and they collected data about drug doses, gas concentrations, and measurements about the length of time it took for people to die. They wrote field notes on their observations, documenting their subjective views about the peacefulness of a death in order to inform the NuTech program about which techniques were most effective. These techniques and the science underpinning them are now well documented, and books such as *The Peaceful Pill Handbook* even provide reliability and peacefulness ratings for the methods outlined (Nitschke and Stewart 2009). These are, as Professor Brian Martin (2010, 54) says, "techniques to pass on."

Around late 1999, John Hofsess convinced most fieldworkers to send me anonymized reports of deaths using NuTech methods. Most of the reports provided bare-bones data about the death-hastening method, illness, time to death, and any complications observed. One of the early techniques involved an oxygen deprivation device called the debreather. This was a closed circuit breathing apparatus that depleted the oxygen supply until a person was breathing only nitrogen, which cannot sustain life (Ogden 2001, 2010a). Although effective, the debreather was supplanted by oxygen deprivation with helium.

Between 1999 and 2002, I received over 170 anonymized reports of assisted deaths, mostly from the United States and Canada. About 130 involved oxygen deprivation with helium. In 2002, however, the flow of reports almost completely stopped. The chill on information sharing happened because activists were fearful of sending me data when Reverend George Exoo from West Virginia was snared in an Interpol investigation over a helium suicide in Ireland, and Vancouver Islander Evelyn Martens was arrested in an elaborate RCMP surveillance operation concerning two deaths. Two and a half years later, Martens was acquitted, and more than five years later, a United States district magistrate judge ruled that Exoo would not be extradited to face trial in Ireland. In the interim, I put my data away for safekeeping.

Would You Like to Research My NuTech Death?

Anonymized reports and interviews are no substitute for direct observation. Over the years, I befriended many seriously ill people and I routinely received offers to be with them when they died. From time to time, NuTech field-workers would offer to have me come along to see their work, but for one reason or another the offers never came to fruition. Unsurprisingly, NuTech fieldworkers found it difficult to convince their clients that having a researcher present at their deaths was a good idea. Most of these opportunities were hundreds of miles away, which presented little opportunity to build trust or rapport with a potential participant.

In the autumn of 2004, an opportunity presented itself in the middle of a family meal with out-of-town visitors. Out of the blue, an activist and occasional fieldworker telephoned to invite me to film his assisted death, which he said would take place in two to three weeks. Shaken, I said I needed to check with the university ethics board. That night, I quickly prepared an application to the university REB. Since the death was supposed to be imminent, I requested urgent attention:

> On the weekend of September 25th I was contacted by a person who plans to die in the near term ... The participant also offered to have me witness and document his/her death using NuTech methods, with the help of a "death provider." To date, I have only received reports of deaths using these methods via interview and written materials. Witnessing a NuTech death would allow for firsthand corroboration/refutation of some of the knowledge that I have accumulated. This research may also help to formulate other research questions for investigation. (Ethics application, 26 September 2004)

The REB could not give a quick review and approval of the application. Like me, it was conflicted. One REB member argued, incorrectly, that suicide was a crime and that my observation would make me a party or accessory to the offence. Months later, I learned that this member resigned from the REB because the other committee members were leaning toward approval of the research.

Two weeks after receiving the application, the REB decided that ethics review should only proceed if the research had "scholarly merit." The REB convened an ad hoc external committee and asked me to submit a separate "application for scholarly review." External funding agencies usually assess scholarly merit but this research was different in that it was self-funded.

The application for scholarly review argued that the research had scholarly merit because it was unique. No researcher had attended a planned assisted death before, so this exploration satisfied the scientific imperative for new knowledge and understanding articulated in the *Tri-Council Policy Statement: Ethical Conduct for Research Involving Humans* (CIHR, NSERC, and SSHRC 1998). Additionally, direct observation of a NuTech assisted death had the potential to support or refute the validity of information I had already obtained through interview and anonymous reports.

The scholarly merit was not obvious to the external reviewers. I informed the REB chair that I was concerned the reviewers would focus on the "yuck factor" and not the science, which turned out to be the case. Two of the three ad hoc reviewers concluded that the research lacked sufficient scientific merit. The first reviewer said it raised a "significant potential of harm," but was silent on what the harm was. Since the participants decided on the assisted death before inviting me, I did not see any logical connection that the research could *cause* harm. The assisted death would happen with or without the research. Legally, there was no obligation to dissuade or prevent the death.

The second reviewer speculated somewhat derisively, "Would the researcher have accepted the invitation of the participants if one of the participants was simply proposing to assist the other participant by offering to asphyxiate him/her with a pillow?" The reviewer also volunteered a legal opinion that I would be a "party to the offence" of aiding suicide. For reasons that I outline in the next section of this chapter, one cannot be a party to the offence of aiding suicide.

The same reviewer also asserted that I had an obligation "to intervene to prevent the crime," and a "moral and legal obligation to contribute evidence against the offenders in a court of law." This forced me to argue to the REB that I was under no duty to prevent crime and that there was no moral obligation to give evidence in court. I had to remind the REB that any obligation to give evidence in court is subject to the common law Wigmore criteria that I had successfully applied in the coroner's inquest in 1994 (Lowman and Palys 2000).

As is often the case in external reviews, the third reviewer's opinion was significantly different. It did not conflate risks of harm, morality, and legal opinion with scholarly merit. It agreed with my assertion that the research was unique and needed to be done:

> As Professor Ogden outlines, there is much speculation about physician-assisted death but little first-person data. Thus, the proposed project has much to offer and to commend it and, given Mr. Ogden's experience with controversial projects and protecting participants, he would seem

to be an ideal person to carry it out. Further, the fact that the people involved contacted him indicates that they will likely be open with him instead of being skeptical or resistant. As a result, I believe there is significant scholarly merit and, in fact, think that this could be an important precedent in the end-of-life research field and discussion about these issues.

The one-in-three score satisfied the REB. More than three months after receipt of the original ethics application, the REB agreed that the research had the scholarly merit to warrant ethics review. I was invited to submit a revised ethics application, and, after six more months of deliberation, the REB issued a certificate of approval on 12 July 2005. The person who triggered the process by saying he planned to die was still alive. His decision to continue living was independent from the proposed research because he was not informed of the lengthy processes or outcome in the ethics review.

While the original REB application was for a single case study, the REB approved the observation of multiple cases. However, before the research could be carried out, the university administration stepped in to say the research was criminal. On 11 December 2006, I was called to a meeting of the university administration. The provost and VP-academic read from a script: "you are not to engage in any illegal activity including attending at an assisted death."

What Is Canada's Law on Assisted Suicide?

More than one hundred years ago, common law in Canada regarded suicide as the crime of self-murder (Burbidge 1890). When the first Criminal Code was enacted in 1893, suicide was not specifically prohibited but it was an indictable offence to attempt suicide (Taschereau 1893). Attempting suicide was decriminalized in 1972. Counselling, aiding, and abetting suicide have always been indictable offences. They were originally punishable with life sentences, and in the 1950s the penalty was amended to a maximum of fourteen years in jail. The current law is set out in section 241 of the Criminal Code:

241. Counselling or Aiding Suicide – Every one who

(a) counsels a person to commit suicide, or
(b) aids or abets a person to commit suicide,

whether suicide ensues or not, is guilty of an indictable offence and liable to imprisonment for a term not exceeding fourteen years.

The prohibition against aiding or abetting suicide is unusual in Canada's criminal law. Individuals who aid or abet others in committing a crime are normally considered "parties to an offence," but the principal act in this case, suicide, is not a crime. Under section 241, individuals can either criminally aid or abet a suicide, but the party to an offence section of the Criminal Code does not apply. If it were possible to be a party to the offence of aiding suicide, then the individual who is aided or abetted would be a party, criminalizing suicide and attempted suicide. In *Rodriguez* (1993), Madam Justice Beverley McLachlin noted that the law makes an arbitrary and illogical distinction by making suicide legal and assisted suicide illegal.

I was surprised when the university directed me to not engage in the "illegal activity" of attending an assisted death. After all, Svend Robinson[5] was present at Sue Rodriguez's assisted suicide and a Special Prosecutor's Report concluded that his attendance at the suicide was not an offence: "The fact that Svend Robinson was present at the suicide, without evidence which would show that his opportunity to have committed an offence was exclusive, is not sufficient to lay a charge against him" (Johnston 1995). In addition to the official conclusion in Svend Robinson's case, there was the more recent trial of Evelyn Martens, who was acquitted of charges of aiding two suicides. When instructing the jury about the law, Justice Davies advised that mere presence at a suicide is not an offence and that the words or actions of a person accused of aiding suicide must be active and significant:

> Aiding or abetting in the context of this case requires that there be some active participation by Ms. Martens or some active assistance rendered by her. Ms. Martens must have associated herself with the suicide of either or both of Ms. Charest or Ms. Burchell by participating in it and trying to make it succeed or by actively encouraging it to occur. There must be a significant link between Ms. Martens' words or actions or both and the suicide of either Ms. Charest or Ms. Burchell or both, as the case may be.
>
> Mere presence, without more than that, is not an act of aiding or abetting a suicide. Simply ... agreeing not to intervene to stop or thwart the process, without more, is neither aiding nor abetting.[6]

Four months after issuing its directive, the university obtained a legal opinion to support its position: "It is likely that the proposed research project would be construed by a court as constituting a criminal offence" (L. T. Doust, QC, personal communication, 19 April 2007). The opinion insisted that my presence at an assisted death constituted endorsement and encouragement of the act of suicide. The legal opinion made no reference to *Martens* or the Special Prosecutor's Report. I later learned that my research proposal and ethics application were not provided to the lawyer charged with giving an opinion about my research.

Since the university directive was specific to assisted suicide, I filed a new application to the REB for approval to attend *unassisted* suicide. Some observers in the university community told me this was cheeky, but I believed that the ethical distinction between observing unassisted suicide versus assisted suicide, if there was one, had to be resolved. The REB approved the new application to observe unassisted suicide in less than four months, on 20 April 2007. While the REB reported this new approval to the university administration, the university issued no statement about the probity of observing unassisted suicide.

The Canadian Association of University Teachers (CAUT) was concerned that the original university directive might infringe academic freedom, so it commissioned a legal opinion on the unassisted suicide research. The opinion said my proposed conduct "would likely not be found to contravene s. 241 of the *Criminal Code*" (E.D. Crossin, QC, personal communication, 14 June 2007). By the late spring of 2007, I was caught between opposing legal opinions, a university directive not to attend at an assisted death, and the REB's permission that I could observe both assisted suicide and unassisted suicide. By this time, Marcie presented a concrete research opportunity, so the problem was hardly academic.

Meeting Marcie

Active participant recruitment was not part of the research design to observe either assisted or unassisted suicide; Marcie and I were passively connected by a right-to-die group. Over several months, we got to know one another through long meetings. At our first meeting, Marcie was clear that she wanted to end her life, and she was under the impression that I might help her. She displayed for me an array of prescription medications from her medicine cabinet, and we drank tea while she weighed their pros and cons for lethality. As I have had to do many times before, I explained that my research role precluded giving advice or assistance. Disappointed but undeterred, Marcie befriended me, and she continued with her own research into techniques for self-chosen death. Over the next months, she systematically organized her affairs and got rid of unwanted property. I learned that she and her mother had attempted a double suicide a few years earlier. Her mother succeeded and Marcie regretted failing. Their pact had involved drugs, which Marcie vomited. Because of that, Marcie was interested in non-drug methods that would eliminate the possibility of a second failure because of regurgitation.

It was easy to build rapport with Marcie. She was very likeable, good with conversation, and interested in many things. She was unselfish and concerned with ensuring that her death wish did not harm me. She claimed to enjoy our talks but did not want to burden me. Marcie said that I was the only person that she could talk to about her plans for ending her life. Other people were dismissive if she tried to discuss it with them, and they would force a change in the topic. Her doctor refused to discuss Marcie's wish to die. I would tell Marcie that it was my job to listen, that I was interested in her thoughts. I assured Marcie that I would not stop her, but that I also did not want her to die. She seemed to like hearing me say that.

We both looked forward to our meetings every couple of weeks. I wondered whether our meetings contributed to Marcie postponing or reconsidering her plan to die. Sometimes we would picnic and spend nearly all of our time talking about everything but death. I never knew how to ask if our friendship was causing Marcie to reconsider her plans. I now know Marcie was not staying alive for our friendship. She would talk in general terms about how long she expected to continue living and what she wanted to do before she died. The deadlines would pass and new ones would be made. As the weeks went on, the deadlines grew less distant. Then one day she said, "I think it will be next week."

The Next Week, the Night Before

Days later, on Sunday evening, my telephone rang at 5:59 P.M. It was Marcie. "I'm ready," she said.

"You're ready?" I asked.

"Yes, I've had a wonderful day," she said. "I'm ready to die tomorrow."

Marcie said she had one more person to talk to in the morning and then she would be ready to go. Our phone call was short. I felt rattled. I assured Marcie that I would come to her home, but that she should sleep on her decision and call me in the morning. That night I scrambled to back up computer hard drives and I tried to separate my teaching and research materials, anticipating the possibility of confiscation by the police and hoping that any raid would allow my teaching life to continue without disruption. It was a long night. I conferred hastily with confidants, protected field notes, and notified my university faculty association that the research opposed by the university might soon happen. Earlier in the week, lawyers in Vancouver had couriered a legal opinion to CAUT, but its content was unknown to me.

Death Day

At 7:15 A.M. Marcie telephoned. She said she had slept very well. An hour earlier, I had been trying to reach the CAUT executive director in Ottawa about the legal opinion. He was unavailable and I was getting anxious. Marcie repeated what she had said the night before. She was ready to end her life. Could I come to her house around 10:00 A.M.? I stalled. Marcie was unaware of the university administration's opposition to this research, and I never allowed her to worry about my employment security. I said that I had a few things to attend to and that I would try to arrive around 11:00 A.M. Mostly, I needed advice from CAUT.

Shortly after 9:00 A.M. the executive director of CAUT telephoned from Ottawa. He read out the concluding remarks of a fresh legal opinion and asked me to confirm that it accurately described my research procedures. On that understanding, he said that CAUT, my university faculty association, and the Federation of Post-Secondary Educators believed that I had the academic freedom to proceed. If any legal action was taken against me, the unions would enforce what they believed was a collective agreement obligation to indemnify me and would see to it that I was assisted if the university did not do so. Relieved, I dressed in a jacket and tie and left the house. The drive to Marcie's home was surreal. While driving I dictated field notes into a portable recorder and I asked myself if this was real. Could it be a trap? Was Marcie an actress? Five years ago, an undercover RCMP officer masqueraded as the goddaughter of the former nun who died holding the hand of Evelyn Martens. Evelyn was no fool, but she would tell me later that the detective tricked her, completely. Was I paranoid? I reminded myself that paranoia in this situation was my friend because it would keep my conduct on the right side of the law.

Marcie was waiting for me on her front porch, beaming brightly and smartly dressed in a crisp white blouse and sleeveless vest. "I'm so excited," she said. "Today is the day I can be free." The sky was clear, the temperature was about fifteen degrees, and there was no sign of rain.

Marcie invited me inside. I had been to her home many times, but this time she showed me her sparsely furnished bedroom for the first time. In a vase were the white, long-stem calla lilies that I had cut from my garden and had given to her earlier that week. Near the bed, under cover of a blanket, was a helium tank that Marcie had purchased from a party supply store. "I know where I want to go for lunch," she said, "but can you take me to the library first?" Marcie had books to return.

I waited in the car while Marcie returned her library books. Next, she gave me directions to drive to Queen Elizabeth Park. We strolled for a bit, enjoying the park's view of Vancouver and the mountain backdrop. Marcie wanted "to be in nature," so we ate lunch on the outdoor terrace at the Hilltop Bistro. I ordered ahi tuna, Marcie ordered mushrooms, and we shared them. Afterwards we drank coffee and divided a caramel crème brûlée. A small Japanese wedding party arrived and took its place at several reserved tables. Marcie excused herself and crossed the terrace to greet the bride and groom, saying hello in Japanese. She wished the young couple a happy life together and told them they were beautiful.

When Marcie returned to our table, she was consumed with joy for the newlyweds. Then her thoughts turned to her own prospects, which were diminishing. The future she wanted was irretrievably lost as a result of a heart attack and transient ischemic attacks.

"Small strokes," she said, "but with big consequences."

The strokes had hit Marcie a decade earlier, just when she was planning an early retirement to pursue her passion for travel and helping people in developing countries. The heart attack followed seven years later. To an outsider, Marcie looked relatively robust, but she did not see it that way. She had worked in health care all of her life. She loved caring for others, but she did not want to be institutionalized and surrender her independence. Marcie told me about a friend who was living in a care facility. "They're good there," she would say, "but that's not what I want."

"I'm so glad to have you with me," she said. "I don't have to die alone." Marcie asked a friend to be with her, but her friend could not do it. I remember telling Marcie that this was not unusual, that in Scotland there was a right-to-die organization called FATE, Friends at the End. We agreed that it was a good name.

"What would you say if I could not go through with this, if I could not be with you?" I asked. I wanted to know if my presence could have a causal effect on Marcie's decision.

Marcie's eyes were teary. "I'd be disappointed, but I'd understand," she said. "Are you ... ?"

"No," I said.

Marcie then asked me how I would feel if she changed her mind and decided not to end her life. "If you could not do your research with me, would you be upset?" I told Marcie that I would be very happy if she lived another day. I meant it. Our sentences were getting shorter and the silences were getting longer. Marcie's eyes moistened some more, and so did mine.

After eating, we walked to my car. Crows had raided a garbage bin and scattered food wrappers all over the grass. Marcie could not ignore the mess, and I followed her lead to clean it up. We returned to Marcie's house, and she took me to the basement and insisted I chat with her while she folded her laundry. Then we retired to the living room, and I asked Marcie to review the two forms that we had gone over many times before. The first was a four-paragraph statement intended to ensure that participants consider the possibility that my presence might influence their behaviour and decisions. We read the statement together and then Marcie signed and dated it. The REB did not require a signature, but I wanted to be able to prove my compliance, if necessary:

> Sometimes research participants alter their normal behaviour patterns because they are aware that they are being observed. This is known as "reactivity" to the researcher. Reactivity is defined as "atypical or artificial behaviour produced by the respondent's awareness of being studied." It is a requirement of the Research Ethics Board (REB) that I inform you that my presence as a researcher may influence your behaviour.
>
> I am not asking you to complete this deathing. Even though I am here at your request to document this planned death, you do not have to carry through with it because I am here. You can change your mind.
>
> The REB is concerned that my presence may be a factor in causing this death to take place, because you have asked me to document it. The REB requires that I ask you to consider this possibility.
>
> The REB's ethical approval of this research in no way is intended as a statement about the ethical status of this proposed deathing.

My lawyer had updated the second form the previous week. Its purpose was to protect me from misdirected charges of aiding suicide or culpable homicide. Slowly, we read it together. At the second paragraph Marcie stopped for a moment and then read out loud the part that the lawyer had changed: "not facilitating, advancing, promoting, expediting, inciting, emboldening, urging … Oh my, seven words when just one would do!"

To Whom It May Concern:

> It is my careful and well considered decision to end my life according to my values and beliefs. This decision was made without regard to Mr. Ogden or his research. It is my desire to have Mr. Ogden with me when I decide that it is time for me to end my life.
>
> I am not seeking publicity. I want it known it is clear to me Mr. Ogden is not facilitating, advancing, promoting, expediting, inciting, emboldening, urging or encouraging me to end my life.
>
> My decisions and my actions are carefully considered and I have evaluated the choices available to me. I am clearly aware that I am free

to change my mind if I choose. I understand that Mr. Ogden is equally interested if I choose to continue to live.

I understand that Mr. Ogden is an observer and his purposes are academic research, for the benefit of education and scholarship. It is my wish that no harm come to him as a consequence of his attendance.

"It's eight words," I said. "On the next line is 'encouraging.'" We shared a laugh at the expense of lawyers. I was happy for the humorous moment and could feel the pressure building. For the second time in less than half an hour, I excused myself to use the toilet.

When I returned from the bathroom, Marcie put one of her favourite operas on the stereo, Giuseppe Verdi's *Nabucco*. She fetched a bottle of wine from the kitchen and we toasted her life. I felt awkward and Marcie seemed at ease. The toast was brief, and then Marcie excused herself for a quick bath. In the meantime, I wrote some field notes.

It was surreal. For weeks, I discussed my observations and feelings with my friend and colleague John Lowman, professor of criminology at Simon Fraser University. John had me on guard because of his cautions that Marcie could be a police agent-provocateur. I tried to imagine that Marcie could be a police officer, that the helium tank she purchased did not really contain helium, and that police were waiting for their "gotcha" moment.

Marcie returned from her bath, dressed for bed. She asked me to follow her to the bedroom. Marcie arranged her equipment and verbalized the steps that she had rehearsed for ending her life. We talked about what I would do to call the coroner after she died, and Marcie reminded me to telephone her executrix the next day. I tried to stay cool but I was beside myself with anxiety.

While attempting to loosen the tap on the helium tank, a troubled look came over Marcie. "It won't open," she said.

It was inexplicable. "This is it. It's a set-up," I thought. I had seen Marcie open the tap on a different tank in her rehearsal once before.

Marcie struggled with the valve and she looked frustrated. Her eyes pleaded with me as her hand strained to turn the tap, seeming to beg me to help. "It won't open," she said.

I felt awkward. It is instinctively normal to help someone open a jar, loosen a nut ... but cracking open the valve to a suicide kit was not the same thing. I said nothing.

"Can you?" Marcie asked. I shook my head. I was terrified to speak. If Marcie were an undercover police officer, I could not know how my words might be used.

Then, breaking the silence Marcie remembered that she had pliers in the kitchen. I followed her, feeling helpless and foolish. She could not find the pliers but she eventually settled on a nutcracker tool that would do the trick. It worked. After loosening the tap on the helium tank, Marcie put the nutcracker on her bedside table next to the adhesive tape and other materials that she used to assemble her kit. Later that night as I was driving home I imagined the police standing in Marcie's room, looking at the objects on her bedside table and wondering about the nutcracker.

I do not intend to detail Marcie's death here, as I have already described the technical details as a case report in the *American Journal of Forensic Medicine and Pathology* (Ogden, 2010b). After Marcie died I scribbled field notes and I paced. *Nabucco* played its final minutes on the stereo and then the house was eerily quiet. Moments before I was counting Marcie's final breaths, and now I was acutely alive to my own uneasy breathing as I tried to maintain my composure. Marcie was gone, but she was there too, and her body was slowly cooling. It was awkward being alone in Marcie's home. I felt totally out of place and overwhelmingly sad. It was an uncomfortable honour to be with Marcie when she died.

Post Death

The coroner followed me out the front door, saying that she would be calling the police but she could not make me wait. Standing on the porch were two body-pickup attendants – a young woman, a man, and a folding gurney on wheels. The woman and I exchanged quizzical looks of recognition but we did not speak. The coroner had not yet called the police, and I needed to leave.

As I descended the vinyl-covered stairs leading to the concrete path, the female body-pickup attendant called out, "Are you Russel Ogden?"

I stopped and turned to face her. "Yes."

"Oh! I'm Leena Maplethorpe. Do you remember me? I took your criminology class a couple years ago!"

The strangeness was getting stranger. I did remember Leena. She was a good student. It was awkward. Leena had not yet entered the house, and she would not know the reason I was there. She was on a routine job, but I was not. As graciously as possible I said hello and explained that I needed to go.

Months later I found one of Leena's assignments in my files, ironically titled, "Techniques to Reduce the Psychological Burden on Executioners." I decided to contact her to ask what happened after I left the scene. Leena told me she was no longer working in body pickup. When the police arrived she and her partner were immediately dismissed and recalled several hours later to collect Marcie. Leena did not know that I had attended Marcie's death, nobody had questioned her about me, and she could not remember if the plastic hood was still covering Marcie's face when she removed her from the house.

I did not go straight home. Instead, I went to a colleague's house and telephoned my lawyer to outline the day's events. My field notes, portable voice recorder, and camera were locked up for safekeeping, and then I went home.

The next morning, I called the executrix shortly before 9:00 A.M. She had already been contacted by the Vancouver Police Department. She said the news was a shock, and speculated that Marcie could not tolerate the idea of more strokes and losing the ability to care for herself. The executrix sounded curious about me, remarking that Marcie had never mentioned me. She asked if she could give my name and number to Marcie's friends, and I agreed.

Not long after I spoke with Marcie's executrix, a detective from the Vancouver Police Department telephoned and asked me to make an appointment to come in for an interview. I referred him to my lawyer for an appointment, but the detective's holiday plans got in the way of a meeting. When he was due to return the following month, I heard nothing.

Three days after Marcie's death, I was telephoned long-distance by a woman who described herself as Marcie's dearest friend. She said she got my number from the executrix. I knew about the friend and I was aware that she had visited Marcie the previous month, which is something they did every year. The friend asked some pointed questions about how long I had known Marcie, and whether Marcie died peacefully. Although the friend volunteered that she had not spoken to the police, I made careful notes just in case. It was some consolation that she spoke of Marcie being "free," just as Marcie had said three days earlier: "Well, I think she was probably very ready to go ... Well, I'm sorry to be talking to you about this but I appreciate it. It clears up things. We knew it might happen, but it caught us off guard anyway. And now she is free." Only the police could answer the question of whether my presence at Marcie's suicide was an offence, but they were not communicating. In January 2008, I filed a request under the BC Freedom of Information and Protection of Privacy Act (FIPPA) for the police "general occurrence" file. In stages and subsequent to various appeals, a heavily redacted fifty-one-page report was released a year later, in January 2009.

The police report is revelatory. The investigation was immediately assigned to VPD's "Major Crime Section." Minutes after I departed from Marcie's house, police arrived. That evening, seventeen officers of constable, detective, sergeant, and inspector rank combed what is repeatedly called a "crime scene."

They contained and secured the house, and officers searched garbage containers, looked for security cameras, and talked to neighbours. There are many references to "suspect Ogden," "assisted suicide," and "the victim." While the "Forensic Ident Team" did its work, Marcie's body remained on her bed for nearly eight hours until she was eventually placed in a padlocked body bag and transported under police escort to the morgue.

While I was waiting for the results of the police investigation, the university commissioned a supplementary legal opinion about my research for unassisted suicide. The university's counsel refused my offer to meet and provide further information, but this time the university provided him with copies of my research protocols.

The university's legal opinion was completed nearly one year after Marcie's death. It concluded that passive observation of suicide is not criminal, but that my "prearranged presence" was more than passive and therefore would constitute an offence:

> "Prearranged presence" is just as much evidence of aiding and abetting a suicide as it is evidence of aiding and abetting any conventional offence, and that is so regardless of whether the suicide happens to be assisted or not.
>
> For these reasons, and those outlined in our previous opinion, our view remains that Mr. Ogden's proposed research project would contravene s. 241(b) of the *Criminal Code*. (L.T. Doust, QC, personal communication, 13 June 2008)

The legal opinion left me feeling uneasy. A year had passed since Marcie's death, the police had not interviewed me, and the investigation was "ongoing." Not long after the university gave me its legal opinion, the Vancouver Police Department was concluding its investigation, but I would not see the result until January 2009. I was vindicated:

> Det. Robertson, who interviewed Ogden, also felt that there was no evidence to believe that Ogden had committed a criminal offence.
>
> Det. McCartney and Det. Reid both agree that there is evidence that Russell [sic] Ogden is a researcher as he has published a number of papers on the subject of suicide. While many people would find that the act of Ogden observing people commit suicide is repugnant and ghoulish, there is no legal requirement for Ogden to intervene to stop the suicide and as long as he does not counsel to commit suicide or do anything to assist in the suicide, he does not commit a criminal offence.

Being both a criminology professor and a researcher into suicide, Russell Ogden is no doubt aware of the Criminal Code sections relating to suicide and he would likely know what line would have to be crossed to commit the offence of "Counselling or Aiding Suicide." ... In summary, Det. McCartney, [and] Det. Reid are of the opinion that no evidence of a criminal offence being committed by Russell Ogden has been found in these two cases.[7]

Conclusion

Researching self-chosen death is difficult. A 1995 Senate of Canada report titled *Of Life and Death* recommended that "research be undertaken into how many are requesting assisted suicide, why it is being requested, and whether there are alternatives that might be acceptable to those making the requests" (74). In 2000, a Senate follow-up report noted that the research had not been done: "Direct empirical research into euthanasia and assisted suicide is hindered by the illegality of these actions. Confidentiality is essential and funding bodies such as universities can be extremely vulnerable to public opinion on such sensitive issues. Independent funding needs to be made available to qualified researchers" (Senate of Canada 2000, 32). Separate from government support and funding, it is possible to do smaller-scale research into self-chosen death, which may ultimately lead to larger-scale inquiry. The process by which it was possible to witness Marcie's self-chosen death involves a constellation of variables with origins dating back many years. By upholding ethical principles of participant confidentiality, gaining trust within the right-to-die movement and with individuals who need a safe place to discuss deeply intimate matters, I earned a privileged place for research.

There are a number of lessons to be learned from this process. The social scientist's ethical pursuit of knowledge can be perceived by law enforcers as an opportunity to exploit researchers. Researchers must resist threats from law enforcers and maintain their commitments to participants and independent free inquiry. While the mandate of government agencies may conflict with a researcher's mandate, these conflicts can be managed. It is imperative that researchers understand the relevant laws and do everything possible to acquire external support, such as that afforded me by CAUT.

By resisting the pressures of state agents, my identity as a social scientist was strengthened, and this ultimately helped with my resolve to do my research, even when the university administration did not agree. Most importantly, because I had defended the privacy of past research participants in the face of court subpoenas, it was not difficult to assure future research participants that their privacy would also be protected. Those past experiences were

valuable currency for acquiring information from research participants, negotiating with the REB, and dealing with the police, coroner, and university
administration.

Since first witnessing Marcie's death in 2007, I have continued to accom-
pany research participants at the end of their lives. The experience is still
emotionally wrenching and compounded by coroner prejudice and intimidating encounters with the police. After Marcie's case, the police have always
been sent first to the scene by the coroner, which has resulted in police intimidation and arrest, but never any charge. For me, this is a reflection of
Canada's morality politics, which are resistant to academic inquiry that acknowledges suicide as a possibility. Rather than trying to understand suicide,
the current morality politics regard suicide as a phenomenon to be judged,
prevented, ignored, or swept under the carpet. The consequence is that suicide is underresearched. But other jurisdictions offer a more accommodating
methodological terrain to study suicide. Less than a year after Marcie's death,
I experienced something instructively dissimilar while researching several
suicides assisted by Dignitas, a well-known right-to-die group in Switzerland. For decades, Switzerland has allowed altruistic assisted suicide, and nonprofit societies such as Dignitas have developed transparent practices to help
their members with suicide while endeavouring to protect vulnerable people
and ensure accountability to law enforcers. Assisted suicides are reported to
the police and coroner, and the cooperative and transparent practices foster a
fertile ground for research opportunities.

Early in 2008, I learned from news reports that Dignitas had experi-
mented with helium as a non-drug alternative to barbiturates for assisting
suicides and that video recordings of the deaths had been provided to the police. I contacted Dignitas founder Ludwig Minelli, whom I had once spoken
to in 2005 but never met, and he welcomed me to come to Switzerland to
view the videos. I prepared a research ethics application, and the university
REB that previously took months to consider applications to directly observe
suicide and assisted suicide quickly exempted the prospective video analysis
from REB review, reasoning that videos of assisted suicides did not involve
research with "human participants" (had I known that, the REB application
would not even have been necessary). Mr. Minelli obtained copies of the
videos from the police, but a technical malfunction interfered with playback.
In April 2008, together, we visited the Zurich police station to study the
videos, at which time the police made new copies and gave me a set. Next,
I went to San Francisco to complete moment-by-moment analysis of the
deaths with two retired American professors of anaesthesiology. The final
product was a paper published in the *Journal of Medical Ethics* (Ogden,
Hamilton, and Whitcher 2010). The smooth research experience using Swiss

data contrasts with the rough road experienced in Canada, but one can hope it is also a bell-wether for better trends in this country.

Acknowledgments

I thank the anonymous reviewers for their insights in improving this chapter. I am especially grateful to my Kwantlen Polytechnic University colleagues Jean McKendry, Greg Jenion, and Erling Christensen for their thoughtful input.

Notes

1 *BC Coroners Service Policy and Procedure Manual,* 21 April 1999, sec. 2.2.G.1/1, Suicide – Euthanasia and Assisted Suicide.
2 Larry Campbell would later go on to serve as mayor of Vancouver and then as a senator for Canada. In 2009, he co-wrote *A Thousand Dreams: Vancouver's Downtown Eastside and the Fight for Its Future.* The book describes how he, as coroner, did not aggressively pursue cases of assisted suicide, yet it makes no mention of his *Inquest of Unknown Female* (Campbell, Boyd, and Culbert 2009).
3 *Inquest of Unknown Female* [1994], Oral Reasons for Judgment of the Honourable L.W. Campbell, Coroner (20 October 1994), Coroner file 91-240-0838.
4 The "Wigmore criteria" for deciding claims of privilege in the absence of a statutory basis are recognized by the Supreme Court of Canada (*Slavutych v. Baker et al.,* [1975] S.C.J. No. 29, [1976] 1 S.C.R. 254):

> (1) The communications must originate in a *confidence* that they will not be disclosed;
> (2) This element of *confidentiality must be essential* to the full and satisfactory maintenance of the relation between the parties;
> (3) The *relation* must be one which in the opinion of the community ought to be sedulously *fostered;* and
> (4) The *injury* that would inure to the relation by the disclosure of the communications must be *greater than the benefit* thereby gained for the correct disposal of litigation. (Wigmore, 1905, 3185; emphasis in original)

5 Robinson is a former federal member of Parliament for the Burnaby riding in British Columbia.
6 *R. v. Martens* (4 November 2004), unpublished transcript (Charge to Jury), Duncan, BC, registry 25133-6.
7 Concluding remarks of Detective Robert Reid, Vancouver Police Department, General Occurrence file 2007-117316, 16 July 2008.

References

Burbidge, G.W. (1890). *A Digest of Criminal Law of Canada (Crimes and Punishments).* Toronto: Carswell.
Campbell, L., Boyd, N., and Culbert, L. (2009). *A Thousand Dreams: Vancouver's Downtown Eastside and the Fight for Its Future.* Vancouver: Greystone.
Docker, C.G., and Smith, C.K. (1993). *Departing Drugs.* Victoria, BC: Right to Die Society of Canada.
Farrar, S., and Baty, P. (2003). Exeter Student Wins £63,000. *Times Higher Education Supplement,* 31 October.

Humphry, D. (1991). *Final Exit: The Practicalities of Self-Deliverance and Assisted Suicide for the Dying*. Eugene, OR: Hemlock Society.

—. (2002). *Final Exit: The Practicalities of Self-Deliverance and Assisted Suicide for the Dying* (3rd ed.). New York: Dell.

—. (2008). *Good Life, Good Death*. Junction City, OR: Norris Lane Press.

Johnston, R.T.C. (1995). Special Prosecutor's Report: Investigation into the Death of Susan Jane Rodriguez. Unpublished report.

Last Rights Publications (Ed.). (1995-2000). *The Art and Science of Suicide*. 9 vols. Victoria, BC: Author.

—. (Producer). (2000). *New Technologies for Self Deliverance* [Videorecording]. Victoria, BC: Author.

Lowman, J., and Palys, T. (2000). Ethics and Institutional Conflict of Interest: The Research Confidentiality Controversy at Simon Fraser University. *Sociological Practice: A Journal of Clinical and Applied Sociology 2*, 245-64.

Magnusson, R. (2002). *Angels of Death: Exploring the Euthanasia Underground*. New Haven, CT: Yale University Press.

Mair, G.B. (1980). *How to Die with Dignity*. Edinburgh: Scottish Exit.

Martin, B. (2010). Techniques to Pass On: Technology and Euthanasia. *Bulletin of Science, Technology and Society 30*, 54-59.

Nitschke, P., and Stewart, F. (2009). *The Peaceful Pill Handbook*. Bellingham, WA: Exit International US.

Ogden, R.D. (1994). Euthanasia and Assisted Suicide in Persons with Acquired Immunodeficiency Syndrome (AIDS) or Human Immunodeficiency Virus (HIV). Master's thesis, Simon Fraser University.

—. (2001). Non-Physician Assisted Suicide: The Technological Imperative of the Deathing Counterculture. *Death Studies 25*, 387-402.

—. (2003). No Ring of Confidence. *Times Higher Education Supplement 14*, 7 November.

—. (2010a). The Debreather: A Report on Euthanasia and Suicide Assistance Using Adapted Scuba Technology. *Death Studies 34*(4), 291-317.

—. (2010b). Observation of Two Suicides by Helium Inhalation in a Pre-Filled Environment. *American Journal of Forensic Medicine and Pathology 31*(2), 156-61.

Ogden, R.D., Hamilton, W.K., and Whitcher, C. (2010). Assisted Suicide by Oxygen Deprivation with Helium at a Swiss Right-to-Die Organisation. *Journal of Medical Ethics 36*, 174-79.

Ogden, R.D., and Wooten, R.H. (2002). Asphyxial Suicide with Helium and a Plastic Bag. *American Journal of Forensic Medicine and Pathology 23*(3), 234-37.

Palys, T., and Lowman, J. (2002). Anticipating Law: Research Methods, Ethics and the Law on Privilege. *Sociological Methodology 32*, 1-17.

—. (2010). Going Boldly Where No One Has Gone Before? How REB/TCPS Risk Aversion Is Killing Research on Sensitive Topics. *Journal of Academic Ethics 8*(4), 265-84.

Senate of Canada. (1995). *Of Life and Death: Report of the Special Senate Committee on Euthanasia and Assisted Suicide*. Ottawa: Minister of Supply and Services.

—. (2000). *Quality End-of-Life Care: The Right of Every Canadian*. Ottawa: Minister of Supply and Services.

Smith, C.K., Docker, C.G., Hofsess, J., and Dunn, B. (1995). *Beyond Final Exit*. Victoria, BC: Right to Die Society of Canada.

Stone, G. (1999). *Suicide and Attempted Suicide*. New York: Carroll and Graf.

Taschereau, H.E. (1893). *The Criminal Code of Canada as Amended in 1893 with Commentaries, Annotations, Precedents of Indictments, Etc.* Toronto: Carswell.

Wigmore, J.H. (1905). *A Treatise on the System of Evidence in Trials at Common Law, Including the Statutes and Judicial Decisions of All Jurisdictions of the United States, England, and Canada.* Boston: Little, Brown and Company.

chapter 2   **Ensuring Aboriginal Women's Voices Are Heard: Toward a Balanced Approach in Community-Based Research**

Catherine Fillmore, Colleen Anne Dell, and Jennifer M. Kilty

ABORIGINAL WOMEN'S VOICES are consistently absent in the literature on drug use and treatment, and researchers and treatment professionals alike know little about the destructive impact of stigma on the self-identities and recoveries of First Nations, Inuit, and Metis women in treatment for problematic drug use. Colleen Dell, in collaboration with the National Native Addictions Partnership Foundation and the Canadian Centre on Substance Abuse, secured research funding and assembled a team of researchers and community members to tackle what became a five-year and then an ongoing community-based research project.[1] National Native Addictions Partnership Foundation treatment centres constituted the communities participating in the research. The research team addressed the following questions: What are the experiential paths of Aboriginal women in conflict with the law in the constitution and reconstitution of their self-identity (defined as the healing journey), particularly in view of the stigma associated with illicit drug use, prior to, during, and following treatment? How do treatment program workers influence women's constitution and reconstitution of their self-identity, and what is their role in the healing journey? Over the course of one year, we interviewed sixty-five First Nations, Metis, and Inuit women in treatment, twenty women who had completed treatment, and thirty-eight treatment staff, many of whom were also in recovery. The majority of these individuals were First Nations, which reflects the composition of the treatment centres. All of the quotations that appear here are excerpted from these interviews, which were conducted between 2006 and 2007 in Aboriginal substance abuse treatment centres across the country.

The research team sought additional partners, including Aboriginal elders, treatment providers, women with a history of drug treatment, treatment centre directors, academic researchers, and community agencies working with criminalized Aboriginal women to ensure representation and input from multiple standpoints. We also engaged three expert mentors to provide advice in the specialized areas of traditional Aboriginal healing, drug treatment, and rehabilitation. The expanded team was composed predominately of Aboriginal women from a variety of educational, occupational, geographical, and age categories. As the project's research coordinator, Sheila, explained:

> Working alongside a number of diverse individuals has brought forward the multitude of views that are reflective of each other's experiences, from urban to rural, First Nations to Metis, academic to activist. Each of us brings forward our lived experiences within the project. Our stories shape the way we approach research, and the project has benefitted by our differences, by understanding how we are not a single story.

From the outset, our team's primary consideration was researching with respect, which we defined as "carrying out research with people who have been traditionally excluded from the production of knowledge and considering the rights, beliefs, values and practices of everyone involved in the research process" (Dell et al., forthcoming). To facilitate respectful research, we made reciprocity and recognition cornerstones of our balanced approach so as to inform our relations and activities with participants throughout the project.

The goals of this chapter are twofold. First, we outline how we prioritized women's voices to create a balanced research approach based on reciprocity, respect, and recognition. The key to creating this balanced approach was the development of relationships, friendships, bonds, and connections among and between the research team. Second, by drawing on participation and action in collaborative community-based research, we explore how women's experiences guided the development of the interview and storytelling guide, story (co)production, collaborative analysis, and community-relevant knowledge-exchange activities.[2]

On Creating a Collaborative and Balanced Research Approach

Including Aboriginal women's experiential voices challenges the claim that the Western scientific method is the only way to produce valid knowledge (Gatenby and Humphries 2000; Tickner 2005). It also disrupts the long-standing power inequalities between the researcher and the researched that are characteristic of social science (Hunter 2002; Deutsch 2004; Shope 2006). To carry out our goal of prioritizing the missing voices of marginalized First Nations, Inuit, and Metis women, we combined community-based, Aboriginal, and feminist research approaches to create a balanced approach to research – an extension of what Kirby and McKenna (1989) refer to as doing research "by, for and with" women. Our notion of balance emphasized a relationship based on reciprocity through shared storytelling and giving back to the treatment community. In this case, giving back involved coproducing knowledge and addressing Aboriginal interests. Research was carried out in a respectful way by safeguarding the rights, beliefs, and values of our diverse research team members, community members, and participants. Finally, to achieve a balanced approach, we had to recognize the legitimacy of Aboriginal women's voices in the research arena.

Elders reinforced that reciprocity, respect, and recognition are interrelated and common in community, Aboriginal, and feminist research methodologies. Our balanced approach to research is inherently political, for the team shared three personal and collective goals: empowerment and capacity building, privileging women's experiences and enhancing their lives, and producing knowledge to serve the needs of Aboriginal women.

Community-Based Research: Illustrating Reciprocity

Defined as "a collaborative approach to research that equitably involves, for example, community members, organizational representatives and researchers in all aspects of the research process" (Israel et al. 1998, 177), community-based research focuses on participation, democratic collaboration, and knowledge generation (Brydon-Miller and Maguire 2009, 80). While the socially marginalized are traditionally excluded from the production of knowledge in Western research, community participation, rooted in constructionist and critical theorist evaluations of scientific knowledge, offers a particularly useful alternative (Israel et al. 1998, 176-77; Mance, Mendleson, and Byrd III 2010, 132). Emphasizing shared participation throughout the research process and working with the strengths and resources of community members are critical to increasing the quality of the research (Fletcher 2003), for they help build relationships among partners and co-researchers that in turn encourage reflexivity (Mance, Mendelson, and Byrd III 2010, 132).

For example, when community service workers, all of whom had a history with problematic substance use, pointed out the importance of reciprocity and the need to honour the women who shared their stories with a meaningful gift, the research team agreed that a fiscal honorarium (already a contested issue in research ethics) (Fry et al. 2005) was not appropriate. Subsequently, upon discovering the teachings of the oyster totem from Herb Nabigon's autobiography, *The Hollow Tree* (2006), we decided that following each story-telling session, we would offer the gift of a natural oyster and enclosed pearl. While the oyster was being opened, the researcher would share Nabigon's story of the pearl:

> The strongest example I can find in Nature comes from Sister Water, the cradle of Mother Earth's womb. In her depth can be found the teachings of the oyster totem. Here the oyster's precious jewel, a pearl that starts out as a grain of sand, is nothing more than an irritant that has entered the barnacle or oyster at some point and cannot be removed. That oyster has lodged in its folds something that is very painful to its habitat-being. The sand cannot be removed and now the oyster must contend with it, using its natural abilities to deal with the situation. Unlike humans who pretend "it" will go away, the clam pulls from its inner qualities a working solution. The clam totem's teaching resembles our own feeble attempts to make peace with our emotions. It didn't ask for the lesson, but it was forced to take a negative aspect of life and work with its principles. In this instance Nature teaches the oyster to tap into its intrinsic abilities to protect itself from corrosion. The oyster now heaves up its own mucus in multiple layers until it polishes smooth the intrusive entity – the grain of sand. Time then becomes the key. The outcome is a jewel that is admired by all. (52-53)

Establishing a reciprocal relationship with participants fosters reflexivity. Drawing on the symbolic story of the pearl and oyster, the women similarly came to identify their problematic drug use as an irritant that required the discovery of their inner strength to overcome drug addiction, and they described the experience as transcendent.

Through reciprocity, members of the research team and treatment community both gained and learned from one another. While team members offered a message of hope through the symbolic gift of the pearl, they in turn received inspiration, insight, and knowledge about the complexity of substance use. Having interviewers with histories of substance use allowed team members to share their own stories as they found points of convergence with the women's experiences. One team member recounted:

> And then reading those stories, too. It just made so much sense. It helps, I guess, reinforces, that this is why Aboriginal women use and abuse alcohol, drugs – because of a dysfunction of their families, the stuff they've witnessed, the violence, the poverty, the racism; they experienced a lot

of that, and they talked about that in all of the transcripts. And I related to a lot of that because a lot of that I experienced in my own life, coming from the same place. We all want to reach that same goal, you know. We want to be happy. We want to be free. We want that joy. We want that hope. We want that respect. (Jenny)

The exchange of symbolic and culturally meaningful gifts reinforced the importance of reciprocity underlying our balanced approach. Giving the pearl cultivated trust and comfort, demonstrating how the development of creative and project-specific methodologies can strengthen the relationship between researchers and the community. Further, the focus on reciprocal relations demonstrates the ways in which Aboriginal communities and universities can become coproducers of knowledge in ways that benefit Aboriginal women.

Aboriginal Methodology: Illustrating Respect

Aboriginal methodology requires directing research to serve Aboriginal interests or self-determination in the research process (Schnarch 2004), to counter the exploitative research rooted in Canada's history of colonization (Dua 1999; Smylie et al. 2004). Recent studies demonstrate the positive outcomes of incorporating the principles of community-based participatory research with Indigenous communities (Leslie, Hughes, and Braun 2010, 128) that invoke "a balance between leadership by academics and leadership by community" (Nguyen, Hsu, and Kue 2010, 118). Vannini and Gladue (2008, 140) call for a decolonized epistemology that begins with a reflection of one's own historical background and position before beginning "the process of democratizing, discovering, reframing, and claiming knowledge."

In response to the history of exploitative research on Aboriginal peoples, increasingly, individual Aboriginal communities are drafting their own ethical and moral agreements to ensure research is conducted with the guidance and participation of the community. Community involvement necessitates ensuring that the research is not harmful; as such, it holds tremendous potential to provide valuable information and insight into an issue of interest (Fisher and Ball 2003; Castellano 2004). The research was guided by the ownership, control, access, possession (OCAP) principles, the ethical codes adopted by treatment centres involved in the study, the guidelines from the National Native Addictions Partnership Foundation, and an elder's teaching on Aboriginal philosophy and clanship to understand and practice respect. The OCAP principles suggest that to avoid the abuse and mistreatment of First Nations communities under study, the researcher should provide the collective ownership of group information, First Nations control over research and information, First Nations management of access to their data, and the physical possession of data by First Nations (Schnarch 2004), so as to ensure that Aboriginal people are more actively involved in the research process.

To foster respectful relations with the directors, staff, and women at the treatment centres, project coordinators organized an orientation to become familiar with staff and programs and to participate in traditional ceremonies. Additionally, we invited three Aboriginal team members to share their experiences with drug use and criminalization. We offered two of these inspirational stories, printed in a small booklet, to the women at the end of their storytelling session to demonstrate our respect and empathy for women in treatment and to offer them hope in their own healing journeys. One participant expressed how inspirational it was to see "Sharon had made it," and by meeting Sharon in person, she felt a sense of renewed hope for her own future. The inspirational stories helped to legitimate women's lived experiences and to generate mutual compassion and an authentic connection between researchers and participants.

To promote respectful and democratic relations among our team, we developed an open and fluid model of leadership for the project to ensure team members had ongoing opportunities for input and participation at all stages of decision making. An elder reflected: "There's been a lot of energy that went into somebody's vision to make this happen, a reality. And I believe what they're doing is the very best that they can do. They are not doing it alone. They're having a lot of direction. And it's for a good reason. They don't have ownership of this information" (Elder Joyce Paul). Another team member emphasized that establishing a respectful and trusting relationship with a community for the purpose of doing research requires "long-term relationship building" and "working on a level playing field." She stressed the importance of "strict research standards," "a balance between academic and community needs," and "using an Aboriginal approach" to achieve such a relationship. A non-Aboriginal team member noted that "respect is being together on a level playing field," adding that the researcher who spearheaded the project "never pulled rank" and that "everyone got their say" through regular and frequent emails that compiled "everyone's interpretations."

Fostering reciprocal relationships among a nationwide team of community members and researchers took over two years before we were ready to go into the field to begin conducting interviews, and it remains an ongoing process. As principal investigator, Dell was the central figure with whom treatment directors, elders, researchers, and Aboriginal team members had contact. Given the history of exploitation of Aboriginal communities by white researchers (Smylie et al. 2004), this relationship was vital to the project; over time and through face-to-face meetings, group retreats and travel, smudges, and lengthy and oftentimes personal telephone conversations, team members developed a sense of trust in Dell's vision of the project. Developing trust required speaking to one another about personal issues – our families, health, weddings, funerals, school, careers, and any manner of things we were experiencing. Like snowball sampling, the development of interpersonal relationships emerged and grew organically rather than through forced and formalized measures such as those encouraged by traditional research methods that demand objectivity and emotional neutrality. For many Aboriginal team members, participation in this project required reassurance that researchers would not take from the community without giving back – this reassurance emerged as a result of their friendship with Dell. Team members and community members put their faith in Dell as a person they knew intimately rather than Dell as an objective and distanced researcher. In a project DVD titled "Sharing Our Research Journey," Dell states, "It is about people owning their own voices, information about themselves. In this sense, we all own the data, that is, our contributions to it. Although I have taken stewardship for it as the principal investigator, it was a result of your entrusting me with that responsibility."

This is not to say that we did not confront reservations about participation in the project. Initially, some treatment directors felt wary about working with researchers. However, one team member reflexively stated during an informal discussion of the project that "the project demonstrated that a research project could be done with respect and honour, as many projects are not done this way." Our attempts to ensure an ethically grounded research practice received acknowledgment and validation from treatment staff and elders. For example, one director and elder stated:

> What stays with me is the honesty and being addressed all the time with integrity, dignity, and being consistent. 'Cause sometimes people just will touch base, and that's it. You don't hear from them for a while. But I found that the communication, like between our centre and [names team members], at all times was consistent. I was always kept up to date, like, you were an important part of this whole [project]. (Elder Joyce Paul)

Western approaches that emphasize researcher neutrality and nondisclosure (Gatenby and Humphries 2000; Hunter 2002; Deutsch 2004; Tickner 2005; Shope 2006) could be viewed as disrespectful by Aboriginal communities that emphasize mutual storytelling. Therefore, we sought opportunities to build respectful partnerships, whether it was participating in sweetgrass ceremonies and morning prayers or sharing stories with the women at the centres. Throughout the project, elders were invaluable in guiding our efforts to understand and link to spirituality and embrace traditional teachings; as Elder Dexter remarked, "You want that balance in there. Whatever we did, whatever it is that we do, helping a person out there, there's always a prayer."

Feminist Research: Illustrating Recognition

A central feature and goal of feminist research is to improve women's lives (Fonow and Cook 2005; Harding and Norberg 2005). Such an approach accepts as "truth" that women occupy a marginalized position in society, and that social structures seek to maintain a power imbalance through patriarchy, misogyny, and gendered and racialized practices (de Laine 2000). Contrary to traditional social science, and given women's ongoing oppression, feminist research requires privileging their experiences (Cook and Fonow 1986). Addressing women as a homogenous category, however, does not acknowledge power imbalances between women or the intersectional implications of race, class, sexuality, and ability on the recognition (or lack thereof) of women's varied experiential knowledge (Shope 2006).

Feminist, antiracist, and anticolonial critics point out that "disrespectful, insensitive, or unresponsive" conduct by researchers persists in many communities and that Aboriginal women, particularly those marginalized by substance use and poverty, "continue to be treated as objects of study rather than experts of their lives and the conditions that mediate them" (Salmon 2007, 983). In a participatory action research project involving thirteen indigenous female elders, Zohl dé Ishtar (2005, 359) recommends, "For White feminists to forge a partnership with Indigenous women, they need to develop a methodology that can navigate two divergent cultures, two ways of knowing and being." Dé Ishtar describes her model, "Living on the Ground," as "grounded in relationship, bridg[ing] Indigenous and feminist knowledge, requir[ing] the researcher to be passionately involved, and produc[ing] tangible outcomes which immediately benefited the project's hosts" (ibid.). By basing the research on the development of personal relationships, many of which remain and continue to grow, our project captured the importance of bridging Indigenous and feminist knowledge. For example, one team member recounted how bonding with one another evoked the team's compassion and strengthened their commitment to the project: "[We] were sitting around having a meeting discussing the different findings that we found and how emotional all of us got and how passionate all of us got, talking about our findings. And we each talked about it, and we each cried about it, sitting in this academic environment ... It just let me know right there, that we were in the right place" (Jenny).

Recognition occurred through prioritizing women's voices, which one team member articulated as follows:

It's a silenced voice, and that was one of the things that came through so clearly in the interviews. And we know that already. It is a silenced, marginalized voice ... It's so wrong that certain segments of society don't have a voice, and so that is part of what we could do as a collective, to give that voice, to make sure that their voice is heard. People are not able, I don't think, unless you start to understand and you start to feel what others are going through, then you just aren't going to get it. (Colleen)

Similarly, an academic team member reflected on the stark difference between our grounded approach and the Western scientific approach, observing that "it taught me how to be holistic, to work from the ground up, to leave 'expertise' at the door. I was there to learn from the women and their narratives." These outcomes were only possible due to the relationships fostered among the team.

Hence, our project began with recognizing the voices of Aboriginal women. As noted earlier, at the outset of the project we asked three First Nations women on the research team to document the impact of stigma on self-identity in their own healing. The women's stories informed the team's understanding of the significance and meaning of cultural identity; the centrality of family and community; the impacts of stigmatization and the importance of hope; and the need for balance (physical, emotional, intellectual, and spiritual). This knowledge was used to develop the storytelling guide (which we used in lieu of a more traditional interview schedule) for the project.

Beginning the project with the women's stories built trust with the staff and women at the treatment centres.[3] One woman in treatment indicated the project helped her to feel empowered and validated:

It made me feel important, you know, like I was somebody. 'Cause for so long I didn't feel like I was worth anything ... Like now somebody is taking the time to hear my side, my story, you know, things that bothered me. It made a lot of difference because I felt important, you know, like after all those years. Like I was always being everybody's backbone. Now all of a sudden I had a backbone. It made me feel worthy, you know, useful again. (Anita)

An elder similarly observed that "it is empowering [when] people's pain is validated, especially when they look back at it and know they made a difference. To anyone, themselves or their family or other women they've come across, they say, 'If she can do it, I can do it.' It's the power of example" (Elder Joyce). In this way, our nontraditional methodology – built upon the development of real relationships – was central not only to making connections in the community and across the team but in having a positive and inspirational impact upon the participants who make up the communities we researched.

Participation and Action in a Collaborative and Balanced Research Methodology

The trilogy of respect, recognition, and reciprocity that characterizes our balanced research approach provided the foundation for the team and community participation in all stages of the research process; participatory action and involvement in project outcomes are fundamental elements of community-based research (Stoecker 2009, 393). While participation of community members and partners is important throughout the research process, studies suggest that the interview stage requires the greatest community involvement (Stoecker 2009, 392). Stoecker (2009, 398) claims that "bringing equality to the social relations of knowledge production requires supporting people from all walks of life to become producers of publicly exchanged knowledge" that "transforms existing oppressive social relations of knowledge production." Working toward an open and democratic process in collaboration with members of the treatment community entailed promoting participation and action throughout the four stages of the research process: developing a storytelling guide; gathering and coproducing the stories; collaborating in the analysis of the stories; and relaying what we learned to the community.

Developing the Storytelling Guide

The decision to ask three First Nations women on our research team to document their personal healing journeys was a key turning point in shaping and moving the research forward. The objective was for Sharon, Valerie, and Jane to reflect upon their personal healing journeys in relation to areas of investigation – namely, problematic drug use, mothering, stigma, experiences of treatment and criminalization, and identity as an Aboriginal woman. They each shared their story in approximately five thousand words and found the process supportive:

I verbally shared my story so many times in the past twenty years, but never actually sat down to write it. I asked myself, "How do I write this?" As I wrote my story, I realized it was similar yet different than verbally telling my story. Well, words are words that come out of your mouth, and people can misinterpret what you're saying, and some even forget the message you're leaving. Whereas, with writing, you can leave a message of hope and can provide courage to someone who is really searching to understand one's life. Someone may be reading my story fifty years from now, when I have passed this physical life and moved to the spiritual realm. (Valerie)

By drawing upon Aboriginal traditions of oral storytelling (Vannini and Gladue 2008) and Western academic methods of written documentation, the three team members felt transformed by writing their stories with the goal of providing hope to other women. Rather than telling their stories to a counsellor or an institutional authority, they were identifying with aspects of their healing journeys that resonated with, moved, changed, and meant something to them. In this way, their storytelling was self-directed and autonomous rather than extracted by questions posed by others, and it generated connectedness among team members and between participants and researchers as we began to gather and coproduce participant stories. In addition to using these stories to identify key subject areas for the interview guide, we encouraged participants to read them to connect with the project before commencing the interview.

Gathering and Coproducing the Stories

Elder Joyce Paul spoke of the need for respect and hope to guide and move the project forward and felt that these seeds were planted at the first research meeting, observing that "giving [everyone] a pearl was like a seed planted and nurtured along as they looked forward to seeing each other again. No doubt women banded together ... Together they were empowered." We reinforced these relationships by establishing a collaborative approach to the storytelling session, where participants are "co-constructing and negotiating a narrative that is full of care" (Vannini and Gladue 2008, 141). The mutual sharing of stories reflects a talking circle, a traditional form of storytelling among First Nations in Canada (ibid., 142). Vannini and Gladue (2008, 142) identify the common similarities between this kind of interviewing ("reflexive dyadic") and talking circles: "the sharing of experiences, reciprocity, heartfelt speaking, respect, support, honouring, listening, mutual empowerment, compassion, and interconnectedness generated by open sharing." One team member expressed the powerful impact of open sharing: "Women who have gone through these experiences and are telling their story, and they see people are listening, respecting what they say ... It's just so amazing when they see they can be treated with respect" (Sharon C.). Correspondingly, an expert mentor observed,

> I think that the way the research was set up – it was so respectful to the clients that were being interviewed – and it was done in a way that was very respectful to their lives ... And the women, I guess because of that – sort of whatever rapport the interviewers were able to establish – they ended up very forthcoming in terms of talking about real aspects of their lives. I guess healing is recognizing the struggles you've been through. (Greg)

Like talking circles, we expected and welcomed differences and strove to problem solve any difficulties or tensions, often "talking it out" together as a group (in person and through frequent phone conversations and teleconferences) with the support and guidance of our elders. Our commitment and support for the women and their welfare unified our team; for example, as a team member stated, "All of us, every one of us, we work differently, we do things differently. We all have different ways of approaching, but the intent is the same. We all want the well-being of these women and try to articulate to the best of our ability to get a message out there for them" (Val). Showing respect for "the spirit" was fundamental to working through differences on our team. An elder and treatment director affirmed that "when you attack someone's spirit, it is never justified. No one should have to prove they know more because they are more brown – everyone has their own strengths" (Elder Joyce). When team members raised questions about the research process, we resolved them by listening with respect. The early and continued development of close personal ties between team members actually encouraged open discussion, as members felt safe to bring their concerns to the table. One concern, for instance, was the gender imbalance on the team, which called for us to expand the research team to include male advisors and mentors as well as a male elder:

> Some impressions from the women and the centres were that perhaps we hadn't considered something like, for example, the importance of balance between men and women in those relationships. Women want healthy relationships with their partners. And, so when we talk about gender sensitivity, it's not always just women–centred programming ...

it's that balance. So, really, I think that [the research process] is constantly evolving and changing. Because we've encouraged dialogue, there's always been that dynamic process. So, there's that momentum. (Cathy)

Other concerns related to non-Aboriginal team members who felt apprehension about "doing or saying something wrong" to Aboriginal members of the team and treatment community. One team member spoke of being able to work through this "emotional barrier" because "the team was inclusive; no one was afraid to give opinions and teach others who don't know." Non-Aboriginal team members expressed some discomfort, for example, when they were first involved in participating in traditional ceremonies such as smudging. The research team's emphasis on inclusivity and knowledge sharing meant that non-Aboriginal team members were never treated "like outsiders." For another team member, "a great gift was a young Ottawa project coordinator who unfailingly bridged the cultural (and generational) gap with her compassion, deep commitment, and infectious enthusiasm for the project and its participants; she treated us all like family, which we felt deeply, and consistently provided the momentum and imagination to propel the project forward" (Cathy).

To gain insight regarding the effectiveness of the storytelling guide, participants were invited to complete an anonymous evaluation and to submit it in a sealed envelope at the treatment centre. In keeping with the project goals of reflexive, collaborative, and exploratory qualitative analysis, we asked the women to write as much or as little as they wanted about their experience of sharing their stories. The evaluations demonstrated that the women felt the project was meaningful to their lives. Most commented on the fact that they were not simply requested to answer a series of closed-ended questions. One woman, for instance, wrote, "I liked that the questions were designed to get me to tell my story." Other comments included: "I like the idea of you researching to help other women"; "it makes me feel better that there are people looking out for us"; and "finally, someone actually cares about women's issues and wants to address the problem at the root." One participant, who became a team member and assisted with the analysis and dissemination of research findings, reflected:

When I was first interviewed for this project I didn't think much of it because I felt that I had no voice and what could I possibly do to help another person ... Having gotten involved with it [the project] was an amazing experience that helped me to know that I am someone, and that I can help others, and that I do have that voice to be there even if it is just for one other person. (Anita)

Having received overwhelmingly positive feedback from team members and women participating in the storytelling sessions, we incorporated both participation and action throughout the analysis.

Collaborative Analysis of Stories

Our balanced, collaborative approach to analysis emphasized the importance of having researchers, partners, and communities equitably and democratically involved throughout the research project (Mance, Mendelson, and Byrd III 2010). Some methodologists metaphorically describe analysis as crystallization because "crystals grow, change, alter, but are not amorphous. Crystals are prisms that reflect externalities and refract within themselves, creating different colors, patterns, arrays, casting off in different directions. What we see depends upon our angle of 'repose'" (Richardson 1997, 92, qtd. in Lincoln and Guba 2000, 181).

Crystallization allows us to emphasize the multiplicity of voices involved in the interpretation of the interview transcripts and to sustain transparency in our collaborative work. We filtered the experiential stories through the crystal or prism with the aim of gaining a threaded (holistic) understanding of the coproduced stories (rainbow/spectrum). At the centre of the crystal are our team member's diverse lenses that filter the analysis of the women's stories through their experiences and knowledge sets. In order to organize the women's stories, team members participated in identifying discursive themes. In all, we drew from the knowledge sets of different groups and people, including academic researchers, community members, elders, treatment workers (social workers, counsellors), storytelling participants, and transcribers.[4]

Academics brought social science and thus "outsider" knowledge (Kirby and McKenna 1989) from which the team conducted a preliminary organization of discourses. For example, literature reviews helped us to develop key thematic areas of interest: self-harm, identity, surviving violence, criminalization, caretaking, drug use, and mental and physical health. Community members and elders provided an experiential and cultural lens, better described as insider knowledge. These team members drew on their postcolonial worldviews and their own subjective experiences that made sense of the coproduced stories. Elders often provided culturally relevant stories that reflected the experiences and findings as they unfolded, which incorporated Aboriginal oral tradition into our meaning-making process. Treatment providers (social workers and counsellors) offered a third analytic lens and insider knowledge regarding treatment structures, programming, and goals. Finally, transcriptionists recorded the themes they identified during the transcription process, a strategy that Tilley (2003) emphasizes as important in preliminary open coding.

Our "prism" or crystallization approach to collaborative analysis increased the transparency and accuracy of our conclusions.[5] Having multiple people review the transcripts enhanced transparency by increasing the opportunity for discussion, nuanced examination, and thus more accurate theme construction. Themes identified during the preliminary analysis were presented and discussed with staff and women in treatment at the centres,[6] which not only increased analytical rigour but "support[ed] researcher reflexivity, and promote[ed] positive, empowering research relationships" (Forbat and Henderson, qtd. in Salmon 2007, 986). Involving multiple groups of people in a collaborative analysis acted as a community-based form of member checking that increased the believability of our theme construction by ensuring that the themes reflected the patterns represented in the stories (Lincoln and Guba 1985). This kind of regular and ongoing collaborative peer feedback generated a sense of honesty in our interpretation of the discursive messages rather than trying to achieve the impossibility of uncovering "truth" in a discourse implied by traditional Western methods (Creswell and Miller 2000). In the words of one team member, the process of analysis was "slower but the outcomes were stronger ... When doing the analysis, we had ongoing reviews – agreeing, pointing out gaps – and the research process was more rigorous, the results were more reliable."

Knowledge Exchange in Relaying the Findings to the Community

Graham and others (2006, 14) report considerable conceptual ambiguity, misapplication, and inconsistency in describing the terms used in the "knowledge-to-action field," including *knowledge translation, knowledge transfer, knowledge exchange,* and *knowledge dissemination.* The multitude of terms has contributed to their confusion and complicated usage (Pentland et al. 2011; Henry and Mackenzie 2012). A common concern is the linearity of knowledge translation approaches and the need for more fluid and dynamic models of knowledge exchange (Ward et al. 2012) that emphasize a collaborative (Henry and Mackenzie 2012) and interactive approach (Mitton et al. 2007) among team members, participants, and community stakeholders (Graham et al. 2006). For this project, we adopted the term *knowledge exchange* because of its emphasis on respectful collaboration, genuine interaction, and the centrality of relationships in producing knowledge. As Graham and others write, "In contrast, with knowledge translation and transfer, there is no expectation that the same stakeholders will be involved in all stages of the process" (ibid., 17).

However, a common barrier to knowledge exchange activities is the traditional "incentive system" in the academy that requires the dissemination of research findings in peer-reviewed journals and books, for example (Mitton et al. 2007, 739). More recently, critical scholars, such as van den Hoonaard (this volume), argue that the term reflects broader trends in the colonization of qualitative research by biomedical approaches to scientific studies, which, at the same time, have further intensified the pressure for social science scholars to publish (or perish). While we recognize the need for peer evaluation, knowledge exchange in community-based research grounded in Aboriginal and feminist praxis has quite a different meaning. For instance, knowledge exchange reflects the researcher's ability to give back useful and timely results to participants and related communities. Lengthy journal articles and books laden with academic jargon do not provide the necessary accessibility for participating communities.

Treatment staff voiced this concern and urged the research team to provide the centres with practical and helpful results on a regular and ongoing basis. Subsequently, we approached knowledge exchange on two levels: first, the traditional publication path and, second, a more flexible and creative route by generating accessible mixed-media tools for participants, communities, and treatment centres. In the following discussion, we outline three of the unique ways our team translated research findings to participants and treatment communities – namely, through a research reflections video, a song, and a discussion guide.

Research Reflections Video
In February 2009, we held a gathering of thirty members of the research team, community partners, and participants at Cedar Lodge in Dundurn, Saskatchewan. The goals of this gathering were to review research findings, reflect upon the research process, and develop an effective action plan for sharing findings with participants and treatment communities. Dé Ishtar (2005, 358) urges the bridging of Indigenous and feminist knowledge at all stages of research, including knowledge exchange, to encourage passionate involvement so that findings have "direct, immediate use" to the community. Salmon (2007, 985) claims that many women are frustrated by their experiences with community researchers who not only own and guide research, but who "come, do the research, and then it's months or years before we hear from them again." Similarly, team members expressed concern about exploiting Aboriginal communities; one member affirmed, "researchers cannot go into a community and then leave. First Nations have suffered because of researchers, and [I] want instead to contribute to their success." To provide treatment centres and participants with quick accessible feedback on the progress of the research, we shared findings through fact sheets, posters, a website, online forums, and regular informal emails and discussions on the project's progress.

Given that our balanced approach is unique in comparison to most research ventures, while at the Cedar Lodge gathering we formulated a broader action plan for knowledge exchange that included disseminating information specifically about our methodology. The team decided to develop a collaborative and participatory DVD that documented our research process. Videography, described as "an empowering, democratizing method" in interviewing (Kindon 2003, 144), has similar impacts on knowledge-exchange activities. MPet productions interviewed team members about who they were, how they became involved, and what they brought to the project. In order to receive feedback before the video was finalized, we distributed a rough cut to all team members, including those who were not able to attend the gathering. The video, *Sharing Our Research Journey* introduces the basic premise of our research process – that no single form of knowledge has priority over another. In April 2010, we broadcasted a ten-minute clip for SaskTel MAX television in Saskatchewan titled "Saskatchewan: A Healing Journey – Disseminating Knowledge through Song Creation."

With the findings in mind, participants at the Cedar Lodge gathering worked with Violet Naytowhow, a Woodland Cree singer/songwriter, to create a song that reflects the project's findings. Similar to the adoption of storytelling with its links to the talking circle as a tool for decolonizing our research methodologies, the use of music as a vehicle for communicating the findings of the project served to break down the traditional hierarchical relationships between academics and the community. Violet Naytowhow shares:

> Reflecting back, to the song writing event, I saw the hearts and minds of many reflecting holistically, their emotions of a healing process, sharing that in a creative process (song writing) about their lives in motion with others lives. Inspiration for the words to dig deep into themselves was encouraged by the initial focusing meditation, sharing circle and youth who spoke on her own healing journey. It was a true testament of a respectful relationship amongst many human beings gathered to share the message of unified hope and supportive healing.

Various drafts of the song were distributed to team members for feedback; the song, "From Stilettos to Moccasins," was officially released on 13 May 2009, followed by a music video in August 2009. We delivered over six thousand copies of the DVD to treatment centres, conferences, and various community organizations. However, sharing our findings with a broader audience required the use of mass electronic media; therefore, we uploaded the song to YouTube and our Facebook group.[7] Electronic media attracts youth, for whom such technology is a vital part of their social networks (Flicker et al. 2008, 286).

The development of "From Stilettos to Moccasins" was a collaborative, bonding, and transformative experience for many members of the research team. As academic researchers, we initially believed that the process required us to temporarily suspend our training in lieu of artistic creativity. Correspondingly, there was the discomfort of entering the unfamiliar terrain of songwriting for those who had little music background – not dissimilar to how many people feel when they act as a participant in a research project. Research is a method of knowledge coproduction and message sharing, and songwriting as a form of knowledge exchange taps into the very heart of what it is we do as researchers. There is no question that this song has gained a widespread audience; as of February 2014, the video has been viewed nearly twenty-five thousand times on YouTube.

Discussion Guide

Finally, the team developed a forty-minute training video and discussion guide, *From Stilettos to Moccasins: A Guide for Group Discussions,* intended as an educational tool for women in addictions treatment. The training guide is based on the central finding of our study that Aboriginal women need to reclaim a healthy self-identity in order to heal from problematic drug use. This initiative originated from participants' desire to have others experience "walking in their shoes" to understand their lives.

The discussion guide offers a structured three-hour group discussion guide on identity, stigma, and healing, and includes exploration exercises and guiding questions designed to promote self- and group reflection and dialogue and to support women in treatment as they transition back to their communities. The discussion guide reinforces the crucial role of aftercare support, an insight clearly voiced by participants. It is not a treatment program or model of recovery; nor is it designed as a counselling session. The training guide comes with evaluation forms for the facilitator and participant, which can be modified, updated, and improved by the research team.

Conclusion

A major aim of our research project was to examine the role of stigma and identity in the healing journeys of Aboriginal women as they grapple with problematic drug use.[8] By drawing on community-based, Aboriginal, and feminist research methodologies, this research demonstrates that women's multiple voices are necessary to interpret, contextualize, and analyze co-produced stories as well as to identify effective avenues for disseminating research findings. Firmly entrenched in our research approach is the understanding that everything and everyone is interconnected. Congruent with

Aboriginal epistemology, we adopted a holistic approach that recognizes that there is a multiplicity of ways of knowing, the importance of reflexivity, and the value of subjective knowledge through storytelling. In contrast to object- ive, emotionally neutral research models, this approach endorses a democratic and decolonized methodology, working from a base of mutual respect, reci- procity, and recognition in developing long-term relationships with team members, participants, and community partners. Drawing on the work of Little Bear, Christensen (2012, 232) writes that storytelling is "the central medium of knowledge transmission" and a valuable "educational tool" for Indigenous communities. Unlike static linear methodologies, our dynamic balanced approach, with its emphasis on collaboration and relationships, en- abled us to develop highly innovative and culturally meaningful methods of knowledge exchange, such as the coproduction of "From Stilettos to Moccasins," which reflected the women's stories of their complex healing journeys.[9]

Undoubtedly, the team's inspiration was the women who shared their stories and to whom we felt a sense of commitment and responsibility. By maintaining the rule that the team had to approve of all project-related pub- lications, presentations, and dissemination of findings, we avoided becoming academics who legitimized the voices of marginalized women. Rather than "giving a voice to" or "speaking for" the team or the participants, we worked to generate spaces for their voices to be heard and for them to speak on their own – both within their communities as well as in academia, with govern- ment officials, and among treatment services. By securing continued funding for travel, diverse team members were able to participate in conferences and presentations for the project. It was rare that an academic would publish or present findings alone; on those rare occasions, key team members were al- ways listed as copresenters in absentia.[10] Our team members participated in this project because they care about their communities and the research being done; however, most hold other full-time, paid employment. Subsequently, team members took the lead on different components of the project as they fit their interest, skills, and schedules. Rather than "passing through" the community by either seeking tacit approval of academically constructed work by busy community members, the project would halt until there was group discussion, reflection, and agreement. While at times this balanced approach prolonged typical research timelines, Dell argues that

> until we have that knowledge shared amongst everyone and people re- spect that and respect other individuals, I don't think we have a com- plete picture of what we are trying to solve or to create a policy, or

whatever. That voice and that experience has to be there, and it is not any less than what I bring or anyone else brings.

At the same time, commitment to the project meant that team members faced challenges, whether it was juggling the competing demands of caring for a young family or an elderly parent with project deadlines, or travelling long distances with health challenges, or attempting to resolve the tensions between our research goals and those dictated by conservative university administrations. With respect to pressure from universities to produce a scholarly publication record, one team member explained,

> All of the time spent drafting plain language summaries, writing a song, making videos, creating training guides, and engaging in ongoing informal discussions with community members and participants is time away from crafting articles for peer review. There are possible negative implications of these research decisions – for example, failing to focus exclusively on peer review publications or publishing authorship in alphabetical rather than contribution percentage value order – may affect us as we apply for tenure, promotion, or other research grants.

However, what we learned and experienced by working with the treatment community not only made us more compassionate social scientists, it also exemplified a path for researching with respect. Conducting community-based research requires thinking of research as praxis, which Paulo Freire (1993, 36) defines as "reflection and action upon the world in order to transform it." As critical social scientists, we had to challenge much of our academic training that taught us to be neutral and objective and to direct the research project as we saw fit. Ultimately, we sacrificed our position as "principal investigators" and entered the field as novices and outsiders. Moreover, we left the comforts and predictability of academia to engage in activities, such as song and video making, which were beyond our knowledge bases. Correspondingly, treatment providers worked outside their comfort zone by engaging in research activities, such as collaborative storytelling or analysis, rather than counselling. One team member described the challenge of listening as a researcher when she had experiential knowledge of drug use: "I could not take [my] street in there and be tough. [I] had to be patient, to listen." In effect, our project illustrates the coming together of very different communities – namely, academia, National Native Addictions Partnership Foundation treatment centres, marginalized women, and Aboriginal communities. We suggest that this research acted as a point of suture between these different communities and that it was only possible because of the relationships formed among the group.

Mapping the research around the three R's – recognition, respect, and reciprocity – helped to ensure participation and action by the research team, members of the treatment community, and participants. Whether it was building the focus of the project and storytelling guide from the ground up (beginning with the stories of three team members), or finding a way to foster reciprocity in a culturally meaningful way with participants for sharing their stories (offering the pearl in the oyster), or standing outside of traditional academia as we disseminated research findings (in song and music video), we forged innovative entrées to community-based research. These methods require critical scholars to be both reflexive and flexible in their approach – and to avoid trying to fit research into a preconceived methodology. For this research, the strength of the relationships that were formed between team members made the project function. Completely outside traditional methodologies, the fact that many team members came to actually love one another pushed us to work together in a way that reflected an Aboriginal worldview. This is unlikely to occur in most research situations, and we are certainly not advocating for others to begin their research by expecting this to take place. Rather, we suggest that by letting go of predetermined expectations and being creative and open to different ways of thinking about, engaging, and doing research, researchers will be more likely to create a unique research path that bridges academic and community interests.

Notes

1   The Canadian Institutes of Health Research, Institute of Aboriginal People's Health was a major funder of this project.

2   Throughout this chapter, we use the term *story* to emphasize a particular kind of narrative most relevant in the Aboriginal methodology literature (Barton 2004), as well as to avoid confusion with emerging discussions of narrative analysis. Lawler (2008, 33) notes that many use the terms *story* and *narrative* interchangeably to describe "resources and social and cultural productions that people use in their day-to-day lives 'to make sense of' their lives."

3   Another key finding was the benefits the three women identified in telling their stories: discovering the impact of the written word, promotion of healing, recognition of the ability to offer hope to women in need, increase in self-esteem, and increased appreciation of the importance of sharing their lived experiences with others (Acoose et al. 2009).

4   Findings from the interviews with women clients and staff were remarkably similar. For example, both groups identified a core set of helpful traits defining the skills and abilities of treatment workers, including recognizing the impact of trauma, demonstrating care and empathy, fostering open communication, supporting links to Aboriginal spirituality and culture, being non-judgmental, providing inspiration and hope, acknowledging the past with a view to moving toward the future, and fostering community ties (Niccols, Dell, and Clarke 2009).

5 Another major finding of this study is the need for treatment programs to assist women in re-claiming their identity as Aboriginal women through the inclusion of culturally meaningful healing experiences (Niccols, Dell, and Clarke 2009).

6 Where possible, the team members who attended the treatment centres returned in person to discuss the preliminary findings; we also contacted staff by telephone, and in other instances, were able to discuss these findings at research meetings, such as at our Cedar Lodge (Saskatchewan) retreat in February 2009.

7 See "From Stilettos to Moccasins" at http://www.youtube.com/watch?v=1QRb8wA2iHs &feature=channel.

8 For a more detailed discussion of findings related to the Eurocentric construction of Aboriginal women as "expected" offenders, see Dell and Kilty (2013).

9 For further information on how the voices of First Nations women function as an essential teaching tool, see Acoose and Dell (2009).

10 This chapter is the first text solely authored by academics involved in the project.

References

Acoose, S., Blunderfield, D., Dell, C.A., and Desjarlais, V. (2009). Beginning with Our Voices: How the Experiential Stories of First Nations Women Are Contributing to a National Research Project. *Journal of Aboriginal Health* 4(2), 35-43.

Acoose, S., and Dell, C.A. (2009). Hear Me Heal: First Nations Women Healing from Drug Abuse. In Robert Wesley Herber (Ed.), *Indigenous Education: Pacific Nations* (1-8). Regina: First Nations University of Canada.

Barton, S.S. (2004). Narrative Inquiry: Locating Aboriginal Epistemology in a Relational Methodology. *Journal of Advanced Nursing* 45(5), 519-26.

Brydon-Miller, M., and Maguire, P. (2009). Participatory Action Research. *Educational Action Research* 17(1), 79-93.

Castellano, M.B. (2004). Ethics of Aboriginal Research. *Journal of Aboriginal Health* 1(1), 98-114.

Christensen, J. (2012). Telling Stories: Exploring Research Storytelling as a Meaningful Approach to Knowledge Mobilization with Indigenous Research Collaborators and Diverse Audiences in Community-Based Participatory Research. *Canadian Geographer* 56(2), 231-42.

Cook, J., and Fonow, M. (1986). Knowledge and Women's Interests: Issues of Epistemology and Methodology in Feminist Sociological Research. *Sociological Inquiry* 56(4), 2-29.

Creswell, J.W., and Miller, D.L. (2000). Determining Validity in Qualitative Inquiry. *Theory into Practice* 39(3), 124-31.

dé Ishtar, Z. (2005). Striving for a Common Language: A White Feminist Parallel to Indigenous Ways of Knowing and Researching. *Women's Studies International Forum* 28(5), 357-68.

De Laine, M. (2000). *Fieldwork, Participation and Practice: Ethics and Dilemmas in Qualitative Research.* Thousand Oaks, CA: Sage.

Dell, C.A., and Kilty, J.M. (2013). The Creation of the Expected Aboriginal Woman Drug Offender in Canada: Exploring Relations between Victimization, Punishment, and Cultural Identity. *International Review of Victimology* 19(1), 51-68.

Dell, C.A., Lyons, T., Grantham, S., Kilty, J.M., and Chase, W. (Forthcoming). Researching with Respect: The Contributions of Feminist, Aboriginal and Community-Based Research Approaches to the Development of Our Study of First Nations Women's Healing from Problematic Drug Use. In R. Berman (Ed.), *Corridor Talk: Canadian Feminist Scholars Share Their Stories of Research Partnerships.* Toronto: Inanna Publications and Education.

Deutsch, N.L. (2004). Positionality and the Pen: Reflections on the Process of Becoming a Feminist Researcher and Writer. *Qualitative Inquiry* 10(6), 885-902.

Dua, F. (1999). Canadian Anti-Racist Feminist Thought: Scratching the Surface of Racism. In E. Dua and A. Robertson (Eds.), *Scratching the Surface: Canadian Anti-Racist Thought* (7-34). Toronto: Women's Press.

Fisher, P.A., and Ball, T.J. (2003). Tribal Participatory Research: Mechanisms of a Collaborative Model. *American Journal of Community Psychology 32*(3/4), 207-16.

Fletcher, C. (2003). Community-Based Participatory Research in Northern Canadian Aboriginal Communities: An Overview of Context and Process. *Pimatziwin: A Journal of Aboriginal and Indigenous Community Health 1*(1), 27-61. http://www.pimatisiwin.com/online/?page_id=116.

Flicker, S., Maley, O., Ridgley, A., Biscope, S., Lombardo, C., and Skinner, H. (2008). e-PAR: Using Technology and Participatory Action Research to Engage Youth in Health Promotion. *Action Research 6*(3), 285-303.

Fonow, M., and Cook, J.A. (2005). Feminist Methodology: New Applications in the Academy and Public Policy. *Signs 30*(4), 2211-36.

Freire, P. (1993). *Pedagogy of the Oppressed.* New York: Continuum International Publishing.

Fry, C.L., Ritter, A., Baldwin, S., Bowen, K.J., Gardiner, P., Holt, T., Jenkinson, R., and Johnston, J. (2005). Paying Research Participants: A Study of Current Practices in Australia. *Journal of Medical Ethics 31*(9), 542-47.

Gatenby, B., and Humphries, M. (2000). Feminist Participatory Action Research: Methodological and Ethical Issues. *Women's Studies International Forum 23*(1), 89-05.

Graham, I.D., Logan, J., Harrison, M.B., Straus, S.E., Tetroe, J., Caswell, W., and Robinson, N. (2006). Lost in Knowledge Translation: Time for a Map? *Journal of Continuing Education in the Health Professions 26*(1), 13-24.

Harding, S., and Norberg, K. (2005). New Feminist Approaches to Social Science Methodologies: An Introduction. *Signs 30*(4), 2009-15.

Henry, A., and Mackenzie, S. (2012). Brokering Communities of Practice: A Model of Knowledge Exchange and Academic-Practitioner Collaboration Developed in the Context of Community Policing. *Police Practice and Research 13*(4), 315-28.

Hunter, M. (2002). Rethinking Epistemology, Methodology, and Racism: Or, Is White Sociology Really Dead? *Race and Society 5,* 119-38.

Israel, B.A., Schulz, A.J., Parker, E.A., and Becker, A.B. (1998). Review of Community-Based Research: Assessing Partnership Approaches to Improve Public Health. *Annual Review of Public Health 19,* 173-202.

Kindon, S. (2003). Participatory Video and Geographic Research: A Feminist Practice of Looking? *Area 35*(2), 142-53.

Kirby, S., and McKenna, K. (1989). *Experience Research Social Change: Methods from the Margins.* Toronto: Garamond Press.

Lawler, S. (2008). Stories and the Social World. In M. Pickering (Ed.), *Research Methods for Cultural Studies* (32-52). Edinburgh: Edinburgh University Press.

Leslie, J., Hughes, C., and Braun, K. (2010). Engaging Participants in Design of a Native Hawaiian Worksite Wellness Program. *Progress in Community Health Partnerships: Research, Education and Action 4*(2), 121-30.

Lincoln, Y.S., and Guba, E.G. (1985). *Naturalistic Inquiry.* Newbury Park, CA: Sage Publications.

—. (2000). Paradigmatic Controversies, Contradictions and Emerging Confluences. In N.K. Denzin and Y.S. Lincoln (Eds.), *Handbook of Qualitative Research* (2nd ed.) (163-88). Thousand Oaks, CA: Sage Publications.

Mance, G., Mendelson, T., and Byrd III, B. (2010). Utilizing Community-Based Participatory Research to Adapt a Mental Health Intervention for African American Emerging Adults. *Progress in Community Health Partnerships: Research, Education, and Action 4*(2), 131-40.

Mitton, C., Adair, C., McKenzie, E., Patten, S., and Perry, B. (2007). Knowledge Transfer and Exchange: Review and Synthesis of the Literature. *Milbank Quarterly 85*(4), 729-68.

Nabigon, H. (2006). *The Hollow Tree: Fighting Addiction with Traditional Native Healing*. Montreal and Kingston: McGill-Queen's University Press.

Naytowhow, V., and CIHR Project Research Team. (2009). From Stilettos to Moccasins [Music video]. http://www.youtube.com/watch?v=1QRb8wA2iHs&feature=channel.

Nguyen, G., Hsu, L., and Kue, K. (2010). Partnering to Collect Health Services and Public Health Data in Hard-to-Reach Communities: A Community-Based Participatory Research Approach for Collecting Community Health Data. *Progress in Community Health Partnerships: Research, Education, and Action 4*(2), 115-19.

Niccols, A., Dell, C.A., and Clarke, S. (2009). Treatment Issues for Aboriginal Mothers with Substance Use Problems and Their Children. *International Journal of Mental Health and Addiction 8*(2), 320-35.

Pentland, D., Forsyth, K., Maciver, D., Walsh, M., Murray, R., Irvine, L., and Sikora, S. (2011). Key Characteristics of Knowledge Transfer and Exchange in Healthcare: Integrative Literature Review. *Journal of Advanced Nursing 67*(7), 1408-25.

Salmon, A. (2007). Walking the Talk: How Participatory Interview Methods Can Democratize Research. *Qualitative Health Research 17*, 982-68.

Schnarch, B. (2004). Owner, Control, Access, and Possession (OCAP) or Self-Determination Applied to Research: A Critical Analysis of Contemporary First Nations Communities. *Journal of Aboriginal Health 1*(1), 80-95.

Shope, J.H. (2006). You Can't Cross a River without Getting Wet: A Feminist Standpoint on the Dilemmas of Cross-Cultural Research. *Qualitative Inquiry 12*(1), 163-84.

Smylie, J., Kaplan-Myrth, N., Tait, C., Martin, C.M., Chartrand, L., Hogg, W., and Maccaulay, A.C. (2004). Health Sciences Research and Aboriginal Communities: Pathway or Pitfall? *Journal of Obstetrics and Gynecology Canada 26*(3), 211-16.

Stoecker, R. (2009). Are We Talking the Walk of Community-Based Research? *Action Research 7*(4), 385-404.

Tickner, J. (2005). What Is Your Research Program? Some Feminist Answers to International Relations Methodological Questions. *International Studies Quarterly 49*(1), 1-22.

Tilley, S.A. (2003). Transcription Work: Learning through Co-participation in Research Practices. *International Journal of Qualitative Studies in Education 16*(6), 835-51.

Vannini, A., and Gladue, C. (2008). Decolonized Methodologies in Cross-Cultural Research. In P. Liamputtong (Ed.), *Doing Cross-Cultural Research* (137-59). New York: Springer.

Ward, V., Smith, S., House, A., and Hamer, S. (2012). Exploring Knowledge Exchange: A Useful Framework for Practice and Policy. *Social Science and Medicine 74*, 297-304.

chapter 3

Commitment and Participation: A Collective Action to Defend the Rights of Homeless People against Anti-Disorder Policing Practices in Montreal

Céline Bellot, Marie-Ève Sylvestre, and Bernard St-Jacques

As COMMITTED SCHOLARS AND community organizers, we are dedicated to working with marginalized populations to improve their living conditions and ensure that their rights are respected. We emphasize, on the one hand, the responsibility of lawyers to intervene in the political and social world and to refuse to legitimize unjust normative systems and, on the other hand, the responsibility of social scientists to use the unique power of law to question the ways in which it exacerbates patterns of social exclusion. It is our position that scholarship with commitment is not simply a necessity – it also distinguishes itself from other legal contributions because it explicitly pursues political objectives. Being aware of the possible abuses of authority perpetrated in the name of intellectual activity is a necessary condition for engaging in scholarship with commitment.[1]

For jurists, scholarship with commitment goes beyond simple position taking, which is inherent to our disciplinary training and our ethical commitment toward our clients. Here, it is a question of highlighting the responsibility of researchers and/or jurists to intervene in the social and political fields and refuse to legitimize systems or series of rules – in this case, the criminal justice system – that are fundamentally unjust. For Lochak (1996), it is necessary to reaffirm the obligation of researchers and/or jurists to avoid participating in the sanctioning, trivialization, or naturalization of discriminatory policies through their writings and/or actions. Since they have access to the knowledge and language of the law as well as to all the privileges associated with those who can claim to be acting under the force of law (Bourdieu 1986), jurists also have the obligation to criticize the false neutrality of this law when, in the name of "equality," it "forbids everyone, rich and poor, to sleep under bridges, beg in the streets and steal bread," as Anatole France wrote in 1894.

Our contribution, though coming from a political angle, must nevertheless respect a certain number of rules ensuring scientific rigour. Thus, the notion of scholarship with commitment is distinct from the position adopted by most radical relativists, who, by rejecting scientific positivism, fall into the opposite trap by asserting that it is impossible to conduct research uncontaminated by personal and political sympathies, that no facts can exist without values, and that the only valid ethical positioning would be to "take sides for subordinates against their superiors" (Becker 1967, 32). This being said, political objectives and ideological positions should be clarified and disclosed from the outset. We should always be reminded of our own biases as researchers. This permanent investigation of our values and positions, referred to as "reflexive critique" (Bourdieu and Wacquant 1992), is recognition of the fact that researchers are shaped by their objects and subjects of study and are directly influenced by their political standpoints (Harcourt 2000). However, these biases are in no way an impediment to becoming "public intellectuals" or "committed scholars." On the contrary, value commitment is a necessary condition of objectivity (Gouldner 1968, 114).

Accordingly, being committed to our values implies that our loyalty goes first to defending and promoting the values that inspire our research: social justice, human rights, and social recognition. The stigmatization and criminalization of the homeless appear to us as cases of "non rights," built around the denial of rights. This denial of rights is qualified by Honneth as, fundamentally, a denial of recognition (Honneth 2006; Renault 2004). Even though we built this study around injustice, we also try to have empathetic relationships with actors rather than sympathetic ones.

To be faithful to our values as researchers also entails being faithful to the values supporting scientific research, such as transparency, truth, and honesty. In this sense, we agreed to consider and deal with information that was initially perceived as being "hostile" to our values, goals, and points of view (Gouldner 1968). This relationship allows us to conserve some liberty as researchers working at the heart of the dominant relationships under study. Our academic contribution to the political field also aims at combining the specific strengths of law and social sciences to document and reveal the consequences of legal rules and social policies, such as anti-disorder policing programs, on the structures of domination (Geertz 2000; Harcourt 2000). In this chapter, we demonstrate how conducting criminological and legal research under the banner of scholarship with commitment resulted in critical changes to the rights and living conditions of the homeless in Montreal.

Striking an Alliance between Research, Law, Social Intervention, and the Streets

Since the 1990s, in Montreal, the increasing enforcement of anti-disorder programs and zero-tolerance policies has resulted in the use of the criminal justice system as a means of managing homeless people (Wacquant 1999; Young 1999). These policies and programs were inspired by broken window theory[2] (Wilson and Kelling 1982), which, despite its popularity, is not supported by empirical evidence and has been widely criticized in the scientific literature (Harcourt 2001; Wacquant 2004; Bellot and Morselli 2003; Sylvestre 2010). The implementation of the neighbourhood police system in 1997 and its optimization five years later in 2002 were the occasion for the police and city officials to reaffirm their commitment to fight antisocial behaviours. Still, in 2008, the "occupation of urban space" was listed among the eight most important challenges facing the "new generation of neighbourhood police" (SPVM 2008).

In the field, homeless individuals, service providers, and researchers witnessed the increasing issuance of statements of offence as well as their harmful effects on those who live in and off the streets.[3] However, they were not able to systematically measure the phenomenon, as most offences were breaches of bylaws enforced by the municipal court, for which official statistics were not tallied, or to show its disparate impact on the homeless. Nor had they been able to resist the official rhetoric surrounding these apparently neutral policies that promote order, civility, and cleanliness and aim at ensuring a better quality of life for all citizens, or counter the argument raised in support of such programs – namely, that there was a community consensus in favour of controlling the use of public spaces and policing disorderly people.

Aware of the need for community organizations to know more about this phenomenon, develop a collective rights defence strategy, and identify an alternative to penalization, we decided to assume our political obligations and our ethical injunction to address the asymmetries of our unjust world (Torre and Fine 2007) by joining Bernard St-Jacques and other community organizers in the creation of Opération Droits Devants (ODD). Through the process of defining the partnership and balancing the needs of research and action, we ensured that the three levels of alternatives to penalization we would later promote were present from the outset of the working relationship: alternatives to incarceration, alternatives within the penal system, and alternatives to repression.

Drawing on participatory and action research approaches, we worked to develop a partnership in the field of research, the field of practice, and with homeless people themselves in order to produce evidence on penalization and resist official legitimating discourses that were largely based on prejudices and stereotypes about poverty and homelessness. The development of participatory action research (PAR) reflects both our scientific and ethical commitment to creating conditions for social change to be used by the community (Cahill 2007). Participation is a commitment to working with people directly concerned to challenge unequal power relationships and respond to the exclusion of homeless people in our society. PAR is a method that Fine (2006) identifies as "contesting research," leading to the "understanding that people – especially those who have experienced historic oppression – hold deep knowledge about their lives and experiences and should help shape the questions, [and] frame the interpretations" (Torre and Fine 2007, 458). Similar to Dell, Fillmore, and Kilty's chapter in this volume, combining research and action to develop evidence was a way for us to be involved in policymaking from the bottom up. Yet, in contrast with the approach outlined by Dell, Fillmore, and Kilty, the concerned individuals were not directly involved with the scientific direction of the project; rather, we worked as partners with pre-established zones of discourses, roles, and responsibilities.

As we agreed on the objectives, the partnership between research and action offered a multi-angled and innovative picture of the penalization of homeless people. Criminological research demonstrated how the law exacerbates patterns of social exclusion while critical legal analysis allowed us to identify and criticize specific categories and discourses in the criminal justice system and in criminal law that construct homeless people as criminals and justify the use of repressive techniques against them. Given that law's power also lies in its capacity to mobilize resources and provide legitimacy to rights arguments, we united our efforts in the hope that we could mobilize the unique force of law and the multiple layers of meaning of social sciences to defend the rights of the homeless in Montreal. Thus, besides conducting research on penal practices used against homeless people, we also talked about a policy on homelessness that would consider the rights of homeless people.

Opération Droits Devant became a reality in May 2003, involving more than thirty community organizations. The principal idea behind ODD came from an acknowledgment of the need to bring together and promote existing knowledge and practices in order to make up for the absence of data on the penalization of homeless people and to challenge the use of criminal law as a way of dealing with homelessness. Sharing this idea, researchers, community workers, and homeless people developed actions to promote the defence of rights.

Instead of penalizing homeless persons, the goal was to develop an individual and collective approach to defend their rights, centred on these objectives:

- to ensure the training of social intervention workers and encourage them to inform marginalized persons of their rights and possible courses of action (for example, how to file a complaint)
- to gather information about cases where the issuing of statements of offences consists of discrimination and violations of rights, use this data to paint a portrait – as accurately as possible – of the situation, and disseminate knowledge about the penalization of homeless people and its effects
- to exert political pressure, gather support, and carry out various actions for consciousness-raising and denouncement within public opinion.

Our objectives were pursued simultaneously even though, at times, some of them took precedence over others.

Training Strategies

The first team meetings of ODD revealed that, like homeless people, social intervention workers were unfamiliar with the penal process and how to engage with and even challenge it. For this reason, we developed a training strategy to explain the characteristics of the legal system and how to deal with it, based on the researchers' knowledge and social workers' experiences. So, from the beginning, activities were carried out jointly. No one type of knowledge was considered more important than another. The training sessions were based on a factual presentation of the penal system and on experiences both of intervention workers who had assisted homeless people in their proceedings and of homeless people themselves.

Finally, we created a legal guide for workers on the validation of awareness-raising material for youth, for example, the "T'as des droits" card.[4] In the beginning, the ODD functioned as a forum to develop this training strategy and also share information. Afterwards, training sessions were offered directly by community resource groups to intervention workers and people experiencing homelessness.

Information Gathering and Mobilization

Opération Droits Devant organized meetings and forums to share information about the penalization of homeless people, based on social intervention workers' experiences. Workers involved in ODD initially sought to gather and tally all the tickets handed out to homeless people. This process was unexpectedly tedious, and a new strategy was adopted to give an account of the systemic use of penalization practices. With funding, we were able to develop a research project, directed by Bellot, and to draw the information on tickets given out to homeless persons from the databases of Montreal's municipal court.[5] In May 2005, we gathered the first statistics on the penalization of homeless people. Thus, it became possible to analyze more than twenty-six thousand statements of offences (tickets)[6] for violations to bylaws related to their occupation of public spaces, such as public consumption of alcohol or drugs and drunkenness, loitering, soliciting, and sleeping in a park after closing hours, as well as the path such statements followed through the criminal justice system. This investigation led to the discovery of the following results:

- an increase in penalization and judiciarization from 1994 to 2004
- a rise in the social and legal costs inflicted on homeless people and in particular on the ways in which penalization produces homelessness and aggravates social exclusion
- systemic and generalized use of imprisonment for default payment of fines, and the connections between such incarceration and delayed street exit process
- an overburdening of the criminal justice system and an increase in its costs.

Marie-Ève Sylvestre joined us soon thereafter. Trained as a lawyer, she helped to empirically document and support certain key arguments in our strategy for the defence of rights; she also helped us develop our applications for research funding and share the results stemming from each researcher's studies as well as studies we conducted together. Sylvestre's studies, focusing on police strategies and discourses, provided comprehensive knowledge on the legitimating discourses used to justify repressive measures, which we used to improve our own understanding and presentation of the data. In particular, she demonstrated that there was no community consensus on the use of repressive measures against the homeless and that the harmful effects of disorderly behaviour had been largely exaggerated.

Dissemination Strategies

Opération Droits Devant, at that time, played a role as a platform for the dissemination of these results to different target populations. The authors of this chapter gave more than two hundred presentations in five years, from radio and TV clips to three-hour university lectures.

The dissemination of results to social intervention workers and homeless people took place during ODD's regular monthly meetings and forums. This process was made easier thanks to the knowledge provided by the training sessions on the penal system. Quantitative data provided numbers on statements of offences issued and the use of incarceration that supported intervention workers' and homeless people's accounts. First, the fieldworkers and the homeless people became messengers to disseminate the findings in the streets and thus invalidate the idea that these events were "anecdoctal" or happened only "from time to time." The contours of penalization as a phenomenon, rather than as an individual experience, were finally known. Subsequently, monthly meetings and three forums held by ODD made it possible to constantly adjust the strategies of dissemination and awareness-raising by jointly identifying key actors, designing the style of the presentations, and adapting their contents.

Second, we reached the public by disseminating our data through traditional media (the press, radio, television). In order to monitor the message being sent, reach the largest possible audience, ensure the circulation of solid and consistent information, and make sure the ideas were clear to all, we deliberately chose to develop "discourse zones." The zone entrusted to intervention workers and homeless people concerned the consequences of penalization and the discriminatory nature of these practices; the zone entrusted to research specialists consisted of the breadth of the problem and the congestion of the criminal justice system. We decided on these discourse zones based on the fact that we only had quantitative data at the time; we knew that our exclusive data had to circulate outside the boundaries of community groups' claims to be taken up by other actors.

In addition to our quantitative data, we needed to create events where it would be possible to testify to the unjust nature of penalization. At the time, one of our most widely media-covered events was the symbolic delivery of tickets. This event has been held for a number of years as part of an awareness-raising campaign. During a full afternoon, in different downtown locations, street workers team up with homeless people to hand out statements of offences to passersby who commit the same type of violation for which homeless people are commonly punished: not respecting traffic lights as a pedestrian; loitering on the sidewalk; taking up more than one space on a public bench, dropping cigarette ashes on the ground, and so on. Repeated each year, this event gives homeless people the chance to speak, to be heard, and to receive recognition for the absurdity of such sanctions.

Finally, we adapted our discourses to present them to students according to their discipline (sociology, social work, criminology, political science, law) and their level of study (high school, college, university). We accepted all requests made for presentations on the subject, regardless of where the requests came from. We contributed to articles published in various student newspapers – all from schools in Montreal – as well as newspapers, websites, and blogs in the alternative media.

Through the dissemination of our research results and their appropriation by those convinced of the unjust nature of penalization, we were able to sustain and strengthen our process of mobilization. Consequently, we had to widen the debate and build new alliances. Accordingly, the Réseau Solidarité Itinérance du Québec (Network of solidarity for homelessness)[7] launched a process of collective mobilization in all the regions of Quebec, with the goal of producing a social claims document – the 2006 "Policy on Homelessness" (Vers une politique en itinérance). This policy is founded on the need to recognize the human, economic, and social rights of people experiencing homelessness. Its implementation and the claims it puts forward – particularly the right of citizenship for homeless people, which includes the right to occupy public space – grabbed the attention of all the political and judicial leaders in Quebec.[8]

Nevertheless, to support the promotion of alternatives, we needed to do more than raise awareness about the existence of injustices; we needed to break through into other related fields – for instance, law enforcement and the administration of justice. Calling upon officially designated third-party organizations, such as the Commission des droits de la personne et des droits de la jeunesse du Québec (CDPDJQ),[9] and organizations acting out of solidarity with us, such as the Ligue des droits et libertés and the Réseau juridique VIH/SIDA, we shared the results of our research with actors involved in these fields of law enforcement: the police, the security services in the metro, the municipal court, and the Cour du Québec (provincial court).

Besides these distinct strategies used to produce and disseminate data, the work undertaken to promote recognition would be meaningless unless it also gave a chance to the people most directly concerned, the homeless, to embrace the results. With this goal in mind, the research findings on issues surrounding penalization were taken up by individuals experiencing homelessness and made into artistic projects. The most important of these projects were a photo exhibit, community radio and television broadcasts, and reports in alternative and street media. These individuals were given a voice in debates at forums held by ODD. To do this, we extended an invitation to individuals already involved in social and political actions, including members of volunteer committees from services used by homeless people or members of housing committees.[10] At the same time, intervention workers backed by street youth were proposing to issue a complaint to the CDPDJQ.[11]

Toward Recognition of Penalization, Its Effects, and Changes

Throughout these years, ODD was driven by the desire to make the reality of penalization visible, to make it more widely known, and to support alternatives. Though the repression of people experiencing homelessness still exists in Montreal and must be fought, we take a moment here to look at the progress we have made.

Constructing a New Social Problem: The Penalization of Homeless People

When ODD was created, we could hardly discuss issues related to penalization with public authorities as they failed to see it as a problem. Years later, we can see how far we have come. The public consultations held by the City of Montreal in May 2008 were an opportunity for the city to rethink its approach toward homelessness.[12] These and the parliamentary Commission parlementaire sur l'itinérance (Commission on homeslessness), held in the fall of 2008 and spring of 2009, were two highlights in the fight for homeless people's rights.[13] Many statements (Bellot 2008; Sylvestre 2008) and papers produced by homeless people and organizations to whom we offered our support were submitted to elected officials at both municipal and provincial levels. In its statement and presentation, the Quebec Bar called for striking out all charges against homeless people for violations of city bylaws and provincial laws and for denouncing penalization.[14] The president of the CDPDJQ asserted in writing and in person that penalization appears to be a discriminatory practice as it is a form of social profiling, building this concept on the same arguments of racial profiling. In November 2009, the CDPDJQ produced a substantial statement, based in part on our data, showing how repressive measures used in Montreal participate in the production of social profiling of homeless people. In doing so, not only did it confirm the discriminatory nature of the penalization of homeless people, it also created a legal precedent in favour of the protection of persons according to their social condition (Campbell and Eid 2009).

At the end of the fall of 2009, with the submission of the aforementioned statement from the CDPDJQ on the social profiling of homeless people in Montreal and the report of the parliamentary commission on homelessness, we were able to appreciate the distance we had come: these legal and political entities had clearly raised their voices against repressive practices used against homeless people.[15] This political pressure paved the way for a meeting with the minister of justice in December 2009, to establish a work schedule for developing alternatives to penalization and judiciarisation. However, social agencies criticized the Quebec government's *Plan d'action interministériel* (Interministerial action plan) for being too timid, both in terms of the immediate measures it was proposing and the deferral of actual actions to a future date (Gouvernement du Québec 2009).[16]

The last forum held by ODD was, for us, significant. During the forum, the president of the CDPDJQ and the president of the Quebec Bar provided a follow-up on the actions they had carried out after producing the public notices on penalization practices. Furthermore, the Montreal police now produce their own data to monitor their practices. According to our research and theirs, there has been a reduction in the number of tickets handed out to people experiencing homelessness.

Finally, we succeeded in shifting the definition of the problem from "homeless people" to "police practices used towards homeless people." All the reports produced by or with ODD showed that police response to complaints made by residents did not justify such repressive measures. Rather, they pointed to the existence of a form of social profiling,[17] given that many acts for which homeless people are penalized are also committed by the general population without consequence. Significantly, actors in the fields of law enforcement and the administration of justice all agree that penalization is a real problem because the strategy is costly, counterproductive, and unfair.

Building New Relationships

Through the activities of ODD, both social intervention workers and homeless people learned to demystify the penal system and understand how they can work with it. These changes and adjustments represent small gains since they remain tied to the balance of power we established. They were not – in most cases – incorporated into official practices. Nevertheless, these new relations between social intervention workers and people working in the field of law enforcement and the administration of justice exist and are waiting to be reinforced. These new connections may help us, for example, gain access to files, seek alternatives, and come to agreements concerning compensatory work. In a way, the working groups made it possible to renew dialogue between the justice system and the homeless, who were silenced by the automatization of legal procedures. Though our efforts toward dissemination and representation produced some results, they called for enormous amounts of time, as well as self-restraint, given that sharing these findings with more-or-less hostile audiences was rarely an easy undertaking. But, sharing the fact that penalization is not the way to deal with homeless people was the first step toward developing a committee, establishing a working group, and, finally, building new relationships.

Simultaneously, the pressing legal circumstances of the homeless people we encountered and their scarce knowledge in the matter convinced us to open up the ODD legal clinic in 2005. The clinic's mission is to collect information on the legal status of homeless people who request it and support them in the actions they wish to undertake. Its service is based on a model of social support, not legal counsel, since the work is carried out by intervention workers. In other words, the ODD clinic seeks to bring the streets to the justice system by decoding and then deconstructing relations built on authority, mistrust, and sometimes hostility.

Creating Alternatives to Penalization

Working groups were created, both locally and with the Quebec Department of Justice, to contribute to the development and implementation of alternatives to incarceration and to help slow down automated legal procedures and, to a lesser degree, recourse to penalization.[18] For example, one of the most important changes we saw in Montreal is that, because of the dissemination of our research to the municipal court judges, they no longer issue warrants of committal to incarcerate the homeless. This practice began in 2008, although the law was not modified and still allows incarceration for default payment of fines.

The Municipal Court also established a position for a prosecutor specializing in homelessness issues to whom people experiencing homelessness can contest their tickets directly. For the first time, a genuine dialogue is taking place between homeless people and the penal system. Our research demonstrated that the process was almost purely administrative since everything, from the judgment to the decision to incarcerate, was done in the absence of the person experiencing homelessness. Though it is worthy to note that the service exists, it nonetheless presents some limitations. For instance, the prosecutor can only act prior to a judgment.

Another important development is the increased possibility for homeless people to complete compensatory work. With this measure, waiting periods were shortened and special arrangements were made so that they can meet with their supervisors without a previous appointment. These measures allowed homeless people to benefit from extended repayment schedules that are adapted to conditions of poverty and homelessness (monthly payments of two to three dollars). These agreements offer a way out from a status of debtor to the Municipal Court, even though it is difficult for people experiencing homelessness to pay back the full sum of their dues. This alternative received criticism because it places the burden of settling the debt on the homeless person, even though the debt itself is, to a large extent, unlawful. The Quebec Bar's call for striking off homeless people's records was precisely aimed at addressing this issue by cancelling any debt owing instead of by seeking to alter the penal system to obtain payment.

Mediation services and tandem patrols composed of a police officer and a social intervention worker were created to promote alternative solutions to penalization. These most recent strategies help reduce repression, but, more so, they invalidate the recourse to repressive measures as solutions when problems related to the sharing of public space appear. All in all, our research and the social claims we developed with Opération Droits Devant confirm the importance of conducting research in partnership with the fields of practice and with individuals affected by the issue. This approach to research brings real advantages for collective action undertaken in favour of the defence of rights of people experiencing social exclusion.

Scholarship with Commitment: Reflections

To carry out research and action together with actors committed to justice presents many challenges, but collective mobilization helps to position research. Unlike a number of studies on collective action with marginalized populations that tend to adopt an outsider's perspective on the problem, the theoretical framework of the present study implies that we adopt an insider's perspective: that is to say that we consider the problem *with* those affected – the homeless. Our research, like that from other partners, was but one source of knowledge that contributed to the construction of a process of action and defence of rights. Given its scientific nature, our research provided legitimacy and credibility to the broader project goals. In this way, we do not fully deconstruct the power relations between science and society; as researchers, our voice still rings louder than that of our homeless participants. Furthermore, as qualitative researchers, we experienced the power of numbers. The absence of existing data, including from government sources, on the impact of judicial practices against vulnerable populations brought us, by force of circumstance, into the arena of "evidence-based practices." This paradigm contends that scientific data, especially quantitative data, help to justify the use of various resources, cost controls, and outcomes of public action (Lafortune 2009; Couturier, Gagnon, and Carrier, 2009). We were aware that the production of "hard data" or "evidence" would increase the credibility of our research. Hence, we proceeded to produce evidence related to judicial practices, in order to prove the issue was more than "just anecdotal."

However, since we used participatory and action research approaches in our methodology that emphasize the participation of concerned actors at different stages of the research, we produced embedded evidence rather than external evidence, as is often the case in more traditional research. For this reason, the perspective framing our actions and social claims did not stem from evidence based on the logic of standardization; on the contrary, we sought to highlight the ineffectiveness and counterproductive nature of penalizing vulnerable and socially outcast individuals. Our research helped increase wide-ranging legitimacy for the accounts of social intervention workers and homeless people, giving their discourse significant weight in the debate.

Our actions also drew impetus from the force of law and more specifically from the new power balance created by the existence of legal data. Many legal actions undertaken in recent years to protest the discriminatory and unconstitutional nature of legislative or statutory documents have failed because of the lack of empirical data supporting their claims.[19] By combining scientific legitimacy and legal force, and by occupying political space, we were ensuring our claims were solidly supported. While the law plays a unique role in the perpetuation of inequalities and in shaping ideas about certain groups of people – for instance, the centuries-old law holding that vagrants and homeless people are criminals – it can also make change possible. We can hardly think about alternative practices and beliefs without understanding how law influenced them in the first place and how, when grounded in empirical evidence, it has the power to make positive change. Moreover, having access to legal knowledge also facilitated our interventions and exchanges with actors who play key roles in the criminalization process, the criminal justice system, and professional organizations such as the Quebec Bar.

Our concerted decision to use discourse zones helped to gradually increase political and institutional pressure. The ODD, having in its possession the only existing empirical data capable of giving an account of the practices of those who control the penal system – from the police to the penitentiary services – was able to take up public space to criticize these judicial practices and re-define the contours of the debate by incorporating the rights of homeless people.

As a result, it became possible to shed light on the discriminatory nature of penalization practices and to support the institution of a policy on homelessness founded on the rights of people experiencing homelessness as citizens. Presenting penalization as a violation of human rights brought us up against many obstacles. The first was the fact that disorderly behaviour associated with homelessness was understood to cause harm to the residents and to other actors who faced the permanent presence of homeless people in the public space. In response, we challenged the connections made between disorder, homelessness, and harm. While disorderly behaviour is not harmless, its harmful effects have been largely exaggerated, rather relying on *feelings* of insecurity and risk assessment. Moreover, we served the harm argument back to its proponents: repression itself needs to be understood as harmful too in terms of rights violations and impediment to the street exit process and, as such, needs to be weighed accordingly when considered in public policies (Harcourt

1999). The second challenge consisted of mentioning to those working in the field of law enforcement that their practices infringed upon fundamental human rights. The creation of a balance of power gave us enough legitimacy and credibility to hold an alternative discourse and (re)construct an old social problem in a different light.

Consider where we began (giving press conferences, organizing working groups, and having to fight the association between homelessness and criminality) and where we ended up (a public request for amnesty for all statements of offences issued to homeless people, supported by the Quebec Bar). Establishing a balance of power can help change social representations and deconstruct prejudices. Our latest gains, recognition from the CDPDJQ of the existence of social profiling against homeless people and from members of Parliament for the need to cancel statements of offences already issued and develop alternatives to penalization, demonstrates the extent to which our work helped transform the position of political and legal authorities.

The goal of the partnership-based research project we discussed in this chapter was to create space for the recognition of the problem of penalization and the reality of homelessness. Providing space for hearing the voices of those who suffer injustices, while using data to illustrate the systemic nature of those injustices, our research and practices for the defence of the rights of people experiencing homelessness produced a new kind of knowledge on social justice. Positioning ourselves within the framework of the theory of recognition, we were forced to rethink the relationship between theory and the production of knowledge: this theory calls for a unique ethical and epistemological standpoint that largely exceeds existing normative frameworks (Bellot 2001). Consequently, our research and social justice actions to defend the rights of the marginalized, vulnerable, and homeless people themselves become products and sources of critical knowledge on society. Within our partnership, the dissemination of knowledge was organized to create a balance of power founded on the demonstration of the counterproductive nature of penalization practices toward homeless people, the inevitable congestion of the penal system, the absence of arguments supporting the use of repressive measures, and, most importantly, the unjust situations sanctioned by these practices. It is for this reason that the research itself became an actor in the process of mobilization. Considered as one source of knowledge among others, our research contributed to achieving an overall demonstration of how the human rights of homeless people are violated.

Accordingly, we must now proceed with a discussion on alliance strategies between the fields of research and practice and, more specifically, on the position of research as an asset and as a means. Scientific knowledge is too often considered a final authority and, as a result, can no longer play a complementary role in collective action. It was through our joint decision to draw on all of these sources of knowledge as well as by the constitution of discourse zones that we were able to maintain the intrinsic force of each category of knowledge. A researcher will never be as effective as a homeless person to tell what it means to experience penalization. On the other hand, no one is better positioned than a researcher to speak about the quality and scientific validity of data; similarly, the jurist is the most skilled to bring up this issue in the legal arena. The definition of each role and specific contribution thus appears as a necessary condition for research to play an actor's role in the process of collective action.

This is also true of creating an alliance between research, fieldwork, and the population concerned by our collective action; it requires that we transform the usual relationships between people from completely different social statuses, positions, and circumstances. The creation of ODD as a common space for recognition gave us a chance to hear the words of injustice through the various voices and, as a result, to produce a common discourse on the unjust situations generated by penalization. The goal of ODD was not to construct a new common identity but to produce a discourse drawing from three types of knowledge, each one contesting penalization and promoting alternatives.

Looking back, nearly ten years later, we can measure the distance covered while we write this chapter. With hindsight, the challenges, episodes of doubt, and uncertainty fade away. However, the decision to secure our collective action within a strategy of recognition constantly brought us back to the fact that every step was a gain, and that every challenge not only revealed the need for recognition but also drove us forward. Thus, in this sense, and apart from any considerations for secondary gains, our work partnership opened up a space for recognition because, through our decision to welcome and support each person's participation in the creation of an opportunity for social change, we brought about the deconstruction of standardized relationships between researchers, jurists, social intervention workers, and people experiencing homelessness. That is the first step ... for change ...

Notes

1   When we talk about scholarship with commitment – in other words, about researchers who "lend their specific competence and authority to political causes" (Bourdieu 2001, 33) – many in the university and political spheres remain skeptical, even as they readily accept the political engagement of community organizers. Is this not a contradiction in terms? Is it possible to be rigorous on a scientific level while upholding ideals and/or aligning oneself to a cause? Indeed, this goes against a certain conception of legal positivism for which the

science of law is "a descriptive meta-language on the subject of law" (Lochak 1996) and its interpretation neutral and objective, admitting neither prescriptions nor value judgments (Kelsen 1999). It also runs counter to an axiologically neutral conception of social sciences that states that we can distinguish between what stems from "pure logical reasoning" (facts) and what stems from their "practical assessment" (values). According to this conception, researchers must abstain from imposing their value *judgments* in the field (Weber 1917).

2   This theory requires that action be taken against petty crimes in order to prevent further criminality by eliminating signs of disorder, including graffiti or broken glass, and certain acts, such as loitering, panhandling, and consuming alcohol or drugs in the public domain.

3   As was demonstrated in several cities, the increase in the number of arrests and statements of offence issued for minor crimes brought about the criminalization of people who had no previous criminal history and, in the interim, created resentment among those who are especially targeted by these practices and subjected to increased surveillance.

4   Much of this material was created by the Collectif d'intervention par les pairs and by members of the Collectif opposé à la brutalité policière (COBP), some of whom had experienced life on the streets. For more information on the COBP, please visit http://cobp.resist.ca/.

5   For more information on the method and results of this study, please see the 2005 research report on the RAPSIM website, http://www.rapsim.org. To illustrate the inherent challenges of accounting for statements of offence handed out to homeless people, let us call to mind the fact that when they are issued tickets, many homeless people give the address of the organizations they are used to going to – on an irregular basis. The municipal court then sends written notices to those addresses for each default of payment and each step of the judicial process, in order to make the procedures official. Consequently, each organization receives thousands of letters every year addressed to people whom, in some cases, they have lost all trace of, and that can only be opened by the addressees.

6   In comparison, workers had been able to collect fewer than one thousand statements of offences.

7   This is a provincial network aimed at reuniting all the collectives working on homelessness at a local level.

8   For a presentation of our proceedings and the policy on homelessness, please go to www. rapsim.org and consult the section "Réseau Solidarité Itinérance."

9   The CDPDJQ is a legal institution with a mission to inform Quebecers on the protection of their rights and freedoms as defined in the Quebec Charter of Human Rights and Freedoms and to advocate on their behalf. Quebec innovated on charter categories by including protections related to the social condition of a person.

10   Various organizations working with homeless people (Montreal shelters, for instance) have volunteer committees in which homeless people get involved. These committees perform different functions, including offering support to projects centred on rights activism and recognition. The housing committees are associations established in different neighbourhoods whose role is to defend the right to social and affordable housing for the population as a whole but also for individual tenants who are most in need.

11   As of March 2014, no complaint has been presented to the CDPDJQ, mainly because of the lengthy submission procedure, which can extend over many years. By definition, it is difficult for a homeless person to remain present and available throughout this procedure. Following the publication of the results from the first study, groups dedicated to homeless people were able to call upon the CDPDJQ to intervene in this matter. Instead, the CDPDJQ formed a committee – the Tripartite Group (Groupe tripartite) – who, under its supervision, brought together the SPVM (Montreal police service), the security services of the Montreal metro (Service de sécurité du Métro de Montréal), the city's elected officials in charge of public safety, and representatives of community organizations, to debate –

collectively and officially – the question of the penalization of homeless people and its alternatives.

12 For more information on these consultations, please see the Ville de Montréal website, http://ville.montreal.qc.ca, section "Commissions permanentes, Culture et vie urbaine, itinérance, 2008."

13 To read the documents from the commission and view the presentations, go to the Assemblée nationale du Québec website.

14 Marie-Ève Sylvestre, a member of the Quebec Bar, helped to write the statement and present it to the parliamentary commission.

15 To read the report "Itinérance, agissons ensemble" from the parliamentary commission, especially the first recommendations pertaining to use of public space, see http://www.assnat.qc.ca/.

16 To read the Quebec government's action plan, see http://publications.msss.gouv.qc.ca/acrobat/f/documentation/2009/09-846-01.pdf.

17 Many authors insist (see, for example, Harcourt 2001 and Spitzer 1999) that "zero tolerance" policing strategies discriminatorily target specific populations. The use of loosely defined criminal offences gives police much discretion, thus opening the door to social profiling. This term originates from studies on discrimination toward visible ethnic minorities.

18 For more details, see Sylvestre et al. (2011).

19 This was true in Ontario in the case of *R. v. Banks,* [2007] O.J. no. 99, where there was an attempt to establish the unconstitutional nature of the Safe Streets Act, and in British Columbia in the case of *Vancouver Federated Anti-Poverty Groups of B.C. v. Vancouver City,* (2002) B.C.J. No. 493 (C.S.C.-B.), where similar attempts were also defeated. We believe these cases could have ended differently if the claims had been supported by empirical data.

References

Becker, H. (1967). Whose Side Are We On? *Social Problems 14,* 23-39.

Bellot, C. (2001). Le monde social de la rue: Expériences des jeunes et pratiques d'intervention à Montréal. PhD diss., Université de Montréal.

–. (2003). *Alternative à la judiciarisation des personnes itinérantes: Un énoncé de définition.* Produit dans le cadre des travaux du comité aviseur d'Alternatives à la judiciarisation du RAPSIM. Montreal: RAPSIM.

–. (2008). Sortir de la judiciarisation: Soutenir la reconnaissance des droits des personnes itinérantes à Montréal. Mémoire présenté à la Commission Parlementaire sur l'itinérance, Assemblée nationale du Québec. http://www.assnat.qc.ca/.

Bellot, C., and Morselli, C. (2003). La tolérance zéro: Ses racines, ses enjeux. *Politiques sociales 62*(1-2), 4-11.

Bellot, C., Raffestin, I., Royer, M.N., and Noël, V. (2005). *Judiciarisation et criminalisation des populations itinérantes.* Rapport de recherche au Secrétariat National des Sans-abri. Montreal: RAPSIM.

Bourdieu, P. (1986). La force du droit: Éléments pour une sociologie du champ juridique. *Actes de la recherche en sciences sociales 64,* 5-19.

Bourdieu, P., and Wacquant, L. (1992). *Réponses: Pour une anthropologie réflexive.* Paris: Le Seuil.

Cahill, C. (2007). Repositioning Ethical Commitments: Participatory Action Research as a Relational Praxis of Social Change. *ACME: An International E-Journal for Critical Geographies 6*(3), 360-73.

Campbell, C., and Eid, P. (2009). *La judiciarisation des personnes itinérantes à Montréal: Un profilage social.* Commission des droits de la personne et des droits de la jeunesse du Québec. http://www.cdpdj.qc.ca/publications/Documents/itinerance_avis.pdf.

Couturier, Y., Gagnon D., and Carrier, S. (2009). Management des conduites professionnelles par les résultats probants de la recherche: Une analyse critique. *Criminologie 42*(1), 185-200.

Fine, M. (2006). Contesting Research: Rearticulation and Thick Democracy as Political Projects of Method. In L. Weis, C. McCarthy, and G. Dimitriadis (Eds.), *Ideology, Curriculum and the New Sociology of Education: Revisiting the Work of Michael Apple* (145-66). New York: Routledge.

Geertz, C. (2000). *The Interpretation of Cultures.* New York: Basic Books.

Gouldner, A. (1968). The Sociologist as Partisan: Sociology and the Welfare State. *American Sociologist 3*(2), 103-25.

Gouvernement du Québec. (2009). *Plan d'action interministériel en itinérance, 2010-2013.* Quebec: La Direction des communications du ministère de la Santé et des Services sociaux du Québec. http://publications.msss.gouv.qc.ca/acrobat/f/documentation/2009/09-846-01.pdf.

Harcourt, B. (1999). The Collapse of the Harm Principle. *Journal of Criminal Law and Criminology 90*(2), 109-42.

–. (2000). After the "Social Meaning Turn": Implications for Research Design and Methods of Proof in Contemporary Criminal Law Policy Analysis. *Law and Society Review 34*(1), 179-93.

–. (2001). *Illusion of Order: The False Promise of Broken Windows Policing.* Cambridge, MA: Harvard University Press.

Honneth, A. (2006). *La société du mépris: Vers une nouvelle théorie critique.* Paris: La Découverte.

Kelsen, H. (1999). *Théorie pure du droit* (2nd ed.) (Trans. C. Eisenmann). Paris: L.G.D.J.

Lafortune, D. (2009). Introduction au numéro sur l'intervention à l'aune des données probantes. *Criminologie 42*(1): 3-13.

Lochak, D. (1996). Écrire, se taire ... Réflexions sur la doctrine antisémite de Vichy. *Le Genre Humain*, no. 30-31. Paris: Le Seuil.

Pichon, P. (2002). Au nom d'une expérience commune de "sans domicile fixe": Mobilisation collective et entraide. In V. Châtel and M.-H. Soulet (Eds.), *Faire face et s'en sortir,* vol. 2, *développement des compétences et action collective* (15-22). Fribourg: Éditions Universitaires Fribourg.

Réa, A. (2007). Les ambivalences de l'état social-sécuritaire. *Lien social et politiques 57,* 15-34.

Renault, E. (2004). *L'expérience de l'injustice.* Paris: La Découverte.

Ruegg J., Klauser, F., and November, V. (2007). Du citoyen et de la civilité: Réflexions à partir de l'exemple de la vidéosurveillance. *Lien social et politiques 57,* 127-40.

Smith, N. (1996). *The New Urban Frontier: Gentrification and the Revanchist City.* New York: Routledge.

Spitzer, E. (1999). *The New York Police Department's "Stop and Frisk" Practices: A Report to the People of the State of New York from the Office of the Attorney General.* New York: Civil Rights Bureau.

SPVM. (2008). *At the Heart of Montreal: New Service Coverage Framework.* Montreal: SPVM.

Sylvestre, M-E. (2008). La pénalisation et la judiciarisation des personnes itinérantes au Québec: Des pratiques coûteuses, inefficaces et contre-productives dans la prévention de l'itinérance et la réinsertion des personnes itinérantes – Mémoire présenté à la Commission des affaires sociales du Québec dans le cadre de la Commission parlementaire sur l'itinérance, Assemblée nationale du Québec. http://www.assnat.qc.ca/fr/.

–. (2010). Disorder and Public Spaces in Montreal: Repression (and Resistance) through Law, Politics and Police Discretion. *Urban Geography 31*(6), 803-24.

Sylvestre, M.-E., Bellot, C., Couture Ménard, P.A., and Tremblay, A. (2011). Le droit est aussi une question de visibilité: Occupation des espaces publics et parcours judiciaires des personnes itinérantes à Montréal et à Ottawa. *Canadian Journal of Law and Society 26*(3): 531-61.

Torre, M.E., and Fine, M. (2007). Theorizing Audience, Products and Provocation. In P. Reason and H. Bradbury (Eds.), *The SAGE Handbook of Action Research* (407-19). Thousand Oaks, CA: Sage Publications.

Wacquant, L. (1999). *Les prisons de la misère.* Paris: Raisons d'agir Éditions.

–. (2004). *Punir les pauvres: Le nouveau gouvernement de l'Insécurité Sociale.* Paris: Agone.

Weber, M. (1917). Essai sur le sens de la "neutralité axiologique" dans les sciences sociologiques et économiques. In *Essais sur la théorie de la science* (Trans. J. Freund) (399–78). Paris: Plon.

Wilson, J.-Q., and Kelling, G. (1982). Broken Windows. *Atlantic Monthly*, 1 March, 29–38.

Young, J. (1999). *The Exclusive Society*. London: Sage Publications.

chapter 4   **Dance in Prison: Narratives of the Body, Performativity, Methodology, and Criminology**

Sylvie Frigon and Laura Shantz

SINCE THE 1990S, RESEARCHERS have been developing new methodologies that transcend theory/method divisions, research categories, and disciplinary backgrounds. Feminist methodologies first blurred boundaries and made these transitions over thirty years ago (see Harding 1997; Harding and Norberg 2005; Reinharz 1992; Smith 1974; Stanley and Wise 1983, 1993); new, radical methodologies continue this tradition. Early feminist methods sought to reinsert women into research – as theorists, researchers, and active subjects. They changed research perspectives, moving from research "on women" to researching issues that are important to women (Harding and Norberg 2005; Smith 1974). These researchers challenged traditional knowledge – sometimes by shifting the focus of study and sometimes by employing different research methodologies. While this created challenges to their legitimacy and acceptance (see Harding 1986, 1997; Smith 1974), the techniques and topics explored forever changed the shape of academic research. Donna Haraway (1988) and others critically examined the entire research process, including the idea of an objective "truth," noting that all truths are partial and situated in that they emerge from particular philosophical, epistemological, social, and moral positions. Feminist methodological contributions also include the situated researcher, who reflexively engages with the research and both affects and is affected by it, and active subjects, who are given agency within research. Feminist research also includes a reflexive understanding of the larger environment in which research is created, including spheres and axes of privilege and oppression. These innovations have garnered wide praise and were adopted by many researchers, generating new debates and lines of inquiry. The discipline of criminology was part of these innovations (Scraton 1990; Daly and

Chesney-Lind 1988; Frigon 2001). This chapter chronicles some of the continuing shifts and changes in methodologies by using Sylvie Frigon's research on dance with female prisoners as a lens to highlight research approaches involving corporeality, performance, and mobilities.

Feminist Methodology: Old Wine in New Bottles?[1]

Pamela Moss (2007) highlights the innovative potential of feminist research. Feminist research techniques, questions, and analyses are not peculiar to women's or gender studies; there is little, if anything, truly unique about the methods employed. It is, however, the combination of questions, perspectives, and techniques and their innovative use that creates a body of groundbreaking feminist work. Researchers can choose among four paths, combining anticipated or unanticipated questions with familiar or unfamiliar methods to create feminist research (Moss 2007). New methodologies and research approaches continue to grow in this same vein, challenging existing categories and assumptions and creating new intellectual spaces for research and inquiry. These methodologies emerge from various disciplines and perspectives that question reified knowledge and examine new directions for research, including cultural studies, postmodernism, poststructuralism, and queer, trans, and gender studies. These practices, including creative sociologies, postmodern methods, and embodied sociologies, offer an array of new and adapted theories and methodologies to guide research (see Denzin 2003; Shilling 1993; Somerville 2004). New methodologies do not emerge from a vacuum of thought. Rather, they are intimately linked to epistemology and theory. Building on this rich tradition, we discuss the innovative potential of feminist research methods, methodologies, and epistemologies by focusing on the body, corporeality, performativity, and mobility in our explorations of dance in prison.

Dance as an Alternative Research Tool: On the Origins of the Project

Dance and prison? Two unrelated words, or worlds? Dance can provide a space of resistance for prisoners who are, by definition, confined in a restricted, controlled, closed, and monitored space. Dance in prison can also provide a unique entry point for analyzing carceral space and questioning the discipline of criminology (Frigon 2008; Frigon and Jenny 2009, 2010).

Sylvie Frigon met Claire Jenny, contemporary dancer, choreographer, and director of the Parisian dance company Point Virgule, in 2004, when Claire contacted Sylvie about an article that she had written on self-injury, the body, and imprisoned women (see Frigon 2001). Claire came to Ottawa, and their shared vision on empowerment and politics emerged. Point Virgule, created (with Paule Groleau) in 1989, has offered dance workshops in French prisons since 1995.[2] Through fifty to seventy-five hours of dance workshops, the team offers prisoners a unique opportunity to reconnect with themselves. Building on her dance experience at Fresnes Prison in 2000, Claire, accompanied by a troupe of French artists, led a project in Maison Tanguay in 2004. On 18 October 2004, dancers and prisoners performed for other prisoners and outside guests, including Sylvie. This was a fascinating moment that echoed Sylvie's work on the criminology of the body. Another performance led by Point Virgule and Les Productions C took place at Joliette Institution for Women, a federal penitentiary in Quebec. This performance took place in 2006 and involved dance students from the Université du Québec à Montréal.

This collaboration led to the qualitative research project described here; the project examined dance within prison as a form of therapy, a method of learning, a site for critical reflection, and an outlet for artistic expression. The effects – kinaesthetic, emotional, and potentially transformative – of the dance experience were recounted by some of the five prisoners, one ex-prisoner, and ten artists who participated in the workshops. To understand how dance affected the participants, seventeen ($n = 17$) interviews were conducted with choreographers, dancers, artists, actors, video and sound artists, professionals, prisoners, and ex-prisoners on their experiences.[3] The interviews touched on their experiences of dance within prison and how dance affected the women's identities and prison experiences. Excerpts of these interviews are used throughout this chapter. The interviews were conducted in prison (with prisoners) and in cafés in Paris (with the artists of the dance company).

What Is Contemporary Dance?

The twentieth century saw the birth of a modernist approach to dance that emphasizes freedom, the individual, and progress. As early as the end of the nineteenth century, choreographers and dancers were exploring new ways of thinking about the movement of the body. These pioneers of what we now call contemporary dance broke away from the rules that govern classical ballet. For example, Isadora Duncan (1877-1927) freed herself from the corset and the ballerina pointes as she was inspired by the flow of movement in nature (e.g., movements of the sea, wind, etc.).

In the late nineteenth century, the West slowly opened to other cultures, sparking a renewal of artistic approaches. Industrial development in the early twentieth century and the technological innovations that mark the era also had clear impacts on the artistic processes of numerous dancers and choreographers. In a general context of transformation where the outlines of identity are blurred, philosophers and artists question the place, and subsequently the future, of the individual. Contemporary dance develops various ways of understanding the body in motion, and these projects are often directly linked to events in recent history. Some projects cover topics that were highly political and critical at the time: in 1933, German choreographer Kurt Jooss (1901-79) created *The Green Table,* which heralds the absurdity and horror of the Second World War. More recently, the South African choreographer Robin Orlin (b. 1955) developed a work denouncing the apartheid; in *Daddy, I've Seen this Piece Six Times before and I Still Do Not Know Why They're Hurting Each Other* (1999), a black dancer, dressed in a white tulle tutu, performs a very unique version of an excerpt from *Swan Lake* (1877), one of the most famous pieces of classical ballet. In Canada, Quebec choreographer Pierre-Paul Savoie created *Bagne* in 1992, where two dancers perform in the heart of an imposing metal structure that alludes to the prison: the prisoners seek, spy on, and stare at one another.

Unlike how classical ballet shapes the body in a perpetual quest for verticality and maximum elevation, contemporary dance plays with the multiple phenomena of gravity. Representations of imbalance, falling, and suspension are common elements of body language in modern and contemporary dance. The ground is considered a partner that draws or, instead, repels. Finally, a major characteristic of contemporary dance is the use of "ordinary" bodies. According to French researcher Marion Rousset (2006), this is an eminently political approach. Like him, many choreographers choose to use different artists: fat, thin, short, tall, young, old; dancers with heterogeneous bodies or simply amateurs with diverse backgrounds and experiences. In 2002, he reprised German choreographer Pina Bausch's (1940-2009) play *Kontakthof* (created in 1978) with amateur dancers aged fifty-eight to seventy-seven years. In Canada, Gina Gibney Dance has held dance workshops for abused women living in La Dauphinelle shelter in Montreal (Gina Gibney Dance 2010) to help them develop resilience and overcome trauma. Similarly, Point Virgule has produced several productions on and in prisons, including *Résilience* (produced in Fresnes, France, and performed in Montreal); *Cheminement* (a solo produced in Paris, France, and performed in Ottawa); *Prolongement* (performed at Maison Tanguay, Montreal); and *Dé-Tension* (performed at Joliette Institution in Joliette, Quebec).

Dance as Innovative Methodology

Dance is a fluid, dynamic means of expression that allows the researcher to take new perspectives, transcend set categories, and question existing knowledge and practice. Within the prison, dance provides a stark contrast to the physical environment and institutional practices. How does the prison shape the dancers and the dance? How does dance reconfigure penality? One of the goals of this research and its methodology is to provide a positive contribution, even a transformative experience, to the lives of participants as well as contributing differently, in an artistic manner, to the gendered embodied penality.

Bodies, Corporeality, and Criminology

Any social order produces and reproduces a specific corporeal order. This corporeal order mediates a cultural and symbolic system of any given society at a specific historical moment and in a specific political context (Frigon and Kérisit 2000; Préjean 1994). At the dawn of the twenty-first century, the body, both men's and women's, has increasingly become a central part of rethinking theory and practice in many disciplines, including sociology, psychology, medicine, anthropology, geography, history, law, psychiatry, and criminology. The confined body can achieve some spaces of "freedom" through performance and temporarily reclaiming the space of confinement. The pivotal concept of the body serves as a parameter for exploring gendered bodily practices through dance. The institution's power manifests directly and indirectly through its hold on/of the body and is reinforced by practices of subjection and the *political technology of the body*. Dance as a carnal art disrupts and transcends this technological power.

The concept of the body is an important one in criminological and penal practices but is rarely theorized. However, the links between the body and crime, the body as a site of explanation of deviance, marginality, and criminality emerged well before the nineteenth century; they can be traced back to the work of early philosophers. The corporeal metaphor (body-machine; body-politics) was indeed present in the works of Aristotle, Plato, Montesquieu, Bossuet, and Rousseau. In the sixteenth and seventeenth centuries, for example, various body parts (the face, the brain) were taken as explanations and signs of deviance and criminality. From the school of physiognomy, to the development of typologies, phrenology, and the "primitive stigma" emerged a science that located evilness, badness, and wickedness in the brain (see Frigon 2003a for a more in-depth discussion).

Michel Foucault (1977) has shown us that, historically, the body of the condemned was supervised, controlled, tortured, and even decapitated. However, at the beginning of the nineteenth century, punishment-as-spectacle (see van Dülmen 1990) was replaced as the transition from the *macropolitics of the spectacle* to the *microphysics of power* occurred, a transition that involved attempts to transform the individual's mind through punishment. Nevertheless, certain modern elements of punishment continue to concern the body itself: rationing of food, sexual deprivation, loss of freedom, corporal punishment, solitary confinement, strip search, body cavity searches, and segregation, to name a few. The body remains, as it were, central to penality: "it is always the body that is at issue – the body and its forces, their utility and their docility, their distribution and their submission" (Foucault 1977, 25). According to Foucault, we must analyze punishment as a complex social function and as a political tactic through which the body is invested, trained, marked, and tortured. Furthermore, in this penality, the body becomes both a *productive* body and a *subjected* body. This is the culminating point of disciplinary normalization.

More generally, however, feminist theorists have debated the body's role in social inquiry. Historically, bodies hold a tertiary place in social research, considered only insofar as physical embodiment implicates bodies in social interactions; the mind and one's thoughts were considered far more important than one's body (Shilling 1993). While some philosophers, researchers, and theorists (e.g., Pierre Bourdieu, Norbert Elias, Michel Foucault, Erving Goffman) considered bodies, these are relatively recent developments. For some, bodies are concrete objects that are influenced by and, in turn, influence the environment. Many researchers working within positivist paradigms – as well as some early feminist theorists – essentialized the body, locating the "feminine" in a female body (without age, class, or racial attributes; the body was assumed to be white and heterosexual), using physical difference to demarcate "woman" as an analytic category. Here, "female" and "male" are binaries; one's position is determined based on chromosomes, regardless of gender identification or other categories, such as age, race, ethnicity, class, and so on (see Hill Collins 1991; Harding 1986; Ussher 2006).

In contrast, postmodernists, poststructuralists, and some third-wave feminists argue that the body is constructed through discourse, challenging its corporeal existence (Shilling 1993; Somerville 2004). Poststructuralism is more frequently concerned with theoretical, philosophical, or abstract topics such as power, resistance, freedom, language, and discourse – where bodies emerge only when research questions necessitate their existence, such as in studies of illness, pregnancy, or sexual abuse (Somerville 2004). Poststructural perspectives highlight the inherent tensions and contradictions in individual identities and often abandon the body as an analytic category. The perspective notes that reified categories – such as race and gender – are useless and meaningless. Margaret Somerville (2004) problematizes this turn away from the body, countering that bodies matter and are significant. She argues that conventional methodologies, combined with a poststructural theoretical lens, can be transformed into poststructural methodologies:

> In light of the identified need to bring the lived body into a discursive relation with contemporary theoretical formulations of the body, then, certain methodological gestures have been suggested within the context of contemporary body theories. These are: naïve accounts of experience, using the body (at the scene of work) as a strategy, and unearthing bodily and embodied experiences in memory and diary ... *While these methodological strategies are not necessarily poststructural in themselves, by bringing them into relation with contemporary body theory at the site of research, they are changed by such intersections.* (Ibid., 50; emphasis added)

Embodied sociology responds to both positivist, essentialized studies, where the body is merely a research subject like all others, and to postmodern and poststructural works that overlook bodies, focusing instead on discourses and abstractions (Inckle 2010; Shilling 1993). Instead of being *about* bodies, embodied sociology emerges *from* them, examining the complicated, messy, and contradictory nature of corporeality (Williams and Bendelow 1998). This perspective combines traditional and contemporary sociological research, integrating the body and bodily concerns with critical, postmodern, and poststructural discourses. This research takes a middle ground, acknowledging bodily existence whilst problematizing categories and hierarchies based around physical bodies. Tim Newton (2003) argues that the body is not an infinitely pliable canvas on which to act out discourses although it is affected by and affects discourses. As such, some studies acknowledge intersectionality and positionality, where bodily attributes and social discourses interact to create systems of oppression, power, and privilege that shift and vary within and between situations. In criminology, this is particularly significant (Bruckert and Frigon 2004; Frigon 2001; Frigon and Jenny 2009; Kilty 2008).

Feminist research highlights the negative discourses associated with women's bodies; women are considered different and deficient relative to men. Their bodies, even when perfectly healthy, are seen as "other" and abnormal (Koch and Mansfield 2004; Ussher 2006). Embodied sociology reconnects discourses – including idealized accounts of women's bodies, beauty standards, and media images – with women's own experiences. Laura Hurd Clarke (2001), for example, studied older women's perceptions of their bodies, contrasting others' reactions to the women's bodies with their personal feelings. Disparities between how one *looks* and *feels* created dissonance and frustration. Similarly, Debra Gimlin (2007) examines how older women in dieting groups construct identities vis-à-vis societal beauty standards. The women negotiated their corporeal selves (including their weight, age, and capabilities), social discourses and beauty standards in relation to how they felt about their bodies. These studies connect discourse and theory with actual, physical bodies, reconnecting abstract theory and lived reality.

Similarly, in this case study we see the participants' physical bodies as sites where their theoretical and discursive understandings of confinement, imprisonment, and the prison are explored and negotiated, causing psychological and physiological symptoms. At first, the artists were excited to meet the prisoners, but before they could describe their feelings, they expressed their concerns: "Am I able to exist in this singular context? How will I be moved emotionally? When I found myself there for the first visit, we had a tour of the cells immediately. I was not expecting it, I told myself, 'I'll never be able to.' How will I control my emotions?" (Paule Groleau, dancer). The artists also tell of the tension and fatigue experienced after the first day they spent in prison. These experiences are not merely emotional or sensory; rather, they affect one's entire body. Anita Praz, a sound artist, and Jean-Pierre Poisson, an actor, testified to the physical and moral impact of the first experience in Fresnes:

I did nothing that day, I did nothing, but I have never been as tired in my life as after that day. It left a huge impression on me. The weight, like lead, like a ... constant strain ... And I don't know, something palpable, very heavy, [sigh] terrible, when in fact nothing was happening ... It was an uneventful day, I imagine, for the women, for Claire and her team. It marked me, physically I was broken. (Anita Praz)

Jean-Pierre Poisson recounted,

We spent the first day ... I remember ... we did the workshop where I found that people seemed to be very cooperative, that this would go more easily, quote unquote, than I had imagined. Really, the first day, it appeared to be surprisingly easy. I remember when I left, I said to Claire, "It went well and everything," and I went home. I slept for two hours. Really, I was exhausted. I wasn't aware at the time ... The energy that it took was completely unknown to me.

For the artists, the new experience of prison imprints their bodies with stress and exhaustion. In their connections with the prisoners, one sees the cumulative effects of the prison environment. While the experience physically exhausted the artists, its prolonged effects on the prisoners were also apparent. Given the unsettling nature of the location and the prisoners' varied and tenuous relationships to their bodies, the artists' first connections with the prisoners were drawn from the context in which they live and the movements of their bodies.

> The body is what translates the problems, tensions ... We see them immediately in the body. ... It's written on the body, on the face, the expression, tension, on the back, walking, the gaze ... So if the body becomes more harmonious, we can say that we are getting harmony inside as well ... That's what's better after dance, it's that things happen with the body, with the look, with sensations ... and it is more than words. And, in fact, it happens. There's something happening. (Fanny Tirel, dancer)

In the early sessions, the women's bodies reveal their suffering through movement. They bear the stigmata and damage of their life journeys and imprisonment, impeding the physical and vital needs that are essential to their well-being, their futures.

> Sick bodies moving. They look hollow because their sternums are a little loose, their backs bent, they are looking down, their knees ... Their entire bodies, their motor skills are constrained as they are forced to follow the same paths, the same schedules, and then there is no projection, so obviously it has an impact on body posture. (Paule Groleau, dancer)

> I remember it was very difficult. They were very sick in their bodies. They were very rigid; for others, mutilated. There were some who had struggled with body image. That is to say, they had gained weight or were not well in their bodies. Walking while looking straight ahead – it was impossible. They would look at the floor, or they would break the gaze. No balance. To touch themselves, very difficult too. To be touched. Dancing barefoot. Yes, it was very strange. (Juliette Vezat, dancer)

In the study of dance, representations and understandings of bodies are closely linked with movement. Performance and performativity are integral to both dance and individual interactions more broadly. How, then, do performance and performativity play out for prisoners within the confines of the prison?

Performances

Performances involve putting culture in motion, privileging action and experiential thought, knowledge and understanding. Performances – from everyday acts and interactions, to theatrics, to critical explorations – open spaces for critical thought, challenging categories and structures by connecting actions and events (Bell 2006). Norman Denzin (2003) notes that performance texts are multifaceted: they are cultural processes; a form of ethnographic praxis; open for interpretation (as other texts); used for scholarly thought; and used to join biography, pedagogy, and politics in acts of resistance, bridging critical Marxism and symbolic interactionism. Like Judith Butler (1990), Denzin argues that performances are unique attempts to emulate categories or ideals. With each performance, one can imitate, negotiate, re-form, or resist. These myriad opportunities to reify or challenge structures make performances both original and imitative.

Performances utilize varied media, including narratives, spoken words, physical movements, written texts, stories, and dramatic productions or plays. For example, Susanna Poole (2007) explores precariousness and migrancy through drama, as she both acts in and directs productions of plays by Marguerite Duras that feature prisoners from Italian migrancy detention centres. The plays resonate with the women's lives, highlighting the precariousness of their positions and lives in the "non-space" of the detention centre. Performance as a method of inquiry is linked to autoethnography, where autobiography and ethnography converge. Autoethnographies embrace situated researchers, dismantling their privileged positions above subjects by combining the roles; the researcher becomes the researched (Spry 2001). Like earlier feminist theories and methodologies, autoethnography situates "objectivity" and "truth" as always partial. It acknowledges a refracted self with multiple identities that may converge, diverge, or contradict, forming texts that destabilize the author and audience (ibid.). In practice, autoethnographies include narratives, performances, and reflexive theorizing that investigates identity, culture, and communication to create dialectic introspection and analysis.

Maarit Ylonen (2003) merges performativity (creation through doing) and autoethnography, examining meanings and narratives in dance. She is both observer and participant, watching the dance ritual from a distance, then dancing herself and constructing meaning with the dancers. Similarly, Sondra Fraleigh (2000) studies dance through phenomenology and autoethnography, exploring both the dance and her engagement with it. Both authors build on Deidre Sklar's (1991, 2000) work on dance ethnography, which uses a kinesthetic language to describe the dance process. In parallel with the methods, goals, and perspectives associated with performativity and performance research, Rebecca Coleman (2008) borrows from philosophy (see Bergson 1999 [1912]), examining the research method of intuition, where the researcher attempts to know an object by entering into it instead of examining it from a distance. Coleman (2008, 106) explains further:

> Intimacy is not to be found *in* an area of research and neither is intimacy *inherent to* a particular research topic. Rather, understood as and through intuition, intimacy is a research *relation,* a method, in the most open sense of the term. As such, a method of intuition does not "uncover" intimacies but *invents* ways of becoming intimate with objects of research.

She emphasizes ties between the researcher and researched, subjects and objects, bodies and images. Her work bridges ethnography and autoethnography and places participants on an even footing with the researcher, who also participates. By fully involving the researcher, this method destabilizes power relations, engaging the researcher reflexively and corporeally in the work.

Through creative workshops in contemporary dance, artists discover the unique context of imprisonment. The prison permeates them; their postures and artistic works explore their feelings and emotions. Within the prison, the dancers begin to question the distance between their experiences and the realities of everyday life in and outside of prison, relationships with others, time, space, sound, and sensuality. In prison, particularly in detention (remand) centres, the time passes strangely. There is little space to stand or to breathe. Between the obsessive waiting for an unknown tomorrow and the unchanging pace of the daily routines, instability and insecurity set in: "What also struck me is the relationship with time. In prison, I had no idea that everything is so rigid, that one could only work from this time to that time. Then the women would have to leave. Then they would come back. So, the slightest movement ... The rhythms are very overwhelming" (Pierre Cottreau, video artist). This singular relationship to time, the uncertainty, the inability to anchor oneself somewhere, even in the most mundane acts, contributes to the heavy tension that prisoners feel corporeally.

While the environment is undoubtedly destabilizing and disorienting, dance can reinvest the sensations of balance and being anchored. One of the fundamentals of modern dance lies in the notions of body weight and transferring support. In prison, it is hard to let go of weight. Given the restrictive nature of the space, the body is often unable to rest or settle, and any step or movement from one foot to the other while balancing on one leg can be difficult. For many women, this difficulty was present before incarceration, given their lifestyles, marginalization, and exclusion. Their bodies were, for many, in a poor physical state. For some women, imprisonment can be a time for reconstruction; a warm place to stay, regular meals, medical care, and safety can make prison a relatively attractive option compared to street life (Robert, Frigon, and Belzile 2007). The search for a sense of balance and calm may be experienced through supporting one's body with the ground. In the various movements developed with the help of Nathalie Schulmann, a contemporary dancer and professor, there are exercises that will help the prisoner to reconnect with the joy of feeling relaxed or even feel a sense of abandonment. At the beginning of each session, the troupe and the women prisoners share a time where they do self-massage and massage others – hence, a moment to share perceptual explorations. Sometimes, these exercises are part of the final performance. These movements seek to ease the uncertainty and vulnerability of the body and the movement of one's feet on the ground. When interviewed, women who participated commented on their experiences:

> With dance, I don't know how to say this, I leave everything that's inside. And then when I've finished the dance, it is quiet. I feel calm. (Rosa, Joliette)

> At the time, I was in a period where it was a bit critical, where I was always having problems with this and that, so obviously it helps you to breathe a little. You're no longer in this constant struggle that feeds on you inside and that you have with you all the time. It's a permanent tension, really. (Audrey, Fresnes)

As these quotes suggest, dance permits the woman to reveal herself without baring too much, to propose another understanding of herself, to exist differently in the eyes of others:

> I learned that I was beautiful. I realized that your weight didn't matter. There are plenty of things you can do. I also learned that I liked being with other people and creating friendships and learning to know them. I also learned to be happy as a woman. I feel fine. I feel strong. (Tessie, Joliette, our translation)

> It's really good because it shows the good side of our fellow prisoners. Because, here, we're not friends. We don't know each other, so everyone judges each other. But after the show, they greet us – "you did a good job" – everything positive, you know. (Lany, Joliette, our translation)

The artistic process generates other perceptions of self, a reconnection with one's emotions, one's interiority. It allows some expression of intimacy:

> I lived in a pretty negative way: it was sometimes revenge, sometimes self-destruction. So, stuff like that. And if today I managed to move forward, to do what I love, it's tied to that. It stirs things. I didn't feel good about my body. I was expressing myself with words, and that made me want to write. It has given me back that little inner voice and my emotions ... Dance, it really connects you with your childhood emotions. Because, this freedom of movement, you have it when you aren't just being judged – that social judgment, a corset. You just let yourself go. (Audrey, Fresnes)

Through performance, the prisoners and artists gain new connections to themselves and their bodies, and to one another. While the actual workshops can provide only a temporary diversion from the prison, the prisoners report being moved and changed by it. In fact, their descriptions evoke theoretical approaches to the broader meanings and significance of movement.

Mobility and Space

Monika Büscher and John Urry (2009) examine the mobility paradigm, which explores various flows – of people, objects, ideas, and time. Mobility studies combine quantitative and qualitative methods, merging movement data with information about *why* and *how* these movements occur. As Jean-Louis Pan Ké Shon (2007) indicates, census data offer significant detail on local populations. Over time, these data allow us to track mobilities, demographic trends, and population characteristics by following groups or examining who passes through a space – whether a country, city, or neighbourhood (see Statistics Canada 2006). Although these quantitative data are collected only every few years and largely consist of vital statistics (e.g., age, sex, ancestry, occupation, income, etc.), they provide valuable longitudinal insights on mobility (Pan Ké Shon 2007). To answer *why* and *how* questions about movements, one turns to qualitative inquiry.

While qualitative research usually focuses on people, spaces, or events, mobility research examines movement, potential movements, and blocked movements (Büscher and Urry 2009). It examines fleeting phenomena such as sensory inputs, including smell, taste, or sight; emotions, which vary between contexts and in response to events; and the kinaesthetic, the results and consequences of movements and actions (Law and Urry 2004). Mobility research may follow movements (e.g., moving ethnographies, research on commuting), analyze mobile communication (e.g., blogs, text messages, etc.), involve time-space diaries, or examine how people traverse and use public space (e.g., airports, shopping centres, etc.).

It is noteworthy that the theorization of space and mobility is a recent addition to criminological inquiry. Studies on homeless women's presence in and use of public spaces from which they are normally excluded (Casey, Goudie, and Reeve 2008), the criminalization and regulation of public and private spaces (Kilty and DeVellis 2010; Moore, Freeman, and Krawczyk 2011), and male ex-prisoners' efforts to resettle and develop networks and belonging within their new communities (Munn 2009) all draw on the concept of emotional geographies. These themes also appear in this case study. Given the newness of this area of inquiry, we draw upon Andrew Gorman-Murray (2009), who links feelings and geography by examining migration and queer identity. He states, "In this new work on emotional geographies, emotions, feelings and senses are posited as the connective tissue between the embodied self and place" (443-44). Bridging mobility studies and more traditional studies of identity and belongingness, he describes journeys from participants' familial homes to their current locations.

The prison, with its imposing physical structure, regimented movements, and monotonous days, brings space, mobility, and time into sharp focus (see Foucault 1977; Wahidin and Moss 2004). These forces are intertwined and blurred; the space remains constant, yet its rhythms and the motions and movements it contains ebb and flow, and time appears to stand still or wildly accelerate. In French prisons in particular, there are empty spaces, vast spaces, and crowded, confined spaces. This gives the strange feeling of dizziness and spinning. Pierre Cottreau, video artist, eloquently described the prison space:

> Fresnes is a very old prison, very old. It is very impressive to see the controls, doors, locks. And, finally, the little spaces that are reserved for each prisoner. And that's very striking. There is a huge central hall, which is always empty. And there are tiny cells, which are very decrepit. So the conditions are quite terrible ... The show took place in the corridor, what they call the corridor, a kind of huge space in the middle, like a vessel, like that. There is a huge gap in the middle where there is never anyone.

Pierre highlights how the prison shapes and constrains the mobilities of its occupants; its physical structure compresses and constrains movements in small cells, and fleeting movements connect these spaces to other areas of the prison. Linked to the space, there is a universe of sound that both creates and mediates the extreme tension of the prison. The ever-present noises of the prison provide a soundtrack to the space, making it come alive and echo within the consciousness of the prisoners and artists. The mobilities of this sound – echoing, piercing, and pervasive – shape the corporeal experience behind the walls. Anita Praz indicated that the impact of reverberation and the silence of that aural universe still bother her:

> [It is] extremely reverberant, a very, very long reverberation. There is a lot of noise, impact sound, and something which constantly resonates. Nothing dull, nothing soothing, of course. Something like silence, always perturbed, always mixed with a hard echo, metallic, on metal, on hard materials ... The carceral space always echoed. It never left us in peace. This marked me. (Anita, sound artist)

It is not insignificant that the artistic creation combines artists and prisoners. In this regard, the choice of the company is always very clear: "Go where it's not easy to go" (Agnés Fréjabue, actress). By entering these difficult, confined, and forbidding spaces, the artists attempt to conjure an alternative space, free of the constraints of the prison. Dancing encourages the women to utilize and own the space, reclaiming the institutional space as their own. How, though, can one create an imaginary space beyond the prison's walls when you know that often, in France, it is forbidden to look a guard in the eye? On this, dancer Fanny Tirel reflected: "So it was on ... initially, the gaze. Watch the horizon; look away. But also to have space. Even in a small room. How can you begin to take space without having 200 square metres?" (Fanny Tirel). Our focus in the prison was partly on how women's mobilities become restricted, as does their vision and the movement of their gaze. To relax and improve their horizontal vision, the prisoners explored dancing and performing two by two, eye to eye, studying the movements and travel released by their desires and the direction of their gazes. Here, prisoners examine their own mobility to relearn seemingly simple actions as well as to gain new understandings of themselves.

In many cases, including this case study, traditional methodologies and techniques – such as interviews, ethnography, hermeneutics, and content analysis – are coupled with theories that require researchers to examine movement and mobility (and its absence). Mobility research blurs the divisions between static moments and dynamic processes, acknowledging that social actors are not confined to one place, space, or time, and instead interact in myriad places and media.

The Body in Criminology, the Body in Dance

Women's bodies in prison are often betrayed and abused, leaving women with a negative self-image. The phenomenon of self-injury is also very present (Frigon 2001; Kilty 2008). Dance offers a way to reappropriate the body by allowing victimized women to reassert ownership of their bodies (see Gina Gibney Dance 2010). Dance in prison is subversive: working from a denied space to reclaimed space. Through space, rhythm, contraction, release, fall, recovery, rebound, the women find a balance: holding in place, straightening one's back, looking up, going toward the other, being in themselves, recapturing a sense of self. Sylvie, one of the women at Maison Tanguay, the provincial prison in Montreal, recounted,

And I was dancing, turning, twirling among other dancers who were also turning, twirling.
And like them, I was floating in the air, turning on the ground
I was occupying the space, all the space
The light was inundating me, the music was filling me
The rhythm was transporting me to the standing ovation of the public
Of which the screams and applauses still nourish me of the joy that was ours. (Bordeleau 2005, 15)

The dancer's body (skin, muscles), the choreography (solos and trios), the sounds (clanking keys, slamming doors, screams), and the music bring us to the prison setting, highlighting the mechanisms and logic of confinement, control, and resistance. The act of dancing, in juxtaposition to the prison structures, demonstrates dance's potential for resistance and individual transformation. As Paule Groleau (dancer) remarked, "When we come with contemporary dance and all this improvisational study and all that physical work, it questions the organization, justice, the guards, and the prisoners. It requires a letting go, and that, that can only be done by professional artists and creators." For example, one of the difficult concepts in creative work in prison is in the often passionate and sometimes conflicting relational phenomena between dance and prison. A dance piece involves a number of people (performers and creators) in a troupe, which is particularly important in prison dance projects as it allows prisoners to work as equals with dancers, experiencing autonomy and agency, both of which are absent from much of their lives. For example, an intimate male-female relationship was constituted and performed at Maison Tanguay, where the only male artist of the dance company danced with a female prisoner. She had asked to dance a waltz in a flowered dress, like a princess. Jean-Pierre remembered, "And the first time was incredible, I don't know, sensual but at the same time not sexual. We had a blast. It moved me enormously because it just added so much. Completely." For this prisoner, the dance had a very strong meaning: the thirty-second duration of the waltz marked the first time a man had treated her so well. Jean-Pierre reflected on the dynamic with his dance partner:

> What connection could I make with women who never see men? What does this put into play? What is assumed? And how to behave, with what attitude? In fact, it wasn't planned. Modesty worked to protect us. You could have gotten away with anything, really. I didn't have to say, "Careful ... I shouldn't touch you like that. Don't —" I could give her what she wanted. There was no risk.

The depth of the workshops with the prisoners caused some artists to contemplate their own paths as people and as artists. Three positions were expressed: the first referred to a relative confusion of roles, the second to a sense of confinement, and the third to the proximity of the prisoners' suffering, which became a mirror of confinement that allowed the women to release or reveal their vulnerability. As an actress and not a dancer, Agnès reflected on this experience:

> Me, I was really aware of my own confinement. And, well, reflection follows that. Being in prison does not make someone more imprisoned than someone who has had a difficult life. Ultimately, I was maybe, in my movements, closer to being trapped than some people we met in prison. But this difference is not a construction; this difference is a fact. And for a performer, it's hard to accept this fact.

This game of reflection can also change one's vision and perspective on the construction of the other and the permeability of space(s) through mobility and corporality/corporeality. As Juliette Vezat, a dancer, suggested, "I no longer have the same outlook on people. And what I also realize is that I could very well go to jail. I feel a bit borderline, too, not far from the edge. There is a fine boundary between being inside and out." There is also the question of how to become reacquainted through touch (self and other). In prison, the rare moments of relaxation and intimate connection with the senses are experienced intensely. Each of the project sessions began with massage. This experience is quite novel for incarcerated women, given that many have only had violent contact with others through victimization and serious assault (see Comack 1996; Comack and Brickey 2007; Frigon 2001, 2003b). Audrey, a prisoner at Fresnes, observed, "It's so serious, the relationship with the body in prison, among girls who were violated or others who sold their bodies. I think that dance proposes linking oneself, body and spirit, one's sensitivity, to reestablish contact. Simply learning to live. To no longer have this suspicion, to let go a little." Prisoners must move from touching themselves (arms, face, etc.) to touching the other (the other's face and torso, etc.), from the mildest to the most intimate. For some, it is extremely pleasurable to regain contact with the skin, but at the same time extremely disturbing. It is a journey for them to realize that touch is not always serious, dangerous, or deviant. These body-to-body relationships develop knowledge of the self and other. Incarcerated women live in extreme restraint, but in the processes implicated in supporting the other dancers, they learn to project confidence and respect. Also, by being supported by others, they are able to explore sensations of floating or flight:

> Yes, yes, you can climb on my back. Don't worry. I'm used to carrying people. She said to me, "But I'm too heavy." Weight is very important. It was a problem for her. I told her, "Well, no, no. Me, I can carry you. It's not a problem." The moment where she ended up on my back, I felt there was a fullness, as if she really began to fly. And then she started to close her eyes and take her time, to look. (Fanny Tirel, dancer)

The intensity of the ephemeral highlights both the challenges of reconnecting with oneself and dance as a potentially transformative tool for both public perceptions and the prisoners themselves. Although the sessions do not have a therapeutic goal, some women have made this link as it offers a different vision of the future, as evidenced by Vanessa and Rosa:

> This project has touched me as much as seeing the shrink. It makes you discover things about yourself. It makes you keep in touch with your inner self, your child. (Vanessa, Joliette)

> I took out a lot of things that I knew that I had inside. I expressed myself a lot. And I think if I could do that, I can do more now. With this show, I said, "I can do that. I can do anything I want." (Rosa, Joliette)

In prison, many women build a shell to protect themselves. Many described dance as a therapeutic way to free themselves from that shell.

You anesthetize your senses. You really blind your spirit. Your body, it must also be armoured. Because every time you must win. (Audrey, Fresnes)

When we discuss touch, these self-protections are especially felt by the artists. This can harden you, create a shell. You can sense it through touch. It is perhaps more obvious through touch than sight. But at the same time, it is a protection system. I think it can provide a lot of protection, when you're in there. (Agnès Fréjabue, actress)

This questioning can be very destabilizing because it contrasts two experiences: one with the artists in the troupe and the other that is regularly suffered in prison.

The fact that there, one has to speak with one's body while one usually always represses ... Here, it's the opposite movement, so obviously it's difficult. And, yes, that warmth and authenticity that you can find in working with these groups ... After the evening, I had a difficult relationship with the guards for sure: they searched us all the time. They slammed the doors in our faces, small pettinesses. The contrast was even greater. It further brought us back to the inhumanity of the guards, in any case. (Audrey, Fresnes)

Thus, female prisoners can be very vulnerable during sensory exploration and improvisational dance, as their sensitivity is again requested: "It awakens the things I feel at times. Well, being listened to, being watched, working on the body, it awakens things that may be hidden, and they can sometimes be painful things" (Pierre Cottreau, video creator). The violence of these states, even their onset, can destabilize the women. The ephemeral dimension of the projects allows women to experience, express, and transform their "violence" during the limited time the artists are among them, something normally inconceivable in this setting. Therefore, dance transforms the environment as well as prisoners' understandings of it, allowing them to transcend their self-conceptions, roles, and the space.

Conclusion

Dance not only brings us to a new way of understanding imprisonment and its effects. It also contributes to methodological innovation, as the dancers –

prisoners and professionals – learn about themselves, one another, and the carceral environment through the dance project. Inserting dance into criminology moves beyond the dyads of crime and punishment or offender and offence to explore the spaces in which punishments are carried out and to alter our understandings of those who are criminalized. Dance methodologies build on the multidisciplinary nature of criminology, offering a different way to explore carceral institutions and create meaning.

In prison, dance is a therapy, a method of inquiry, a way of analyzing one's experiences, and a conduit for critically examining the carceral space as women reconnect with their bodies and the environment through movement. In an environment that is often perceived as cold, violent, and oppressive, dance serves as a conduit to bring humanity to the space and agency to its inhabitants. As such, it represents a methodology that can provide a positive contribution, even a transformative experience, to the lives of participants as well as meeting the researcher's goal to contribute differently to penality. Dance is a gendered performative that uses choreography to highlight various aspects of the prison and through which we may explore the production and use of space, movement, bodies, and sound.

Dance studies expand the contours of the discipline of criminology, serving as a kinesthetic and transformative experience, for the researcher and the research participants. Specifically, dance enables the researcher to insert women with different mobilities, bodies, and identities into research designs and choreography frameworks. Connecting the artistic and the carceral provides a new lens of analysis in which movements, emotions, and visceral reactions become the texts for interpretation, changing our conceptions about punishment, detention, and prisoners by translating *choreographic* propositions into *criminological* propositions. Thus, dance has the power to subvert traditional ways of conceptualizing prison and prisoners and fractures the discipline's often narrow boundaries and its potential methodological straitjacket. Dance, and art more generally, breathes new life into our academic and feminist journeys.

Notes

1   We borrow from Loraine Gelsthorpe's (1990) title "Feminist Methodologies in Criminology: A New Approach or Old Wine in New Bottles?"
2   The company has always worked with and for children, with imprisoned men, and with urban French youth who are considered "difficult" by others.
3   Access to prisoners for this research was facilitated by a professional working within Joliette institution. No difficulties were experienced in gaining access. I believe this was because this was seen as a very positive project and did not represent any threat to the prison.

References

Bell,V. (2006). Performative Knowledge. *Theory, Culture and Society 23*(2/3), 214-17.

Bergson, H. (1999 [1912]). *An Introduction to Metaphysics*. Indianapolis, IN: Hackett.

Bordeleau, S. (2005). Une soirée mémorable à la Maison Tanguay. *Femmes et Justice 20*(1), 12-13.

Bruckert, C., and Frigon, S. (2004). Making a Spectacle of Herself: On Women's Bodies in Strip Clubs. *Atlantis: A Women's Studies Journal 28*(1), 48-62.

Büscher, M., and Urry, J. (2009). Mobile Methods and the Empirical. *European Journal of Social Theory 12*(1), 99-116.

Butler, J. (1990). *Gender Trouble: Feminism and the Subversion of Identity*. London: Routledge.

Casey, R., Goudie, R., and Reeve, K. (2008). Homeless Women in Public Spaces: Strategies of Resistance. *Housing Studies 23*(6), 899-916.

Clarke, L. (2001). Older Women's Bodies and the Self: The Construction of Identity in Later Life. *Canadian Review of Sociology and Anthropology 38*(4): 441-64.

Coleman, R. (2008). A Method of Intuition: Becoming, Relationality, Ethics. *History of the Human Sciences 21*(4), 104-23.

Comack, E. (1996). *Women in Trouble: Connecting Women's Law Violations to Their Histories of Abuse*. Halifax, NS: Fernwood Publishing.

Comack, E., and Brickey, S. (2007). Constituting the Violence of Criminalized Women. *Canadian Journal of Criminology and Criminal Justice / La revue canadienne de criminologie et de justice pénale 49*(1), 1-36.

Daly, K., and Chesney-Lind, M. (1988). Feminism in Criminology. *Justice Quarterly 5*(4): 497-538.

Denzin, N. (2003). The Call to Performance. *Symbolic Interaction 26*(1): 187-207.

Foucault, M. (1977). *Discipline and Punish: The Birth of the Prison*. New York: Vintage.

Fraleigh, S. (2000). Consciousness Matters. *Dance Research Journal 32*(1): 54-62.

Frigon, S. (2001). Femmes et enfermement: Le marquage du corps et l'automutilation. *Criminologie 34*(2), 31-55.

—. (2003a). Body Talk: Women's Experiences of Corporality in Prison. In A. Martinez and M. Stewart (Eds.), *Out of the Ivory Tower: Taking Feminist Research to the Community* (131-54). Toronto: Sumach Press.

—. (2003b). *L'homicide conjugal au féminin: D'hier à aujourd'hui*. Montreal: Éditions du Remue-ménage.

—. (2006). *Écorchées*. Montreal: Éditions du Remue-ménage.

—. (2008). Quand la danse entre en prison: De la reconquête de soi aux enjeux pour la criminologie. With the collaboration of Claire Jenny. *Érudit*, 241-52.

Frigon, S., and Jenny, C. (2009). *Chairs incarcérées: Une exploration de la danse en prison*. Montreal: Les éditions du Remue-ménage.

—. (2010). La danse en prison: Analyse d'une expérience singulière. In V. Strimelle and F. Vanhamme (Eds.), *Droits et Voix / Rights and Voices* (219-36). Ottawa: University of Ottawa Press.

Frigon, S., and Kérisit, M. (Eds.). (2000). *Du corps des femmes: Contrôles, surveillances et résistance*. Ottawa: Les Presses de l'Université d'Ottawa.

Gelsthorpe, L. (1990). Feminist Methodologies in Criminology: A New Approach or Old Wine in New Bottles? In L. Gelsthorpe and A. Morris (Eds.), *Feminist Perspectives in Criminology* (89-106). Bristol, PA: Open University Press.

Gimlin, D. (2007). Constructions of Ageing and Narrative Resistance in a Commercial Slimming Group. *Ageing and Society 27*, 407-24.

Gina Gibney Dance. (2010). Gina Gibney Dance – Community. http://www.ginagibneydance.org/.

Gorman-Murray, A. (2009). Intimate Mobilities: Emotional Embodiment and Queer Migration. *Social and Cultural Geography* 10(4), 441-60.

Haraway, D. (1988). Situated Knowledges: The Science Question in Feminism and the Privilege of Partial Perspective. *Feminist Studies* 14(3), 575-99.

Harding, S. (1986). *The Science Question in Feminism*. Ithaca, NY: Cornell University Press.

–. (1997). Comment on Hekman's "Truth and Method: Feminist Standpoint Theory Revisited": Whose Standpoint Needs the Regimes of Truth and Reality? *Signs* 22(2), 382-91.

Harding, S., and Norberg, K. (2005). New Feminist Approaches to Social Science Methodologies: An Introduction. *Signs* 30(4), 2009-15.

Hill Collins, P.H. (1991). *Black Feminist Thought: Knowledge, Consciousness, and the Politics of Empowerment*. New York: Routledge.

Inckle, K. (2010). Telling Tales? Using Ethnographic Fictions to Speak Embodied "Truth." *Qualitative Research* 10(1), 27-47.

Kilty, J. (2008). Resisting Confined Identities: Women's Strategies of Coping in Prison. PhD diss., Simon Fraser University.

Kilty, J., and DeVellis, L. (2010). Transcarceration and the Production of "Grey Space": How Frontline Workers Exercise Spatial Practices in a Halfway House for Women. In V. Strimelle and F. Vanhamme (Eds.), *Droits et Voix/Rights and Voices* (137-58). Ottawa: University of Ottawa Press.

Koch, P., and Mansfield, P. (2004). Facing the Unknown: Social Support through the Menopausal Transition. *Women and Therapy* 27(3/4), 179-94.

Law, J., and Urry, J. (2004). Enacting the Social. *Economy and Society* 33(3): 390-410.

Louppe, L. (1997). *Poétique de la danse contemporaine*. Brussels: Éditions Contredanse.

Moore, D., Freeman, L., and Krawczyk, P. (2011). Spatio-Therapeutics: Drug Treatment Courts and Urban Space. *Social and Legal Studies* 20(2), 157-72.

Moss, P. (2007). Emergent Methods in Feminist Research. In S.N. Hesse-Biber (Ed.), *Handbook of Feminist Research: Theory and Praxis* (371-89). London: Sage.

Munn, M. (2009). "Falling out of the Rabbit Hole": Former Long-Term Prisoners' Negotiation of Release, Reentry and Resettlement. PhD diss., University of Ottawa.

Newton, T. (2003). Truly Embodied Sociology: Marrying the Social and the Biological? *Sociological Review* 51(1), 20-42.

Pan Ké Shon, J.-L. (2007). Le recensement rénové français et l'étude des mobilités. *Population* (French Edition) 62(1), 123-41.

Poole, S. (2007). Voicing the Non-Place: Precarious Theatre in a Women's Prison. *Feminist Review* 87(1), 141-52.

Préjean, M. (1994). *Sexes et pouvoir: La construction sociale des corps et des émotions*. Montreal: Les Presses de l'Université de Montréal.

Reinharz, S. (1992). *Feminist Methods in Social Research*. New York: Oxford University Press.

Robert, D., Frigon, S., and Belzile, R. (2007). Women, the Embodiment of Health and Carceral Space. *International Journal of Prisoner Health* 3(3), 176-288.

Rousset, M. (2006). Danse contemporaine: Éloge du corps ordinaire. *Regards*, April 1.

Scraton, P. (1990). Scientific Knowledge or Masculine Discourses? Challenging Patriarchy in Criminology. In L. Gelsthorpe and A. Morris (Eds.), *Feminist Perspectives in Criminology* (10-25). Bristol, PA: Open University Press.

Shilling, C. (1993). *The Body and Social Theory*. London: Sage.

Sklar, D. (1991). On Dance Ethnography. *Dance Research Journal* 23(1), 6-10.

–. (2000). On Dance Ethnography. *Dance Research Journal* 32(1), 70-77.

Smith, D. (1974). Women's Perspective as a Radical Critique of Sociology. *Sociological Inquiry* 44(1), 7-13.

Somerville, M. (2004). Tracing Bodylines: The Body in Feminist Poststructural Research. *International Journal of Qualitative Studies in Education* 17(1), 47-65.

Spry, T. (2001). Performing Eutoethnography: An Embodied Methodological Praxis. *Qualitative Inquiry* 7(6), 706-32.

Stanley, L., and Wise, S. (1983). *Breaking Out: Feminist Consciousness and Feminist Research.* London: Routledge.

—. (1993). *Breaking Out Again: Feminist Ontology and Epistemology.* London: Routledge.

Statistics Canada. (2006). *Census of Population.* Statistics Canada catalogue no. 97-551-XCB2006005. Ottawa: Statistics Canada.

Ussher, J. (2006). *Managing the Monstrous Feminine: Regulating the Reproductive Body.* London: Routledge.

van Dülmen, R. (1990). *Theatre of Horror: Crime and Punishment in Early Modern Germany.* Cambridge: Polity Press.

Wahidin, A., and Moss, D. (2004). Women Doing and Making Time: Reclaiming Time. *International Journal of Sociology and Social Policy* 24(6), 76-111.

Williams, S.J., and Bendelow, G. (1998). *The Lived Body: Sociological Themes, Embodied Issues.* London: Routledge.

Ylonen, M.E. (2003). Bodily Flashes of Dancing Women: Dance as a Method of Inquiry. *Qualitative Inquiry* 9(4), 554-68.

chapter 5

Producing Feminist Knowledge: Lessons from the Past

Dorothy E. Chunn and Robert Menzies

Since the 1950s, researchers working from critical perspectives have developed or rediscovered methodological approaches to the study of human experience that are grounded in a critique of positivism and, in particular, the assumption that the social world can be studied "scientifically" in the same way as the physical world. More specifically, they have prioritized approaches that require face-to-face interaction with participants over large-scale studies organized around surveys and statistical analysis. Feminists built on the work of earlier critical researchers who resurrected the social constructivist legacy of the Chicago School of sociology and focused attention on less powerful, often marginalized populations, constructing the latter as "underdogs" (Becker 1963, 1967). With an emphasis on unheard "voices from below," both historical and contemporary, they embraced research methods that would break the silence, including ethnography, interviews, participant observation, life histories, participatory action research, and documentary research based on case files (Eichler and Lapointe 1985; Harding 1986, 1991; Iacovetta and Mitchinson 1998; Reinharz 1992; Smith 1987, 1999; Stanley and Wise 1993).

None of these methods is uniquely feminist, but feminists arguably have made distinctive contributions to the production of knowledge, not least through the deconstruction of the gender-blindness that has historically characterized most of the extant mainstream, malestream research on (marginalized) women (DeVault 1996). For much of the twentieth century, even critical researchers who were acutely aware of how social relations of class and race were linked to marginalization did not see the need to address gender relations in their studies (see, e.g., Hall et al. 1978; Mills 1959; Taylor, Walton, and Young 1973, 1975). Among criminological researchers, for example, criminalized women were generally considered "too few to count," and/or researchers implicitly or explicitly assumed that their analyses of men were equally applicable to women (Adelberg and Currie 1987, Heidensohn 1985; Naffine 1987; Smart 1976). Feminists begged to differ, and their critiques of traditional criminological research and, eventually, their own research helped to create some awareness and space for gendered analyses of the moral-legal-social regulation of marginalized women and men (Balfour and Comack 2006; Daly and Maher 1998; Rafter and Heidensohn 1995).

These and other feminist contributions to the research enterprise are often taken for granted and obscured (Smart 2009, 296-97). Yet, viewed retrospectively, feminist research in this critical tradition has raised a number of important, overarching questions that have stimulated ongoing debate among feminists themselves and continue to be highly relevant in our contemporary world. That said, a comprehensive review of epistemological debates among feminists and how they play out in sociolegal/criminological research is beyond the scope of this chapter. Instead, we examine two sets of broad, recurrent questions about feminist methodologies, drawing on selected authors as well as aspects of our own research involving marginalized populations from the 1980s onwards.

First, what counts as a feminist analysis? Does feminist research always have to focus on women? Can men do feminist research? If yes, how can we conduct research that includes men as both researchers and participants without flattening and obscuring still-existing power differentials between women and men in the current neoliberal context? How do we conduct research that encompasses intragender differences as well as intergender commonalities? Is feminist analysis wholly distinct from other methodological approaches? Are quantitative methodologies antithetical to a feminist analysis?

Second, how can we ensure that we really hear the voices of the marginalized, living or dead? How do we negotiate our relationships with research participants – the dynamic interplay of regulation and resistance, agency and necessity, autonomy and necessity – in engaging the lived experience of human subjects, both men and women? How do we analyze and interpret their stories without either reconstructing their specific perceptions and experiences as more general "truths" or imposing our own framework on what they tell us (i.e., imposing order on messiness)? How do we maintain a respect for, and attentiveness to, the voices of research participants who may be marginalized but are also normatively conventional? How do we respond, politically and strategically, when participants say things that we do not want to hear (for example, by voicing beliefs and opinions that are racist and [hetero]sexist) or when they accept "authoritative" constructions of themselves as deficient, dangerous, or otherwise deviant?

In addressing these questions, we concomitantly consider the status of feminist analysis more generally as an amalgam of intense methodological discourses and practices that both challenge convention and raise profound questions about our political and moral identities as critical social researchers. We argue that the production of feminist knowledges can and does encompass a range of distinctive epistemological positions. We conclude that feminist analysis (no less so than other critical methodological approaches) is more relevant than ever as a tool for mapping and deciphering our social worlds, notwithstanding claims that we are all equal now and have entered a postfeminist era.

What Counts as Feminist Analysis?

Feminists in Canada and other liberal states entered the academy in growing numbers from the 1970s onward (even if they were, admittedly, concentrated heavily in the humanities and social sciences), and they began to generate their own assemblage of research and publications. From the beginning, feminist researchers espoused different, often contradictory, ways of conceptualizing "feminist analysis." Initially, however, the dominant feminist approaches to research rested on the shared assumption that, at its core, a feminist analysis was "by women, on women, and for women" (Stanley and Wise 1993, 30-33). Indeed, during the early 1960s, an analysis produced by a (feminist) woman that centred women's experiences and perceptions of their subordinate status vis-à-vis men historically with the goal of bringing about change (legal, social, etc.) "seemed strikingly original to those who were doing it" (Reinharz 1992, 214). Feminists assumed that an emphasis on (Her)story was needed to counter the androcentric bias of (His)story that had been universalized to subsume women, and that this "corrective" would move women toward equality with men (Stanley and Wise 1993, 31).

Running through debates about feminist analysis was what Sandra Harding (1986) called the "science question" in feminism. In the context of rejecting the prevailing positivist model of research as neither objective nor value- and gender-neutral, many feminist researchers eschewed quantitative analysis altogether (Westmarland 2001). Some feminists, however, adopted an empiricist approach, focusing on the replacement of "bad" science with "good" science that added women/gender to the analysis (Reinharz 1992, chap. 4). Still others, following Harding, maintained that no social research method or analytic model, from the most quantitative experimental design to the most dynamic participatory ethnography, is intrinsically "feminist" or "nonfeminist" in its own right (Maguire 1987). Rather, ideology, epistemology, and research practice were seen by these observers to combine in complex ways.

The proof, as it were, was in the political pudding. Feminist praxis could thrive in the most seemingly conventional of research contexts. Conversely, to adopt a critical qualitative lens did not guarantee that one's research would further the causes of women's rights, nor of social justice concerns more generally (the field of qualitative inquiry, though arguably less so than positivism, is littered with studies that have both contributed to the marginalization of their subjects and reinscribed prevailing power relations) (Horowitz 1967; Mauthner et al. 2002).

Within criminology, the feminist empiricist approach generated a spate of "women and" research studies that examined and critiqued conventional explanations of and responses to women in conflict with the (criminal) law. For example, feminist criminologists challenged the thesis (Moulds 1980; Pollak 1961) that women are treated more leniently than men in the criminal justice and correctional systems because of the operation of chivalry-paternalism. On the contrary, feminists argued that the numerous quantitative studies on chivalry-paternalism were not conclusive one way or the other and that conventional quantitative methodologies are themselves epistemologically suspect (see, e.g., Daly 1994). Some feminists went even further to assert that women are often treated more severely than are men in criminal law, criminal justice, and the correctional system. As exemplars of the inherent gender bias of the law, they pointed to the historically discriminatory treatment of women who sell sex (Brock 2009) and women's notable inability to use the self-defence provisions of the criminal law in cases where they use lethal force to defend themselves against long-time abuse by a male partner/spouse (Browne 1987).

The shortcomings of the empiricist, additive approach to knowledge production elicited powerful critique among feminists (see, e.g., Harding 1986). In particular, the tendency to conceptualize gender as simply a variable, and the assumption that "good" science was primarily a matter of eliminating the sexism in existing research methodologies through the adoption of a "just add women and stir" approach, stimulated the development of feminist-standpoint epistemologies. The latter were based on the assumption that research conducted from a feminist standpoint "produce[d] more complete, less distorted knowledge" (Westmarland 2001). But early formulations of the feminist standpoint also came under challenge for seemingly giving some knowers "an 'epistemic privilege' associated with their identities" (DeVault 1996, 40). Whether their allegiances were empiricist or standpoint, then, when feminist researchers talked about "women," they were most often talking about women like themselves – white, heterosexual, able-bodied, able-minded, and middle-class. As a result, "white feminism" theoretically and methodologically centred feminist research and knowledge production on white, heterosexual, able-bodied, able-minded, middle-class men as the norm toward which "women" should aspire. In so doing, empiricist and standpoint feminists were accused of simply flipping the historical emphasis from men to women, making it impossible to talk about how differences among women and commonalities between women and men affected the forms and degrees of male oppression that differently situated women experienced.

The response to internal and external critiques of standpointism led feminists in two directions. Some concentrated on a reworking of feminist standpointism (Harding 1986; Hartsock 1998; Hill Collins 2000; hooks 2000; Smith 1999). As Dorothy Smith (1999, 96) put it, "women's standpoint means beginning in the actualities of people's lives as they experience them ... [but] this method ... *is not exclusively about or for women*" (emphasis added). Revised standpointism also acknowledged more explicitly differences among women and among men that are generated by the interconnectedness of social relations of class, race, sexuality, (dis)ability, and related axes of subordination and alterity. Other feminists who were not persuaded by either empiricism or standpointism began to explore poststructuralism and postmodernism (Jackson and Mazzei 2009; Lather 1991). The deconstructionist influence of these perspectives stimulated a rethinking of the assumptions underpinning the dichotomous conceptualization of gender relations solely as intergender relations between Women and Men writ large (Smart 1992). Strongly influenced by Michel Foucault's legacy, feminist poststructuralists and postmodernists challenged the essentialism of categories such as "Woman" that rendered differences among women invisible (Riley 1988; Smart 1992).

The dual influences of standpointism and deconstructionism are evident in feminist criminological research. Both perspectives challenge essentialism and illuminate difference and diversity. In response to ongoing efforts to determine whether women are treated more leniently or more severely than are men in the criminal justice system, exponents of both perspectives argue that the answer depends on *which* women (and men) are being considered. Standpointism led feminist criminologists to focus on how conformity or nonconformity to normative masculinity/femininity, family form, motherhood/fatherhood, and other normative categories was linked to the differential treatment of women in the criminal justice system (Comack 1996; Gavigan 1988, 1993; Daly 1989, 1994). Similarly, deconstructionism illuminated the ways in which authoritative discourses (legal, medical, etc.) simultaneously construct Woman in contradistinction to Man and constitute different types or categories of women – married versus unmarried mothers, virgins versus "sluts," "normal" versus "mad" women, and so forth (Smart 1992; see also Diduck 1998).

Meanwhile, two particularly influential findings had emerged from the ever-growing archive of feminist criminological research. First, study after study revealed that the interconnected social relations of gender, race, class, (dis)ability, sexuality, and generation (among others) are central determinants through which women are able or willing to embrace conformity (see, e.g., Balfour and Comack 2006; Chan and Mirchandani 2002; Daly 1992; Grabham, Cooper, and Herman 2009; Roberts 1995; Robson 2004). In the main, white, middle-class women are the "good" mothers, wives, and daughters who are treated more leniently overall than are their racialized, poor, and otherwise subordinated sisters. Second, far from being singular or seamless, human identity is multiple and often contradictory. This fragmented, fluid, and dynamic quality of women's identity has many consequences, including the prospect that marginalized women (and men) may be simultaneously threatening and endangered, unruly and compliant, criminal and victim (Comack 1996; Kilty and Frigon 2006; Swift and Callahan 2009; see also Donzelot 1979).

Clearly, then, there is no consensus within feminism about what makes an approach to research and knowledge production "feminist." Nonetheless, there are points of considerable agreement. For instance, most feminists would concur with Stanley and Wise (1993, 188-89) that there is no "distinct feminist method, in the sense of a technique of data collection and analysis that is specific and unique to feminist social science," but that distinctive epistemologies and methodologies do still exist. Likewise, many feminists would agree with Marjorie DeVault's (1996, 32-34) observation that what makes feminist methodologies distinctive is a commitment to centre "the locations and perspectives of (all) women"; to "minimize harm and control in the research process"; and to use methodologies that contribute to "social change or action beneficial to women."

As DeVault (1996, 34-45) goes on to document, however, methodological diversity still prevails in feminist attempts to achieve these generic goals. Some researchers continue to embrace feminist empiricism, others utilize standpoint methodologies, still others remain in poststructuralist/postmodern deconstructionist mode, and increasingly, many draw on all three traditions. Similarly, some feminists focus primarily on intergender relations, others on intragender relations, and yet others on both. Likewise, some (including men) maintain that men cannot be feminists and cannot conduct research on women since they have not experienced the world in the same way that women have. Others believe that whether they identify as feminists or profeminists, men are still capable of conducting nonsexist, gendered research. Some feminists remain wedded to qualitative approaches and suspicious of quantitative approaches, which, among other things, they consider to be irredeemably linked to positivism. Others reject such a divide and argue that the quantitative/ qualitative distinction "is something of a modern invention" (Atkinson and Delamont 2010), that methodological approaches are inherently neither "good" nor "bad" and that a combination of the two can yield a more comprehensive analysis than can a reliance on one or the other (Kimmel 1998; Kremer 1990; Watts 2006; Westmarland 2001; see generally Fonow and Cook 1991; Kirby, Greaves, and Reid 2006; Letherby 2003; Ribbens and Edwards 1998; Ramazanoglu and Holland 2002; Reinharz 1992; Stanley and Wise 1993).

Our position on the above issues derives in part from our collaborative, historical work on the forensic assessment of women. We were fortunate to have access to two extremely rich sources of data that together spanned more than a century, enabling us to conduct a variety of feminist analyses. First, our analyses of Order-in-Council women and men in British Columbia drew on a wealth of archival, documentary data, including detailed psychiatric case files, over a sixty-two-year period from the 1888 opening of the Public Hospital for the Insane in New Westminster, through to the mid-twentieth century (Chunn and Menzies 1998; Menzies and Chunn 1998, 2005, 2006).[1] Although the case files were not without gaps, they were unusually intact given that archival materials are often destroyed through indiscriminate weeding, fire, and flood, or are closed to researchers for a variety of reasons.[2] As a result, we were in a position to compare all thirty-eight Order-in-Council women who were institutionalized in BC public psychiatric institutions during that period with a matched sample of thirty-eight Order-in-Council men.

Second, we managed to access data from a large-scale, longitudinal study of the women and men subjected to multidisciplinary clinical assessment for mental disorder, fitness to stand trial, and dangerousness at the Metropolitan Toronto Forensic Service (METFORS) during the first year of that agency's operation in 1978.[3] In this more recent historical context, the number of men assessed was still greater than the number of women, but we were able to draw a matched sample of fifty-seven men for comparison with all fifty-seven women who were forensically assessed pretrial or pre-sentence in 1978 (with a follow-up of their subsequent institutional experiences extending through to 1984). Our gendered analyses of forensic decision making at METFORS tapped extensive databases that were generated through both qualitative and quantitative methodologies (Chunn and Menzies 1990; Menzies, Chunn, and Webster 1992). Case files included police reports, clinicians' reports, ward notes, psychiatric letters to the court, and judicial and mental health outcome data on women and men who were brought to METFORS for mental evaluation.[4]

With access to so much data, we were able to conduct a variety of feminist analyses with different foci: historical case studies of "criminally insane" women in British Columbia (Chunn and Menzies 1998; Menzies and Chunn 2005, 2006); documentary analyses that foregrounded all of the women who were forensically assessed but also included statistical data from matched samples of men (Menzies and Chunn 1998; Menzies, Chunn, and Webster 1992); and qualitative, comparative analyses of the women and men assessed at METFORS (Chunn and Menzies 1990).

The findings from these collective studies were extremely illuminating, sometimes unanticipated, and could not have been obtained had we opted to employ only one approach to data collection and analysis. Our detailed case study of "Charlotte Ross,"[5] who stabbed her husband to death in the 1940s, was based on a psychiatric file of more than one thousand pages that spanned her institutionalization as an Order-in-Council "patient" into the early 1970s. While it was ostensibly the unique story of one individual, her case reveals much about gender relations, gendered conceptions of "double deviants" (both "mad" and "bad"), and gendered responses to women more generally during that historical period (Menzies and Chunn 2005, 2006). Although "treatments" changed throughout her forensic confinement, medico-legal authorities consistently viewed Charlotte Ross as a "double deviant" who had breached the requirements of normative femininity – a "Black Widow" who had preyed on a sick, unsuspecting, affluent man and a "Mad Woman" who turned on a sick, unsuspecting spouse who had treated her with generosity and tolerance.

Our comparative, quantitative/statistical analyses provided us with different and valuable findings about the subjects and the process of forensic assessment. In the aggregate, they revealed surprisingly few significant differences between the marginalized women and men who were assessed by medico-legal authorities. To the contrary, our analyses underscored many commonalities that we attributed primarily to their shared socioeconomic subjugation (Menzies and Chunn 1998; Menzies, Chunn, and Webster 1992).

Finally, our qualitative, comparative analysis (Chunn and Menzies 1990) of women and men assessed at METFORS showed how police, forensic decision makers, and judges were beginning to emphasize "sameness," responsibility, and identical treatment as neoliberalism took shape in the late twentieth century. Psychiatrists held most of the women and men they assessed "accountable" for their crimes – "madness" was not often viewed as a mitigating factor – but they arrived at their decisions via ideological and normative channels that were intensely gendered. Both women and men were found "guilty" of flouting conventional standards of femininity and masculinity, respectively, and these violations translated into a clinical emphasis on criminalization rather than medicalization in the psychiatrists' reports.

In retrospect, we can see clearly how our collaborative research experience has shaped our current stance on the question of what constitutes a feminist analysis. Generally speaking, we find ourselves in agreement with Stanley and Wise (1993) and DeVault (1996) about the existence of distinctive feminist epistemologies and methodologies. By the same token, we also want to emphasize that our conceptualization of feminist research and knowledge production has always been, and steadfastly remains, a work in progress. We did not embark on our research with master epistemological and methodological frameworks in mind. Rather, we started with some shared assumptions about feminist/critical approaches to research that were derived in large part from the distinct yet often overlapping critiques of positivism that underpinned critical psychiatry and "underdog sociology" in the 1960s; from the outpouring during the 1970s and 1980s of Marxian-influenced critical criminologies and cultural studies; and from the ever-widening range of feminist sociologies and criminologies that has characterized the past three decades. While these assumptions have been subject to ongoing reflection, qualification, or modification in reaction to our own research and that of others, we have always assumed that: (1) men can be feminists, and they can both conduct and be the focus of feminist research; (2) feminist knowledges about the social world need to challenge structured inequalities that are based on gender and other, intertwined social relations of alterity and subjugation; (3) researchers and research participants must be situated within their broader historical, cultural, structural contexts; and (4) the research topics selected and research questions posed are more important than the particular methodological approach adopted.

These assumptions are in keeping with the epistemological position of "fractured foundationalism" outlined by Stanley and Wise (1993, 8-9), but they are not restricted to one feminist epistemological and methodological position. On the contrary, our own collaborative research experience indicates that not all feminist projects can or should be conducted using the same feminist template. For example, while we assume that, in theory, men can be feminist researchers and participants, we also are keenly aware that the production of feminist knowledges always occurs in a context of structured inequalities. In keeping with this political, social-change dimension of the research enterprise, one of us has always identified as a feminist and the other as a profeminist – a symbolic acknowledgment that men can contribute to and benefit from ending gender inequality, although they do not themselves directly experience gender oppression.

Similarly, although the "ideal" feminist analysis would be as comprehensive as possible – that is, it would be based on both qualitative and quantitative data, focused on both inter- and intragender relations, and historically, culturally, structurally contextualized – researchers are often unable to generate or obtain access to the data that would yield such an analysis. This does not disqualify less comprehensive research as feminist. Rather, it means that the kind of feminist analysis researchers can conduct is heavily dependent on their objectives and the data they have to work with. While this is true of most research, feminists and other critical researchers confront problems such as denial of access to marginalized, often institutionalized, people, that researchers working within conventional paradigms do not. In short, producing feminist knowledge is about working within the boundaries imposed by an imperfect world.

In the next section, we zero in on specific aspects of the research process that have generated ongoing debates among feminists and profeminists about the production and dissemination of knowledge, and that are key to realizing the goal of developing epistemologies and methodologies that "can most directly and far-reachingly challenge nonfeminist frameworks and ways of working" (Stanley and Wise 1993, 188-89).

How Can We Really Hear the Voices of the Marginal?

Feminists, and critical researchers more generally, are concerned about listening to and liberating the voices of marginalized individuals and groups that historically have been heard only faintly or not at all – moving them, in bell hooks's oft-repeated words (2000), from "margin to centre." Epistemological and methodological debates focus on how to access these "voices from below" and on the possibility of really hearing and, just as important, incorporating into text and praxis the diversity of voices among subaltern populations. Two issues of central concern to critical researchers are the negotiation of the researcher-participant relationship and the analysis and interpretation of the voices of research participants.

When it comes to the researcher-participant relationship, the challenge facing university-based researchers – especially those who apply a critical lens to their craft – is the inherent inequality that exists between them and participants who are marginalized, oftentimes along multiple dimensions (see, e.g., Culhane 2003-04; Robertson and Culhane 2005). This inequality cannot simply be willed away by well-intentioned researchers, even if some feminists have taken such an idealist approach. Many others have acknowledged the inequality and attempted to organize the research process in ways that will eliminate, or at least reduce, power differentials between researcher and research participant through the empowerment of the latter. Research methods aimed at empowerment include placing the emphasis on the coproduction of knowledge that is based on researcher reflexivity and participant input (e.g., revision of transcripts by removing text or adding to it) and/or the training and employment of community-based researchers who share the same marginalized status as research participants.

At this point, however, feminists have conducted enough research in this vein to know that a collaborative approach to research with marginalized women (and men) is dual-edged. While empowerment strategies can be innovative and contribute to more equal researcher-participant relationships, they cannot erase the cavernous social distance that separates academic researchers from the marginalized women who participate in their studies, nor remove the structured inequities that characterize the broader context in which the research is conducted. As Culhane (2003-04, 104) has argued, "Looking closely at how researchers and researcher subjects are differently located in class and race hierarchies brings into focus the limitations to the possibilities for establishing more egalitarian relationships within research projects, which are themselves embedded within contexts of privilege."

Another debate among feminists and other critical researchers that speaks to the issue of foregrounding and hearing "voices from below" centres on the question of how researchers should approach their data. Some – for example, feminists working in the grounded theory tradition (Olesen 2007; Plummer 2010) – say that researchers should adopt a minimalist stance, letting their participants speak for themselves both substantively (recording their words verbatim) and technically (preserving grammar and syntax), rather than trying to "read," "interpret," or impose order on what they say. Others express concern about the implications of this approach, vehemently rejecting the argument "that presenting data as if it speaks for itself is an answer to the problem of voice" (Mazzei and Jackson 2009, 3).

A minimalist stance suggests, among other things, that feminist and other critical researchers should bracket off issues that are of concern to them and concentrate on excavating the voices of their research participants. But there are dangers attendant to relying entirely on – in failing to critically interrogate or contextualize – what research participants say. For one thing, like their more privileged counterparts, subaltern women (and men) may not talk about things that show them in a negative light. Moreover, while marginalized women have much in common, they are far from homogeneous in their perceptions and experiences of marginalization, and some will offer words that researchers may not want to hear. How should feminist researchers react when marginalized research participants reinforce the status quo by making racist, homophobic, or sexist comments; or by accepting negative, authoritative constructions of themselves as mad or bad; or by presenting themselves as normatively conventional women (and men) who do not identify with feminism? As Carol Smart (2009, 301) has observed, "Allowing participants more control over the direction of the interview may seem a 'democratic' way forward, but it can mean that we (as sociologists) are deflected away from precisely the things that we think matter."

Feminist researchers must therefore confront the challenging question of how they can empathize with their marginalized research participants without accepting everything they say as "the truth" and without conceptualizing them as one-dimensional victims devoid of agency or human frailties. Like the "underdog" sociologists and criminologists of the 1960s and 1970s, feminists have sometimes been guilty of romanticizing marginalized women and acting like the "zookeepers of deviancy" reproached some four decades ago by Jock Young (1970). As a consequence, they have avoided the analysis of certain issues and topics, in the process leaving the door open for antifeminist researchers to monopolize these areas of study. With a few exceptions (see, e.g., Comack 1996; Comack and Brickey 2007; Daly 1992), for instance, feminists were virtually silent until recently on the question of (marginalized) women who commit acts of serious violence that cannot be justified or explained away. The absence of these women's voices from feminist analyses created a gap that was quickly filled by antifeminists (see, e.g., Pearson 1997), and feminists have found themselves waging an uphill struggle to counter the antifeminist conceptualization of women's violence that now pervades public culture (Lamb 1999).

The difficulties feminist researchers have experienced in their attempts to *really* hear what marginalized research participants are telling them have fuelled arguments to radically decentre "voice" in feminist analysis and knowledge production. As Mazzei and Jackson (2009, 3-4) succinctly put it, "We assert that in our zeal as qualitative researchers to gather data and make meaning, or to make easy sense, we often seek that voice which we can easily name, categorize, and respond to." These authors go on to argue that we need to "strain" the concept of voice and prioritize "the voice that escapes easy classification and that does not make easy sense" – a "transgressive" voice, not a "normative" one (ibid.).

Our own research suggests that there can be no fixed responses to these questions about voice because alternative methodological approaches will differentially shape researcher-participant relationships and how subaltern voices are heard. Our above-described studies of forensic clinical assessment, for example, are primarily historical documentary in content and not grounded in face-to-face interactions with the women and men who are the focus of our analyses. Negotiating the researcher-participant "relationship" obviously takes on a much different meaning when research subjects are dead and cannot consent or contribute directly to the narratives that researchers (re)construct. Likewise, the task of *really* hearing their voices in texts produced and assembled by authoritative others (e.g., clinicians) is also deeply challenging. Sifted through the filters of time, and refracted as they traverse institutional and cultural boundaries, the words and experiences of marginalized and criminalized women often reach us in forms that would scarcely be recognizable to the women who spoke and lived them.

That said, as observed by (among others) the contributors to Iacovetta and Mitchinson's important collection on historical case file research (1998), the voices of subaltern women, men, and children still resonate memorably in these texts, even if they are mediated and papered over, and even if their original interlocutors ignored or failed to hear them. The same is true of the women and men who appear in our historical data on forensic assessment and decision making. Their voices are present but not *really* heard by the medico-legal authorities who determined their respective fates. We are not suggesting that the authoritative knowers (or, for that matter, those who found themselves the subjects of psy-classification) spoke in exactly the same voice. Nonetheless, we found it difficult not to notice that medico-legal authorities consistently transformed the narratives of the women and men being forensically assessed – narratives that often pointed to the influence of structural factors on their personal troubles – into authoritative accounts of individual failings and inadequacies.

The case of a twenty-two-year-old woman sent to METFORS for assessment after being charged with public mischief – she threw a brick through the window of a provincial government building – is typical. The report of the arresting police officer contained this woman's explanation of her action: "she had no place to stay, was down and out, and wanted to be arrested." The clinicians at METFORS, however, determined that she was suffering from "acute situational maladjustment," a diagnosis that was "supported with descriptions of [her] multiple defects" (Chunn and Menzies 1990, 42). This individuation process was a routine feature of expert assessments at METFORS, as it is elsewhere (Pfohl 1978; Allen 1987). Recurrently, clinicians succeeded in depoliticizing and pathologizing the thoughts, words, and deeds of psycho-criminalized women – all the while underscoring the latter's blameworthiness, accountability, and risk (Barron 2012; Ericson and Baranek 1982; Hannah-Moffat 2001) through the peculiar alchemy of neoliberal discourse.

Consistent with the experiences of feminist researchers navigating a diversity of other institutional and cultural contexts, our research in the realm of psychiatry and law has made us acutely aware of the unequal power relations that prevail between researchers and their marginalized participants as well as the inevitably mediated nature of their interactions. Further, we concur with the argument that there are no "authentic," unmediated voices for researchers to excavate (see, e.g., Mazzei and Jackson 2009, 2). Largely because of the agentic qualities of the historical material we work with, however, we are equally convinced that centring what our research participants say, and working to carve out an epistemological and political space in which their voices may be heard, is an imperative of critical research (although admittedly, this stance is more a pragmatic, political one than a position grounded in unassailable, epistemological logic). Thus, we are less persuaded than others that the problems with voice are intractable and that researchers should radically decentre voice in feminist analysis and knowledge production (see Jackson and Mazzei 2009). That said, we do certainly agree with critics of voice to the extent that marginalized people are diverse and that what individuals say always needs to be examined in historical and structural context – all the more so when the words, both spoken and written, of research participants are being filtered through the lenses of powerful and strategically positioned others. On this point, it is worth remembering C. Wright Mills's (1959, 143) classic observation that "social science deals with problems of biography, of history, and of their intersections within social structures."

We find echoes of Mills's argument in feminist debates about the need for cultural, social, and historical specificity in conducting feminist research. Feminists who assume that gender is universally the primary reason for women's historical subordination to men are less concerned about such specificities. From this perspective, patriarchy is transhistorical and transcultural; therefore, *plus ça change, plus c'est la même chose.* In contrast, feminists who assume that gender operates in tandem with other social relations such as race and class – relations that may sometimes be equal to or more important than gender in the marginalization of individuals and groups – argue that the content of patriarchal relations is not always and everywhere the same, and that feminists therefore need to locate their analyses in historical, structural, and human context.

As indicated above, we strongly agree that historical, cultural, and social specificity should be a defining feature of feminist research and the production of feminist knowledge. Even a cursory examination of the overall context in which research was conducted from the late nineteenth century to the present in Canada reveals how the dominant ways of conceptualizing, hearing, and responding to marginalized populations shift as patriarchal and other social relations are (re)formed and reconfigured. In the context of a developing and realized welfare state through the first half of the twentieth century, the primary emphasis was on difference. In stark contrast, in the context of its contemporary counterpart, the neoliberal "minimalist" state, the primary emphasis is on sameness.

When criminology came of age in the early twentieth century as a positivist discipline (Garland 1985), most criminological research drew a line between the "normal" and the "deviant" and, among the deviant, between women and men. From Lombroso and Ferrero's (1895) writings onward, this differentiation translated into intensely gendered explanations of deviance. Theories of women's deviance were few, and those that did enter the criminological canon were typically driven by a hard determinism that largely ignored women's experiences and subjectivities in favour of bio- and psycho-genetic explanations that pointed to individual and sexual pathology. For their part, men were increasingly viewed through the soft determinism of sociological explanations that pointed to pathological circumstances or environments (e.g., family, community, peers) (Heidensohn 1985; Naffine 1987).

With the ascendancy of neoliberalism in the late twentieth century, the emphasis shifted from gender difference and sex-specific, individualized responses (see Glasbeek 2009 on "feminized justice") to sameness and equal (i.e., identical) treatment. While many feminists supported the implementation of legislation and policy based on notions of formal equality, they quickly learned that formal equality did not necessarily translate into positive equal outcomes. Feminist criminologists discovered to their dismay, for instance, that advocating for parity of treatment for women with men in the criminal justice and correctional systems did not advance the causes of either gender. The implicit assumption of this argument – namely, that criminalized and psychiatrized men actually received just treatment and adequate resources – was fatally flawed, as a generation of research by critical penologists and mental health scholars had convincingly shown (Sim 2009; Whitaker 2010). Contradictorily, such equality-informed advocacy often merged with the state's coercive machinery to actually increase the levels of punitiveness targeting both women and men (Daly 1992; Gavigan 1989-90; Snider 1994).

More generally, the formal erasure of difference within the neoliberal political regime of the late twentieth century created a situation whereby still-existing power differentials between women and men, as well as those among women and among men, became increasingly flattened and obscured. As a consequence, non- and antifeminist legal and criminological research, which rests on the belief that men and women are equal, increasingly supports the conclusion that men are victims of reverse discrimination. This body of "backlash" writing asserts that, among other travesties, men are being treated unfairly by the courts relative to women and that men allegedly suffer unacknowledged abuses and other harms in equal measure to their female counterparts (Farrell 1993; Goldberg 1976).

The challenge for feminist researchers is how to avoid the dichotomous analytical framework that traps them within the narrow parameters of male and female, sameness and difference, and is premised on the assumption that only one set of ideas about (marginalized) men and women is operating at any given moment and social location. On the contrary, as sociolegal and criminological researchers have illustrated across a wealth of contexts and subject areas, old ideas continue to circulate and affect our thinking, even as new ideas become the dominant influence on law and policy (Brock 2003; Cunliffe 2011; Swift and Callahan 2009). The fact that laws and policies governing marginalized women and men have become officially value-free and gender-neutral does not mean that long-standing ways of thinking about gender, race, class, and sexual difference are no longer in play. Still, as we have argued in this chapter, examining differences among women and among men, while simultaneously engaging commonalities between women and men, offers one way to undercut such dichotomous thinking. In this respect, Patricia Hill Collins's justly celebrated use of black feminist thought to reconceptualize the "social relations of domination and resistance" – a theoretical approach that differentiates between intersectionality and what she calls "the matrix of domination," and illuminates the linkages between these two phenomena – continues to open up exciting windows of opportunity for feminist/critical researchers. As she has explained,

> Intersectionality refers to particular forms of intersecting oppressions, for example, intersections of race and gender, or of sexuality and nation. Intersectional paradigms remind us that oppression cannot be reduced to one fundamental type, and that oppressions work together in producing injustice. In contrast, the matrix of domination refers to how these intersecting oppressions are actually organized. Regardless of the particular intersections involved, structural, disciplinary, hegemonic, and interpersonal domains of power reappear across quite different forms of oppression. (2000, 18)

Additionally, following Mills (1959), linking individual biographies and stories to broader historical and structural contexts offers a second theoretical and tactical means to avoid dichotomization. Assuming that individuals embody a range of identities, and that being a criminalized or psychiatrized woman or man is only one of many identities, is yet a third strategy (Comack 1996, 2008).

Conclusion

If nothing else, the enduring debates about the politics and epistemologies of feminist methods signal the continuing need for such analysis in the pursuit of critical social research. Assorted proclamations to the contrary, we have yet to enter a postfeminist era, either in the academy or in the wider social order.

Where do we go from here, then? While we are by no means suggesting that "anything goes," our experience of collaboration on feminist analyses of marginalized women and men suggests that we need to adopt an inclusive model of what counts as feminist analysis. History suggests that feminist epistemologies and methodologies are works in progress and that feminists need to engage in an ongoing process of retooling old and developing new analytical frameworks that will most effectively challenge patriarchal and other hierarchical social relations (Stanley and Wise 1993, 188-89).

This objective may require feminists to take methodological risks. As Carol Smart (2009) has argued, the text-based focus of much (feminist) qualitative research of the past generation – in particular, of studies informed by feminist postmodernism and poststructuralism – has made researchers' publications more abstract and less accessible to readers. Moreover, feminist researchers who conduct ethnographic and interview studies frequently lament that the voices of harder-to-access research participants among the marginal are often less "articulate," or that they are not heard at all. As a result, (feminist) researchers may be tempted to gravitate toward those marginalized women who are easier to recruit, who are more "eloquent" according to conventional middle-class standards, and who accordingly provide richer data.

As a means of combating this bias, some feminists have advocated the use of new methodological approaches that will enable participants to "talk" through images, music, drama, and collaborative storytelling, as well as through the coproduction of textual narratives (Smart 2009, 303; Frigon and Shantz, this volume). That said, in the contemporary context of the neoliberal corporate university – where critical research occupies such a precarious status – for the most part it will need to be tenured, senior feminists and allied critical scholars who take these methodological risks. Those women and men who are so positioned need to mount a collective challenge to the extant privileging not only of textual modes of analysis but also of the positivist approaches to research that, with some exceptions (see, e.g., Platt 2012), continue to dominate the practice of social "science" in this second decade of the twenty-first century.

Acknowledgments

We thank the editors for the invitation to participate in this innovative project and for their comments, patience, and other assistance along the way. We also want to express our appreciation to the anonymous reviewers for their constructive comments on our chapter.

Notes

1 Orders-in-Council were special regulatory directives issued by the provincial cabinet under the authority of the Crown. Empowered by the federal Criminal Code, s. 542(2), they provided for the indeterminate confinement "at the pleasure of the Lieutenant-Governor" of persons found not guilty by reason of insanity or unfit to stand trial and those transferred from provincial jails and federal penitentiaries as insane. Parliament abolished these indefinite psychiatric sentences in 1992.
2 Archives often impose restrictions (e.g., a "hundred-year rule") on access to records for privacy or confidentiality reasons that will not always be waived for researchers.
3 METFORS was a secure unit located in Toronto's Queen Street Mental Health Centre. It no longer exists, but forensic assessments continue under the administration of the Centre for Addiction and Mental Health.
4 We did experience some restrictions that limited our ability to examine intragender similarities and differences. The files contained no systematic information about sexuality/sexual orientation of the women and men assessed at METFORS and, as a means of preserving confidentiality, information about race and ethnicity was blacked out on all documents.
5 "Charlotte Ross" is a pseudonym used to protect the confidentiality of the paper's main protagonist.

References

Adelberg, E., and Currie, C. (Eds.). (1987). *Too Few to Count: Canadian Women in Conflict with the Law.* Vancouver: Press Gang.
Allen, H. (1987). *Justice Unbalanced: Gender, Psychiatry and Judicial Decisions.* Milton Keynes, UK: Open University Press.
Atkinson, P., and Delamont, S. (2010). Introduction. In P. Atkinson and S. Delamont (Eds.), *Sage Qualitative Research Methods* (xxi-xxxvii). London: Sage.
Balfour, G., and Comack, E. (Eds.). (2006). *Criminalizing Women: Gender and (In)justice in Neoliberal Times.* Halifax, NS: Fernwood.
Barron, C. (2012). *Governing Girls: Rehabilitation in the Age of Risk.* Halifax, NS: Fernwood.
Becker, H. (1967). Whose Side Are We On? *Social Problems* 14(3), 234-47.
Becker, H. (Ed.). (1963). *Outsiders: Studies in the Sociology of Deviance.* London: Free Press of Glencoe.
Brock, D. (Ed.). (2003). *Making Normal: Social Regulation in Canada.* Toronto: Nelson Thomson.
–. (2009). *Making Work, Making Trouble: The Social Regulation of Sexual Labour* (2nd ed.). Toronto: University of Toronto Press.
Browne, A. (1987). *When Battered Women Kill.* New York: Free Press.
Chan, W., and Mirchandani, K. (Eds.). (2002). *Crimes of Colour: Racialization and the Criminal Justice System in Canada.* Peterborough, ON: Broadview Press.
Chunn, D.E., and Menzies, R. (1990). Gender, Madness and Crime: The Reproduction of Patriarchal and Class Relations in a Psychiatric Court Clinic. *Journal of Human Justice* 1(2), 33-54.
–. (1998). Out of Mind, Out of Law: The Regulation of "Criminally Insane" Women inside British Columbia's Public Mental Hospitals, 1888-1973. *Canadian Journal of Women and the Law* 10(2), 306-37.
Comack, E. (1996). *Women in Trouble: Connecting Women's Law Violations to Their Histories of Abuse.* Halifax, NS: Fernwood.
–. (2008). *Out There/In Here: Masculinity, Violence, and Prisoning.* Halifax, NS: Fernwood.
Comack, E., and Brickey, S. (2007). Constituting the Violence of Criminalized Women. *Canadian Journal of Criminology and Criminal Justice* 49(1), 1-36.

Culhane, D. (2003-04). Domesticated Time and Restricted Space: University and Community Women in Downtown Eastside Vancouver. *BC Studies 140*(Winter), 91-106.

Cunliffe, E. (2011). *Murder, Medicine and Motherhood.* Oxford: Hart Publishing.

Daly, K. (1989). Rethinking Judicial Paternalism: Gender, Work-Family Relations, and Sentencing. *Gender and Society 3*(1), 9-37.

–. (1992). Women's Pathways to Felony Court. *Southern California Review of Law and Women's Studies 2,* 11-32.

–. (1994). *Gender, Crime and Punishment.* New Haven, CT: Yale University Press.

Daly, K., and Maher, L. (Eds.) (1998). *Criminology at the Crossroads: Feminist Readings in Crime and Justice.* New York: Oxford University Press.

DeVault, M. (1996). Talking Back to Sociology: Distinctive Contributions of Feminist Methodology. *Annual Review of Sociology 22,* 29-50.

Diduck, A. (1998). Conceiving the Bad Mother: "The Focus Should Be on the Child to Be Born." *UBC Law Review 32,* 199-225.

Donzelot, J. (1979). *The Policing of Families.* New York: Pantheon.

Eichler, M., and Lapointe, J. (1985). *On the Treatment of the Sexes in Research.* Ottawa: Social Sciences and Humanities Research Council.

Ericson, R.V., and Baranek, P.M. (1982). *The Ordering of Justice: A Study of Accused Persons as Dependants in the Criminal Process.* Toronto: University of Toronto Press.

Farrell, W. (1993). *The Myth of Male Power: Why Men Are the Disposable Sex.* New York: Simon and Schuster.

Fonow, M.M., and Cook, J. (Eds.). (1991). *Beyond Methodology: Feminist Scholarship as Lived Research.* Bloomington: Indiana University Press.

Garland, D. (1985). *Punishment and Welfare: A History of Penal Strategies.* Aldershot, UK: Gower.

Gavigan, S.A.M. (1988). Law, Gender and Ideology. In A.F. Bayefsky (Ed.), *Legal Theory Meets Legal Practice* (283-95). Edmonton, AB: Academic Publishing.

–. (1989-90). Petit Treason in Eighteenth-Century England: Women's Inequality before the Law. *Canadian Journal of Women and the Law 3,* 335-74.

–. (1993). Paradise Lost, Paradox Revisited: The Implications of Feminist, Lesbian and Gay Engagement to Law. *Osgoode Hall Law Journal 31,* 589-624.

Glasbeek, A. (2009). *Feminized Justice: The Toronto Women's Court, 1913-34.* Vancouver: UBC Press.

Goldberg, H. (1976). *The Hazards of Being Male: Surviving the Myth of Masculine Privilege.* New York: Signet.

Grabham, E., Cooper, D., and Herman, D. (Eds.). (2009). *Intersectionality and Beyond: Law, Power and the Politics of Location.* New York: Routledge-Cavendish.

Hall, S., Critcher, C., Jefferson, T., Clarke, J., and Roberts, B. (1978). *Policing the Crisis.* London: Macmillan.

Hannah-Moffat, K. (2001). *Punishment in Disguise: Penal Governance and Federal Imprisonment of Women in Canada.* Toronto: University of Toronto Press.

Harding, S.G. (1986). *The Science Question in Feminism.* Ithaca, NY: Cornell University Press.

–. (1991). *Whose Science? Whose Knowledge? Thinking from Women's Lives.* Ithaca, NY: Cornell University Press.

Hartsock, N.C.M. (1998). *The Feminist Standpoint Revisited and Other Essays.* Boulder, CO: Westview.

Heidensohn, F. (1985). *Women and Crime.* Basingstoke, UK: Macmillan.

Hill Collins, P.H. (2000). *Black Feminist Thought: Knowledge, Consciousness, and the Politics of Empowerment* (2nd ed.). New York: Routledge.

hooks, b. (2000). *Feminist Theory: From Margin to Center* (2nd ed.). Cambridge, MA: South End Press.

Horowitz, I.L. (Ed.). (1967). *The Rise and Fall of Project Camelot: Studies in the Relationship between Social Science and Practical Politics.* Cambridge, MA: MIT Press.

Iacovetta, F., and Mitchinson, W. (Eds.). (1998). *On the Case: Explorations in Social History*. Toronto: University of Toronto Press.

Jackson, A.Y., and Mazzei, L.A. (Eds.). (2009). *Voice in Qualitative Inquiry: Challenging Conventional, Interpretive, and Critical Conceptions in Qualitative Research*. New York: Routledge.

Kilty, J.M., and Frigon, S. (2006). From a Woman in Danger to a Dangerous Woman, the Case of Karla Homolka: Chronicling the Shifts. *Women and Criminal Justice* 17(4), 37-61.

Kimmel, M.S. (1998). Who's Afraid of Men Doing Feminism? In T. Digby (Ed.), *Men Doing Feminism* (57-68). New York: Routledge.

Kirby, S., Greaves, L., and Reid, C. (2006). *Experience Research Social Change: Methods beyond the Mainstream*. Peterborough, ON: Garamond.

Kremer, B. (1990). Learning to Say No: Keeping Feminist Research for Ourselves. *Women's Studies International Forum* 13(5), 463-67.

Lamb, S. (Ed.). (1999). *New Versions of Victims*. New York: New York University Press.

Lather, P. (1991). *Getting Smart: Feminist Research and Pedagogy with/in the Postmodern*. New York: Routledge.

Letherby, G. (2003). *Feminist Research in Theory and Practice*. New York: McGraw-Hill.

Lombroso, C., and Ferrero, G. (1895). *The Female Offender*. London: T.F. Unwin.

Maguire, P. (1987). *Doing Participatory Research: A Feminist Approach*. Amherst: University of Massachusetts Press.

Mauthner, M., Birch, M., Jessop, J., and Miller, T. (Eds.). (2002). *Ethics in Qualitative Research*. London: Sage.

Mazzei, L.A., and Jackson, A.Y. (2009). Introduction: The Limit of Voice. In A.Y. Jackson and L.A. Mazzei (Eds.), *Voice in Qualitative Inquiry: Challenging Conventional, Interpretive, and Critical Conceptions in Qualitative Research* (1-13). New York: Routledge.

Menzies, R., and Chunn, D.E. (1998). The Gender Politics of Criminal Insanity: "Order-In-Council" Women in British Columbia, 1888-1950. *Histoire social/Social History* 31(62), 241-79.

–. (2005). Charlotte's Web: Historical Regulation of "Insane" Women Murderers. In W. Chan, D.E. Chunn, and R. Menzies (Eds.), *Women, Madness and the Law: A Feminist Reader* (79-100). London: Glasshouse Press.

–. (2006). The Making of the Black Widow: The Criminal and Psychiatric Control of Women. In G. Balfour and E. Comack (Eds.), *Criminalizing Women: Gender and (In)justice in Neoliberal Times* (174-94). Halifax, NS: Fernwood.

Menzies, R., Chunn, D.E., and Webster, C. (1992). Female Follies: The Forensic Psychiatric Assessment of Women Defendants. *International Journal of Law and Psychiatry* 15, 179-93.

Mills, C.W. (1959). *The Sociological Imagination*. New York: Oxford University Press.

Moulds, E.F. (1980). Chivalry and Paternalism: Disparities of Treatment in the Criminal Justice System. In S. Datesman and F. Scarpitti (Eds.), *Women, Crime, and Justice* (227-99). New York: Oxford University Press.

Naffine, N. (1987). *Female Crime: The Construction of Women in Criminology*. Boston: Allen and Unwin.

Olesen, V.L. (2007). Feminist Qualitative Research and Grounded Theory: Complexities, Criticisms, and Opportunities. In A. Bryant and K. Charmaz (Eds.), *The Sage Handbook of Grounded Theory* (417-35). Thousand Oaks, CA: Sage.

Pearson, P. (1997). *When She Was Bad: Violent Women and the Myth of Innocence*. New York: Viking.

Pfohl, S.J. (1978). *Predicting Dangerousness: The Social Construction of Psychiatric Reality*. Lexington, MS: Lexington Books.

Platt, J. (2012). Making Them Count: How Effective Has Official Encouragement of Quantitative Methods Been in British Sociology? *Current Sociology* 60(5), 690-704.

Plummer, M. (2010). Grounded Theory and Feminist Inquiry: Revitalizing Links to the Past. *Western Journal of Nursing Research* 32(3), 305-21.

Pollak, O. (1961). *The Criminality of Women*. New York/Philadelphia: A.S. Barnes/University of Pennsylvania Press.

Rafter, N., and Heidensohn, F. (Eds.). (1995). *International Feminist Perspectives in Criminology*. Milton Keynes, UK: Open University Press.

Ramazanoglu, C., and Holland, J. (2002). *Feminist Methodology: Challenges and Choices*. Thousand Oaks, CA: Sage.

Reinharz, S. (1992). *Feminist Methods in Social Research*. New York: Oxford University Press.

Ribbens, J., and Edwards, R. (1998). *Feminist Dilemmas in Qualitative Research: Public Knowledge and Private Lives*. Thousand Oaks, CA: Sage.

Riley, D. (1988). *Am I That Name? Feminism and the Category of "Women" in History*. London: Macmillan.

Roberts, D.E. (1995). Motherhood and Crime. *Social Text 42*, 99-123.

Robertson, L.A., and Culhane, D. (2005). *In Plain Sight: Reflections on Life in Downtown Eastside Vancouver*. Vancouver: Talonbooks.

Robson, R. (2004). Lesbianism and the Death Penalty: A "Hard Core" Case. *Women's Studies Quarterly 32*(3-4), 181-91.

Sim, J. (2009). *Punishment and Prisons: Power and the Carceral State*. London: Sage.

Smart, C. (1976). *Women, Crime and Criminology: A Feminist Critique*. London: Routledge and Kegan Paul.

–. (1992). The Woman of Legal Discourse. *Social and Legal Studies 1*, 29-44.

–. (2009). Shifting Horizons: Reflections on Qualitative Methods. *Feminist Theory 10*(3), 295-308.

Smith, D.E. (1987). *The Everyday World as Problematic: A Feminist Sociology*. Boston: Northeastern University Press.

–. (1999). *Writing the Social: Critique, Theory, and Investigations*. Toronto: University of Toronto Press.

Snider, L. (1994). Feminism, Punishment, and the Potential of Empowerment. *Canadian Journal of Law and Society 9*(1), 75-104.

Stanley, L., and Wise, S. (1993). *Breaking Out Again: Feminist Ontology and Epistemology*. London: Routledge.

Swift, K., and Callahan, M. (2009). *At Risk: Social Justice in Child Welfare and Other Human Services*. Toronto: University of Toronto Press.

Taylor, I. Walton, P., and Young, J. (Eds.). (1973). *The New Criminology: For a Social Theory of Deviance*. London: Routledge and Kegan Paul.

–. (1975). *Critical Criminology*. London: Routledge and Kegan Paul.

Watts, J. (2006). "The Outsider Within": Dilemmas of Qualitative Feminist Research within a Culture of Resistance. *Qualitative Research 6*(3), 385-402.

Westmarland, N. (2001). The Quantitative/Qualitative Debate and Feminist Research: A Subjective View of Objectivity. *Forum for Qualitative Research 2*(1). http://www.qualitative-research.net/index.php/fqs/article/view/974.

Whitaker, R. (2010). *Mad in America: Bad Science, Bad Medicine, and the Enduring Mistreatment of the Mentally Ill* (2nd ed.). New York: Basic Books.

Young, J. (1970). The Zookeepers of Deviancy. *Catalyst 5*, 38-46.

chapter 6

The Evolution of Feminist Research in the Criminological Enterprise: The Canadian Experience

Jennifer M. Kilty

EACH YEAR, I ATTEND the Canadian Federation for the Humanities and Social Sciences Research Congress as a member of the Canadian Law and Society Association. Not only do I present new or ongoing work; I reconnect with friends, colleagues, mentors, and scholars whose work I admire and am inspired by. And without fail, each year, I revisit the same conversation with one or more people, conversations in which we commiserate over our communal experiences of failing to get access to imprisoned or institutionalized populations about, or as Kirby and McKenna (1989) state, "by, for, [or] with" whom we conduct research. In Canada, those of us working with marginalized and criminalized populations appear to be unofficially banned from access to incarcerated people, a long-standing practice that was first documented by prison abolitionist Claire Culhane in her groundbreaking trilogy.[1] Given the increasingly strict ethical protocols enacted in universities across Canada (see Felices-Luna, this volume; van den Hoonaard, this volume) and the even stricter application procedures carried out by federal and provincial government agencies and departments such as the Correctional Service of Canada (CSC) and the Ontario Ministry of Community Safety and Correctional Services, critical scholars are finding themselves without access to the groups and populations they wish to study (Chunn and Menzies 2006). Granted, the bureaucratically driven influx of undergraduate and graduate criminology programs in university departments across the country since 2000 naturally sees an increase in graduate students and scholars doing this kind of work and thus wishing to gain access. Subsequently, one typical narrative used to justify gatekeeping and denial of research access is that prisoners (especially women) are over-researched.

In my efforts to understand why we are not allowed to speak with prisoners, I found myself posing a question that is likewise critical of the discourse I repeatedly hear from colleagues across the country – namely, do critical qualitative researchers construct themselves as intellectual martyrs? Or are we marginalized in terms of research and participant access, credibility, and recognition as a result of gatekeeping and what Martel describes as the "policing of criminological knowledge"? Martel (2004, 163) writes that

> Feminist research and writing may have found itself even more pushed to the margin of scientific legitimacy in recent years due to reflexive styles that upset dominant social, political, cultural and scientific categories and question "objective" or overly abstracted knowledge claims. In turn, feminists who occupy relatively more marginal positions in scientific communities are less likely to be noticed, cited and to have their work published.

Given that my area of specialization revolves around issues pertaining to criminalized women and my epistemological stance as a critical feminist, this chapter begins with an examination of the key principles that emerged from the major shifts in feminism, which are typically characterized as representing three distinct waves (Aikau, Erickson, and Pierce 2007). These principles act as the foundation upon which we build and link feminist work in the larger sense and appear to transcend time and the boundaries produced by trying to differentiate feminist goals and foci by era or wave. In addition to the widely acknowledged role of voice in feminist works (Fabian 2008; Hill Collins 2000; hooks 2000; Kirby and McKenna 1989), there are three principles common to feminist efforts that I dubbed the three P's: positionality, politics, and praxis. The overview that follows serves as a backdrop for the later discussion of the growth of "institutionalized feminism" as a new form of backlash and its impact on the larger feminist criminological project.[2]

Voice, the Three P's, and the First Three Waves

Conceptualizing feminism as a series of eras or waves evokes a sense of linearity in its evolution, but feminism has never been uniform, nor has it evolved without tension, conflict, and unrest (Moore 2008). Each successive wave "ended" because of heightened critical questioning by feminists and nonfeminists alike. This lack of unity is what makes feminism – be it a political, theoretical, epistemological, or methodological concept – contentious; moreover, feminism inspires fear and apprehension from those who stand outside or are challenged by it and resentment from those who feel threatened by what changes it aspires to and calls upon us to undertake. As such, *feminism* is a term laden with much conceptual baggage (Kirby and McKenna 1989) that remains conceptually confused among both lay citizens and academics.[3] Instead of trying to define "feminism," I espouse that there are basic principles that most critical feminist social researchers and activists embrace – namely, the notion of voice[4] (the different ways individuals and groups construct and interpret issues and their position in relation to those issues) and what I identify as the three P's of feminist research: positionality (recognizing the differences among women and the situatedness of their oppressions), politics (politicizing social, economic, scientific, and legal issues through deliberate action), and praxis (working to enact social change regarding the politicized social, economic, scientific, and legal issues). These four principles epistemologically differentiate feminist research from other types of critical research because they require that social enquiries produce tangible results that help effect change in support of the advancement of women; they are also consecutively interdependent – one cannot have praxis without the previous three. For example, to politicize an issue, one has to recognize and contextually understand the social positionalities and voices of the group under study; and to enact praxis the researcher must politicize those positionalities and voices.

The notions of voice, politics, and praxis remain central premises of feminist efforts throughout the different eras, as women strive to "be heard" and, also, to have their voices reflected in equitable laws and policies. For example, in their efforts to have a legally recognized and thus political voice with which to evoke sociopolitical and personal change, first-wave feminists fought to rectify preliminary de jure inequalities, such as the right to vote and be persons under the law. Second wavers continued the political fight for legal rights for women (including affirmative action, criminalization of marital rape, and increased reproductive rights – for example, legal abortion), as well as increased de facto rights (regarding domesticity, education, and work) (Aikau, Erickson, and Pierce 2007). Particularly relevant for the later discussion of the importance of critical feminist research, second-wave feminism saw increasing numbers of women in academia (Pierce 2007); however, Dorothy Smith's (1987) work illustrates the ongoing difficulties women face even among those considered the most socially open-minded and progressive.[5] While a shift in women's representation in tenured faculty positions is slowly taking place, fewer women hold upper-level rank or full professor positions – meaning that equality in terms of voice and political representation in academia (in research and at the institutional level) will take yet another fifteen to twenty years to achieve. The Canadian Association of University Teachers (2008, 1) reports that "overall, between 1984 and 2004, the total number of full-time university teachers in Canada increased by about 9,000.

Of this number, more than 6,000, or 67 per cent, were women, bringing the percentage of women to just under one-third of all university faculty."[6]

Despite the advancements made by the politicization of second-wave feminist voices, the 1980s and 1990s saw feminism come under fire externally by anti- and postfeminists (Cudd 2002) as well as internally by black, Latina, Indigenous, lesbian, and other marginalized feminist scholars and activists (hooks 2000; Hill Collins 2000).[7] Third wavers criticized second-wave feminism for advancing a falsely homogenous depiction of women and, worse still, a universal woman's voice and consciousness that by and large echoed that of white, middle-class, educated women. Heavily influenced by the works of bell hooks, Patricia Hill Collins, Angela Y. Davis, and Kimberlé Crenshaw, third-wave feminism emphasized the need to recognize positionality, or the intersectional effects of race, class, gender, sexuality, and ability, and the realization that there is no universal woman's consciousness or experience but rather a plurality of women's experiences. Third-wave feminism attempted to account for the missteps of the second wave, which failed to consider what Hill Collins (2000) calls the matrices of oppression that contributed to the creation of a kind of hierarchy of feminist voice. This hierarchy emerged for a number of reasons, including the absence of other (more marginalized) feminist voices from academia, institutional, and state discourses, and the media; by speaking for (Alcoff 2009) women as a composite group, second wavers ensured that the voices, criticisms, and work of white academic feminists largely became *the* feminist voice. I do not mean to advance a realist approach to voice but rather a constructivist one that coincides with the important third-wave criticism that feminism must value the role of material experience in the generation of diverse voice(s).

The ongoing third wave of feminism is characterized by increased diversity and pluralism and thus much debate and tension in terms of political positioning. Considering the slow evolution of gender equality, this is not surprising. Early on, it was necessary to challenge the obvious and universal legal and political inequalities women faced (to be persons, to vote, and, later, reproductive rights and equal pay for equal work) ; of course, this was championed by women with some social or political clout – meaning that they were middle- or upper-class, white, and educated. However, once these basic rights were established and other social movements such as civil rights began to gain momentum, racially minoritized women began to speak out about the falsity of a universal woman's voice that ignored the implications of race, class, sexuality, and ability, among other potential forms of oppression.

In spite of these advancements in feminism and their solidification of the value of voice and the three P's in much feminist work, there is no "correct" way of doing feminism. I do not propose, even with these principles, that there is *a singular* point of entry or lens through which feminists enter the research domain. Feminism is not only about broader gender equality; rather, it is intersectional equality and the elimination of institutional marginalization that is of importance. This brief description of the evolution of feminist goals provides a context for understanding the feminist backlashes that have contributed to the rise of what I call "institutionalized feminism" in corrections for women in Canada. It is important to understand what Chunn, Boyd, and Lessard (2007) term *backlash narratives* not only because such narratives have influenced feminist attempts to reform and shape law and policy in Canada, but also because they provide the foundation upon which critics either call for the end of feminism or block feminist research and goals by coopting feminist language so as to suggest that women are receiving equitable treatment despite their continued marginalization.

Backlashes: The Lingering Effects of Anti- and Postfeminism

Feminism is nearing the end of its third wave and, as such, is characterized by a state of flux and unrest in the larger feminist project (Rogers and Garrett 2002; Moore 2008). This unrest is linked to feminist backlash that primarily takes shape through antifeminist discourses (Chunn, Boyd, and Lessard 2007; Moore 2008), more recent postfeminist discourses, and institutionalized feminism that fosters disconnect from the communities, groups, and causes within which feminists are striving to support and enact change. As we encroach upon the dawn of the next wave, feminist social researchers are called upon to respond to competing discourses that question feminism's value and political usefulness. Chunn, Boyd, and Lessard (2007, 2) identify three main backlash narratives: first, feminism worsened women's (and all citizen's) social positioning by "luring them out of their proper sphere" in the home; second, we are now in an era of postfeminism because women have achieved equality, thus rendering feminist warnings passé; and finally, women are achieving more than equality and have thus started to "take from men's share of the pie." These narratives have emerged across disciplines, and feminist scholars have outlined their impacts in education and academia (Cudd 2002; Moore 2007), criminology and law (Gotell 2007; Moore 2008), politics (Wiegers 2007), race and multiculturalism (hooks 2000; Hill Collins 2000), and the broader feminist and women's studies projects (Burgess-Jackson 2002; Rogers and Garrett 2002; Klein 2002).

Backlash to feminism is the base of antifeminist discourses. While Susan Faludi first documented the emergence of backlash to feminism in 1991, critics of feminism, or even the goal of equality between men and women, have always challenged the notion that women experience disadvantage due to their sex. This disadvantage is obvious given the challenges our foremothers faced in securing de jure and de facto rights throughout the first three eras of feminism; if backlash were new and unique to the postmodern era, earlier feminist efforts would have witnessed a smooth and universally agreed upon shift to protect women's legal, social, and human rights. The claims made by antifeminists that feminism advances misandry and/or reverse sexism are therefore unsurprising – they are simply a continuation of age-old criticisms of feminism rooted in a fear of disrupting patriarchal power and gender relations.[8] By and large, feminists will continue to respond to antifeminist criticisms that will likely never dissipate. According to Faludi (1991, xxii), however, the more important consideration is that

> [a] backlash against women's rights succeeds to the degree that it appears not to be political, that it appears not to be a struggle at all. It is most powerful when it goes private, when it lodges inside a woman's mind and turns her vision inward, until she imagines the pressure is all in her head, until she begins to enforce the backlash, too – on herself.

One result of turning backlash inward is the unhelpful evolution of postfeminism – or the belief that we now live in an era beyond the need for feminism (Bean 2007). The crux of postfeminist arguments actually embody the worst of second-wave liberal feminist ideals that push for sameness as equality between men and women and ignore women's positionalities, gender and sexual politics, and praxis altogether. Postfeminist discourses often espouse that "radical" feminism actually damaged women's fight for equality (Rogers and Garrett 2002); for an example of this type of work, see Neil Boyd's 2004 book *Big Sister: How Extreme Feminism Has Betrayed the Fight for Sexual Equality*. Interestingly, these arguments should signal an alarm to critical scholars as the sympathetic focus is once again brought back to the group that continues to hold the most power in most Western societies – men – and more specifically, middle-class white men.

Each year, I survey my undergraduate classes when we turn to discussions of feminism and women's rights to generate dialogue about who identifies as a feminist, who refuses to do so, and who believes that women are no longer disadvantaged based on their sex or gender. It is important to question the assumption of gender equality when, for example, women are still blamed for their sexual victimization, as illustrated by *Toronto Star* and *National Post* headlines "A New Form of Victim Blaming in Rapes" (Zerbisias 2011) and "No Jail for Rapist Because Victim 'Wanted to Party'" (McIntyre 2011). What I typically uncover among my undergraduate students is a general misunderstanding about what feminism is – including the beliefs that men and women have reached equality in Canada and that to be a feminist you must be angry, lesbian, and unfeminine or masculine (sometimes referred to as "femi-Nazis") (Klein 2002). With secured de jure rights, gender inequalities in contemporary Western societies are often much more entrenched and difficult to identify than they were in the past. Subsequently, there is a disjuncture between feminist goals and what the public, especially younger generations, understand about women's position in society. As Aikau, Erickson, and Pierce (2007, 33) write, "While some conclude that feminism is in a state of disarray, others maintain that the newest generation is complacent, lazy, or politically disengaged, and still others argue that feminism is flailing, if not dead."

In criminology, postfeminist discourses suggest that feminism damaged women's fight for equality by overemphasizing women's victimization. In her discussion of women's violence, Patricia Pearson (1997), for example, argues that the third-wave goal of identifying the victimization-criminalization continuum (Comack 2006; Moore 2008; Pollack 2006) set women up as permanent victims who are treated too leniently or, in Pearson's words, "chivalrously" by a criminal justice system that fails to recognize that women can be just as violent as men. To be clear, I am not claiming that all women who use violence do so because of their experiences of victimization; however, this should not be misinterpreted to mean that women achieved equality and that feminism is now pushing for leniency rather than equitable sentencing. The result is the simultaneous failure to consider how structural marginalization leads some people to come in conflict with the law and a "tough on crime" mindset that fails to acknowledge disadvantage as a mitigating factor in criminality.

Postfeminist discourses coupled with the policing of critical criminological scholarship (Martel 2004) and Canada's increasingly conservative political climate are contributing to the growth of the crime control industry (Christie 2000), which is being realized through a number of initiatives, including the construction of new and larger prisons, increased security to combat women's riskiness in lieu of measures to address their needs, mandatory minimum sentences, and the continued use of restraints, strip searching, and segregation, despite feminist claims that these practices do greater harm to most incarcerated women (Acoby 2011; Arbour 1996; Comack 2006; Hannah-Moffat and Moore 2005; Pollack 2006; TFFSW 1990). Moreover, the lack of correctional transparency in Canada is well documented (Arbour 1996; Culhane 1979, 1985, 1991; Martel, Hogeveen, and Woolford 2006; Moore 2008; Sapers 2008) and is partially held up by denying critical and feminist researchers access to prisons as a site of ethnographic research in favour of in-house research. Correctional research on criminalized women has been widely criticized for adopting feminist language to couch traditional correctional goals of security, surveillance, and punishment (Hannah-Moffat and Moore 2005; Martel 2004;

Martel, Hogeveen, and Woolford 2006; Moore 2008). I call this "institutional-ized feminism" and suggest that it is a form of backlash that contributes to the policing of critical scholarship by prohibiting the production of feminist criminological research.

Canadian Corrections and Institutionalized Feminism as a New Form of Backlash

Feminist sociolegal scholar Emma Cunliffe describes feminism as a personal yet sociohistorically, culturally, and politically situated worldview:

> Feminists, just like anyone else who wants to change the world, have to be prepared to take responsibility for the changes they make and they often have to put a lot of work in well after the battle has seemingly been won. This is often unfair – for my mother, as for many women, it meant doing a triple shift of paid work, housework and volunteer activ-ities. Mum was my first role model in how to get something done and then how to make it work even when you are sleep deprived. (Cunliffe, qtd. in Llewellyn et al. 2005, 71-72)

For Cunliffe and other feminists, this position requires action, albeit action that does not *have* to be "revolutionary" in the larger political sense; rather, feminist goals remain dedicated to manifesting some degree of social change (i.e., politics and praxis rooted in voice and positionality) to facilitate gender equality. Like Cunliffe, many feminist scholars enter their work with similar conceptual baggage that shapes and frames their vision of gender practices and inequality. In fact, one of my earliest memories is of a morning in kinder-garten when I refused to participate in a game of "kissing tag." Despite vocal-izing that I did not want to participate, another male youngster kissed me anyway. My reaction, given the context, was inappropriately aggressive, but it was also political – I responded by punching my male classmate. Upon being sent to the principal's office to explain and to await my mother, I remember distinctly that no one in a position of authority (my class teacher or the prin-cipal) asked me about, and I did not volunteer, what had happened to provoke this violent outburst that did not befit my regular behaviour. It was not until my mother arrived that I was asked this question. And while she indicated that violence in this circumstance was unacceptable and she encouraged me to go directly to the teacher should something like this occur in the future, she also stated that if a boy ever kissed me against my wishes and I needed to make him stop, I had her permission to punch him. This subjective experi-ence later shaped how I entered into relationships with men; as a young and then adult woman, it encouraged me to think about men's sexual wishes and my relationship to those wishes, in light of my own desires.

Critics may question my mother's advice, but it taught me that different context-dependent options were available (speaking to an authority versus resorting to violence) in terms of claiming a voice. Echoing this point, much contemporary feminist research involves politicizing the structural and institutional barriers that oppress and confine women in different ways and thus reflect different positionalities and voices. In my case, the educational authorities responded by sending me home from school, while the young boy who instigated the incident was told to listen the next time a child refused to play. And while I do not question having been disciplined (hitting my classmate was certainly unnecessary),[9] the failure to discipline the boy for kissing me against my wishes illustrates but one example of how notions of acceptable behaviour are gendered and how institutional responses can normalize male sexual advancements and work to silence the voices of women and girls. My voice and positionality as a girl who felt violated was marginalized by gendered institutional rhetoric.

Similarly, correctional discourses speak about criminalized populations thus maintaining their marginal and stigmatized status (see Hannem and Bruckert 2011). With this premise in mind, when conducting research by, for, and with (Kirby and McKenna 1989) criminalized women, critical feminist scholars frequently begin with the position that it is essential to speak with the women and to allow the voices and positionalities of women in prison to be the centre of, rather than marginal in, the methodological and theoretical design, execution, and analysis of our research and data (Martel 2004; Moore 2008). However, increasingly complex institutional barriers such as ethics boards, correctional rhetoric and policy, and a growing lack of transparency in correctional management prohibit many of us from speaking with incarcerated men and women (Chunn and Menzies 2006; Hannah-Moffat and Moore 2005; Martel 2004; Martel, Hogeveen, and Woolford 2006).

The lack of critical and ethnographic prison research and the growth of in-house corrections research, whose discourses mirror the language of but fail to embody feminist principles in action, gave rise to institutionalized feminism. While extensive work by Canadian feminist criminologists documents the correctional usurping of feminist language and the correctional transformation of women's needs into institutional risk factors (Comack 2006; Comack and Balfour 2006; Dell, Fillmore, and Kilty 2009; Hannah-Moffat 1999, 2006, 2008; Hannah-Moffat and Moore 2005; Hayman 2006; Kilty 2006; Martel 2004; Moore 2008; Shantz, Kilty, and Frigon 2009), the impact of institutionalized feminism more broadly and in the criminological enterprise specifically remains largely unexamined.

Institutionalized feminism is a nonthreatening, watered-down, middle-ground approach to seeking gender equality that may be conceptualized as the redux version of second-wave feminism, which sought sameness between the sexes and advocated for a universal woman's voice. For example, in their efforts to respond to ongoing criticism from critical and feminist criminologists, since the close of the 1990s, corrections has adopted pseudofeminist language (i.e., gender-responsive, women-centred) and has coopted feminist concepts like "empowerment" to appear as though corrections for women is feminist in nature. In this instance, institutionalization offers a subtle but transformative turn in feminist advancement; on the surface, it gives the appearance of placating feminist criticisms and warnings. It appears to take feminist concerns into consideration as policies, laws, and practices are reviewed and revised, but all too often it simply incorporates feminist discourses into the problematic existing policies, laws, and practices that are detrimental to women.

In terms of doing criminological research, institutionalized feminism surfaced on a number of key fronts, one of the most important being researchers' increasingly restricted access to enter and conduct research inside correctional facilities. The Correctional Service of Canada (CSC) developed the Women Offender Research Branch, which helps it to justify denying outside research in order to prevent women from becoming "over-researched." Subsequently, the CSC produces much of the research done in the prison context (Hannah-Moffat and Moore 2005), with little if any consideration for the obvious conflicts of interest this poses – namely, how can a government agency effectively evaluate its own practices and consider the voices of the marginalized population it imprisons, especially when those voices oppose the agency's practices, policies, and discourses?

While second-wave feminism presented a (falsely) universal woman's voice, institutionalized feminism in the correctional context – at least on the surface – claims to address some differences across groups of women. For example, the CSC holds an Aboriginal research and policy branch and conducts research on the different needs of Aboriginal women. However, feminist criminologists argue that correctional attempts to address these different needs often result in overly punitive practices such as higher rates of the use of segregation, the strict management protocol, and maximum security for Aboriginal women (Acoby 2011; Arbour 1996; Martel 2004). In this case, "difference" is racialized, "need" is transformed into risk (Hannah-Moffat 1999, 2006, 2008), and institutional practices become more punitive for Aboriginal women who are already overrepresented in the criminal justice system (Acoby 2011; Arbour 1996; Comack 2006).

Effectively incorporating the voices of prisoners in research and policy requires an active engagement of difference (Gunaratnam 2003) so as to recognize positionality. Feminists maintain that traditional epistemologies systematically exclude women as knowers or agents of knowledge (Martel 2004), which means that the questions oppressed groups (including criminalized women) want answered are "queries about how to change [their] conditions and how to win over, defeat, or neutralize forces arrayed against [their] emancipation, growth, or development" (Harding 1987, 8). Given that the criminal justice system is a key actor in the repression of prisoners' voices, correctional officials readily transform the standpoints of incarcerated women and researchers who take a feminist position into not only personal affronts to correctional research and researchers but potential threats to institutional security.

Denying critical feminist scholars access to incarcerated populations is then presented as a legitimate response and allows CSC to save face through (repressed) bureaucratic transparency. In the larger correctional project of managing risk, critical feminist scholars are frequently denied access; only CSC (or other like-minded) researchers or those conducting research perceived as noncritical of CSC appear to be permitted access to conduct research inside the prison setting.[10] For instance, a graduate student in my department, whose research did not examine CSC practices or discourse in any critical way and was supported at the institutional (prison) level, was asked by CSC national headquarters to include a disclaimer in any presentation of her work that stated, "These findings are the result of a student thesis project, primarily a learning exercise, which does not have sufficient methodological rigour to allow for confidence in its conclusions or extrapolation of its findings beyond the current sample." Perron, Holmes, and Jacob (this volume) discuss the difficulties in navigating research agendas in institutional settings because they have the ability to "hinder the research process, for example, by restricting access to certain areas or people, intimidating the researcher with legal implications, prohibiting publication of the results, or going before professional ethics committees to limit the scope of the study." As all outside (noninstitutional) researchers must apply for access to do research about or with prisoners, the unique difficulty facing feminist and other critical criminologists is not just that we do not have easy or unencumbered access, but that the institutional evaluative criteria used to determine if the research project is acceptable do not respect the rigour of qualitative research.[11]

The above disclaimer reflects what Martel (2004) describes as the bipolarization of subjective (qualitative) and objective (quantitative) research. With this proviso, CSC demonstrates its political goal of discrediting outside and namely, small-scale qualitative research through the use of positivist evaluative criteria that dismiss voice, positionality, and the value of exploratory and/or praxis oriented work. Martel (ibid., 170) suggests that "in "scientific" terms, this comment amounts to saying that nonrepresentative samples cannot possibly reveal anything worth knowing, and that the study was "scientifically invalid." In this way, correctional administrators discredit small-scale qualitative research that gleans its empirical power from showcasing positionality and voice and calling for praxis in the form of prison reform and social change. In a personal communication, the student in question described feeling discouraged by conducting the research, stating: "I was more of a public relations statistic than a researcher who could provide valued information. I felt like CSC (at the national level) was using me with very little risk to them, to say, 'See! We allow outside research! Look at this study!'"

Even more problematic, CSC continues to deny prisoners the option of speaking with critical scholars, which is a gatekeeping procedure that results in the larger setback of prisoner-voice appropriation. That the Correctional Service of Canada claims authority over both prisoners' and researchers' voices – in terms of who prisoners may speak with and when they may do so, as well as the topics we as critical researchers are able to study if we are to gain access to criminalized persons and correctional environments and staffs – is the very antithesis of what feminists and convict criminologists advocate (Alcoff 2009; Harding 1987; Martel 2004; Smith 1987, 1999; Gunaratnam 2003). The correctional claiming of others' voices occurs on a number of levels. During the application process to enter federal prisons for women to conduct my doctoral research, I was criticized for using the term *prisoner* in my research proposal. CSC officials told me that "we don't use that term anymore, it's offensive; *inmate* is CSC terminology." This is a minor example of the appropriation of voice and of the desire to launder all institutional research through a CSC-approved lens.

My epistemological position as a feminist drawing on principles laid out in convict criminology taught me that prisons make prisoners and that correctional terms like *inmate* reflect an institutional attempt to sanitize penal language in order to make correctional practices more politically correct and thus palatable for the public. Similar to their use of feminist terms such as *empowerment,* appropriating (feminist) language and terminology allows "CSC first to adopt and then to determine the language's subsequent interpretation" (Hayman 2006, 239). However, the etymology of the word *inmate* indicates that it was originally used to describe borders or house dwellers and was later adapted to describe students residing in dormitories and patients in hospitals, and finally as a euphemism for prisoners. The core of the term suggests the syllable *in* from the word *inside* and *mate* from the word *companion;* but prisoners are not inside with companions – they are incarcerated against their will.

The official CSC response to my 2005 application for access to federal prisons for women was no – not because the topic of my study was over-researched, as CSC began its own national examination of self-injurious behaviour three years later (see Gordon 2010; Power and Ussher 2010). Rather, I was told that because I was not a trained (or as a student, in training to be a) psychologist or psychiatrist, I was not qualified to ask questions about or to conduct research on self-injurious behaviour. This decision was made despite the fact that I received institutional approval from my university's research ethics board and that my project was approved by my doctoral committee[12] – which was made up of three well-known scholars with a combined total of over seventy-five years of research experience on sensitive topics with marginalized, criminalized, and otherwise institutionalized populations. Instead, correctional officials told me that should I conduct research on how women spend their leisure time, a topic about which they felt they were lacking information, I would be granted access to federal prisons.[13] This exemplifies institutional control over who is permitted to do specific types of research as well as bureaucratic diversion tactics at play. By trying to divert my attention to a nonthreatening alternative topic, CSC exhibited an attempt to control what I, as an outside feminist researcher, would be able to write about. Ultimately, CSC did not want a critical feminist researcher entering federal prisons for women to conduct an exposé on penal practices and self-injurious behaviour and hoped I would be sidetracked by the rare offer of access in return for a change in topic.

This lack of transparency and correctional cover-up is not simply the stuff of conspiracy theories. To offer a practical example, in 2007, eighteen-year-old Ashley Smith was transferred to Grand Valley Institution for Women from the New Brunswick juvenile offender system.[14] Smith was a chronic self-injurer, resistant to correctional demands, and for all intents and purposes a difficult prisoner for frontline staff to contend with (Sapers 2008). Rather than privileging Smith's voice (and needs) and actively engaging in difference so as to acknowledge the effects of her positionality, correctional officials from high-ranking bureaucrats to prison administrative and frontline staff spoke *to* and *about* Smith (Alcoff 2009). They responded to her difficult behaviour by leaving her in segregation for her entire eleven-month period of incarceration in federal prison, when she took her own life in plain sight of correctional officials who were instructed not to intervene until she was unconscious (Sapers 2008). Despite Smith's parents' and the media's desire to air the video footage of Ashley Smith being physically restrained, left in her own urine, and then of her eventual death, the CSC fought for months to prohibit the public from seeing what transpired – namely, the continued stripping and segregation of women who self-injure. This was the same legal tactic the CSC used in 1994 following the illegal strip-search, by men, of mostly Aboriginal women prisoners in the now closed Kingston Prison for Women (Arbour 1996).

Institutionalized feminism is partially the result of individuals with reform rather than feminist or resistant and critical agendas working within the bureaucracy of government and other powerful agencies. It meshes well with what Hannah-Moffat and Moore (2005) call the "liberal veil" that shadows the punitive nature of Canadian punishment in neoliberal times by responsibilizing individual offenders to participate in their own change processes. The subsequent outcome is reformed or sanitized penal language that pays homage to feminist criticism without actually situating knowledge within the discourses and narratives of the marginalized population under study, which would instead call us to politicize their positionalities, and without enacting praxis called for by feminist research. Consequently, correctional discourses couch this noncritical and nonfeminist work in language such as "woman-centred," "gender-responsive," "gender-conscious," "needs-based," and "empowerment" (Hannah-Moffat 2006, 2008; Hayman 2006). At first glance, these terms appear to reflect feminist goals and give the public the impression that we have and are continuing to strive for women's equality and rights. With this in mind, it is no surprise that my undergraduate students in criminology believe we have achieved equality and that feminism is no longer needed. The cycle then continues as noncritical students enter institutional jobs to secure normative things like career success, financial security and/or status, and power or capital in their field, while failing to consider the larger picture of state repression and social control.

Conclusion: In Response to Backlashes and the Dawn of the Fourth Wave

Feminist scholars start from what is difficult or problematic in the lives, material realities, and experiences of women in order to create a research design by, for, and with women (Kirby and McKenna 1989). As Burgess-Jackson (2002, 32) suggests, in order for the movement to evolve, "[n]o self-respecting feminist scholar, whether liberal, radical, or otherwise, wishes to avoid criticism. It is the lifeblood of academia. But scholarly criticism goes hand in hand with – or should go hand in hand with – constructive work."

Our work is thus situated in and by women's voices and positionalities. At the same time, the growth of institutionalized feminism and pervasive postfeminist discourses caused many feminist scholars to become increasingly detached from their former linkages with activism and organization outside the academy. Argues Smith (1999, 21), "This is partly a result, no doubt of the changing organization of the women's movement itself, of the growth and advances that have meant more specialization and less place for the multi-connected activism of the earlier movement." Being detached from the cause and the women at the centre of the research risks rendering women's voices mute; it also works to disrupt efforts to use research as a way to politicize a particular issue or group. Correctional research on criminalized women is described as "women-centred" rather than as feminist, subsequently making it apolitical and thus lacking the praxis that ensures that change happens for the group – the long-term goal and one of the key principles of feminism.

This sociopolitical disconnect from the individuals and populations we study has encouraged many critical and feminist scholars (see Bruckert; Munn; Bellot, Sylvestre, and St-Jacques; and Dell, Fillmore, and Kilty, this volume) to call for us to remember our roots, our communities, the issues that drive us, and the need to lend our support to and learn from those working on the front lines for women's causes. Participatory action research (PAR) presents a way to re-involve communities, groups, and frontline workers in feminist research, to promote praxis through grounded theoretical and methodological research that is done by, for, and with women and other marginalized groups. In a way, PAR is the reincarnation of feminist methodological goals and values, and, not surprisingly, it is currently experiencing the same types of critiques regarding its validity and rigour that feminist research has faced historically (see Fine 1994; Harding 1987). However, while PAR methods may offer feminist researchers a way to remain grounded in women's positionalities, without access to prisoners, feminist criminologists remain hard-pressed to carry out such a research initiative.

Finally, it is important to return to the question I posed at the start of this chapter. Do we, critical and feminist qualitative researchers, *want* to feel like intellectual martyrs, or are we actually marginalized in the research process, by ethics, and in terms of access, credibility, and recognition? I wish I could say that academics are exaggerating the degree to which institutionalized feminism, bureaucracy, and the continued lack of government transparency has an impact on their ability to conduct critical research inside correctional institutions in Canada. However, the examples provided in this text paint a picture of a system that is actively working to ensure that the goings-on inside Canadian prisons are not made public. When we consider CSC's historical response to criticism of corrections for women in particular, this is predictable. For example, despite numerous inquiries and royal commissions calling for the closure of the first prison for women, including the 1938 Archambault Report published only four years after the Kingston Prison for Women opened in 1934, the prison was not closed until 2000.

Instead, the Correctional Service of Canada's adoption and reinterpretation of feminist and critical language has become an effective political strategy to waylay criticism. In response, I urge my fellow critical and feminist criminological scholars to band together in documenting their interactions with federal and provincial correctional services. As feminists have noted for decades, voices are powerful – so powerful that academics are denied access to speak with criminalized people or to observe and thus witness correctional activities in daily practice. We must remember that correctional facilities are public institutions and, as members of the public, we have every right to enter them. And finally, we must remember that prisoners (not inmates) are citizens, who, while legally deprived of their liberty, have every right to speak out publicly about their experiences of criminalization and incarceration – including the right to choose whether they speak with critical and feminist scholars.

Notes

1 Culhane wrote three books on the subject: *Barred from Prison* (1979), *Still Barred from Prison* (1985), and *No Longer Barred from Prison* (1991). The books commence by documenting her inside experience of one of the worst prison riots and hostage takings in Canadian prison history, her role in securing a memorandum of understanding between the Correctional Service of Canada and the prisoners, and her subsequent ban from and public fight to be able to re-enter federal prisons in Canada.

2 *Institutionalized feminism* refers to the cooptation of feminist language by oppressive institutions and discourses (like corrections) to suggest that the institution is responsive to women's differences; it is a strategy to appear as though there is no need for (and thus to block or silence) outside feminist research.

3 Kirby and McKenna (1989, 32) define *conceptual baggage* as "a record of your thoughts and ideas about the research question at the beginning and throughout the research process ... By making your thoughts and experience explicit, another layer of data is revealed for investigation. The researcher becomes another subject in the research process and is left vulnerable in a way that changes the traditional power dynamics/hierarchy that has existed between researcher and those who are researched."

4 Voice in qualitative research reflects the need to recognize that researchers *interpret* both authors' texts and participant narratives as well as how reality is epistemologically and ontologically constructed (Fabian 2008).

5 Smith notes that when she began teaching she was the only woman in her department – not atypical given that only 15 percent of university faculty at the time were women (1987, 27-28).

6 This division is further stratified by discipline (with more women in the social sciences than science or engineering) and by race (with the vast majority of university professors being white). For example, while my own department has five racially minoritized scholars, the remaining twenty-eight full-time faculty members (ranging from assistant to full professor) are white anglophones and francophones.

7 Antifeminists are those who either do not believe in equal rights between men and women or those who believe that feminism advances unequal power by awarding women unfair advantages. Postfeminists are those who believe that we have moved beyond the need for feminism because we have secured equality; they purport that to continue with feminist efforts results in unfair disadvantages for men.

8 In criminology, antifeminist discourses often advance positivist explanations of women's criminality that are rooted in biological reductionism. Lombroso and Ferrero's (1895) references to atavism and criminals as evolutionary throwbacks are coupled with gendered discourses of acceptable behaviour for women that systematically construct criminalized women as "non-women" whose criminal actions are more terrible than men's. Theorizing in this vein continues in contemporary criminological discourses as we see legal defences built around "premenstrual syndrome" and blaming women's criminality on their liberation via the women's movement, empowerment, or desire to "be like men" (Comack 2006; Moore 2008).

9 I do not presume to suggest that a boy who responded similarly to an unwanted sexual advance at the hands of a female classmate would go undisciplined.

10 For example, in this volume Frigon and Shantz describe their work on dance, which they conducted inside Quebec provincial and federal prisons for women. Although they firmly situate themselves as critical feminists, they were able to present their research as a benign exercise and support for the women. By avoiding direct examination of correctional practices and policies, their work was seen as nonthreatening to institutional strategies of governance.

11 For a critical discussion of rigour in terms of qualitative research and methods, see van den Hoonaard, this volume; he asserts that quantitative or positivist interpretations of rigour are inappropriate for assessing the value of qualitative research – whose empirical power comes from the detailed and immersed description of smaller samples or cases rather than statistically significant sample sizes, replication, and other standard scientific modes of evaluating research rigour.

12 For a related discussion of institutional restrictions running contrary to ethics approval, see Ogden, this volume, and Lowman and Palys, this volume. While Ogden received ethics approval for his research on witnessing assisted suicide, the university later failed to support his work and attempted to end the project.

13 For a related discussion of government constraints on analysts conducting research for the state, see Fabian, this volume.

14 Ashley Smith was sentenced to a period of incarceration in a juvenile facility in New Brunswick for throwing crab apples at a postman. Her "unruly" behaviour (Dell, Filmore, and Kilty 2009) resulted in the provincial system seeking out federal aid by supporting her transfer to the federal system for adult women.

References

Acoby, R. (2011). On Segregation. *Journal of Prisoners on Prisons 20*(1), 89-93.

Aikau, H.K., Erickson, K.A., and Pierce, J.L. (2007). Introduction: Feminist Waves, Feminist Generations. In H.K. Aikau, K.A. Erickson, and J.L. Pierce (Eds.), *Feminist Waves, Feminist Generations: Life Stories from the Academy* (1-45). Minneapolis: University of Minnesota Press.

Alcoff, L.M. (2009). The Problem of Speaking for Others. In A.Y. Jackson and L.A. Mazzei (Eds.), *Voice in Qualitative Inquiry: Challenging Conventional, Interpretive, and Critical Conceptions in Qualitative Research* (117-38). New York: Routledge.

Arbour, Mme Justice L. (1996). *Commission of Inquiry into Certain Events at the Kingston Prison for Women*. Ottawa: Ottawa Public Works.

Bean, K. (2007). *Post-Backlash Feminism: Women and the Media since Reagan-Bush*. Jefferson, NC: McFarland and Company.

142   Jennifer M. Kilty

Boyd, N. (2004). *Big Sister: How Extreme Feminism Has Betrayed the Fight for Sexual Equality.* Vancouver: Greystone Books.
Burgess-Jackson, K. (2002). The Backlash against Feminist Philosophy. In A.M. Superson and A.E. Cudd (Eds.), *Theorizing Backlash: Philosophical Reflections on the Resistance to Feminism* (19-47). Lanham, MD: Rowman and Littlefield Publishers.
Canadian Association of University Teachers. (2008). The Tenure Gap: Women's University Appointments 1985-2005. *CAUT Equity Review 4* (September), 1-4.
Christie, N. (2000). *Crime Control as Industry.* New York: Routledge.
Chunn, D., Boyd, S.B., and Lessard, H. (2007). *Reaction and Resistance: Feminism Law and Social Change.* Vancouver: UBC Press.
Chunn, D., and Menzies, R. (2006). "So What Does All This Have To Do with Criminology?" Surviving the Restructuring of the Discipline in the Twenty-First Century. *Canadian Journal of Criminology and Criminal Justice 48*(5), 663-80.
Comack, E. (2006). The Feminist Engagement with Criminology. In E. Comack and G. Balfour (Eds.), *Criminalizing Women* (22-57). Blackpoint, NS: Fernwood Publishing.
Comack, E., and Balfour, G. (2006). *The Power to Criminalize.* Halifax, NS: Fernwood Publishing.
Cudd, A.E. (2002). Analyzing Backlash to Progressive Social Movements. In A.M. Superson and A.E. Cudd (Eds.), *Theorizing Backlash: Philosophical Reflections on the Resistance to Feminism* (3-16). Lanham, MD: Rowman and Littlefield Publishers.
Culhane, C. (1979). *Barred from Prison.* Vancouver: Pulp Press.
–. (1985). *Still Barred from Prison.* Montreal: Black Rose Books.
–. (1991). *No Longer Barred from Prison.* Montreal: Black Rose Books.
Dell, C., Fillmore, C., and Kilty, J.M. (2009). Looking Back 10 Years after the Arbour Inquiry: Ideology, Practice and the Misbehaved Federal Female Prisoner. *Prison Journal 89*(3), 286-308.
Fabian, S.C. (2008). Voice. In L.M. Given (Ed.), *The Sage Encyclopedia of Qualitative Research Methods* (944-45). Thousand Oaks, CA: Sage Publications.
Faludi, S. (1991). *Backlash.* New York: Anchor Books.
Fine, M. (1994). Working the Hyphens: Reinventing Self and Other in Qualitative Research. In N.K. Denzin and Y.S. Lincoln (Eds.), *Handbook of Qualitative Research* (1st ed.) (70-82). Thousand Oaks, CA: Sage Publications.
Gordon, A. (2010). *Self-Injury Incidents in CSC Institutions over a Thirty-Month Period.* Ottawa: Correctional Service of Canada.
Gotell, L. (2007). The Discursive Disappearance of Sexualized Violence: Feminist Law Reform, Judicial Resistance, and Neo-liberal Sexual Citizenship. In D. Chunn, S.B. Boyd, and H. Lessard (Eds.), *Reaction and Resistance: Feminism Law and Social Change* (127-63). Vancouver: UBC Press.
Gunaratnam, Y. (2003). *Researching "Race" and Ethnicity: Methods, Knowledge, and Power.* London: Sage.
Hannah-Moffat, K. (1999). Moral Agent or Actuarial Subject: Risk and Canadian Women's Imprisonment. *Theoretical Criminology 3*(1), 71-94.
–. (2006). Pandora's Box: Risk/Need and Gender-Responsive Corrections. *Criminology and Public Policy 5*(1), 183-92.
–. (2008). Re-imagining Gendered Penalties: The Myth of Gender Responsivity. In P. Carlen (Ed.), *Imaginary Penalties* (193-217). Collumpton, UK: Willan.
Hannah-Moffat, K., and Moore, D. (2005). The Liberal Veil. In J. Pratt, M. Brown, S. Hallsworth, and W. Morrison (Eds.), *The New Punitiveness* (88-100). Collumpton, UK: Willan Publishing.
Hannem, S., and Bruckert, C. (2011). *Stigma Revisited: Implications of the Mark.* Ottawa: University of Ottawa Press.
Harding, S. (1987). *The Science Question in Feminism.* Ithaca, NY: Cornell University Press.
Hayman, S. (2006). *Imprisoning Our Sisters.* Montreal and Kingston: McGill-Queen's University Press.

Hill Collins, P.H. (2000). *Black Feminist Thought*. New York: Routledge.

hooks, b. (2000). *Feminist Theory: From Margin to Centre*. Cambridge, MA: South End Press.

Kilty, J. (2006). Under the Barred Umbrella: Is There Room for a Women-Centred Self-Injury Policy in Canadian Corrections? *Criminology and Public Policy* 5(1), 161-82.

Kirby, S., and McKenna, K. (1989). *Experience Research Social Change: Methods from the Margins*. Toronto: Garamond Press.

Klein, E.R. (2002). *Undressing Feminism: A Philosophical Exposé*. St. Paul, MN: Paragon House.

Llewellyn, K., Cunliffe, E., Kelly, F., Riley, T., and Wall, S. (2005). The F Word(s): A Five-Part Conversation by Gen-X Feminists. *Atlantis: A Women's Studies Journal* 29(3), 61-75.

Lombroso, C., and Ferrero, G. (1895). *The Female Offender*. New York: Appleton and Co.

Martel, J. (2004). Policing Criminological Knowledge: The Hazards of Qualitative Research on Women in Prison. *Theoretical Criminology* 8(2), 157-89.

Martel, J., Hogeveen, B., and Woolford, A. (2006). The State of Critical Scholarship in Criminology and Socio-Legal Studies in Canada. *Canadian Journal of Criminology and Criminal Justice* 48(5), 633-46.

McIntyre, M. (2011). No Jail for Rapist Because Victim "Wanted to Party." *National Post*, 24 February.

Moore, D. (2008). Feminist Criminology: Gain, Losses and Backlash. *Sociology Compass* 2(1), 48-61.

Moore, W.L. (2007). "I Thought She Was One of Us!" A Narrative Examination of Power and Exclusion in the Academy. In H.K. Aikau, K.A. Erickson, and J.L. Pierce (Eds.), *Feminist Waves, Feminist Generations: Life Stories from the Academy* (250-69). Minneapolis: University of Minnesota Press.

Pearson, P. (1997). *When She Was Bad: Violent Women and the Myth of Innocence*. Toronto: Penguin.

Pierce, J.L. (2007). Traveling from Feminism to Mainstream Sociology and Back: One Woman's Tale of Tenure and the Politics of Backlash. In H.K. Aikau, K.A. Erickson, and J.L. Pierce (Eds.), *Feminist Waves, Feminist Generations: Life Stories from the Academy* (109-39). Minneapolis: University of Minnesota Press.

Pollack, S. (2006). Therapeutic Programming as a Regulatory Practice in Women's Prisons. In E. Comack and G. Balfour (Eds.), *Criminalizing Women* (236-49). Blackpoint, NS: Fernwood Publishing.

Power, J., and Ussher, A. (2010). *A Qualitative Study of Self-Injurious Behaviour in Women Offenders*. Ottawa: Correctional Service of Canada.

Rogers, M.F., and Garrett, C.D. (2002). *Who's Afraid of Women's Studies? Feminisms in Everyday Life*. Walnut Creek, CA: AltaMira Press.

Sapers, H. (2008). *A Preventable Death*. Ottawa: Office of the Correctional Investigator.

Shantz, L., Kilty, J.M., and Frigon, S. (2009). Echoes of Imprisonment: Women's Experiences of Successful (Re)integration. *Canadian Journal of Law and Society* 24(1), 85-106.

Smith, D. (1987). *The Everyday World as Problematic*. Boston: Northeastern University Press.

–. (1999). *Writing the Social*. Toronto: University of Toronto Press.

TFFSW (Task Force on Federally Sentenced Women). (1990). *Creating Choices*. Ottawa: Correctional Service of Canada.

Wiegers, W. (2007). Child-Centred Advocacy and the Invisibility of Women in Poverty Discourse and Social Policy. In D. Chunn, S.B. Boyd, and H. Lessard (Eds.), *Reaction and Resistance: Feminism Law and Social Change* (229-61). Vancouver: UBC Press.

Zerbisias, A. (2011). A New Form of Victim Blaming for Rapists. *Toronto Star*, 4 March.

part 2   Ethical Quagmires:
            Regulating Qualitative Research

The Politics of Threats in Correctional and Forensic Settings: The Specificities of Nursing Research

Amélie Perron, Dave Holmes, and Jean Daniel Jacob

QUALITATIVE INQUIRY CONSTITUTES an attractive approach to generate firsthand accounts of individuals or groups who experience various forms of oppression, discrimination, and vulnerability. Although qualitative research is a valuable, legitimate, and scientific method of inquiry for investigating human processes and phenomena, some critics have noted a tendency among qualitative researchers to romanticize their work, especially when investigating politically, ethically, and emotionally charged topics. Research accounts may present sentimental descriptions of participants (Harrison, MacGibbon, and Morton 2001) or portray the researcher as "the hero on a quest of mythic proportions" who "battles the usual adversaries" (Thorne and Darbyshire 2005, 1110). Several authors have cautioned against the tendency to romanticize research (see, for example, Harrison, MacGibbon, and Morton 2001; Roulston 2001; Thorne and Darbyshire 2005; Walker 1985), which may come about in researchers' intentions to "give voice to the voiceless" or "tell the stories" of the "oppressed" or "forgotten." Yet conducting qualitative inquiry can be distinctly unromantic. For instance, there is a risk of ontologizing certain groups and situating them in rigid categories that can be equally damaging, disempowering, and difficult to shake (e.g., vulnerable, disabled, victim, marginalized, socially excluded, disenfranchised, minority, etc.). Furthermore, research that involves marginalized groups and/or settings that are heavily regulated by rules, norms, and procedures (and in which issues of marginalization and oppression abound) add another layer of complexity with which the researcher must grapple. As nurse researchers who work in the field of corrections and forensic psychiatry, we continuously negotiate such politics and make numerous decisions that are less than heroic. In this chapter, we characterize our research as sensitive research and explore the ethical, political, professional, and methodological issues that mark nursing research activities in prison and forensic settings. We use interview excerpts from five different studies we conducted between 2004 and 2010 in various psychiatric secure settings. We discuss the way traditional ethical frameworks, such as those proposed by professional codes of ethics, are insufficient to address the politics of sensitive health research. We present some of the strategies we have come to develop to safeguard the integrity of the research process and, at times, the nursing profession itself. While our discussion focuses on nursing, some of the lessons learned are also applicable to other health-related professions such as medicine, psychology, and social work.

Correctional and Forensic Nursing as an Object of Inquiry

We have accumulated over twenty years of qualitative research experience in correctional and forensic psychiatry settings in federal and provincial/state institutions in Australia, Canada, and France. Our work typically focuses on nursing practice in these highly regulated environments, where nurses' behaviours, as prescribed by correctional settings, may not fit with nursing principles, values, and ethics (Jacob and Holmes, 2011a, 2011b; Holmes 2002, 2005; Holmes and Murray 2011; Holmes, Perron, and Michaud 2007; Holmes et al. 2005; Perron 2011; Perron and Holmes 2011; Perron, Holmes, and Hamonet 2004; Perron and Rudge 2012). Grounded theory, ethnography, and critical discourse analysis constitute our preferred research methods. Studying nursing practice in normative and tightly regulated environments is not limited to the examination of care techniques; it moves beyond them and touches on broader issues of subjectivity and identity, power, resistance, risk, oppression, professionalism, and ethics (as both professional and political practice).

The distinctive feature of nursing practice in forensic and secure milieus stems from the fact that nurses must formally endorse two distinct mandates: to care for inmates and to support or partake in activities aimed at their custody, surveillance, and control. We have discussed the extent to which the ideological bases of these two mandates are antithetical (see Holmes 2005; Jacob 2012; Perron and Holmes 2011; Perron and Rudge 2012; Perron, Holmes, and Hamonet 2004). Current literature largely supports this idea (Dunbar 2003; Fisher 1995; Martin 2003; Mason and Mercer 1998; Mason, Richman, and Mercer 2002; Martin and Street 2003), although many authors make great efforts to reconcile these paradoxical mandates. Nursing practice in forensic and/or secure settings is rife with difficulties mainly because it is based on principles and values (such as critical thinking, individualized care, collaboration, confidentiality, and patient rights and advocacy) that may clash with the broader institutional demand for conformity, obedience, standard-ization, visibility, suspicion, and social distance toward the care recipient (Holmes and Murray 2011). Nurses are still expected to provide care (in every sense of the word), but institutional rules and regulations often impede ethical care provision as it is dictated by current standards of practice (Burrow 1991a, 1991b, 1992, 1993a, 1993b, 1998; Martin and Street 2003; Mason and Mercer 1998).

Because offenders constitute a highly vulnerable population, nurses are ex-pected to be careful to protect their rights, for instance, through the negotia-tion of treatment options (especially psychiatric treatment) and the upholding of ethical interventions. Nurses also have the professional obligation to report instances of abuse or neglect toward patients, especially if it is carried out by nurses (see, for instance, American Nurses Association 2010; Australian Nurs-ing Federation 2006; Canadian Nurses Association 2008; College of Nurses of Ontario 2011; International Council of Nurses 2006; Turner et al. 2006). In some Canadian provinces, this mandatory reporting is formalized through legislation. However, correctional and forensic psychiatric nurses interviewed in various studies have discussed the way this professional obligation is in direct opposition to the "code of silence" that is prevalent in their workplace (Holmes 2005; Perron and Holmes 2011; Perron, Holmes, and Hamonet 2004). This code of silence suppresses such reporting or, if reporting is carried out, it gives rise to "disciplinary" measures, such as the ostracization of the nurse responsible for the report and covert threats about his or her safety. The fol-lowing quotation from one of our research participants (Perron, Holmes, and Hamonet 2004, 127) provides a stark example of this phenomenon:

Participant: [Inmates] will say they injured themselves falling out of bed or playing soccer. But we know they were beaten up by other inmates who heard what they've done on TV. It's like a code of honour in prison, a punishment within a punishment. But nobody talks about it, even though everyone knows it exists. Nurses don't dare to report those incidents because everyone knows some officers participate. If a formal complaint was filed, there would be repercussions for sure.
Researcher: What kind of repercussions?
Participant: Well, the word would go around and the next time that nurse would need their assistance, they wouldn't go. They would just leave her with it.
Researcher: Even if her life was threatened?
Participant: Oh, they would go but after a little while, after she'd been scared good, you know ... so she would learn.

This account is consistent with Storch and Peternelj-Taylor's (2009, 113) observation that, in prison, issues around whistle-blowing "are magnified because staff rely on each other for personal safety: a powerful deterrent to speaking up, even when it is the right thing to do." Similar results from another one of our studies (Jacob 2010) show that the nursing group operates as a disciplinary (and disciplined) body in which the dominant view may be imposed over alternative ways of thinking and doing. Opposition to hegemonic viewpoints may cause some nurses to become excluded from the dominant group and, consequently, to lose the safety of being part of such a group. One female nurse explains this process:

> The people that feel that way are very powerful or kind of intimidating people, so everybody else just sits quiet. Because you do not want to be seen as an opposer to the thing. I have had male nurses saying to me, "Well you know, you could be in a lot of trouble one night; you could be in a lot of trouble and we'd be awfully slow to get there." (Jacob 2010, 111)

The literature on forensic nursing emphasizes correctional and forensic nurses' obligation to practice according to their code of ethics because correctional settings often have features that make ethical professional practice difficult – or, in some cases, impossible to achieve (Storch and Peternelj-Taylor 2009; Bonner and Vandecreek 2006). Nurses speak about how they must eliminate aspects of their practice that do not fit with the prevailing custodial order; they add that they face a number of "reminders" in their daily work regarding this obligation. For instance, nurse participants reported that patient confidentiality is very difficult to uphold because officers often ask nurses about patients' health and personal information (e.g., whether they have a mental illness, have addictions problems, or are HIV-positive), and some have nearly breached patient confidentiality by attempting to peer into medical records. Refusing to provide such information can lead to reprimands or jokes that nurses are "siding with the crims" instead of protecting "their own." Nurse participants also described the way correctional officers would harshly correct nurses who called inmates "patients" or who addressed them as "Sir" (Holmes et al. 2005; Perron and Holmes 2011; Perron and Rudge 2012). Such reprimand often occurred in front of patients, nurses, and/or correctional staff, which sends a clear and public message about nurses' proper conduct vis-à-vis the inmate population. Nurses were also identified as posing a threat to the correctional institution because of their perceived overly trusting and empathetic attitude toward offenders. This, correctional officers argued, made them easy to manipulate by inmates who were trying to circumvent security regulations and gain particular privileges (Holmes et al. 2005; Perron and Holmes 2011; Perron, Holmes, and Hamonet 2004). The fact that most correctional and forensic settings harbour male offenders and employ male officers, coupled with the fact that nursing remains a predominantly female profession, constitutes a determining feature of this blanket attitude toward nurses; it also adds a gendered layer to the understanding of nurses' professional practice in such hypermasculine settings (Jacob 2012; Holmes 2005).

The disciplining of nurses who exhibit what are deemed to be "caring," "maternal," and "soft" behaviours and attitudes is carried out in both overt and covert ways. Admonishing nurses who display courteous behaviours toward inmates, making nurses wait for no particular reason for an officer to open a gate, or mocking a nurse's concern for a patient's state of health are all examples of behaviours that have been reported by nurses participants in our studies. Some nurses reported having their personal property vandalized (e.g., their car) after a confrontation with a correctional officer. One instance of physical assault was reported in one study, where a nurse defending her clinical interventions was brutally pushed against a wall by a correctional officer who forbade her to document her assessment and interventions in a patient file. Such behaviours are meant to convey a form of professional hierarchy within the institution, and nurses are clearly and repeatedly made aware that nursing and health concerns are superseded by correctional imperatives of security, conformity, and obedience. Recognizing that they are subjected to the same expectations of appropriate and compliant behaviour as are inmates, nurse participants discussed the ways in which they must submit themselves to these institutional demands. Much like inmates, nurses are seen as posing· a risk to the institution, first because their professional standards and values are antithetical to prison culture and therefore challenge this culture on a day-to-day basis and, second, because nurses are deemed to be a liability in face of offenders who may display manipulative or exploitative behaviours. This assumption is especially true with regard to female nurses working with male populations: due to their "naturally" trusting and caring inclination, they are assumed to lack the objectivity, suspicion, and distance that are called for in prison settings. These two levels of risk must therefore be curtailed namely through the modification of nurses' professional behaviours (Perron and Holmes 2011; Perron and Rudge 2012).

Our work with nurses in secure settings has shown that nurses develop various ways of adapting their practice to institutional demands. They may reduce interactions with patients; they may call them by their last name, as many correctional officers do; they may partake in officers' jokes about patients and/or nurses; and they may adopt a more custodial approach to patient care (such as resorting to the seclusion room or medication more often, sometimes at officers' demand). All three authors have also observed that nurses may nurture their relationships with officers and administrators through acts of camaraderie or flirting. They may also remain silent about witnessing illicit practices carried out by staff. These behaviours are in direct opposition to standards of nursing practice and could lead to disciplinary action by nurses' professional bodies if they were brought to their attention. Because these practices are questionable and problematic in light of nurses' professional obligation to uphold standards of care, examining them in the context of research can lead to significant challenges for the investigator. Recognizing the complex context of health care provision leads us to consider nursing research in correctional and forensic settings as highly sensitive, if not downright contentious.

A Word on Sensitive Nursing Research in Secure Settings

Correctional and forensic institutions, in which most of our research is conducted, fit the description of highly controlled and normative systems. Researchers must learn quickly to navigate these systems in a way that will safeguard the integrity of the research process and the reliability of the data and protect the participants themselves. It may prove difficult to maintain anonymity and confidentiality in a setting where these two principles are perceived as potentially risky and where opposing principles – namely, detection, identification, and the amplification of inmates' and staff's visibility – constitute the modus operandi. In prison and secure environments, security imperatives dictate the necessity to monitor people's movements within the institution (e.g., card swipes, log sheets, escorts, cameras, and the notification of peers of one's absence). Unless interviews are conducted outside the institution, it is impossible for research participants to go unnoticed because they will need to inform others of their participation and/or they will be seen in the company of the researcher at some point.

There are clear advantages to examining the way correctional and other secure institutions come to function, and much can be learned about the reciprocity between, and the blurring of, individual and institutional social processes in closed environments. Our research involves the sharing of personal information by participants; it also carries deep political ramifications that add an extra layer of caution and constraint over the research process. The articulation of these various features gives rise to sensitive research as described by Lee and Renzetti (1990) and thus create methodological, legal, and ethical issues for the researcher.

Several authors have attempted to define what constitutes sensitive research. For instance, Sieber and Stanley (1988, 49) suggest that sensitive research is research in which "there are potential consequences or implications, either directly for the participants in the research or for the class of individuals represented by the research [and that] can have broad social implications." This definition is general enough that it can include just about any form of investigation with social repercussions. It also points toward the investigator's social responsibility in carrying out this type of research (Sieber 1993). However, Lee (1993) argues that we have no insight into the types of consequences or implications referred to by Sieber and Stanley, and this renders their definition too broad. For example, any research with social effects, such as applied research, could fit this definition. Lee further suggests that such definition also overlooks potential methodological hurdles, though he does not explain what such hurdles might be.

As an alternative, Lee and Renzetti (1990, 512) propose the following definition: "A sensitive topic is one that potentially poses for those involved a substantial threat, the emergence of which renders problematic for the researcher and/or the researched the collection, holding, and/or dissemination of research data." What makes this definition attractive is the fact that the sensitive nature of research is not so much "embedded" in the research problem itself as it is rooted instead in the articulation of particular contingencies linked to its sociopolitical context. These authors identify four areas in which research can be perceived as threatening:

(a) where research intrudes in the private sphere or delves into some deeply personal experience; (b) where the study is concerned with deviance and social control; (c) where it impinges on the vested interests of powerful persons or the exercise of coercion and domination; (d) where it deals with things sacred to those being studied which they do not wish profaned. (Ibid.)

Lee (1993) identifies three types of threats that both arise from and produce "sensitive" research; these threats are directly linked to the four areas described above:

- *Intrusive threat:* This threat stems from research that penetrates participants' private sphere and uncovers information that is deemed too personal, emotionally charged, and stressful. This information would likely have not been shared in any other context, and it may bring both relief and intense anxiety to the participant.
- *Threat of sanction:* A threat of sanctions occurs when participants fear the researcher because the information being gathered could be used against them. Such information is often about behaviours that do not comply

with a given set of rules, either formal or informal. Sanction may also refer to derogation or exploitation, especially if the group being studied is disadvantaged socially and/or economically (Lee 1993).

- *Political threat:* This type of threat affects the interests of particular actors involved directly or indirectly in the research process. Mason (1997, 85) further emphasizes this point, arguing that a political threat is felt when "the research findings are viewed as dangerous as they may destabilize the existing situation and challenge stakeholders' vested interests." A political threat is proportional to the degree to which findings are to be disseminated.

Interestingly, these types of threats are often discussed as being experienced at the individual level, such as when a participant is uncomfortable with the disclosure of certain information. However, we argue that these threats may also be "felt" at the level of institutions, such as correctional and forensic settings, where there can be clear disadvantages of having internal rules and processes scrutinized by "outsiders." A researcher could therefore be seen as posing a significant risk to host institutions that are regulated by potentially controversial processes because he or she represents "a relatively uncontrollable element in an otherwise highly controlled system" (Spencer 1973, qtd. in Lee 1993, 9). The correctional institution itself may therefore hinder the research process, for example, by restricting access to certain areas or people, intimidating the researcher with legal implications, prohibiting publication of the results, or going before professional ethics committees to limit the scope of the study (Lee 1993, 1995; Mason 1997; Punch 1998). Kilty's chapter in this book clearly exposes the way institutions restrict access to critical scholars because their research may question, challenge, or disrupt institutional processes, policies, and practices.

We strongly believe that nursing and health-related research in prison and secure settings carries particular political undertones that situate it within the realm of sensitive research. Interviewing nurses and health professionals about their professional practice involves an examination of highly subjective (and possibly private) features such as emotions, intuition, meanings, values, and judgment. Although such research is concerned with the articulation of professional practice within a particular setting (such as a prison or secure institution), we argue it is hardly possible to distinguish between the personal and the professional domains that make up one's practice. Nurses may thus be compelled to disclose highly personal information in their discussion of professional practice.

We must also take into account the fact that research in prison and secure settings is, in itself, a delicate endeavour, one that is consistent with Lee and

Renzetti's second domain of sensitive research because it is directly concerned with issues of deviance and social control. What is of interest for our particular research program is the way nurses' and health professionals' specialized knowledge, skills, and competencies have become instrumentalized in carrying out discipline, surveillance, and (social) control activities that are consistent with correctional imperatives. Foucault (1995, 248) has addressed this aspect as the third dimension of the prison, upon which modern carceral society is modeled: "the technico-medical model of cure and normalization." However, as nurses (and perhaps other health professionals) strive to preserve standards of care, their resistant behaviours are likely to be constituted as "deviant" behaviours insofar as they may oppose dominant discourses and bring on conflicts with correctional staff and administrators (Holmes 2005; Perron and Holmes 2011). These aspects may be deemed difficult to discuss in the context of research.

The sensitive nature of research is likely to be linked to its ethical implications. In the case of research performed by health care professionals about health care professionals in secure settings, this is particularly problematic. Few would argue that following one's professional code of ethics is fundamental in contexts where patient/offender rights are threatened. This is a crucial ethical issue with which nurse researchers must grapple; it is perhaps the most obvious because nurse researchers must abide by the same professional rules and regulations as practising nurses. They are expected to protect patient rights throughout the research process and report wrongdoings or poor standards of care that may occur when nurses exert their functions inappropriately. This situation is consistent with Lee's (1993) description of potential threats listed above. When investigating nursing practice in correctional or forensic milieus, a researcher may therefore generate discomfort and suspicion by asking questions about nurses' daily behaviours and decisions. Nurse participants may perceive a sense of intrusion, or they may fear that what they say will be used against them. They could fear sanctions from their employers for "having said too much," for example. Conversely, they might worry that their statements will be used against them as proof of substandard practice, which would lead to the imposition of disciplinary measures by their professional organization. Such concerns are likely to arise if researchers are perceived as evaluators of nurses' professional practice who will relay sensitive information to competent authorities.

These ethical conundrums incur further challenges, such as gaining access to the setting, recruiting participants, and ensuring trustworthy accounts by informants. The perception of threats is likely to induce a climate of discomfort, suspicion, or cynicism. It may also skew the researcher's findings, particularly if participants tell the researcher textbook accounts of practice that have been purged of controversial elements. Furthermore, recording participants' statements creates additional anxiety for some. For example, in one study (Perron and Rudge 2012), a participant feared her voice would be recognized by her superiors, despite the fact that the researchers had repeatedly ensured her of data confidentiality and informed her that any identifying marker (e.g., age, ethnicity, title, country or city of origin, etc.) was eliminated during the transcription process. These measures were not sufficient to reassure this participant about the researcher's commitment to safeguarding confidentiality, as the following exchange shows:

> *Participant:* Oh, God ... I just put my name in there ... [ellipses
>   indicate hesitation]
> *Researcher:* It's deleted, I don't leave names.
> *Participant:* They're going to know who I am anyway.
> *Researcher:* This is not going to be shared with anyone ...
> *Participant:* God I hope this tape gets destroyed!
> *Researcher:* Do you want me to turn it off?
> *Participant:* Oh no, it's all right. I've said too much anyways, so what
>   difference does it make?

Lee (1993, 1995) has argued that examining ethical dimensions is not enough to comprehend the complexity of sensitive research. Along with Bonner and Vandecreek (2006), we further argue that ethical frameworks, such as those provided by professional codes of ethics, are insufficient to address the ethical and methodological problems encountered in sensitive research.

Epistemological Considerations in Conducting Sensitive Research

Understanding nurses' practices, discourses, and subjectivity construction in prison and secure environments is at the very heart of our research. To do this, nurses' practices must be recognized not simply as individual endeavours but as expressions and products of broader institutional processes that promote particular discourses (e.g., corrections, security, custody, and control) and eliminate alternative discourses, including those consistent with professional discourses of nursing (e.g., holistic and individualized care, nurse-patient relationship, critical thinking, professional autonomy, the use of the least restrictive measures, and patient confidentiality). It is well accepted that prison and secure settings rely on an intricate web of power relations that manifest themselves in various ways (Storch and Peternelj-Taylor 2009). Penitentiaries and forensic hospitals are designed to manage all aspects of inmates' lives. They closely regulate and monitor the way time and space are used. They create spaces where conventions and traditions are to be strictly observed and where interactions are forced, codified, even ritualized. Secure institutions rest on the creation and enactment of particular categories, including risk categories, which entail a careful and systematic process of labelling, describing, positioning individuals in particular spaces, enhancing visibility, and so on (Holmes and Murray 2011). While it is agreed that inmates' lives are regulated down to their most intimate details, we can also conceive that many aspects of health professionals' lives are also constrained in secure settings. Nurses, for example, are subjected to numerous directives (overt and covert) that dictate how they are to dress and present themselves; if and how they are allowed to speak; with whom to associate and whose interests they may advocate for; if and how they are allowed to circulate in the setting; how they are to prioritize daily (care) activities; which aspects of one's professional and ethical obligations to forego; and so on.

Nurses and other health professionals partake fully in these interlocking power relations as both subjects and objects of power (Holmes 2005). As objects of power, practising nurses are also subjected to political processes with mortifying and depersonalizing effects, and despite intense moral distress and suffering (Storch and Peternelj-Taylor 2009; Perron and Rudge 2012), they benefit from limited recourse and protection (Perron, Holmes, and Hamonet 2004). Hence, they also constitute a vulnerable population in these settings, albeit not to the same extent as inmates, but one that speaks nonetheless to the multiple ethical contingencies that make up nursing practice in highly regulated and secure settings. Conducting critical qualitative research to uncover the way these power relations emerge necessarily involves an examination of domination and oppression processes. Importantly, we argue that nurses constitute both targets and facilitators of these processes, which regulate the way they interact with offenders and with the correctional institution as a whole. Challenging this (im)balance of power through critical qualitative research can therefore be perceived as threatening by both prison administrators/officers and health professionals, which renders recruitment and data collection highly delicate.

Following one's code of ethics is insufficient to address the complexity and intricacy of health care provision in secure settings because ethical practice in research comes to encompass more than the application of ethical principles in solving a particular dilemma (e.g., to report or not a nurse to his or her professional body). Along with Foucault, we believe that "the ethico-political choice we have to make every day is to determine which is the main danger"

(Dreyfus and Rabinow 1983, 232). In the context described here, we believe that there are two main dangers to consider: first, that reporting individual nurses will fail to resolve institutional shortcomings regarding the protection of vulnerable groups; second, that by taking this stance, nurse researchers run the risk of being shut out of potential study sites or of being boycotted by potential nurse participants, thereby reducing possibilities of gaining insights into professional practices that are still little known (especially in light of the fact that correctional and forensic nurses are seldom identified "as prominent research subjects).

We wish to emphasize that, as researchers, we are not advocating for the support or endorsement of unprofessional practices; abusive behaviours or neglect toward patients should be reported. However, our research and clinical experience show that the disciplining or removal of a few individual nurses does not address the systemic issue of complex power structures (of which nurses form a part). These power structures govern individual behaviours in such a way that issues of repression and domination become institutionalized and normalized – and therefore perpetuated – in everyday practice. Individuals may thus be replaced by others who will be subjected to the same (gradual or brutal) processes of socialization and regulation with deep personal effects.

It is important to note that nurses, despite many important problems that impede their clinical practice, are very much aware of the necessity to create and maintain "resistant" spaces where ethical practice can be maintained alongside practices that are the result of a compromise with the correctional discourse. Pockets of resistance should be seen not as a failure in the face of institutional power but as a potent sign of nurses' political consciousness. This resonates in a very specific way in the context of research. Research, in this regard, can be seen as a practice and a strategy aimed at uncovering (and perhaps cultivating) such resistant behaviours. Capitalizing on resistant behaviours constitutes a way of ensuring that care provision to offenders is maintained, perhaps not in its ideal(ized) form but in a form that is consistent within the realm of institutional possibility. Reporting nurses in this context, then, would situate nurses in yet another category of institutional risk, which would spell additional regulatory mechanisms and further constrain care interventions that resist correctional imperatives.

We believe that providing nurses with an opportunity to describe their experiences of oppression in secure settings is part of a researcher's ethical practice. For instance, we view interviews as one of the few safe spaces where they can discuss their situation, confide in a person that is not part of the setting, and vent feelings of anger and powerlessness. Private interviews allow participants to problematize their practice, work environment, and paradoxical social mandates. They make possible the development of "a domain of acts, practices, and thoughts that seem ... to pose problem for politics" (Rabinow 1984, 384). Interviews help participants take a step back and consider their position in the matrix of (correctional and health) technologies that form the prison or forensic environment. Questions raised during interviews may bring new light to issues that have become normalized or taken for granted. Interviews may therefore promote a renewed sense of (political) agency, partly through the examination of current policies and the questioning of their underlying assumptions about risk, security, custody, punishment, and health care provision – assumptions that situate nursing practices and discourses at the margins of "prison work."

Interviews are not the only channel where political research can be enacted. Conducting research rests on a multiplicity of decisions that are made before recruitment or encounters with participants. An ethical perspective in sensitive nursing research encompasses more than deontological obligations; it must also include an examination of the researcher's own philosophical and political stance vis-à-vis the object under study. It includes practices in relation to oneself and others so as to achieve ethical action; it involves managing the research issue, the participants, the environment, and the researcher's self (Brackenridge 1999). One way to achieve this, before the study begins, is to use politically charged frameworks, such as those proposed by Foucault, Arendt, Agamben, Castel, Goffman, and others in critical theory and feminist studies. Such frameworks speak to the researcher's duty to uncover and critique existing power relations within a particular setting, to challenge power and oppression processes, and to disrupt the status quo (see, for example, Holmes and Murray 2011). This requires an understanding of political action as ethical action (Rabinow 1984). It also focuses on the social, cultural, historical, and political contexts of particular objects (e.g., institutional policies) and uncovers the way their presentation as value-neutral entities works to conceal their political nature. Critical or radical perspectives therefore shed light on the way language is used, first, to identify and categorize certain groups (e.g., nurses) as being problematic or posing a risk, and second, to prescribe adequate procedures to mitigate such risk. This political mindset allows one to understand the inner workings of correctional and forensic institutions, leading us to consider the potentially limited effects (and perhaps even the detrimental effects) of professional discipline in a context where health professionals are already heavily disciplined (in a Foucauldian sense). Research thus becomes inscribed in the realm of both ethics and politics. Such theoretical frameworks may be perceived to be too critical or radical by the selected research setting, thus rendering access more difficult to secure; it may therefore be necessary to "silence" these critical perspectives. This may involve the withholding of some information from the selected study site, or its articulation in a form that does not stir controversy or a defensive stance by prison administrators or staff. As we shall now see, other strategies need to be considered in carrying out research that bears clear ethical and political undertones.

Practical Considerations in Conducting Sensitive Nursing Research

Managing Ethics Committees

When preparing an ethics application, a basic rule of thumb is that the investigator must plan all her/his activities so as to protect participants. In sensitive research, one must be aware of the study group's vulnerable position, and that the research process may add another layer of constraint that could spell additional hardships. For instance, in one particular project, a nurse told the first author that she was mocked by colleagues about her participation and questioned about the information she had shared during the interview. Despite the investigator's precautions, in settings such as prisons, people's whereabouts are easily detectable because of intricate surveillance systems (e.g., cameras, card swipes, log-ins, etc.). Thus, it may be impossible to conceal a meeting between a researcher and a participant if it takes place within the workplace. Investigators should therefore be prepared to conduct interviews at another location should participants make this request. Other possible hardships endured by participants may take the form of significant distress during data collection. In our experience, participants have expressed significant distress or have broken down while discussing difficult situations. At the very least, the researcher is expected to offer to refer them to their employee assistance program (EAP coordinates should be sought prior to commencing the study). We choose to offer additional options (e.g., crisis lines, counselling resources) as well, as participants may distrust employer-related services. Measures to be implemented in the event of a crisis during interviews need to be planned and outlined for the ethics committee.

Rather than neglect or minimize potential issues when preparing an ethics application, an investigator should indicate that she or he is aware of such challenges and describe the steps that will be taken to minimize potential adverse effects. Aside from offering potential participants the opportunity to meet outside their workplace, we also suggest that they avoid communicating with the research team via their work email or phone. We also offer to turn off the recorder during the interview when a particularly sensitive topic is raised, and we provide participants the opportunity to review interview transcripts before they are analysed. When an investigator is aware of the issues faced by study participants, it is easier to explain in the consent form how they may translate into particular risks for participants, contrast them with the benefits of the study, and offer strategies to mitigate those risks.

An ethics committee will closely examine the recruitment process. In restricted settings such as prisons, where access to participants can be a complicated process, recruitment often necessitates the involvement of a middle person, such as a manager, who can relay information to staff and who may escort the researcher around the premises (this may be the case, for instance, when a researcher is not granted a circulation permit). It should be made clear that the names of those who will be enrolled in the study will not be revealed to this person, and this condition needs to be conveyed to the ethics committee as well as to potential participants. We have only recruited nurses in the course of our work; however, should we work with forensic patients, we are aware that recruitment would involve another layer of scrutiny meant to ensure that only subjects who are able to consent are approached and that issues that may affect consent (e.g., inmate's illiteracy) are properly addressed (Pont 2008). It would also involve the need to ensure that participation in the study is not used by administrators as a condition for granting particular privileges to and secure compliance by the inmate.

Despite stressing that participants are under no obligation to partake in a study, we have noted that a middle person facilitating the recruitment process may (wilfully or not) exert pressure upon individuals. We take care to highlight this point in our ethics application, alongside explanations as to how we counter this. For instance, during encounters with participants, we always emphasize the fact that they don't need to participate, regardless of what they may have been told by their manager, and that should they choose to withdraw, this decision will not be shared with others. We have had a few individuals take this opportunity to withdraw instantly, which speaks to the coercion that participants may experience when administrators become involved in the recruitment process.

Overall, participants should be free to make their own decisions as much as possible. The investigator's role, then, is to offer options (e.g., time and place of meeting, participants being allowed to withhold their real name from the researcher, choice of pseudonym/code, digital recording or note taking during the interview, handling of off-the-record information, withdrawal from the study, permission to quote participant directly or not, etc.) and to discuss the advantages and the risks of each option with the participant. Other issues such as data handling, storage, and ownership are also key when undergoing an ethical review. To preserve the confidentiality of the data in the context of prison research, we are adamant about storing research data in a location other than the research setting, even when an office is provided to us onsite. We keep all research material (e.g., consent forms, questionnaires, digital recorders, notebooks, etc.) in opaque binders or pocket files that no one is allowed to handle or examine, and we carry these on our person at all times.

It is also clear that data in any shape or form are never discussed with anyone, not even with participants who casually ask, as some have, "if anyone else mentioned the same issues" they had. To this, we simply respond in a concise manner that we cannot comment as it would breach confidentiality. Data confidentiality is a key aspect of the ethics review process, and investigators must describe in a realistic way how they will preserve it. It is important to note that some research sites may claim ownership of any data collected by the researcher and require her/him to hand over all material during or at the end of the project. This may make confidentiality issues particularly troublesome. Researchers should negotiate data ownership at the beginning of the process and stress their obligations to participants. Should the institution be unwavering about this aspect, investigators must inform potential participants (as well as the ethics committee) of this condition and its possible consequences with regards to data confidentiality. Alternatively, the investigator may consider conducting research at another facility.

Generally speaking, ethics committees will be concerned with the researcher being able to perform the intended study with as little interference as possible so that participants' interests and rights are protected and the integrity of the data is preserved. The researcher will be expected to function within the realm of what is permitted by the institution but to do this as independently as possible.

Matters of Researcher Independence

The issue of independence may generate heated discussions, especially in relation to qualitative research, as it is often associated with the criterion of objectivity. At the risk of oversimplifying a complex issue, we would like to discuss the notion of independence, not as a matter of methodological rigour, but as a matter of politics. We therefore discuss independence in two ways: first, in relation to administrative structures; second, in relation to study participants.

First, from an administrative point of view, independence constitutes a powerful strategy in sensitive qualitative research. Remaining an independent researcher refers to the collection of decisions that will allow a researcher to speak as freely as possible of her or his results and that will not depict the researcher as though she or he belongs with the institution. It may involve a decision as seemingly trivial as avoiding the use of an institutional email address. Moreover, it means avoiding, as much as possible, any circumstances or conditions that grant third parties control over the collection, handling (e.g., sharing, storage), analysis, or publication of research data. For instance, carefully choosing a funding body (e.g., public or governmental sources of funding) or avoiding conducting studies at the request of an institution (e.g., correctional institution, professional organization) are strategies that afford the researcher the necessary latitude to analyze and disseminate findings. Provisions must be made so as to safeguard the independent nature of the project. In our experience, for example, some correctional research settings have required that investigators submit their findings prior to publication in order to authorize their release and have imposed the signature of a binding form to ensure compliance. As stressed earlier, it was thus important to clarify data ownership issues prior to commencing the study. By remaining as free as possible, we have maintained our independence more easily and have been able to publish uncensored research data. This may, of course, trigger strong reactions from the research setting that seeks to control the impact of critical or damaging information, a point we shall return to later.

Examining the matter of "independence" in relation to study participants leads to an entirely different kind of reasoning. Becker (1967, 244) describes the way sociologists inevitably harbour sympathies for one study group or another and that most will "take the side of the underdog." To this, we add those researchers, such as ourselves, who are not sociologists but whose preferred theoretical frameworks are nonetheless grounded in the social sciences. We contend that establishing the researcher's independence from study participants is neither possible nor desirable. We go so far as to suggest, contentiously perhaps, that such independence is unethical when conducting research with groups that are subjected to oppressing and often violent processes, such as nurses practising in prison settings. In light of our research, we suggest that nurses are comparable to "subordinates," as described by Becker (ibid., 240) because they are routinely seen as violating the "approved and official morality" of the prison order (e.g., empathizing with an inmate or calling him "Sir") and because they are expected to comply fully with prison rules and regulations. We find value in

> investigat[ing] their complaints ... about the way things are run just as though one ought to give their complaints as much credence as the statements of responsible officials ... We assume, for the purpose of our research, that subordinates have as much right to be heard as superordinates, that they are as likely to be telling the truth as they see it. (Ibid., 241)

Through our work, we have firmly established that nurses' views and experiences are significant and that they allow us to shed new light on the way prison settings organize socially and politically. We therefore disrupt what Becker calls the hierarchy of credibility, that is, the taken-for-granted belief that the most reliable and authoritative accounts are uttered by individuals situated at the top of any social/institutional hierarchy. This disruption further exemplifies the political nature of sensitive research, and it is in keeping with our paradigmatic and theoretical underpinnings.

Alliances

This desire to give precedence to prison nurses' experiences points to a crucial element: alliances. Alliances are pivotal to the research process, partly because they potently signal the politics of research. In contexts of tense relationships between certain groups (between officers and administrators on the one hand, and nurses on the other, for instance), one may assume that a neutral stance is a strategic choice. Given the power relationships described earlier, being "neutral" in prison will bring on suspicion rather than trust because the neutral researcher may be perceived as unaware, naive, indifferent, or deceitful – four qualities that considerably hinder his or her credibility. Citing Burton, Lee (1995, 23) describes this position as that of "a 'social eunuch' devoid of views and principles ... someone who plays both sides against the middle." The matter of alliance is also critical in the sense that it touches on issues of subjectivity and the negotiation of power relationships. In our case, it has involved endorsing subjectivities that are marginalized in the prison setting (e.g., nurse, researcher, outsider, and, for the first author, female) and displaying behaviours and attitudes that are consistent with these subjectivities. Endorsing such marginalized subjectivities was strategic because it helped foster trust among potential participants and facilitated recruitment. It also avoided the very risky space of "neutrality."

Carefully choosing one's alliances involves a variety of behaviours, such as remaining polite but distant with particular groups; accepting invitations to join participants during meal or coffee breaks; declining the use of a private office that is situated near an administrator's office, and so on. These behaviours can become topics of conversations among staff. Decisions that seem mundane or inconsequential may bear significant political implications for the study and influence recruitment or participants' willingness to share critical information.

Recruitment

Recruitment activities offer an opportunity to clearly establish the researcher's ethical obligations regarding the handling of the data. In all our research endeavours, speaking in clear terms, avoiding empty words or statements, and answering questions in a concise and straightforward manner (using basic language) have been essential in this regard. We have been careful to convey our awareness of nurses' difficult context of practice and believe this has been effective in building rapport and trust with potential participants. Offering options as to how the interview will unfold also facilitates recruitment. Recruitment is a time when participants negotiate their willingness to partake in the study. Care should thus be taken to express the researcher's concern for participants' needs. Our experience shows that this stance may generate anxiety or raise questions on the part of the setting's administrators. However, we have not come across a situation where we were denied access to the premises, but we are aware this could be an issue, for example, in privately run organizations.

During the recruitment process, several commitments are (publicly) made. It is essential to uphold these commitments throughout the research process. For instance, during a research project in a federal penitentiary, the first author had assured potential participants that the research data would be kept safe and secure at all times. During her multiple visits to the site (several hours away from her office), she gathered her digital recorder and research documents in an opaque carry case that she carried everywhere she went (interviews, in-services, meal breaks, toilet, etc.). She refused to lock it in an office that had been provided for her and always kept it within her reach when she conducted interviews or observations. While some participants noted with humour that she monitored her carry case "like a hawk," she took it to mean they had taken note of her strict diligence regarding the handling of confidential research data.

Being the Object of Inquiry

The research endeavour can be seen as a collection of opportunities for the investigator to keep his or her promise to participants. In this regard, staff may indulge in a variety of behaviours that test the investigator's attitudes and trustworthiness (Lee 1995). While these are often carried out in humour, they do provide hints into a subject's concern with the (possibly disruptive) presence of the researcher in the setting. Therefore, one should not take these events lightly because reactions are scrutinized and noted. For instance, during the first author's above-mentioned study, correctional officers made sarcastic remarks about the validity and the relevance of nursing research and asked her what was to be gained from it. During a particular visit, a staff member asked, in front of others, if she had made any particular "discoveries" yet. On another occasion, upon the researcher entering the nursing station, one nurse stated in a joking manner that "the researcher had arrived" and that they would need to "watch what they said from now on." Responding in a concise, matter-of-fact way has been the approach that has worked the best in our experience. In some cases, responding with humour allowed us to defuse the slight tension caused by the skeptic. Anticipating these situations and thinking beforehand about the best way to react is possibly the best strategy. Whatever the approach, however, one should remember that, in a setting where assertiveness and authority are deemed desirable traits, answering in a defensive or vague manner or showing discomfort will hinder one's efforts to appear confident and trustworthy.

Managing Researcher-Participant Relationships

Interviews may provide participants with a much-needed outlet to discuss particular experiences. Conducting an interview on sensitive topics typically involves reiterating the researcher's obligations regarding confidentiality and the independent nature of the study. Participants may be critically aware of the potentially threatening nature of their accounts. In our experience, adopting a conversation style (rather than a straight question-and-answer format) may put participants more at ease during interviews. Understanding how to time questions and asking these in a straightforward, nonjudgmental, and supportive manner are key skills in sensitive research; as is showing awareness of participants' situation and its (social, ethical, emotional, legal) impact. Participants may request to provide "off-the-record" information (Alty and Rodham 1998). In our experience, much information shared off-the-record provides highly valuable insights into the intricacies of the research problem. Some participants may be open to the use of this material, as long as its source remains completely anonymous (that is, not linked to a particular research code or pseudonym), but others may refuse that the information be used altogether, fearing that it will somehow be traced back to them. Researchers must therefore negotiate whether the data will be used or eliminated entirely and follow through with the resolution.

Several participants in distinct studies commented on the fact they had no one to turn to for effective support and guidance, that they felt isolated, and that their spouse, family members, and friends could not understand their plight. In two separate studies, nurses broke down while describing experiences of harassment, bullying, belittling, ostracization, and powerlessness. Although they refused a referral to a support or counselling service, such incidents show the extent to which researching sensitive topics may obscure the line between "researcher" and "counsellor." Alty and Rodham (1998, 278) describe this process as the "researcher versus therapist dilemma," which leads to the blurring of the space that traditionally typifies researcher-participant relationships. The researcher must therefore be ready to manage potential situations where a participant may ask for advice or request staying in touch with the researcher after the study. Issues surrounding the researcher-participant relationship have been discussed at length in the context of ethnography, and their implications in terms of over-involvement have been stressed (see, for instance, Glesne 1989). However, in a paradigm where ethical action rests on a political mindset, one cannot ignore the fact that relationships developed with participants, while not being a form of friendship per se, go well beyond the traditional participant-researcher rapport, into the realm of human fellowship.

Managing Oneself

The necessity to manage and support participants leads to another issue: the management of the researcher him/herself. Brackenridge (1999, 400) discusses the importance of reflecting on which of the researcher's "selves" is embodied at any given time and, therefore, which agenda is promoted and furthered: "the personal, the scientific, or the political," to which we add "the professional." This may be difficult because self commands a particular line of action that may be in direct opposition to another self's agenda. For example, protecting participants' privacy may be in support of ethical conduct, if ethics is understood as falling within the realm of an ethics of the self (personal domain and, in the context of critical theory, political domain). However, it may also oppose ethical conduct if ethics is understood as being strictly guided by formal codes of ethics and standards of practice (professional domain). Furthermore, the scientific self, in establishing rigour, may be dedicated to being fully transparent about his or her literature review, theoretical framework, and data collection tools. However, in exposing the full scope of the study, he or she may elicit concerns from the research setting and jeopardize the possibility of conducting the study at all. If he or she is sensitive to the political nature of the research process and elects to conceal the critical nature of the research, access to the setting may be granted and invaluable information and insights may be gained, but such behaviour may be cast as highly deceptive, unethical, and possibly unscientific. We argue that deception is a small transgression in light of the significant understandings that can be gained in inaccessible settings where systemic bullying and censorship constitute the norm. It follows from that point of view that, in order to understand the dynamics at play and bring on change, access to the setting must be safeguarded, even if it means downplaying or concealing one's theoretical perspective. These various examples make clear that selves do not constitute distinct ways of being and that overlap occurs, as evidenced by one's ongoing struggle over the proper (ethical) course of action (Brackenridge 1999). Such struggle points to the researcher's embodiment of political research, in that he or she becomes an instrument of political change in every sense of the word.

Dissemination of the Results

Disseminating the findings is a critical component of research and bears significant implications. For instance, presenting the results in the setting itself may constitute a powerful act because it may present – and therefore legitimate – divergent views, discourses, and practices. Participants may realize that colleagues share similar concerns and aspirations for change. Presenting results may foster solidarity among oppressed groups, which may lead to more organized, consistent, and systematic political actions. Dissemination outside the setting may trigger strong opposition. Findings that expose controversial, or even illegal, practices may prompt the institution to prohibit further dissemination or to demand that findings be subjected to institutional review and authorization first. This may entail allusions or threats about the possibility of legal action should the researcher fail to comply. In the second author's experience, following the publication of disconcerting results, an administrator repeatedly demanded access to the confidential research data and other documents (Holmes and Murray 2011). The administrator also contacted the journal that had published the results and questioned the validity of the data. These allegations persisted despite several independent reviews of research evidence by competent authorities.

Proceeding with the dissemination of research is facilitated considerably if the researcher has remained independent. Should actions or accusations such as the ones above occur, it is essential to seek support from one's organization and its ethics committee. Seeking legal counsel may also be necessary, as occurred in Holmes's case. The requirement to document every decision made throughout the research process cannot be overstated. For instance, Holmes and Murray had kept all the communication (paper and electronic) that established without doubt that proper authorizations (institutional and ethical) had been granted. If insufficient care had been taken to record or store relevant correspondence, the integrity of the study and the researchers would have been more difficult to establish. Letters and emails, both formal and informal, ethics certificates, and other research-related documents must be securely kept, and we believe it is wise to keep these several years after the study has ended. Vague or ambiguous statements by research setting administrators should be clarified and the researcher's ethical and legal responsibilities (e.g., confidentiality of the data) need to be explicitly stated and documented.

These strategies constitute some of the ways to prevent and deal with difficulties arising from conducting sensitive research. They are the result of our own experiences in a particular context, that of prisons and forensic environments. In spite of the precautions taken, investigators can still be subjected to intimidation, overt and covert threats, and personal attacks. In our view, the degree of violence evident in the example provided speaks to the paranoid and pathological nature of total institutions such as correctional settings. The strategies discussed here may or may not provide the answers or guidance a researcher needs, but they do raise awareness regarding an investigator's expectations about the research problem at hand, the investigation process itself, and the vested interests of the research subjects as well as the administrators of the selected research site. What is important to remember is that engaging in critical qualitative research requires more than incorporating buzz words and radical frameworks in a research proposal. It involves the embodiment of ethics and politics well beyond the confines of a single research project. It involves an ongoing reflection about the situatedness of thoughts, beliefs, and actions crystallized in particular discourses and practices, including professional and research practices. It also requires a high level of independence so as to maintain a certain distance with particular institutions (including research and teaching institutions) so that one can keep reflecting on "what constitutes the main danger."

Conclusion

The unique nature of correctional and forensic environments gives rise to particular tensions regarding the potential threats of research. Conducting research in such environments remains delicate, since personal, professional, and organizational practices and discourses are subject to scrutiny and critique. In this sense, we argue that research brings into play ethics and politics in a process that seeks to disrupt the status quo and encourage (or impose) change. This process is not without challenges. In this chapter, we have attempted to bridge theoretical (epistemological) and practical issues and propose some strategies that support conducting sensitive research while being true to one's political and ethical commitments to the participants and the wider community. Despite the challenges associated with doing so, engaging in sensitive research and ensuring the independence of the researcher enable the use of research as a tool for ethical practice as they force greater institutional transparency.

References

Alty, A., and Rodham, K. (1998). The Ouch! Factor: Problems in Conducting Sensitive Research. *Qualitative Health Research 8*(2), 275-82.

American Nurses Association. (2010). Position Statement: The Nurse's Role in Ethics and Human Rights: Protecting and Promoting Individual Worth, Dignity, and Human Rights in Practice Settings. http://nursingworld.org/.

Australian Nursing Federation. (2006). *Competency Standards for Nurses in General Practice.* www. anf.org.au/nurses_gp/resource_03.pdf.

Becker, H.S. (1967). Whose Side Are We On? *Social Problems 14*(3), 239-47.

Bonner, R., and Vandecreek, L.D. (2006). Ethical Decision Making for Correctional Mental Health Providers. *Criminal Justice and Behaviour 33*(4), 542-64.

Brackenridge, C. (1999). Managing Myself: Investigator Survival in Sensitive Research. *International Review for the Sociology of Sport 34*(4), 399-410.

Burrow, S. (1991a). The Special Hospital Nurse and the Dilemma of Therapeutic Custody. *Journal of Advances in Health and Nursing Care 1,* 21-38.

–. (1991b). Special Hospital: Therapy vs. Custody. *Nursing Times 87,* 64-66.

–. (1992). The Treatment and Security Needs of Special Hospital Patients – A Nursing Perspective. *Journal of Advanced Nursing 18,* 1267-78.

–. (1993a). An Outline of the Forensic Nursing Role. *British Journal of Nursing 2,* 899-904.

–. (1993b). The Role Conflict of the Forensic Nurse. *Senior Nurse 13,* 20-25.

–. (1998). Therapy versus Security: Reconciling Healing and Damnation. In T. Mason and D. Mercer (Eds.), *Critical Perspectives in Forensic Care: Inside Out* (171-87). London: Macmillan.

Canadian Nurses Association. (2008). *Code of Ethics for Registered Nurses.* Ottawa: Canadian Nurses Association.

College of Nurses of Ontario. (2011). *Mandatory Reporting: A Process Guide for Employers, Facility Operators and Nurses.* Pub. No. 42006. Toronto: CNO. www.cno.org/Global/docs/ih/42006_ fsMandReporting.pdf.

Dreyfus, H.L., and Rabinow, P. (1983). *Michel Foucault: Beyond Structuralism and Hermeneutics.* Chicago: University of Chicago Press.

Dunbar, C. (2003). Correctional Nursing: A Practice in Contradiction. *Nursing Spectrum (New York/New Jersey Metro Edition),* January 27. news.nurse.com/apps/pbcs.dll/article?AID= 2003301270367#.Ux4Hj02Yapo.

Fisher, A. (1995). The Ethical Problems Encountered in Psychiatric Nursing Practice with Dangerous Mentally Ill Persons. *Scholarly Inquiry for Nursing Practice 9*(2), 193-208.

Foucault, M. (1995). *Discipline and Punish: The Birth of the Prison.* (Trans. A. Sheridan). New York: Vintage Books.

Glesne, C. (1989). Rapport and Friendship in Ethnographic Research. *International Journal of Qualitative Studies in Education 2*(1): 45-54.

Harrison, J., MacGibbon, L., and Morton, M. (2001). Regimes of Trustworthiness in Qualitative Research: The Rigors of Reciprocity. *Qualitative Inquiry 7*(3), 323-45.

Holmes, D. (2002). Police and Pastoral Power: Governmentality and Correctional Forensic Psychiatric Nursing. *Nursing Inquiry 9*(2), 84-92.

–. (2005). Governing the Captives: Forensic Psychiatric Nursing in Corrections. *Perspectives in Psychiatric Care 41*(1), 3-13.

Holmes, D., and Murray, S. (2011). Civilizing the Barbarian: A Critical Analysis of Behaviour Modification Programs in Forensic Psychiatriy Settings. *Journal of Nursing Management 19* (3), 293-301.

Holmes, D., Perron, A., and Michaud, G. (2007). Nursing in Corrections: Lessons from France. *Journal of Forensic Nursing 3*(3-4), 126-31.

Holmes, D., Perron, A., Michaud, G., Montuclard, L., and Hervé, C. (2005). Scission entre le sanitaire et le pénitentiaire: Réflexion critique sur les (im)possibilités du soin infirmier au Canada et en France. *Journal de réadaptation médicale* 25(3), 131-40.

International Council of Nurses. (2006). *Position Statement: Nurses' Role in the Care of Detainees and Prisoners.* Geneva: ICN. www.icn.ch/images/stories/documents/publications/position_ statements/A13_Nurses_Role_Detainees_Prisoners.pdf.

Jacob, J.D. (2010). Fear and Power in Forensic Psychiatry: Nurse-Patient Interactions in a Secure Environment. PhD diss., University of Ottawa.

–. (2012). Working in a Violent Environment: The Pitfalls of Integrating Security Imperatives into Forensic Psychiatric Nursing. In D. Holmes, T. Rudge, and A. Perron (Eds.), *(Re)Thinking Violence in Health Care Settings: A Critical Approach* (315-30). Surrey, UK: Ashgate.

Jacob, J.D., and Holmes, D. (2011a). The Culture of Fear: Expanding the Concept of Risk in Forensic Psychiatric Nursing. *International Journal of Culture and Mental Health.* doi:10.1080/ 17542863.2010.519123.

–. (2011b). Working under Threat: Fear and Nurse-Patient Interactions in a Forensic Psychiatric Setting. *Journal of Forensic Nursing* 7(2), 68-77.

Lee, R.M. (1993). *Doing Research on Sensitive Topics.* London: Sage.

–. (1995). *Dangerous Fieldwork.* Thousand Oaks, CA: Sage.

Lee, R.M., and Renzetti, C.M. (1990). The Problems of Researching Sensitive Topics. *American Behavioural Scientist* 33(5), 510-28.

Martin, P.M. (2003). Exploring the Nature of the Nurse-Patient Relationship in an Acute, High Security Forensic Psychiatry Unit. D.N. diss., La Trobe University.

Martin, T., and Street, A.F. (2003). Exploring Evidence of the Therapeutic Relationship in Forensic Psychiatric Nursing. *Journal of Psychiatric and Mental Health Nursing* 10(5), 543-51.

Mason, T. (1997). Censorship of Research in the Health Service Setting. *Nurse Researcher* 4(4), 83-92.

Mason, T., and Mercer, D. (1998). Introduction: The Silent Scream. In T. Mason and D. Mercer (Eds.), *Critical Perspectives in Forensic Care: Inside Out* (1-8). Hampshire, UK: Macmillan.

Mason, T., Richman, J., and Mercer, D. (2002). The Influence of Evil on Forensic Clinical Practice. *International Journal of Mental Health Nursing* 11(2), 80-93.

Perron, A. (2011). The Forensic Patient's Moral Career as a Measure of Institutional Disciplinary Processes. *International Journal of Culture and Mental Health* 5(1), 15-29. doi:10.1080/17542863 .2010.540819

Perron, A., and Holmes, D. (2011). Constructing Mentally Ill Inmates: Nurses' Discursive Practices in Corrections. *Nursing Inquiry* 18(3), 191-204. doi:10.1111/j.1440-1800.2011.00526.x.

Perron, A., Holmes, D., and Hamonet, C. (2004). Capture, mortification, dépersonnalisation: La pratique infirmière en milieu correctionnel. *Journal de réadaptation médicale* 24(4), 124-31.

Perron, A., and Rudge, T. (2012). Exploring Violence in a Forensic Hospital: A Theoretical Experimentation. In D. Holmes, T. Rudge, and A. Perron (Eds.), *(Re)Thinking Violence in Health Care Settings: A Critical Approach* (89-106). Surrey, UK: Ashgate.

Pont, J. (2008). Ethics in Research Involving Prisoners. *International Journal of Prisoner Health* 4(4), 184-97.

Punch, M. (1998). Politics and Ethics in Qualitative Research. In N. Denzin and Y. Lincoln (Eds.), *The Landscape of Qualitative Research* (156-84). Thousand Oaks, CA: Sage.

Rabinow, P. (1984). *The Foucault Reader.* New York: Pantheon Books.

Roulston, K. (2001). Data Analysis and "Theorizing as Ideology." *Qualitative Research* 1(3), 279-302. doi:10.1177/146879410100100302.

Sieber, J.E. (1993). The Ethics and Politics of Sensitive Research. In C.M. Renzetti and R.M. Lee (Eds.), *Researching Sensitive Topics* (14-26). Newbury Park, CA: Sage.

Sieber, J.E., and Stanley, B. (1988). Ethical and Professional Dimensions of Socially Sensitive Research. *American Psychologist* 43, 49-55.

Storch, J., and Peternelj-Taylor, C. (2009). Ethics for Health Care Providers: Codes as Guidance for Practice in Prisons. In D.C. Hatton and A. Fisher (Eds.), *Women Prisoners and Health Justice: Perspectives, Issues and Advocacy for an International Hidden Population* (109-16). New York: Radcliffe Publishing.

Thorne, S., and Darbyshire, P. (2005). Land Mines in the Field: A Modest Proposal for Improving the Craft of Qualitative Health Research. *Qualitative Health Research 15*, 1105-13.

Turner, M., Catlin, A., Dickey, S.B., Michel, D., Mace, D., and Lattanzi, K. (2006). Ethics and Issues in Prison, Forensic and Other Similar Nursing Settings. *Online Ethics Newsletter* (Fall). http://www.nursingworld.org.

Walker, J.C. (1985). Rebels with Our Applause? A Critique of Resistance Theory in Paul Willis's Ethnography of Schooling. *Journal of Education 167*(2), 63-83.

chapter 8 ## How Positivism Is Colonizing Qualitative Research through Ethics Review

Will C. van den Hoonaard

QUALITATIVE RESEARCH IS CAUGHT in the cross-hairs of relentless ethics-codes regimes inhabited by the principles and practices derived from positivist, biomedical research. These regimes refer to the whole panoply of laws, codes, or guidelines that purport to promote and sustain ethical research. Through the need to follow the mandates of these regimes, qualitative research is being colonized by positivist research standards. This chapter, however, explores how qualitative researchers themselves enable this colonization through the adoption of the cultural signals, symbols, and norms and values of positivist research.[1] Colonization occurs in a variety of social settings, whether political, economic, scientific, ecological, or urban. Its success hinges on the willingness of the host setting to accommodate the new paradigm and the extent to which it does so. Qualitative research resembles a colonized country whose indigenous values and approaches are gradually being dissipated by the dominant, neopositivist model of research.

The Trouble with the Ethics-Codes Regimes

There is little disagreement among social researchers that ethics-codes regimes are having a troubling influence on their research. Encapsulated in such ethics regimes is a positivistic outlook on how research ought to be done. It should be clearly stated that one should not conflate positivism and ethics codes. Ethics codes adumbrate a diversity of issues, such as ethical principles, but when those principles touch philosophy of science and methodology, they express a positivistic stance. We learn from Sue Richardson and Miriam McMullan (2007, 1123), for example, that 27 percent of 130 surveyed social scientists in the United Kingdom proclaim the irrelevance of the state's ethics regime for social science. Annette Hemmings (2006, 13), as another example, shows that ethics committees, since their inception, have "been largely modeled on standard clinical trials," and Ann Hamilton (2005, 193), another social researcher, avers that the ethics review system "is often nonsensical when applied to social research; the rules are not right or wrong, but irrelevant." In the experience of Christine Halse and Anne Honey (2007, 336), research ethics committees that work with national ethics codes hold the view that research "proceeds in a linear way." "The dissonance," they continue, "between research practice and the governing practices of the institutional discourse of research ethics is more than bothersome, galling, or benignly unsettling. It exposes an epistemological rupture – an ethical schism (ibid., 342-43) (see also Hauck 2008, 1).

Social researchers have mounted these criticisms in light of many federal codes' obdurate inability to take their particular approaches, especially qualitative research, into account.[2] Charles Bosk and Raymond De Vries (2004, 258) worry about the "trained incompetence [of ethics committees] when it comes to the inductive methods of qualitative research."[3] And increasingly, according to Hamilton (2002, 7), "many qualitative and survey researchers are being squeezed into an ill-fitting regulatory space." As Ian Shaw (2008, 411) makes clear, a 2001 statement by the United States National Institutes of Health on ethics in research shows a commitment to quantitative methods. In the eyes of Raymond De Vries and Carl Forsberg (2002, 199), ethics committees "are structured to review medical, not social scientific, research." Franklin Silva (2008, 325) speaks of the biomedical basis of ethics codes as an inappropriate model for social research, referring to it as the "sovereignty of traditional [scientific] paradigm" (see also Tilley and Gormley 2007, 369; Kellner 2002; SSHWC 2004; AAUP 2001). According to the United States National Communications Association (2005, 219), the ethics review committees "inappropriately view social science research through perceptual lenses and policies shaped by experimental biomedical research."

Elsewhere around the world, scholars voice similar troubles. In their research in five countries, Martin Tolich and Maureen Fitzgerald (2006, 71) declare, "we have yet to find an ethics committee that reflects qualitative epistemological assumptions." In Finland, Klaus Mäkelä (2006, 6, 8) worries that "an extremely strict interpretation of the Personal Data Act [in his country] and an unfounded extension of the legislation on medical research to cover social research will seriously hamper social research without actually improving the position of research subjects." In Sweden and Norway, there are similar extensions to social research.

Colonization of Qualitative Research by Positivist Standards

It is hard today to visualize doing research without having to resort to apply-ing for formal research ethics review of one's planned research – a now ubi-quitous process. As new generations of social researchers are entering their disciplines, they are not necessarily familiar with the time when formal ethics review was not part of planning research. This situation would not necessarily be problematic if the ethics review system were not driven by paradigms that originate in biomedical research.

What makes the colonization by the biomedical ethics regime so robust is that it is propelled by its agents of social control – that is, the state, its funding mechanisms, and an increasingly vast bureaucratic structure in universities that annually absorbs an estimated \$35 million in Canada, and \$500 million worldwide (van den Hoonaard 2011). When that social control is vertically integrated throughout all levels of scholarly endeavours – nationally, regionally, locally, and involving granting agencies and editorial decisions of journals – we speak of "vertical" ethics. This vertical system is not dissimilar to corporate entities that exercise control up and down the market chain. Thus, vertical ethics is penetrative because it brings into line lower-level ethics committees, journals, graduate schools, and academic societies, many of which require an ethics certificate before a researcher can publish an article or gradu-ate with a higher degree. Moreover, universities, departments, and journals invoke ethics codes to protect themselves.

Embedded in the new ethics regime is the dominant approach to science that privileges traditional, positivist, scientific outlooks and methods. In other words, the new ethics regime pushes qualitative research into the embrace of positivism. Elizabeth Paluck (2010, 59), for example, shares a view that might puzzle many qualitative researchers:

> Over the past few decades, a productive exchange in political science has explored the idea that qualitative research should be guided by the logic of mainstream quantitative and experimental methods ... Quali-tative researchers can aspire to use experimental logic for constructing counterfactuals and drawing causal inferences ... but cannot use actual experiments.[4]

Reinforced by the ethics regime, neopositivism undercuts and changes the research habits of social researchers. Conforming to those ethics codes means that social researchers must now surrender their traditional epistemologies and methodologies.

There are, moreover, forces other than ethics codes at work that make the colonization of qualitative research by neopositivism possible – namely, the extent to which the host paradigms (i.e., the social sciences and qualitative research in particular) respond to and accept this colonizing process. Indeed, this chapter specifically explores the ways that qualitative researchers are adopting these norms.

Many have already accepted this near-inevitable process. Others exercise a judicious form of secondary adjustment (Goffman 1961, 54).[5] Secondary adjustments involve a quiet, beneath-the-surface undermining of the biomedical parameters of the research ethics review system (such as by purposely offering vague project descriptions). Still others resist the colonization, usually at great personal sacrifice. In terms of full resistance, researchers might abandon all thought of conducting research in full light of the university (see, for example, Ferrell and Hamm 1998; Ogden, this volume). On all accounts, however, qualitative researchers invoke cultural signals, symbols, and norms and values of positivism as their new normative form of doing research.

Cultural Signals

Language constitutes a significant cultural signal. It is critical to one's cultural participation and identification (Haas and Shaffir 2009, 45). In effect, when two disciplinary cultures meet, one of the most profound differences relates to the particular use of language and terminologies. However, as Howard S. Becker points out, when two scholarly communities meet, the question is always raised, in what language should the discussions take place?

> Quantitative researchers always want to know what answers qualitative researchers have to their questions about validity and reliability and hypothesis testing. They do not discuss how they might answer the questions qualitative researchers raise about accuracy and precision and breadth ... They want the discussion to go on in their language and the standards of qualitative work translated into the language they already use. (2001, 329)

Becker reminds us that the quantitative researchers' insistence that qualitative researchers use their language is not premised on epistemology or logic but on the hierarchical social organization and power differential between the two systems of thinking. After all, he avers, superordinate groups "think everything should be translated so that it makes sense in their language" (2001, 329). Occupying a subordinate place, qualitative researchers use the language and terms that originate in positivist research settings. Qualitative researchers are adopting such terms as *protocol* and resort to writing in the passive voice. Social researchers use these and other words to signal to ethics committees that they comply with their commonly held concepts. By engaging in a variety of language strategies to placate research ethics boards (REBs), we are learning to emphasize the use of particular words over others to remove potential barriers toward receiving approval for the ethics review application.

The most significant cultural signal involves the use of "performative language."[6] Its use denotes an attempt to bridge differences between the interactants. The weaker or more marginal the group to which members belong, the more likely they will use performative language because they may feel a moral obligation to create that bridge. Performative language implies that "to say something is to do something." Therefore, to make the statement, "'I promise that ...' is to perform the act of promising as opposed to making a statement that may be judged true or false" (Cline 2002, 24). As the National Communications Association (2005, 206) (of the United States) emphasizes, it is important to use "the right language" when submitting an application to an ethics review committee. Alexander Clark, moreover, wants qualitative research to build its influence in the sphere traditionally reserved for clinical research – namely, evidence-based practice; he speaks against qualitative researchers' bemoaning or undermining the merits of this practice (2008, 310).

However, the challenge is even greater for qualitative researchers because ethics committees are unfamiliar with the language of qualitative research (Hamilton 2005, 199). Often, they must change words to meet the ethics committee's needs (NCA 2005, 227). One researcher admitted to her readers to having modified her language into more "post-positivist" terms (ibid., 228).[7] In my case, my research ethics board told me to specify in advance how long my interviews would take, regardless of the circumstances and the desire of the research participants or me as researcher. The desire for full knowledge and disclosure prior to research engagement creates a precarious position for qualitative researchers whose research is so dependent on context and the individual participants. Knowing in advance exactly how long an interview will last or how long one will remain in the field is nearly impossible; the demand for such knowledge pushes qualitative researchers to structure their research in and on positivist terms.

The researcher's adoption of the same language that appears on application forms is an acknowledgment, on the part of the researcher, that he or she finds that language meaningful. The "start" dates and "end" of projects, the "length" of interviews, "written consent," "confidentiality," "anonymity," and "destruction of data" are powerful concepts, some of which have no, little, or a different meaning to many social researchers.[8] As I observed at a qualitative research symposium, one researcher went so far as to say, "Say anything to make the [ethics committee] happy. You have to say something. Make it up! You invent possible research findings," and "you must recycle the bureaucratic language (almost like plagiarism). Use the same protocol as someone else" (Couch-Stone Symposium, 7 February 2003, Phoenix).

I wish to comment on four usages of language that highlight the problematic aspects of the colonizing process internalized by social researchers: the use of the term *protocol,* the passive voice, *best practices,* and *investigator.*

Protocol

The term *protocol* is significant in ethics application forms. Increasingly, social researchers use the term despite its ill-advised meaning in social research. It appears faithfully in communications principally from and secondarily to ethics committees. Upon closer inspection, one sees that the term *protocol* signifies something that is not subject to interpretation. The *Oxford English Dictionary* defines *protocol* as a "formal or official statement of a transaction or proceeding; spec. the detailed record of the procedure and results in a scientific experiment; hence, experimental procedure."[9] According to the *Random House Dictionary of the English Language,* a protocol involves "a statement reporting an observation exactly and without attempting an interpretation"[10] – an intriguing use of the term in the interpretative sciences! The term has become so ubiquitous that some social researchers might be hard pressed to come up with an alternative or with what the previous generation of researchers conventionally used in its place – namely, *research plan, design,* and the like.

The term directs the gaze of the research ethics reviewer to the minutiae of data gathering, not the conceptual or theoretical scheme behind it, or any other potentially challenging ethical issues in the research. Are the data gathered "reliable"? Can the research question be operationalized? What kinds of ethical issues are likely to emerge from implementing the protocol? How should the researcher deal with those issues? The emergent nature of qualitative research makes it impossible to offer details about one's research plans, particularly if the researcher has not yet visited the research setting.

The Use of the Passive Voice

If culture implicates language, then surely the use and the promotion of the active or passive voice as a writing style are key. Author- and agency-evacuated styles of writing – so common in positivism – represent a victory for quantitative research but distort the culture of qualitative social research itself. After researchers have submitted articles, journals frequently change the active voice to the passive voice. As Becker (1986, 79) claims, "sentences that name active agents make our [i.e., social researchers'] representations of social life more understandable and believable." Following Becker, when we say that "interviews were conducted," we hide the interviewer and the research participant, too. The expressions reduce the interview experience to an impersonal research act, lacking human agency.

For social researchers, however, it is important and relevant that they indicate human agency. Symbolic interactionism – one of several perspectives in the study of society – acknowledges that humans are constantly engaged in, partaking in, and shaping institutions and roles. Such a culture must also indicate the engagement of the researcher with the social setting: it not only lends more credence to the research but also reflects a key theoretical and ethical position in social science writing in which humans are agents who are not worked over. This particular use of language reflects the researcher's attitude towards data as something that requires interpretation, not simply as representing truth per se. Using the passive voice, the researcher takes away this fundamental aspect of his or her work and subsequent analysis. Ironically, the use of the passive voice offers an imprecise and inaccurate description of the research act. "Interviews are conducted," but by whom? "Data were gathered," but by whom? The passive voice is destined to make the research sound objective and scientific, but it misses the mark in terms of precision and accuracy.

Best Practices

Best practices are a technique or methodology that, through experience and research, has proven to lead reliably to a desired result. Apparently, a commitment to using best practices in any field is a commitment to using all the knowledge and technology at one's disposal to ensure success. Such fields as health care, government administration, education, project management, hardware and software product development, and others make extensive use of this term.[11] One commonly finds its usage in fields where positivism holds sway. Despite its increasing usage by qualitative researchers to accommodate the dominance of positivism, *best practices* is not a term one conventionally associates with basic social research where no immediate applications are anticipated. From a social perspective, *best practices* connotes de-skilling, suggesting that there is *one* way of doing things, rather than using judgments that would allow a researcher to figure out the approach that would best suit each particular research setting.[12]

Investigator

Another term inhospitable to the social sciences is *investigator.* While the term is often an administrative one, we must note that its original usage connotes the "lead scientist or engineer for a particular well-defined science (or other research) project, such as a laboratory study or clinical trial."[13] It confirms the idea that the (principal) investigator is the "individual designated by the grantee, and approved by NSF [National Science Foundation], who will be responsible for the scientific or technical direction of the project" (NSF 2002, 8). In the context of social science research one would be hard pressed to define the term's usage. Still, it has become quite conventional for the term to appear on social science research grant applications and especially on research ethics review applications.

The usage has become so commonplace that we are unable to loosen it from actual social research. The term *investigator* is typically absent from, or is an anomaly in, North American ethnographies, whether classical or contemporary. In Europe, however, the use of *investigator* is not an anomaly, given the shorter tradition of qualitative research there. Daniel Figaredo (2006), for example, in his review of a Spanish ethnography in education, uses the term quite freely. So, too, do disciplines in North America where ethnographies are generally quite new or where they stand close to the biomedical model of research, such as nursing.

As a qualitative researcher, I see myself more as a "learner" rather than an "investigator," for the plain reason that I am trying to be open about learning a new (sub)culture, and all the research participants are teaching me about how they see the world and make meaning of it. To portray myself as an investigator would misconstrue what I am doing. An investigator viscerally "others" the subjects of research, which is contrary to the interpretivist approach that seeks connections through interaction. When one has been researching an area for a number of years, one becomes an expert in gathering data, but ultimately one must still take the stance of a learner or researcher, without the hierarchical, detective-like innuendo that *investigator* implies. When resorting to using *investigator,* one assumes that truth is something that can be uncovered; for many social researchers, truth is always in the making and is, at best, quite fluid.

Symbols

A symbol is the outward, visible sign of a culture. A sign is something that stands for something else. It can be a thing or an event. For example, smoke can signify fire (Hewitt 2007, 36). In our case, symbols formally signify to the colonizer that the researcher has accepted the demands of the adopted, colonizing culture. Partly through research ethics review, the use of the signed informed consent form and the reluctance to write monographs stand out as prime symbols of positivist research.

The Signed "Informed Consent" Form

Ethics codes widely advocate the use of the signed informed consent form. It involves a highly stylized approach that is counter-effective because, inevitably in qualitative research, its usage breaks the trust between the researcher and the research participant. Its use, however, has a staying power in ethics regimes in Canada and elsewhere and continues to receive increasing attention in ethics codes. When one compares the first *Tri-Council Policy Statement* (*TCPS*) (MRC, NSERC, and SSHRC 1998) and the *TCPS 2* (CIHR, NSERC, and SSHRC 2010), one sees that while the first version refers to consent 210 times, the second refers to consent 388 times.

More important than the sizeable increase in numbers between these current and proposed guidelines is the idea that informed consent itself is the perceived lynchpin in the ethical conduct of all research. There is no application to an ethics committee that ignores informed consent. It is a boilerplate issue, ready to be invoked in any research, which, even in positivistic research, has problematic aspects. For example, a court case involving Arizona State University and the Havasupai Tribe in the Grand Canyon highlights the kind of research to which the tribe initially consented. Members had agreed to provide blood samples, but researchers took a further step by analyzing the blood samples, which the tribe had not consented to (Brinkerhoff 2010).

In the case of ethnographic research, Lesley Gotlib Conn, a self-described neophyte as a medical anthropologist, describes the painful uselessness of signed consent forms in her research on medical doctors, who interpreted her plan to use the forms as an inversion of the power and control that the doctors customarily exercise when they ask patients for their consent. She found that the ethics review procedures "drastically alter[ed] the epistemological relationship between the anthropologist and her informants, which has negative consequences for medical anthropologists in clinical field sites" (Gotlib Conn 2008, 500). The doctors saw themselves as "waiving control over [their own] involvement" in the study – the very opposite of the doctors' typical control of a research setting (ibid., 506). Prior to her plans of using consent forms, Gotlib Conn had a collaborative and productive relationship with the doctors as her research participants. After her pressing the doctors to sign the consent forms, some doctors withdrew from the study.

The need to obtain informed consent seems a compelling one, and it would be difficult to challenge such a need. However, there are natural limits in social research to obtaining consent. Section B in Chapter 3 of the *TCPS 2* (CIHR, NSERC, and SSHRC 2010) deals with departures from the general principles of consent. These departures are predicated on whether there is no more than minimal risk to participants, whether the welfare of research participants is not adversely affected, and whether the research design makes it impossible to carry out the research if consent is sought. Specifically, non-participant, covert, and observational research in public areas requires ethics committees to waive the need for consent so long as social researchers address concerns about privacy and confidentiality (ibid.). In another instance, field-work often involves initial visits to a setting to explore the feasibility of conducting a study where using consent forms is premature, especially if one has not yet committed himself or herself to that research setting. Researchers use these visits to sharpen their own understanding of the phenomenon or setting they hope to study. By far the most common practice is for researchers to take notes of settings or experiences that have not yet been formally selected as areas for research. Typically, researchers collect these notes, not knowing whether they serve as a launching pad for more formal research. Seeking consent of an individual in a crowd, in another locale, whose faces or identity researchers have either forgotten or never knew in the first place, makes informed consent work impossible or absurd.[14]

The Reluctance to Write Monographs

There is pressure on quantitative researchers for publications to appear in a "timely fashion" (CSA 2010, 59), and this pressure is seizing qualitative researchers. The proverbial trend toward "salami" publications in journals speaks to this urgent pressure. Salami publications involve cutting up one's research results into several publications or duplicating similar or near-similar publications to effect higher visibility of one's research either as part of one's career or within the discipline as a whole. This problem is so universal that at least seventy journals have devoted editorials to this phenomenon (Firth 2002, 1). While the trend started in the biomedical field, more and more social researchers are increasingly resorting to this practice. According to Ian MacLachlan (2010, 88), "many believe that research findings can and should be sliced and diced in as many different ways as possible to maximize the number of publications reporting the work." Ethnographic writing, which generally involves monographs or books, cuts across this trend and potentially reduces one's visibility.

The monograph, in particular the ethnography, remains one of the most influential segments of social research. *Contemporary Sociology*, the principal journal that publishes book reviews in sociology, conducted a long-range review of books in 1996. Of the nineteen most widely known books in sociology, there were ten ethnographies. A book based on the reviews in the same journal (Clawson 1998) discovered that, of the fifty-three sociology books with sales greater than fifty thousand, twenty-two were ethnographies. Ironically, systems that count citations completely ignore them in books (CSA 2010, 192), including monographs, despite the influential nature of ethnographic research.[15] The research and writing of a book can take between six and fifteen years, while writing articles occupies less time (although, within the disciplines, there are also considerable variations between ethnographic articles and more purely quantitatively driven ones).[16] In some respects, one might refer to the authoring of monographs as "total scholarship," something that one engages in through "slow scholarship."

Norms and Values

The final aspect of colonization involves internalizing neopositivist norms and values that also shape the ethical dimensions of qualitative research. Norms and values refer to goals. Norms are guidelines to everyday, routine goals of research while values concern overarching desired principles. Colonization imposes a panoply of norms and values. It redesigns qualitative research in ways that were not indigenous in that research, while it also signifies an attachment to overt expressions of a new allegiance. Norms and values embrace "rigour" in research, finding the "best practices," seeing ourselves primarily as "investigators" (rather than as "researchers"), establishing "audit trails," engaging in "evidence-based" research, and, finally, advocating "mixed methods." These notions are indeed quite foreign to qualitative researchers, but some resonate with the monitoring demands of the ethics regime. As Susan Boser (2007, 1060) avers, "the framework typically used by an IRB [institutional review board] for monitoring research ethics is predicated on postpositivist epistemological assumptions of a distanced objectivist research stance."

Rigour

In recent years, rigour has commanded considerable attention. Kristie Saumure and Lisa M. Given (2008, 795) claim that rigour depends on how transparent the research process is, whether it has achieved "maximal validity or credibility," or dependability and reflexivity, among other things. Health researchers in particular see an urgent need to ground their qualitative research in rigour. Some scholars argue that qualitative research can be made rigorous and suggest research strategies to achieve rigour to assess the trustworthiness or merit of qualitative research (Sandelowski 1986; Krefting 1991). Interestingly, even those who argue that rigour is not applicable in qualitative research (such as Davies and Dodd 2002) suggest alternative strategies in qualitative research that could meet the standards of rigour – namely, attentiveness, empathy, carefulness, sensitivity, respect, and reflection, among others. Still, Deidre Davies and Jenny Dodd frame their list of qualities as a compensation for rigour, which, after all, seems to remain as the standard.

Audit Trails

In the search for rigour, some qualitative researchers now advocate "audit trails" that consist of a "thorough collection of documentation regarding all aspects of the research" (Rodgers 2008, 43). This approach seems particularly attractive to some qualitative researchers in nursing, such as Beth Rodgers, who sees audit trails as a means of providing justifications for decisions that researchers take while doing the research. They are, in effect, retroactive assessments. The auditor looks at documentation, field notes, and "notes about data collection experiences," (ibid.) changes in design, and memos, among other things.

The work of an auditor can be vast. The data I collected for one of my later research projects for my book *The Seduction of Ethics* (2011) cover at least two thousand pages of notes, four hundred pages of interview transcripts, and at least two metre stacks of official documents, not to mention another three metres of files in a filing cabinet. Aside from the fact that it is not possible to record every research decision, whether large or small, it would be exceedingly difficult and time-consuming to detail all the decisions that helped me interpret the data or helped me make decisions before I started gathering the data. The audit trail would also have to include a close examination of how my data have found their way into the writing of *The Seduction of Ethics* and into a number of other publications. How long would it take for an auditor to mount a trail covering research that took six years to conduct? In the final analysis, whose interpretation could be genuinely counted as valid? Would audit trails make the research rigorous, an ostensible goal for those who adopt a positivist cloak of research? The problematique of audit trails is well worth a separate chapter or article.

Evidence-Based Research

As a rule, the origins of evidence-based research lie in "the care of patients using the best of the growing volume of available research evidence to guide clinical decision making" (Spinal Cord Injury Network 2010). A key article on the subject (Sackett et al. 1996, 71) best summarizes evidence-based medicine as "the conscientious, explicit, and judicious use of current best evidence in making decisions about the care of individual patients." Its connection to clinical practice is a paramount part of its decision. The desire to mount evidence-based research has its roots in political, ethical, practical, educational, and ideological considerations. Evidence-based practice dates back to the nineteenth century, but with the rise of policy research since the early 1990s, it has gained renewed attention (Clark 2008, 308). Policymakers see "randomized control trials and/or systematic reviews as the strongest, most reliable forms of evidence" (ibid., 309). Clark couches his pitch toward fuller inclusion of strategies in positivist research by framing it in terms of expectations of research-funding bodies and public policy. The concept of knowledge translation, however, is so firmly rooted in the medical perspective that it is difficult to appreciate that qualitative researchers are more likely to turn such studies upside down: instead of investigating how clinicians can translate medical knowledge to the bedside, qualitative researchers explore how the experience and knowledge of patients can or should also travel up the hierarchical chain of knowledge, specifically from the bedside to the medical researcher (see, e.g., van den Hoonaard 2009).

The universal acceptance of knowledge translation involves a specific social theoretical perspective in health research that discounts the research participants' perspective of their world but adheres, instead, to an approach more amenable to medical research. Increasingly, certain facets of social research are rejecting the "top-down" model of knowledge translation. Research in Aboriginal communities and more generally community-based research take the perspective that knowledge comes from the communities themselves, not from the experts. Ultimately, one must pose the question: on whose perspective should evidence in research be based?

Mixed Methods

Increasingly, researchers are trying to shoehorn the discourse on quantitative versus qualitative research into research that embodies mixed methods.[17] The intent is to validate qualitative research, especially when it can be pursued within a framework that privileges quantitative research. The attempt to bridge the gap seems laudable but it faces inherent challenges. When one contrasts talk by quantitative and qualitative researchers, it becomes apparent that the former see themselves as using the dominant, "natural" model for doing scientific work. The talk assumes an ideological character, evoking "feeling rules," which Arlie Hochschild (1979, 561-75) describes as the underside of ideology: the object of attention by the dominant group is the members of the group with less power who are then expected to demonstrate the proper "feeling rules," regardless of how one feels. Feeling rules, according to Hochschild (1983, 56), "are what guide emotion work by establishing the sense of entitlement or obligation that governs emotional exchanges."

As Martha McMahon and Sheryl Kleinman (1995, 19) remind us, qualitative researchers feel a moral pressure to present themselves as methodological pluralists to conduct research on the terms of the dominant group. However, qualitative researchers lose their authenticity as they try to grapple with competing demands about their methodology, and thereby violate the ethical integrity of their research. Interestingly enough, it is the quantitative researchers wanting to "make us feel at home" who go to great lengths to claim that the boundaries between interpretative and positivistic paradigms are a chimera and are, in fact, "unnecessary and unhelpful" (ibid.). When qualitative researchers do assert epistemological differences, they are "accused of methodological arrogance" (ibid.). Qualitative researchers become the "unsociable sociologists who refuse others' welcoming overtures." McMahon and Kleinman remind us that "talk of partnership among unequals can become epistemetically and ethically disempowering for the less powerful partner" (ibid.).

Crystallization of the Colonization Process

Not unlike the colonization in a new political landscape, a certain amount of crystallization occurs for the colonizing process to take hold. What processes stand affiliated with crystallization? On one hand, the bureaucratization of the research ethics review system solidifies the incursions made by the dominant positivistic frames into areas inhabited by qualitative research. On the other hand, the perception that knowledge can or should be commodified moves qualitative research into the dominant paradigm too.[18]

Despite our not knowing the precise number of research ethics boards (I estimate three hundred in Canada, and Hamilton [2005, 192] estimates there are three thousand to five thousand in the United States),[19] we do know of the tremendous amount of resources that universities must pour into the functioning of local ethics review regimes, whether making physical spaces available, having a salaried staff at an ethics or research office, or paying for all the accoutrements related to communications, meetings, and the like. These investments of resources, money, and time result in obligations that create a unique space in which researchers are "being worked over" by that space, rather than allowing researchers to position themselves to "work within, and on" (Cheek 2007, 1051-52).

As it currently stands, researchers believe that they ought to comply with the dictates of ethics committees even though those dictates might compromise their research. Moreover, the particular configuration of membership of ethics review committees also plays a hand in redirecting the epistemology and methodology of social research. Self-censorship, too, has become a key factor. REBs develop checklists and flow paths for easier assessments of very diverse research activities on campus. It is inevitable that the biomedical perspective, with its hypotheses, clinical trials, and deductive reasoning, shapes these processes. Only the rare REB can step outside these dominant perspectives.

The conditions that promote colonization of social research ethics also involve the commodification of knowledge and the development of competing obligations to pursue capital-intensive research and satisfy the demands of ethics review committees. The analogy to colonizing a country is remarkable: the developed world sees no use for resources if they cannot be commodified. Similarly, the more persistent and dominant ideology of seeing knowledge as a commodity is submerging the intrinsic value of research. Some researchers believe that these compromises are a relatively small burden to bear when measured against the need to get on with the research, get research grants, employ students, uphold careerism, and qualify for tenure. Others aver that grantsmanship has suffused scholarship with competition and materialism, leaving little room for contemplation and introspection or even time to do proper research.[20]

Conclusion

Inevitably, a dominant school of thought will colonize a peripheral one. This chapter suggests that ethics regimes display ethical conundrums because they reflect concerns in positivist disciplines that have begun to inhabit qualitative research. What facilitates the process of colonization, as I have noted, is the ready adoption by qualitative researchers themselves of the culture, symbols, and norms and values of the dominant, positivist paradigm. In the case of culture, qualitative researchers resort to using language, speech, and terms that resonate with positivist researchers. Regarding symbols, qualitative researchers find themselves adopting the use of consent forms while also redirecting their energies from writing ethnographies to so-called salami publications. In terms of the newly acquired norms and values, qualitative researchers now pay heightened attention to rigour in their research, develop audit trails, and promote evidence-based and mixed-methods research.

There is a way out of this dilemma. At the bureaucratic level, the Ethics Rupture Summit, held in Fredericton, New Brunswick, in October 2012, showed that some elements in ethics codes were negotiable while others were not. Social researchers, for example, could rely on ethics committees to negotiate the start and end days of projects, the number of research participants, or the length of interviews. Such things as informed consent, however, are usually not negotiable. More significantly, however, the summit pointed to the desperate need for ethics committees to treat researchers in the same way that committees expect researchers to treat research participants. Describing the outcomes of the summit in his blog, Zachary Shrag wrote, "It's only a page long and therefore hardly bears summarizing, but I would note its desire to 'encourage regulators and administrators to nurture a regulatory culture that grants researchers the same level of respect that researchers should offer research participants.' That shouldn't be a radical demand, but it is."[21] The ethics summit formally produced the "New Brunswick Declaration on Ethics in Research and Governance," which not only outlined the central, ethical path ethics committees need to follow (which involves treating researchers with respect), but also incorporated other elements that could undo the colonization of social research by medical researcher paradigms.[22] For example, the declaration points to the importance of presenting critical and analytical ideas whenever policymakers present emerging policy concepts so as to generate thoughtful and analytically informed discussion. Ethics is always about human relationships. If such a premise is ignored, the ethics review procedure falls short of its intended aim to stimulate a culture of ethics. On this point, it is noteworthy that the TCPS 2 requires researchers to follow at least twenty-three personal virtues, but does not specify any such virtues for individual members of REBs (although it does assign some virtues to REBs as a body [W.C. van den Hoonaard 2013]).

On an individual level, qualitative researchers cannot easily reject or dismiss the practices associated with positivist research in light of the weight given to them by ethics regimes. However, one can hope that the current crisis as a result of the colonization process might also yield a refurbishing of social research, leading to new methods and practices beyond the pale of neo-positivism. Researchers can exercise a modicum of choice but, for now, the choice is personal. Although some may regard these choices as acts of resistance, others, like me, see them as a reaffirmation of traditional values associated with qualitative research. Interpretive scholars can choose to publish in journals that discourage the use of the passive voice. They can procure more modest grants without the fanfare of capital-intensive research. They can engage in "self-work," and commit themselves to doing their own data gathering and analysis. These efforts, however, may come at a great sacrifice, and because the burden falls primarily on younger or novice scholars, senior scholars who are already tenured have the paramount duty to mount the kind of resistance that would help their junior colleagues.

Researchers need to remind themselves that, without raising their voices, the culture of positivism will leave social research pauperized and homogenized. Ironically, the much-vaunted interdisciplinary or multidisciplinary approaches bring together the more popular forms of research, such as doing interviews, and minimize the value of research approaches that are traditionally associated with qualitative research, such as participant observation and more explorative and contemplative research that go beyond the artificially set starting dates and end periods of research. Neopositivism, through ethics codes regimes, is pulling qualitative research from its moorings of slow and total scholarship, colonizing it. Sadly, qualitative researchers themselves are facilitating this process.

Acknowledgments

I wish to thank Dr. Andrew Achenbaum of the University of Houston and Dr. Deborah K. van den Hoonaard of St. Thomas University, Fredericton, New Brunswick, for their helpful comments on earlier drafts of this chapter. I also wish to acknowledge the Social Sciences and Humanities Research Council for a grant (No. 410-2003-0318) that I received in conjunction with doing an ethnography on research ethics committees.

Notes

1 My chapter uses the term *positivist research standards,* although several other terms come to mind, too, such as *biomedical research, traditional scientific outlooks,* and so on. I use *neopositivism* when I want to emphasize the contemporary recrudescence of belief in positivist research standards.

2 After Canada's Interagency Panel on Research Ethics issued an appeal to receive comments about the 1998 version of the *Tri-Council Policy Statement: Ethical Conduct for Research involving Humans (TCPS)* on 1 August 2003, it received 60 submissions, which represented 60 departmental chairs, 1,400 professors, and 5,000 academic association members (a total of 6,400 individuals) who expressed an overwhelming desire to have the *TCPS* move away from its biomedical template when discussing research in the social sciences and humanities. Chapter 10 of *TCPS 2* incorporates many of the suggestions.

3 Management researchers also see ethics codes lacking relevant parameters for them (Bell and Bryman 2007).

4 Using direct quotes is something quite familiar to qualitative researchers; it conveys the embedded meanings of the quoted author more faithfully or evocatively than paraphrasing.

5 Even in total institutions, inmates engage in practices that allow them to "obtain forbidden satisfactions" (Goffman 1961, 54). However, many practices ("secondary adjustments") do

not directly challenge the staff of an institution. Similarly, social researchers find ways of subtly changing the demands of research ethics review without necessarily resisting it openly.

6   I discuss the role of performative language in greater detail in van den Hoonaard (2010).

7   I think the researcher has meant to say "positivist" rather than "post-positivist." The latter would include qualitative research, and, from the context, one gathers that is not what the author had intended to say. It is a common error.

8   Mertens and Ginsberg (2008, 486) make the case that ethical issues involving "power, consent, confidentiality and beneficence" take on a particular meaning when one is researching "communities who are pushed to the margins of society, either by virtue of an inherent characteristic associated with stigma, discrimination and oppression."

9   *Oxford English Dictionary,* 2nd ed., s.v. "protocol."

10   *Random House Dictionary of the English Language,* 2nd ed., s.v. "protocol."

11   "Definition: Best Practice," Tech Target, February 2007, http://searchsoftwarequality. techtarget.com/definition/best-practice.

12   I thank Dr. Deborah van den Hoonaard, Canada Research Chair in Qualitative Research and Analysis, St. Thomas University, Fredericton, NB, for sharing her insights on this topic.

13   *Wikipedia,* s.v. "principal investigator," http://en.wikipedia.org/wiki/Principal_investigator (last modified 1 January 2014).

14   Kakali Bhattacharya (2007) offers a number of interesting insights about the informed consent form process, outlining a number of difficulties in the field.

15   Along those lines, one notes that of the 17,124 journals ranked in 2008 by SCImago Research Group (http://www.scimagojr.com/) there is not one social sciences or humanities journal listed in the top one thousand. Another interesting aside: the so-called common CV, used by Canada's research-granting agencies to "manage ... CV data in a single repository and generate multiple CVs to member organizations" ("Canadian Common CV," https://ccv-cvc.ca/indexresearcher-eng.frm), downplays entries related to ethnographies because one's scholarly activity is considered in relation to that of biomedical researchers, not social scientists. The common CV accords the writing of monographs a minor place in the hierarchy of scholarly activities and displaces fundamental aspects of social research, such as the production of full-length monographs, which often alone can encapsulate the full research experience writing about social settings.

16   Vicki Smith (2002, 228) looked at the fieldwork behind fifty research monographs and discovered that it took 8.14 years on average after the start of field work to see its appearance as a book. For anthropology, the figure is even higher – specifically, 10.7 years. It is this intensity of time and energy that would entail ever-shifting aspects of the ethical dimensions in one's field work. Arlie R. Hochschild's 1989 study *The Second Shift,* arguably one of the most influential studies of the past thirty years, about how couples share housework took six years to publish after thirteen years of field work. Daniel R. Wolf took three years to do field research among outlaw bikers, but it took fifteen years before his book, *The Rebels* (1991), appeared in print. Studying student culture took Cheryl and Dan Albas (see, e.g., 2009) more than twenty-five years of detailed observation and recording.

17   Research involving mixed methods can evoke ambiguity. Some researchers employ both qualitative and quantitative methods, but they do so more in a parallel fashion. Each method does not inform the other as different arms of the project specialize in one method or the other. Still, for all intents and purposes, researchers style this research as using so-called mixed methods.

18   Positivism is not always synonymous with biomedical research. We see more and more biomedical researchers using narratives. Ethnography is not synonymous with qualitative research. Much of qualitative research eschews field research; some qualitative researchers do not regard content analysis as part of qualitative research.

19 Cary Nelson's (2004, 209) estimate comes close to this figure: in 2000, there were four thousand IRBs in the United States, mainly in universities, hospitals, and private research facilities.

20 A contemporary example where a university encourages contemplation and a slowing down of scholarship is Naropa University, a Buddhist-inspired institution in Boulder, Colorado (Overall 2010).

21 Zachary Shrag, "New Brunswick Declaration Seeks Respect for Researchers and Participants," *Institutional Review Blog,* 26 February 2013, http://www.institutionalreview-blog.com/.

22 See the declaration at http://the-sra.org.uk/sra_resources/research-ethics/the-new-brunswick -declaration/.

References

AAUP (American Association of University Professors). (2001). Protecting Human Beings: Institutional Review Boards and Social Science Research. http://www.aaup.org/IRBCdoc. htm.

Albas, D., and Albas, C. (1989). Modern Magic: The Case of Examinations. *Sociological Quarterly 30*(4), 603-13.

–. (2009). University Student Life and Exams: A "Behind the Scenes" Look at Concept Building and Concept Expansion. In W. Shaffir, A. Puddephatt, and S. Kleinknecht (Eds.), *Ethnographies Revisited: The Stories Behind the Story* (105-20). London: Routledge.

Becker, H.S. (1986). *Writing for Social Scientists: How to Start and Finish Your Thesis, Book, or Article.* Chicago: University of Chicago Press.

–. (2001). The Epistemology of Qualitative Research. In R.M. Emerson (Ed.), *Contemporary Field Research: Perspectives and Formulations* (2nd ed.) (317-30). Long Grove, IL: Waveland Press.

Bell, E., and Bryman, A. (2007). The Ethics of Management Research: An Exploratory Content Analysis. *British Journal of Management 18*(1), 63-77.

Bhattacharya, K. (2007). Consenting to the Consent Form: What Are the Fixed and Fluid Under-standings between the Researcher and the Researched? *Qualitative Inquiry 13*(8), 1095-115.

Boser, S. (2007). Power, Ethics, and the IRB Dissonance over Human Participant Review of Participatory Research. *Qualitative Inquiry 13*(8), 1060-74.

Bosk, C.L., and De Vries, R.G. (2004). Bureaucracies of Mass Deception: Institutional Review Boards and the Ethics of Ethnographic Research. *Annals of the American Academy of Political and Social Science 595*(1), 249-63.

Brinkerhoff, N. (2010). Arizona Tribe Wins First Case Involving Misuse of DNA in Research, 23 April. http://www.allgov.com/.CCA (Canadian Council of Academies). Report of the Expert Panel on Research Integrity Honesty and Trust: Research Integrity in Canada. 5 May. Unpublished report.

Cheek, J. (2007). Qualitative Inquiry, Ethics, and Politics of Evidence: Working within These Spaces Rather Than Being Worked over by Them. *Qualitative Inquiry 13*(8), 1051-59.

CIHR, NSERC, and SSHRC (Canadian Institutes of Health Research, Natural Sciences and Engineering Research Council of Canada, and Social Sciences and Humanities Research Council of Canada). (2010). *The Tri-Council Policy Statement: Ethical Conduct for Research Involving Humans.* Ottawa: Department of Supply and Services.

Clark, A.M. (2008). Evidence-Based Practice. *International Encyclopaedia of Qualitative Research* (vol. 1, 308-11). Thousand Oaks, CA: Sage.

Clawson, D. (1998). *Required Reading: Sociology's Most Influential Books.* Boston: University of Massachusetts Press.

Cline, A.R. (2002). Understand and Act: Classical Rhetoric, Speech Acts, and the Teaching of Critical Democratic Participation. PhD diss., University of Missouri.

CSA (Canadian Sociological Association). (2010). Research Notes: 45 Years of the *Canadian Review of Sociology (and Anthropology)*. *Canadian Review of Sociology* 47(2), 191-97.

Davies, D., and Dodd, J. (2002). Qualitative Research and the Question of Rigor. *Qualitative Health Research* 12(2), 279-89.

De Vries, R., and Forsberg, C. (2002). What Do IRBs Look Like? What Kind of Support Do They Receive? *Accountability in Research: Policies and Quality Assurance* 9(3-4), 199-216.

Ferrell, J., and Hamm, M.S. (Eds). (1998). *Ethnography at the Edge: Crime, Deviance, and Field Research*. Boston: Northeastern University Press.

Figaredo, D.D. (2006). Educational Ethnography beyond Scholarly Ethnography: Transferring Meanings to Cyberspace. Review of Honorio M. Velasco Maillo, F. Javier García Castaño and Ángel Díaz de Rada (Eds.) (2003). Lecturas de antropología para educadores: El ámbito de la antropología de la educación y de la etnografía escolar [Readings on anthropology for educating: The field of educational anthropology and scholar ethnography]. *FQS: Forum: Qualitative Social Research / SozialForschung* 7(2), Art. 2.

Firth, A.Y. (2002). Editorial Stance on Duplicate and Salami Publication [Editorial]. *British Orthoptic Journal* 59, 1-2.

Goffman, E. (1961). *Asylum: Essays on the Social Situation of Mental Patients and Other Inmates*. Garden City, NY: Anchor Books.

Gotlib Conn, L. (2008). Ethics Policy as Audit in Canadian Clinical Settings: Exiling the Ethnographic Method. *Qualitative Research* 8(4), 499-514.

Haas, J., and Shaffir, W. (2009). *Becoming Doctors: The Adoption of a Cloak of Competence*. Cowichan Bay, BC: Jack Haas Printing.

Halse, C., and Honey, A. (2007). Rethinking Ethics Review as Institutional Discourse. *Qualitative Inquiry* 13(3), 336-52.

Hamilton, A. (2002). Institutional Review Boards: Politics, Power, Purpose and Process in a Regulatory Organization. PhD diss., University of Oklahoma.

–. (2005). The Development and Operation of IRBs: Medical Regulations and Social Science. *Journal of Applied Communication Research* 33(3), 189-203.

Hauck, R. J-P. (2008). Symposium: Protecting Human Research Participants, IRBs, and Political Science Redux [Editor's introduction]. American Political Science Association. www.apsanet.org/.

Hemmings, A. (2006). Great Ethical Divides: Bridging the Gap between Institutional Review Boards and Researchers. *Educational Researcher* 35(4), 12-18.

Hewitt, J.P. (2007). *Self and Society: A Symbolic Interactionist Social Psychology* (10th ed). Boston: Allyn and Bacon.

Hochschild, A.R. (1979). Emotion Work, Feeling Rules and Social Structure. *American Journal of Sociology* 85, 551-75.

–. (1983). *The Managed Heart: Commercialization of Human Feeling*. Berkeley: University of California Press.

–. (1989). *The Second Shift: Working Parents and the Revolution at Home*. New York: Avon.

Kellner, F. (2002). Yet Another Current Crisis: The Ethics of Conduct and Representation in Fieldwork-Dependent Social Science. In W.C. van den Hoonaard (Ed.), *Walking the Tightrope: Ethical Issues for Qualitative Researchers* (48-62). Toronto: University of Toronto Press.

Krefting, L. (1991). Rigor in Qualitative Research: The Assessment of Trustworthiness. *American Journal of Occupational Therapy* 45(3), 214-22.

MacLachlan, I. (2010). Tips for Journal Contributors. *University Affairs / Affaires universitaires* 51(8), 88.

Mäkelä, K. (2006). Ethical Control of Social Research: Rules of Research Ethics and Their Interpretation. *Nordisk Alkohol and Narkotika Tidskrift* 23 (English Supplement), 5-19.

McMahon, M., and Kleinman, S. (1995). Mixing Methods: Inclusiveness or Cooptation. *Abstracts of the Canadian Qualitative Analysis Conference*. McMaster University, Hamilton, ON, 19-20 May.

Mertens, D.M., and Ginsberg, P.E. (2008). Deep in Ethical Waters: Transformative Perspectives for Qualitative Social Work Research. *Qualitative Social Work 7*, 484-503.

MRC, NSERC, and SSHRC (Medical Research Council of Canada, Natural Sciences and Engineering Research Council, and the Social Sciences and Humanities Research Council). (1998). *Tri-Council Policy Statement: Ethical Conduct for Research Involving Humans*. Ottawa: Department of Supply and Services.

NCA (National Communication Association). (2005).Communication Scholars' Narratives of IRB Experiences. *Journal of Applied Communication Research 33*(3), 204-30.

Nelson, C. (2004). The Brave New World of Research Surveillance. *Qualitative Inquiry 10*(2), 207-18.

NSF (National Science Foundation). (2002). "NSF 02-151 July 2002 Chapter II – NSF Awards: Definitions." *Grant Policy Manual*. http://www.nsf.gov/.

Paluck, E.L. (2010). The Promising Integration of Qualitative Methods and Field Experiments. *Annals of the American Academy of Political and Social Science 628*(1), 59-71.

PRE (Interagency Advisory Panel on Research Ethics). (2009). Draft 2nd Edition of the Tri-Council Policy Statement: Ethical Conduct for Research Involving Humans (*TCPS*). http://www.pre.ethics.gc.ca/.

Overall, C. (2010).The Non-Tech Classroom: A Place to Talk, to Write, to Listen. *University Affairs 51*(9), 42.

Richardson, S., and McMullan, M. (2007). Research Ethics in the UK: What Can Sociology Learn from Health? *Sociology 41*(6), 1115-32.

Rodgers, B.L. (2008). Audit Trail. *International Encyclopaedia of Qualitative Research* (Vol. 1, 43-44). Thousand Oaks, CA: Sage.

Sackett, D.L., Rosenberg, W.M., Gray, J.M., Haynes, R.B., and Richardson, W.S. (1996). Evidence-Based Medicine: What It Is and What It Isn't. *British Medical Journal 312*(7032), 71-72.

Sandelowski, M. (1986). The Problem of Rigor in Qualitative Research. *Advances in Nursing Science 8*(3), 27-37.

Saumure, K., and Given, L.M. (2008). Rigour in Qualitative Research. In L.M. Given (Ed.), *The Sage Encyclopedia of Qualitative Research Methods* (Vol. 2, 795-96). Los Angeles, CA: Sage.

Shaw, I. (2008). Ethics and the Practice of Qualitative Research. *Qualitative Social Work 7*, 400-14.

Silva, F.L. (2008). Methodological Procedures and Ethical Decisions. *Ciênca and Saúde Coletiva 13*(2), 324-28.

Smith, V. (2002). Ethnographies of Work and the Work of Ethnographers. In P. Atkinson, A. Coffey, S. Delamont, J. Lofland, and L. Lofland (Eds.), *Handbook of Ethnography* (220-33). London: Sage.

Spinal Cord Injury Network. (2010). Glossary. https://spinalnetwork.org.au/node/64.

SSHWC (Social Sciences and Humanities Research Ethics Special Working Committee). (2004). *Giving Voice to the Spectrum: Report of the Social Sciences and Humanities Research Ethics Special Working Committee*. June. Ottawa: Interagency Advisory Panel and Secretariat on Research Ethics. http://pre.ethics.gc.ca/english/workgroups/sshwc/SSHWCVoiceReport June2004.pdf.

Tilley, S.A., and Gormley, L. (2007). Canadian University Ethics Review: Cultural Complications Translating Principles into Practice. *Qualitative Inquiry 13*(3), 368-87.

Tolich, M., and Fitzgerald, M.H. (2006). If Ethics Committees Were Designed for Ethnography. *Journal of Empirical Research on Human Research Ethics 1*(2), 71-78.

van den Hoonaard, D.K. (2009). Moving toward a Three-Way Intersection in Translational Research: A Sociological Perspective. *Qualitative Health Research 19*, 1783-87.

van den Hoonaard, W.C. (2011). *The Seduction of Ethics: The Transformation of the Social Sciences through Ethics Review.* Toronto: University of Toronto Press.

–. (2010). An Idiosyncratic and Inconsistent World: Exploring Communications between Ethics Committees and Researchers. Paper presented at the 27th Qualitative Analysis Conference, "Social Pragmatism as a Conceptual Foundation," Wilfrid Laurier University, Brantford, Ontario, 13-15 May.

–. (2013). Are We Asked to "Other" Ourselves? Social Scientists and the Research-Ethics Review Process. Paper presented at Symposium II (Values), Generic Ethics Principles in Social Research, Academy of Social Sciences, London, England, 15 April.

Wolf, D. (1991). *The Rebels: A Brotherhood of Outlaw Bikers.* Toronto: University of Toronto Press.

chapter 9

Fighting the Big Bad Wolf: Why All the Fuss about Ethics Review Boards?

Maritza Felices-Luna

As RESEARCHERS, WE OFTEN moan and roll our eyes at the thought of having our projects go through ethics review boards (ERBs). They are seen by some as unnecessary, irrelevant, and obstructive (Nelkin 1994) and by others as a mere formality, even a hurdle to conducting our research (Guillemin and Gillam 2004). Yet these boards were established as a means to avoid questionable practices by medical and military research as well as by social science researchers (Pimple 2008; Speiglman and Spear 2009).[1] Given the long list of infamous cases, it would be difficult to argue against the need for a mechanism to prevent or at least reduce the possibility of harming, causing distress, or publicly embarrassing unwilling or unknowing subjects. So why do researchers, particularly those in the social sciences working with qualitative methodologies and nonpositivist epistemologies, dread applying for ethics approval?[2] Why do we react negatively to ERBs? The argument I develop in this chapter is twofold. First, ERBs in their current form are usually not equipped to deal with ethical issues that arise in qualitative, nonpositivist research.[3] Second, ERBs, in some instances and unbeknownst to their members, play a significant role in influencing the type of research produced and therefore the type of scientific discourses that are allowed to exist and circulate. An alternative logic to the current procedural and absolute approach to ethics is possible, however, if ERBs instead aim to develop a negotiated ethics based on principles of mutual moral responsibility.

Fearing the Wolf in Sheep's Clothing

Precisely because ERBs developed in response to the harm and exploitation of vulnerable populations by biomedical research, ethical principles were constructed to regulate biomedical and other experimental research (Pimple 2008). Therefore, the positivist epistemology and quantitative methodology that characterize biomedical research shaped and defined ERBs' philosophy (van den Hoonaard 2002). ERBs are ill-equipped and in some instances not equipped at all to deal with what they consider to be nontraditional research models (Lincoln and Tierney 2004).[4] Although there are some attempts to accommodate qualitative research, accommodation is usually an exception to the "normal" procedure. For instance, Canada's *Tri-Council Policy Statement: Ethical Conduct on Research Involving Humans* dedicates one chapter to issues specific to qualitative research. This demonstrates that research policy that is established according to one model is assumed to be applicable to other models, less minor tweaking. Furthermore, attempts to regulate ethics in qualitative research are often unsuccessful because committees frequently lack the necessary expertise (Speiglman and Spear 2009), which leaves them wary and skeptical of nontraditional methodologies as an "unknown entity" (Allen 2009, 401).

The positivistic model of science and the underlying logic of quantitative methodology have been built into the way that ERBs think about ethics in research, and, as a result, "ethics and models of science now flow into one another. IRB [Institutional Review Board] panels can simultaneously rule on research that is ethically sound, and of high quality" (Denzin 2009, 144). This means that ERBs establish not only what is ethical but also the proper and effective way to conduct research (Gotlib Conn 2008). This can be seen in the fact that ERBs tend to demand that applicants think and "speak white"[5] – in other words, formulate their projects using the logic and language of positivist or postpositivist paradigms (see van den Hoonaard, this volume). When projects do not correspond to this logic and language, ERBs attempt to render them more conventional – that is, positivist (Lincoln and Tierney 2004) – by influencing methodological procedures (Denzin 2009; Lincoln 2009) and requesting significant modifications to the project (Speiglman and Spear 2009). A common suggestion is to change the methodological tools and adopt "transparent" techniques such as questionnaires or surveys that can be reviewed by authorities and ERBs instead of the more "obscure" and unpredictable semi-structured or unstructured qualitative interview guides, observational fieldwork, or ethnography.

Through these solutions, ERBs shape how research is conducted and establish what constitutes good or meaningful research. As a result, they implicitly hamper, if not censor, nontraditional research (Haggerty 2004) and even silence certain researchers and potential participants[6] (Cheek 2003). If we accept that scientific knowledge serves specific interests (Baarts 2009) and protects the "sacred quality of certain social arrangements and conventions" (Nelkin 1994, 365), by granting or refusing approval of research projects, ERBs are (consciously or not, willingly or not) serving the administrative function of knowledge gatekeepers (Gotlib Conn 2008). Thus, ERBs can be thought of as political entities that, tainted by ideology, limit academic freedom (Gotlib Conn 2008): they structure which truth can be spoken and by whom (Librett and Perrone 2010). This can have a paralyzing effect on nontraditional projects as researchers might opt for "easy" choices to avoid potential difficulties with ERBs (Haggerty 2004; Speiglman and Spear 2009).[7]

Although the way ERBs think of research is closely linked to a positivistic model of science, the driving force behind them seems to be a concern over legal matters and pursuits (see Ogden, this volume; Lowman and Palys, this volume). As a result, ERBs have become liability-oriented (Adler and Adler 2002; Gotlib Conn 2008) bureaucracies (Haggerty 2004; Librett and Perrone 2010) performing institutional risk management assessments (Speiglman and Spear 2009) to protect their institution (Christians 2003; Lincoln and Tierney 2004) from legal repercussions through an arbitrary process (Israel and Hay 2006).[8] In other words, ERBs appear to use policing and legalistic solutions to ethical problems (Johnson and Altheide 2002), which is a narrow and inadequate view of ethics for many researchers (Muzychka et al. 1996; Pimple 2008).

The creation of ERBs has resulted in "discourses of ethics folding or collapsing into discourses of institutional control" (Johnson and Altheide 2002, 59). The individual's ability to pursue research is hindered by the hegemonic relationship between the state and scholarship (Goode 2001). ERBs' efforts to disguise their "hierarchical and paternalistic roots" as well as downplay their "coercive and punitive implications" have failed (Shore and Wright 1999, 59). Governmental ethics regimes are now recognized as a form of scientific governance (Braun et al. 2010) where ERBs are part of a system of government (Librett and Perrone 2010) that dictates researcher conduct and research possibilities (Allen 2009). Furthermore, ERBs have grown and extended their mandate from funded research to nonfunded research (Guillemin and Gillam 2004), from biomedical research to the social sciences (Bosk and De Vries 2004), and from academic research to the teaching of methods (Nelson 2004). This process is known as "mission creep" or "ethics creep," given that ERBs are going outside their mandate to include new activities and institutions as well as intensifying the regulation of activities within their mandate (Haggerty 2004; Lincoln 2009; Librett and Perrone 2010).

The current approach to research ethics is the basis of some social scientists' and qualitative researchers' fear of the wolf in sheep's clothing: claiming the need for research ethics (something most researchers would favour), research governing agencies have created a regulatory body (ERBs) whose powers can lead to the marginalization and even delegitimation of nontraditional research or alternative scientific models and, by extension, the knowledges they produce.

Inadequacies with the Current Model

ERBs have the mandate to deal with two fundamental questions: the ethical way of collecting, processing, and reporting data and the ethical way for researchers to behave toward participants (Kitchener and Kitchener 2009). In order to deal with those issues, ERBs have attempted to identify the underlying "law" of ethical research to predict, evaluate, and control ethics. As a result, ERBs have established a series of highly structured procedures based on objectivized relationships (Bosk and DeVries 2004). By adopting a procedural form of ethics, codified by experts and informed through policy research, ethical research no longer signifies morality and ethics, given that the discursive and subjective quality that defines them is lost (Gotlib Conn 2008). In fact, the term *ethics* seems to have been coopted by institutional and administrative bodies. Consequently, researchers opting for nontraditional methodologies and epistemologies believe that, in their current form, ERBs are ill-equipped to address the complex ethical issues involved in their research (see also Perron, Holmes, and Jacob, this volume).

In the following pages, I draw on my experiences researching political violence and armed conflict to discuss more in-depth what I consider to be the most salient inadequacies of the current model.[9] I call attention to issues that are not addressed by ERBs or that are inappropriately, inadequately, or insufficiently addressed.

Loopholes in the Three Keystone Ethical Principles

The key ethical principles can be summarized thusly: (1) research should not cause harm to participants (in response to researchers who infected people with syphilis and other viruses and to Nazi experiments on exposure to the natural elements); (2) participants should be involved in the research voluntarily (in response to research done with captive and/or vulnerable populations such as prisoners, the mentally ill, and orphans); and (3) participants should be thoroughly informed of the procedures and the associated risks so that they can give informed consent (in response to research where people were deceived, as in the Milgram experiment).

Explicit loopholes exist for principles one and three: if we prove that it is absolutely necessary to cause harm or to deceive participants, we will be allowed to do so after a risk/benefit analysis is conducted by the ERB. With regard to the second principle, the loophole is embedded in the principle itself because it is impossible to ensure that research participation is voluntary rather than out of need, implicit coercion, or the belief that by appearing collaborative the participant will get something in return. For example, while I was studying in Montreal, I encountered flyers posted by a firm that offered one million dollars to cut off and reattach a pinkie finger and one hundred thousand dollars to allow your heart to be stopped and restarted. Although as a student I did briefly consider how attached I was to my little finger, I find it hard to believe that individuals would freely have their finger cut off or their heart stopped out of sheer scientific devotion rather than economic need. Granted, participants are still "choosing" how to solve their economic need; however, we fail to see many people, particularly those with economic resources, queuing up as volunteers.

What about the less controversial twenty or fifty dollars offered for participating in an interview? This practice opens up a whole other array of ethical issues. For instance, when I was interviewing women who had been involved in the Peruvian and Irish struggles, I had to decide whether it was ethical for me to give money to people who were talking about their involvement in activities that had resulted in the pain and suffering of others. In the Democratic Republic of Congo (DRC), I had to consider the ethical consequences of giving money to participants when local researchers do not have the economic resources to do so. Given the existing social practice of giving people money for "transportation" (which is the socially correct way of tipping someone without insulting them), the problem was not in the giving of money but in the amount that should be given to ensure that I would not jeopardize the ability of local researchers to get participants in the future.[10] I was also confronted with the difficulty of compensating participants of evidently very different social classes to whom the amount given would not have the same meaning: should I give the same amount to all or should I give different amounts according to their social ranking? The first option risked insulting those who belonged to the upper classes by giving them five dollars; the second option meant creating or at least reinforcing the idea that the upper classes deserve more than the lower classes for participating in the same activity.

Regardless of how we solve these problems, the core issue is the researcher's need to compensate participants in order to avoid exploiting them. In fact, it appears as if the fear of exploiting participants renders us incapable of simply accepting their involvement as a gift to be cherished, respected, and used but not abused.[11] This attitude is ethically problematic because we are letting our pride and arrogance get in the way by refusing to be indebted and thankful to them; instead, we are trying to find a way to make it even, either by claiming that we are giving voice and that we are letting the participants be heard or by financially compensating them.[12] By opting for the latter, we are transforming their experiences into commodities, the researcher into a consumer, and the participant into a dealer. So, why do we limit ourselves to thinking that giving back needs to be monetary? Is it an easy way out instead of choosing to give back in a more involved and time-demanding fashion? By opting for financial compensation, is it actually the researcher who is giving back or is it the funding agency?

Aside from the role that monetary compensation can play in voluntary participation, we need to consider participants' beliefs (unbeknownst to us) that they can obtain something in exchange for their participation. For example, a military judge in the DRC asked what I could do to "get him to Canada" following an interview. Similarly, at the end of an interview, a police commander asked me if I could help his son through the immigration procedure by calling in a favour. In the middle of an interview in Peru, the interviewee asked me out of the blue if I could help her brother find a job. To what extent did these interviewees consent to the research expecting or at least hoping for a favour in return? How could I anticipate this and take the necessary measures to ensure that participants were not misguided or participating out of misconceptions about what I could or would do to help them? Given that it is impossible to guarantee absolute voluntary participation, ERBs play an important role in determining how researchers should go about obtaining voluntary participation. Some ethics experts have suggested introducing a cooling-off period between the time the research is presented and the time participants agree to partake in the project (Haggerty 2004). This type of solution would be a significant hurdle to those doing research with difficult-to-access, clandestine, and/or transient populations.

Ambiguities in the Notion of Harm

Because the ethical understanding of harm evolved from biomedical experiments, it was initially conceptualized in terms of physical harm (pain, injuries, illness, or death) (Pimple 2008; Speiglman and Spear 2009). Since its application to social science research, the concept of harm has broadened to incorporate psychological, economic, legal, and social detrimental consequences (Goode 2001; Haggerty 2004). In their efforts to establish criteria to evaluate the level of harm, ethics codes tend to indicate that the risk to the participant must not be a greater risk or consequential injury than those inherent to their particular life situation (Levine 1979). However, this position is problematic and quite unethical given that it lowers the "acceptable risk" standards for those in the most vulnerable situations.

Researchers further point to the need to differentiate between risk of harm and risk of discomfort, embarrassment, or mere inconvenience (Levine 1979; Gabb 2010).[13] As a case in point, how can we predict, evaluate, or measure the harm caused to someone who is asked to discuss difficult or traumatizing experiences? For certain people, talking about a traumatizing experience is a relief, particularly when they have been unable to discuss it despite their desire to do so. Several of the Peruvian interviewees who were unable to talk about their experiences of being involved in the armed struggle with their families and friends pointed this out. They actually thanked me for listening and acknowledging their own suffering and the suffering they caused others (see also Waldrop 2004). In other instances, participants might be willing to share difficult experiences for what they consider to be a higher cause. In Belfast, two women from an organization that continued with the armed struggle after the peace agreement of 1998 agreed to share their experiences because they wanted voices other than those of IRA members to be heard.

It is impossible to know what participants are going to say or do; therefore, researchers cannot really evaluate the risk of a particular research project (Guillemin and Gillam 2004). When we are evaluating the potential impact of our project, are we expected to take into consideration all possible negative consequences or adverse situations their participation might entail? For example, many of the Irish and Peruvian interviewees spoke about having problems with their families because they did not agree with their decision to participate in my research. Was I expected to imagine this and make them aware of it as a potential problem in order to obtain informed consent? (see also Perron, Holmes, and Jacob, this volume). Is it my ethical responsibility to be concerned by any sort of impact participating in my project might entail? Doesn't this type of thinking lead to conceptualizing participants as potential victims? Is this not a disempowering process and therefore a morally questionable one?

I am by no means suggesting that researchers do not need to think about and discuss potential negative consequences with participants.[14] But these concerns need to be negotiated rather than imposed on them. The reality is that we cannot predict or evaluate these potential forms of harm in the same way we do physical harm. How can researchers measure potential harm when what is difficult to some might not be to others? How can we determine what will or will not be traumatizing in an interview? It is this "unforeseen emotional reaction" that causes concern for ERBs (Waldrop 2004, 246) and makes them wary of unstructured interviews. For instance, those seeking asylum have had to tell their stories so many times throughout the process that what is difficult for them is not telling the story one more time but sharing what would appear to be mundane things. In these instances, it is the trivial things in their life that have been untouched by public scrutiny that become intimate and thus difficult to share. If we cannot have a standardized measurement of harm, we cannot have a standardized response to it (Nelkin 1994). For instance, ERBs often suggest providing some sort of psychological support after the interviews, but what if the required infrastructure or necessary resources do not exist? What if culturally or individually the strategies we put in place are not the best suited to help participants?[15] Furthermore, should we provide support only for the harm caused by the interview, or do we have a moral and perhaps ethical responsibility to offer it for what participants experienced and not simply for our part in it? How many sessions should we make available to participants? How do we finance this? What about those not "lucky" enough to be chosen as participants? Would it not be *more* ethical for support to be accessible to the whole population being studied? What about taking it a step further and finding relevant ways of helping the community?[16]

Predicting Problems, Predicting Solutions: Ethical Guesswork

When conducting qualitative social science research, it is impossible to predict how the project will unravel. For example, what doors are going to open up? How are the different people connected with the phenomenon going to react? What issues or hurdles will arise throughout the research? What concerns or reactions to the research might participants have? In fact, it is impossible for researchers to know what is going to happen during and after the fieldwork (O'Neil 2002). Furthermore, potential risks and benefits are not stable but vary across time and space (Bosk and De Vries 2004). Most certainly our methodological expertise and experience, our knowledge of the research domain, and insights from key informants allow us to foresee some issues that are likely to arise (Thompson 2002). For example, a key informant in the Congo made me aware that for multiple reasons – such as not wanting their name to appear anywhere, being ashamed by their lack of reading and writing skills, feeling that the consent form implies a lack of trust in them – most participants would be uncomfortable signing a consent form.[17] I used this knowledge in the ethics application to explain why I would be using oral consent.

The problem is that not only are we expected to imagine and predict what is going to happen, but there is also an implied homogenization of potential participants and research sites. Not all participants in one project (and least of all across research) have the same concerns, incur the same risks, react in the same manner, and, by the same token, find solace in all those issues through the same responses (Taylor 1987). Furthermore, ERBs forget that they function through codes that are culturally based (Glesne 2011). For the 2010 project in the DRC, the ERB came back with comments regarding my use of snowball sampling, which was not considered problematic in a similar project conducted three years earlier. They were concerned about participant anonymity given that someone would have referred the participant to me, and suggested that I use recruitment posters in different parts of the city. I had to explain to the ERB that no one in the DRC would call a number on a recruitment poster precisely because there was no knowledge of who the researcher was and whether he or she could be trusted. Trust is established precisely through common acquaintances; the only way that people know that they can trust you is if someone they know and trust refers you to them. In fact, I was only able to interview women involved in anti-establishment armed groups because I had developed trusting relationships with key informants who vouched for me. Furthermore, in those instances, the common acquaintance created the "moral bond" between the researcher and the participants, not the consent form. Yet the ERB for the 2010 project was still not satisfied with my explanation and required that the contact give my phone number to the potential interviewee who would then call me if interested. At this point, I explained that, aside from the fact that as part of the social arrangement people introduce one another in person and do not simply give out each other's phone number, due to the precarious economic situation of potential participants, it would be an undue burden to have them call me.

The ERB was operating according to what they imagined would be a concern regarding anonymity for potential interviewees, based on North American thinking. The solutions they proposed were not applicable to the situation in the DRC; while the cost of a phone call might not be a big deal in Canada, it is a big deal in the DRC – even for professionals. It is quite common for participants not to be concerned with the same things that we are or that we thought would matter to them. According to Goode (2001, 246), as researchers we are actually quite arrogant when we assume that "our ethics are identical with subjects' ethics." Even worse, in certain instances, "sociologically ethical" behaviour might actually harm participants because it forces researchers to say or do something unethical, risky, or simply stupid according to the participant's standard (Goode 2001).

Nonetheless, ERBs establish protocols to manage a host of what are highly speculative situations and make precautionary decisions based on the illusion of entirely risk-free research (Haggerty 2004; Librett and Perrone 2010). The breadth of the unknown in qualitative research leads ERBs to *imagine* all sorts of situations and possibilities that *may* arise; thus, they often come back to the researcher with a series of "what ifs" that need to be addressed. The problem with generating a list of what ifs is that once the researcher enters this realm of the imagination the list of what ifs becomes infinite (Haggerty 2004). In the context of a risk-averse and litigious society (Librett and Perrone 2010), ERBs tend to overestimate potential risks (van den Hoonaard 2002). Contrary to other forms of research, qualitative research does not allow the researcher to control the environment or the participants. Researchers cannot foresee how the fieldwork is going to pan out, and, therefore, we cannot lay out the what, when, or how of what we are going to do. All we can do is present the broad strokes of what we intend to do and how we intend to do it, based on reasonably foreseeable scenarios. Anything else is simply ethical guesswork, albeit educated ethical guesswork.

Evaluating Hypotheticals: Seeing into the Future

ERBs can only evaluate the reasonably foreseeable scenarios knowing full well that the reality might end up being different. Attempting to evaluate a project based on the researcher's predictions of possible courses of action, problems, solutions, and outcomes adds up to evaluating hypotheticals instead of a detailed and fixed design.

As a researcher, I have at times found myself in unforeseeable and ethically challenging situations. Although not ethical quandaries, these situations were not ethically trivial – they were what Guillemin and Gillam (2004) call "ethically important moments." For example, at a social event with potential participants for my project in the DRC, I found myself in a conversation with a member of the military. While he was talking to me, a higher-ranking officer started talking over him, demanding my attention. I did not know how to react: by stopping my original conversation and acknowledging the inter-ruption, I would be going against my own principles of equality and respect. However, by not giving him my attention, I would be contravening local social arrangements, imposing my own values, and, furthermore, putting the lower-ranking individual in a difficult and potentially harmful situation. By continuing my conversation, I would be forcing a subaltern to show dis-respect to a commanding officer, which could have material and physical consequences for him.

I faced another "ethically important moment" while interviewing women involved in anti–establishment armed groups in a Peruvian prison. I was con-ducting life history interviews with women from different organizations, which involved meeting the same women on several occasions. One day, I was invited by one of the interviewees to have lunch with four or five of her friends. Although I was ambivalent, I accepted the invitation.[18] They decided we would eat in a workshop to have more privacy. When we got there, I saw that a woman I was interviewing from a different organization was eating alone. I felt uncomfortable because of my relationship with her; I thought it rude not to ask her to join us. However, the politics between the different organizations, the internal dynamics in that pavilion (the woman was considered an outsider by many), and my role as the guest and the fact that this lunch was a kind of test prevented me from doing anything but saying hello.[19] Given that she was insinuating herself by hanging around as close as it was possible, the leader of the group allowed her to join us.

I became even more uncomfortable when nobody made room for her at the table. I was sitting between two people and could not move, and she just stood at the corner of the table two steps behind everyone else. I felt that I was participating in the process of demeaning this person. I compensated by looking at her while talking to the group (something none of the others did) and finding different ways of acknowledging her. However, by doing this I knew that I could be making things worse, as my interaction with her was a constant reminder that I was a witness to a humiliating situation. Furthermore, as it was a kind of test, the "leader" kept asking questions about what I thought of their involvement and of the armed struggle. I had to find ways to answer honestly while being mindful that my access to the field was at stake. At the same time, given that I was interviewing two women who were present during the conversation, I needed to make sure that my answers did not make them feel that I was judging them or breaching confidentiality. Obviously, I had not prepared for such a situation; nor could I draw on the protocol of ERBs to find the proper way to deal with it. Just as it is impossible to think of every possible situation a researcher might encounter; it is always possible to come up with new situations or events that the qualitative researcher might have to face. Thus, ERBs do not certify whether a project is ethical; rather, they certify that the ERB trusts that the researcher will be able to make the *ethical* decision on the spot, based on the list of potential problems and solutions researchers describe in their ethics applications and in their responses to the what ifs presented by the ERB.

Despite how problematic or questionable it might be, the proof of our trustworthiness as ethical researchers is obtained through the answers provided to a long and detailed questionnaire. Through this process, the ability of the researcher to act ethically is not initially recognized; in fact, the ERB questions or strips away the researcher's credibility only to grant or restore it at the end of a tedious process, based on nothing other than the researcher's word that he or she will act in accordance with the information provided.

The system has gone from one that assumes the professional competence and responsibility of the researcher to one based on institutionalized distrust, where researchers are presumed to require additional oversight to ensure they act ethically (Haggerty 2004, 393). The researcher's credibility is only restored by providing answers consistent with the ERB's philosophy. Thus, ERBs certify that the researcher is capable of telling them what they need to hear. The decision is based on the researcher being able to deploy "ethic speak" and perform ethics throughout the process (Halse and Honey 2007). In such a context, researchers have become savvy and now use the appropriate discourse to get their projects approved (Guillemin and Gillam 2004). Yet the reality is that researchers can say they are going to do something and do something else (Halse and Honey 2007). In fact, procedural ethics have little or no impact on how research is conducted (Guillemin and Gillam 2004) because there is no way of knowing that researchers will actually do what they say they are going to do (Bosk and De Vries 2004).[20] To add insult to injury, at the end of this process, it is not really the researcher who is certified and recognized as ethical but the project – and only for a specific period of time. As the clock strikes twelve, after midnight the project becomes unethical again.

Experts, Technocrats, and the Disenfranchisement of Research Participants

The issues discussed thus far should not be read as strikes against ERBs themselves but as strikes against the idea that we can predict behaviour and therefore control ethics. For example, a colleague whose project was certified by an ERB was conducting interviews through an interpreter who, out of the blue, started asking inappropriate questions. Although the researcher took the necessary steps to ensure that the situation was not repeated, it did happen once and participants were exposed to a potentially harmful situation, despite ethics certification and acting in accordance with what was indicated in the ethics application. In other words, it was outside the researcher's control.

Researchers need to acknowledge and work through the fact that research and ethics are messy and ethical guidelines only provide a false sense of security (Brogden and Patterson 2007). Being able to control ethics and ensure all research is ethical is no more than an illusion. In fact, the idea that a project is ethical simply because it has been approved by an ethics board is actually misleading. ERBs can, in fact, become a distraction when we become focused on the procedural and bureaucratic components and neglect of the serious ethical issues in our research (Bosk and De Vries 2004). ERBs can create the "illusion that moral concerns, power issues, justice, protection of human beings (and so on) have been addressed with no further need of concern"

(Cannella and Lincoln 2007, 315). The problem is precisely that ERBs are attempting to make aseptic something that cannot be so: ERBs cannot find a solution to neutralize all of these issues; in fact, no paradigm or methodological approach could. Being an ethical researcher is not finding a way to make power relations disappear but rather finding a way to deal with them and working within them in an ethical manner.

By the same token, the notion that it is possible to establish criteria to distinguish between behaviours that are intrinsically ethical and behaviours that are intrinsically problematic or unethical, regardless of circumstances or other issues and considerations, is delusional and deceptive. Notwithstanding, "ethics experts" have been appointed to determine whether an action is ethical and, if not, the measures required to render it so (Halse and Honey 2007; Gabb 2010). The expert creates guidelines and policies while the technocrats working within ERBs apply them, sometimes with the advice of a lawyer. Such decisions are presented as objective even though they are influenced by their own normative positions, emotions, and concerns over liability.

One of the reasons so many researchers experience a knee-jerk reaction to ethics review boards is that we view the process as an affront to our moral persona and an attack on our professional integrity. We are not bad people out to harm participants; we are not mad scientists or so-called Nazi doctors oblivious to the consequences of our actions. Moreover, we too are trained experts. Some may argue that this is an emotional response by our overly inflated egos, in which case we should simply "get over ourselves." However, the problem is about more than hurting the researchers' pride; forcing researchers to go through ethical review questions, and even challenges, the researchers' ethics, trustworthiness, and professionalism. To make my point more explicit, consider having to pass a driver's exam each time you drive to certify that you are not a danger on the road. The problem is that, inadvertently or not, the researcher is now considered unethical until proven otherwise. Under such circumstances, it is not surprising that obtaining ethics certification is a time-consuming and bureaucratic exercise in protecting from liability the university institution, where research is construed as risky and the researcher as unethical (Halse and Honey 2007; Allen 2009).

On the other hand, this process has taken away participant agency, leaving them passive bystanders who are dependent on the ethics expert for their protection and well-being. In fact, ERBs often construct participants as vulnerable, defenceless, innocent, in need of protection and, in some instances, as irresponsible and unable to make good decisions on their own (Allen 2009; Halse and Honey 2007). Participants are also constructed as potential victims of exploitation by researchers (Glesne 2011; Goode 2001). Researchers and ERBs seem to forget that participants are social actors capable of deploying strategies to protect and sometimes advance their own interests. In a conference in Ottawa in April 2011, one of the presenters talked about conducting interviews with members of a marginalized group where participants were compensated with thirty dollars. He described how one of the interviewees, after answering questions in such a way that the researcher felt like he was being taken for a ride, told other potential participants that "there was a guy giving away $30 and all they had to do was blab for a while." This example shows how someone construed by ERBs as a vulnerable individual who could potentially be exploited by the researcher was actually the one who "exploited" the researcher by taking his money in exchange for what the interviewee himself described as blabbing. To be clear, I am in no way suggesting that potential participants are not vulnerable to exploitation. Rather, I am indicating that construing them exclusively as vulnerable is unethical because it effectively disempowers participants.

ERBs position the ethics experts and the technocrats as the guardians of potential participants. This means that an outsider who does not know the participants and who has limited knowledge (if any) of their world is determining what might or might not harm them; evaluating the risks associated with partaking in the project and deciding for participants whether the risks are acceptable; deciding on the best way to deal with any possible harm or risk; and establishing the ways the researcher should interact with participants to prevent any exploitation. In other words, participants are no longer experts of their own lives; they are no longer seen as equipped to determine what they are capable of doing or evaluate the possible consequences that participating may have on their own lives. Is the ERB or the researcher in the best position to decide on the possible consequences for a police officer in the DRC who participates in a research project? Are participants not better equipped to know if their superior is going to cause them problems and whether they want to participate regardless? What do the ERBs know about what is at stake for ex-political prisoners in Peru or Belfast? Should I decide for them that they should not participate because security forces *might* confiscate the recordings or my notes? Should I have refused an interviewee who wanted to conduct the interview in a public park because of issues of confidentiality, despite the fact that it was where she felt safest?

Despite the fact that the research relationship takes place between the participant and the researchers, an absent and mysterious third party determines the context in which participants and researchers interact and the rules framing their interactions. These rules are established by ERBs, not based on the specifics of each project but on universal and abstract principles that may or may not make sense in the participants' world.

The Pitfalls of an Absolute Approach to Ethics: The Disappearance of Moral Responsibility

As we have seen, ethics are more complicated and more situated than the procedures and protocols of ERBs (Brogden and Patterson 2007). ERBs cannot address the breadth and complexity of empirical studies and compensate by establishing standardized rules on how to react instead of guiding the researcher to make ethical decisions (Gabb 2010). There is too much to cover with one set of regulations (Bosk and DeVries 2004), and ethical dilemmas in the field cannot be dealt with by following universal procedures (Baarts 2009). It is impossible from both an epistemological and pragmatic position to conduct ethical research simply by abiding by what can be seen as a list of dos and don'ts. Ethical codes represent an attempt to eliminate all autonomous and uncontrolled sources of moral judgment by assuming that in any life situation there is only one logical choice (Bauman 1994). Instead of establishing a one-size-fits-all solution, research ethics should be based on a commitment to ethical self-examination and sensitivity toward relations with others (Clegg and Slife 2009).

Ethical research is not the product of "prosecutorial inquisition but of shared discourse and dialogue between parties" (Angrosino and Mays de Pérez 2003, 143); therefore, it is highly contextual (Cannella and Lincoln 2007; Glesne 2011). In fact, ethics are a dialogue "dialectically constituted in confrontation with what is recognised as unacceptable, unreasonable and inhumane" (Gotlib Conn 2008, 509). Ethics do not exist in a vacuum, as a set of absolute or universal principles cut off from the material world. Acting ethically or being ethical is always contextually based. This means that research is fraught with moral and ethical issues that go beyond the scope of ERBs' mandate (Clegg and Slife 2009). The current ethics model ignores the broader spectrum of actors involved in or affected by the research: friends/family of participants, other members of the population being studied, people who are not part of the population but who are somehow concerned with or affected by it, and, finally, the population as a whole (Gohier 2004). In other words, we reduce ethics to the individual and forget about the community and wider society.

As a result, ERBs actually take on only a small part of what ethics in research entails. While ERBs endorse procedural ethics, other researchers advocate for a broader conceptualization of ethics, such as situational ethics, ethics in practice, or relational ethics. (Thomas 2009). These perspectives are based on the belief that moral research behaviour goes beyond ethical knowledge and cognitive choices; it involves sensitivity and commitment to moral issues and actions (Kvale 1996). Ethical relationships cannot be limited to following rules but need to be based on a constant awareness of the responsibilities we have toward others (Haggerty 2004). These broader forms of ethics are unpredictable and subtle, given the ethical obligation to remain true to one's character and be responsible for one's actions and its consequences (Thomas 2009). Ethical research needs to be based on democratic values of autonomy, freedom, equality, and mutual respect (Caron 1993; Dell, Fillmore, and Kilty, this volume). As such, we cannot think about ethics without thinking about power: power between people but also how power relations are connected to institutions, historical circumstances, economics, gender, race, class, cultural backgrounds, and experiences and actual locations (Lincoln 2009, 152).

What is ethical depends on the parties involved, the specific and general context of the research, the circumstances, the potential outcomes or consequences for the parties involved, the time period, and the stakes not only for the researcher and the participant but also for other people somehow involved in the phenomenon being studied. What is ethical also changes with hindsight; therefore, what might appear as ethical at one point might appear as unethical after time passes or given new information or knowing a particular outcome or consequence. Moreover, ethics evolve through time and space: what is acceptable and unacceptable depends on normative values, priorities, and forms of social relations. Ethics are culturally informed, meaning that we cannot simply draft a set of abstract principles; we need to look at ethics as a dynamic and relational process that takes place through actions as well as inaction. To do this, we need to think in terms of research morality and not only abstract and absolute ethical principles stipulated by a research council and applied by ERBs. According to Bauman (1994), morality is in fact an ambivalent condition that cannot be exhausted by an ethical code.

A Way Forward: Negotiated Ethics

Researching the social world through qualitative methodologies and postmodern, constructivist, or critical paradigms implies a logic as well as premises, values, and principles that are different from those associated with positivism; different epistemological systems imply different ethical concerns (Glesne 2011). Currently, researchers working under alternative epistemologies and methodologies do not readily identify with the philosophy and policy governing ERBs, which precludes them from establishing a fruitful dialogue in which ethical issues and concerns may be addressed and discussed.

To encourage sincere dialogue and exchange, it is important to stop thinking about ethics as composed of only three actors playing very specific roles: participants viewed as passive beings in need of protection from victimization and exploitation; researchers as potential threats to the participants because of their "predatory" role; and, finally, ERBs as experts of ethics and arbiters in the tricky relationship between researchers and participants. Doing so involves recognizing the agency of the people involved in the research (key informants, contacts, and potential participants) and considering them as competent social actors and as equal partners. We need to recognize that we are dealing with experts: they are experts of their own lives and experts of the environments in which they live. They are also autonomous beings who can make their own decisions regardless of whether a third party might consider them "risky" or "potentially harmful."

We also need to transform the role of the ERB from one of arbiter, judging and deciding on the ethics of a project, to one of adviser, discussing with researchers the ethical concerns of their project at different stages (Ginsberg and Mertens 2009). The expertise of the board would be based on having a combined vast experience on ethical issues in research (Angrosino and Mays de Pérez 2003) instead of its knowledge of the Tri-Council policy, the standard "what if?" questions, and the accepted solutions to those questions. For this to be achievable, we need to learn to negotiate between three forms of expertise: the theoretical, scientific, and methodological knowledge of the researcher; the self-expertise of the participant (knowledge of themselves, their environment, and the context in which they live); and the comprehensive erudition of the ERB.

It is also necessary to think beyond the three key principles of ethical research and away from concerns over harm-risk-liability to focus on broader issues of morality in research. Instead of conceiving ethics within an absolute model, we need to think of ethics as contextual, dynamic, and relational. This implies not only that there is more than one formula for ethical behaviour but also that ethics need to be negotiated at multiple levels between the researchers and the potential participants, the researcher and the site/population being investigated, and the researcher and the institutional or academic world.[21] Only by accepting that an ambiguity-free moral situation is a utopia (Bauman 1994) and by learning to negotiate among multiple social actors can we strive to achieve ethics in research.

Notes

1 Immersing subjects in cold water; administering radioactive iron and calcium to pregnant women; and injecting subjects with cancer cells, diseases (malaria, dysentery, syphilis), poison, gasoline, LSD, and so on are examples of problematic biomedical and military research (Beecher 1966; Haggerty 2004; Halse and Honey 2007; Librett and Perrone 2010). By contrast, Humphreys's study on homosexuals engaging in public sex, Zimbardo's prisoner-guards project, and Milgram's obedience research (Waldrop 2004; Kitchener and Kitchener 2009) are examples of controversial research in the social sciences.

2 This is not intended to indicate an antagonistic stance toward researchers who use quantitative methodologies and/or drawing from positivist or postpositivist epistemologies. The purpose of this statement is to delineate the type of research addressed in this chapter in a concise way, instead of listing all the possibly relevant epistemological positions (e.g., constructivist, critical, postmodern, participatory, postcolonial). Although researchers who use quantitative methodologies and draw from positivist or postpositivist epistemologies might also "huff and puff" over ERBs, they do so for their own reasons, which, I contend, are different from those presented in this chapter.

3 I do not ignore the fact that ERBs function in very different ways, and it is always possible to find examples of ERBs that support nontraditional research (see Ogden's chapter in this book, for instance). However, the existence of such cases does not undermine the arguments presented in this chapter; it demonstrates that ERBs can work differently and break away from their own constraints.

4 *Nontraditional methodologies* and *epistemologies* are terms used to indicate ways of producing scientific knowledge outside of that designed within a positivist epistemological or methodological framework, such as qualitative methodologies and constructivist, critical, postmodern, participatory, and postcolonial epistemologies.

5 The Royal Commission on Bilingualism and Biculturalism (1963-69), chaired by André Laurendeau and Arnold Davidson Dunton, recorded anecdotal evidence that English Canadians used this expression toward French Canadians and immigrants when speaking in public in a language other than English.

6 For instance, ERBs' requirement for researchers to obtain official authorization from the site prior to conducting a study affects not only who researchers can speak with but which researchers are allowed to speak. Researchers considered critical or unsympathetic to institutions or government might be denied entry into the site (see Kilty, this volume, as well as Perron, Holmes, and Jacob, this volume).

7 This situation is problematic in and of itself but also because, as a consequence, some researchers are opting to use secondary sources or public documents to avoid going through an ethics review process. Equally troublesome is that, for the same reasons, some professors are more and more inclined to direct graduate students toward methodologies and populations that do not require ethics review, which impacts not only the type of knowledge produced but also the type of researchers we are training or, more to the point, not training (Fisher, Wertz, and Goodman 2009).

8 To my knowledge, there is no empirical research on the role played by university lawyers and managers in how ERBs work.

9 This discussion is based on three different projects: my doctoral research on women involved in anti-establishment armed groups in Peru and Belfast; a 2007 project in the Democratic Republic of Congo (DRC) with people working in the area of justice; and a 2010 project on the military and the police in the DRC.

10 I was faced with a similar ethical problem applying for funding to SSHRC: should I pay the same wages to research assistants (RAs) in Canada and in the Congo, or should I pay according to the local norm? On one hand, by being "fair" and paying them the same for doing the same job, I would be creating a problem with the professors at the university in the DRC, who would be getting paid a tenth of what my RAs received. On the other hand, by respecting the local norm, I would be establishing a difference between the Canadian RA and the Congolese RA, and I would be participating in the exploitation of the latter. Given that the funding agency dictated I had to pay according to local fares, I decided to provide the Congolese RA with the opportunity to attend international conferences. However, I was instructed that the project could only finance conference expenses for student RAs. In this

case, the funding rules and regulations from the grant agency forced the researcher into an unethical situation, hampering possible solutions without actually providing an alternative.

11 See Munn, this volume, and Bruckert, this volume, for a discussion on the fears of exploiting participants and the different steps taken to avoid it. See Dell, Fillmore, and Kilty, this volume, for a discussion on finding a meaningful way to compensate participants through the gift of the oyster.

12 This notion of being heard is highly problematic, as Bruckert and Munn discuss in this volume. Furthermore, the only one who in fact listens to the participant is the researcher. Once participants' words are transformed into published form, we no longer hear the participants themselves but only bits and pieces of what they say, and, let's face it, a scientific journal is far from being the most effective way of letting participants "be heard."

13 In fact, what does minimal risk mean? The "infinitesimal chance of substantial harm occurring or the substantial chance of infinitesimal harm?" (Levine 1979, 24).

14 See Perron, Holmes, and Jacob, as well as Munn, in this volume, for example, of how they talked to participants about potential consequences.

15 See, for example, the dilemma of how to help women deal with the consequences of mass rape when researchers or practitioners come from a culture of therapy while the women come from a culture of silence (Folnegovic-Smalc 1994).

16 See Dell, Fillmore, and Kilty; Bellot, Silvestre, and St-Jacques; Munn; and Bruckert, this volume for examples of alternative ways to "give back."

17 Particularly within marginalized populations and postcolonial societies, the idea of signing the consent form or "research contract" is problematic (see Glesne 2011). For an in-depth discussion of informed consent, see Thomas (2009).

18 I was looking forward to the opportunity to share with the interviewee in a different context, but I felt that I would be taking away food, which is a scarce commodity in prison. I solved this problem by coming to terms with the fact that it was not up to me to decide whether they could do without my portion. While I was genuinely concerned, I realized that I had also assumed to know better than the participants what means were available to them and how they should use them. It was not only disempowering but also insulting to refuse their invitation.

19 At different moments during the three weeks I visited the prison, I had to deal with the highly hierarchical structure of the prison and anti-establishment armed groups, with an environment in which people I had befriended were ignored and treated as irrelevant by my companions. Although I refused to go along with the behaviour implicitly expected of me, I was unable to stop what I considered disrespectful behaviours and attitudes.

20 I am by no means advocating a "policing researchers" attitude, although, according to Haggerty (2004), the possibility has been discussed. See also van den Hoonaard, this volume, regarding the implementation of audit trails and the need to ensure all research decisions are trackable.

21 See Dell, Fillmore, and Kilty; Perron, Holmes, and Jacob; Bruckert; Munn; and Ogden, all in this volume.

References

Adler, P., and Adler, P. (2002). Do University Lawyers and the Police Define Research Values? In W.C. van den Hoonaard (Ed.), *Walking the Tightrope: Ethical Issues for Qualitative Researchers* (34-42). Toronto: University of Toronto Press.

Allen, L. (2009). "Caught in the Act": Ethics Committee Review and Researching the Sexual Culture of Schools. *Qualitative Research* 9(4), 395-410.

Angrosino, M., and Mays de Pérez, K. (2003). Rethinking Observation: From Method to Context. In N. Denzin and Y. Lincoln (Eds.), *Collecting and Interpreting Qualitative Materials* (107-54). London: Sage.

Baarts, C. (2009). Stuck in the Middle: Research Ethics Caught between Science and Politics. *Qualitative Research* 9(4), 423-39.

Bauman, Z. (1994). *Postmodern Ethics*. Oxford: Blackwell.

Beecher, H. (1966). Ethical and Clinical Research. *New England Journal of Medicine 274*, 1354-60.

Bosk, C., and De Vries, R. (2004). Being Here and Being There: Fieldwork Encounters and Ethnographic Discoveries. *Annals of the American Academy of Political and Social Science 595*, 249-63.

Braun, K., Herrmann, S.L., Könninger, S., and Moore, A. (2010). Ethical Reflections Must Always Be Measured. *Science Technology and Human Values 35*(6), 839-64.

Brogden, L., and Patterson, D. (2007). Nostalgia, Goodness and Ethical Paradox. *Qualitative Research 7*(2), 217-27.

Cannella, G., and Lincoln, Y. (2007). Predatory versus Dialogical Ethics: Constructing an Illusion or Ethical Practice as the Core of Research Methods. *Qualitative Inquiry 13*(3), 315-35.

Caron, A. (1993). Les exigences éthiques d'une recherche en partenariat. *Revue de l'association pour la recherche qualitative 9*, 68-75.

Cheek, J. (2003). An Untold Story? Doing Funded Qualitative Research. In N. Denzin and Y. Lincoln (Eds.), *Strategies of Qualitative Inquiry* (80-111). London: Sage.

Christians, C. (2003). Ethics and Politics in Qualitative Research. In N. Denzin and Y. Lincoln (Eds.), *The Landscape of Qualitative Research* (208-44). London: Sage.

Clegg, J., and Slife, B. (2009). Research Ethics in the Postmodern Context. In D. Mertens and P. Ginsberg (Eds.), *The Handbook of Social Research Ethics* (23-38). London: Sage.

Denzin, N.K. (2009). The Elephant in the Living Room: Or Extending the Conversation about the Politics of Evidence. *Qualitative Research 9*(2), 139-60.

Fisher, C., Wertz, F., and Goodman, S. (2009). Graduate Training in Responsible Conduct of Social Science Research: The Role of Mentors and Departmental Climate. In D. Mertens and P. Ginsberg (Eds.), *The Handbook of Social Research Ethics* (550-64). London: Sage.

Folnegovic-Smalc, V. (1994). Psychiatric Aspects of the Rapes in the War against the Republic of Croatia and Bosnia-Herzegovina. In A. Stiglmayer (Ed.), *Mass Rape: The War against Women in Bosnia-Herzegovina* (174-79). Lincoln: University of Nebraska Press.

Gabb, J. (2010). Home Truths: Ethical Issues in Family Research. *Qualitative Research 10*(4), 461-78.

Ginsberg, P., and Mertens, D. (2009). Frontiers in Social Research Ethics: Fertile Ground for Evolution. In D. Mertens and P. Ginsberg (Eds.), *The Handbook of Social Research Ethics* (580-612). London: Sage.

Glesne, C. (1989). Rapport and Friendship in Ethnographic Research. *International Journal of Qualitative Studies in Education 2*(1), 45-54.

—. (2011). *Becoming Qualitative Researchers*. Montreal: Pearson.

Gohier, C. (2004). Se la démarcation entre critères d'ordre scientifique et d'ordre éthique en recherche interprétative. *Recherches Qualitatives 24*, 3-17.

Goode, E. (2001). The Ethics of Deception in Social Research: A Case Study. In M. Miller and R. Tewksbury (Eds.), *Extreme Methods* (239-57). Toronto: Allyn and Bacon.

Gotlib Conn, L. (2008). Ethics Policy as Audit in Canadian Clinical Settings: Exiling the Ethnographic Method. *Qualitative Research 8*(4), 499-514.

Guillemin, M., and Gillam, L. (2004). Ethics, Reflexivity and "Ethically Important Moments" in Research. *Qualitative Inquiry 10*(2), 261-80.

Haggerty, K. (2004). Ethics Creep: Governing Social Science Research in the Name of Ethics. *Qualitative Sociology 27*(4), 391-414.

Halse, C., and Honey, A. (2007). Rethinking Ethics Review as Institutional Discourse. *Qualitative Inquiry 13*(3), 336-52.

Israel, M., and Hay, I. (2006). *Research Ethics for Social Scientists: Between Ethical Conduct and Regulatory Compliance*. London: Sage.

Johnson, J., and Altheide, D. (2002). Reflections on Professional Ethics. In W.C. van den Hoonaard (Ed.), *Walking the Tightrope: Ethical Issues for Qualitative Researchers* (59-69). Toronto: University of Toronto Press.

Kitchener, K.S., and Kitchener, R. (2009). Social Science Research Ethics: Historical and Philosophical Issues. In D. Mertens and P. Ginsberg (Eds.), *The Handbook of Social Research Ethics* (5-22). London: Sage.

Kvale, S. (1996). *Interviews: An Introduction to Qualitative Research Interviewing*. Thousand Oaks, CA: Sage.

Levine, R. (1979). Clarifying Concepts of Research Ethics. *Hastings Centre Report 9*, 21-26.

Librett, M., and Perrone, D. (2010). Apples and Oranges: Ethnography and the IRB. *Qualitative Research 10*(6), 729-47.

Lincoln, Y. (2009). Ethical Practices in Qualitative Research. In D. Mertens and P. Ginsberg (Eds.), *The Handbook of Social Research Ethics* (150-69). London: Sage.

Lincoln, Y., and Tierney, W. (2004). Qualitative Research and Institutional Review Boards. *Qualitative Inquiry 10*(2), 219-34.

Muzychka, M., Poulin, C., Cottrell, B., Miedema, B., and Roberts, B. (1996). *Feminist Research Ethics: A Process*. Ottawa: Canadian Research Institute for the Advancement of Women.

Nelkin, D. (1994). Forbidden Research: Limits to Inquiry in the Social Sciences. In E. Erwin, S. Gendin, and L. Kleiman (Eds.), *Ethical Issues in Research* (355-70). New York: Garland.

Nelson, C. (2004). The Brave New World of Research Surveillance. *Qualitative Inquiry 10*(2), 207-18 .

O'Neil, P. (2002). Good Intentions and Awkward Outcomes: Ethical Gatekeeping in Field Research. In W.C. van den Hoonaard (Ed.), *Walking the Tightrope: Ethical Issues for Qualitative Researchers* (17-25). Toronto: University of Toronto Press.

Pimple, K. (2008). Introduction. In K. Pimple (Ed.), *Research Ethics* (xv-xxxi). Burlington, VT: Ashgate.

Shore, C., and Wright, S. (1999). Coercive Accountability: The Rise of Audit Culture in Higher Education. In M. Strathern (Ed.), *Audit Culture: Anthropological Studies in Accountability, Ethics, and the Academy* (57-89). New York: Routledge.

Speiglman, R., and Spear, P. (2009). The Role of Institutional Review Boards: Ethics – Now You See Them, Now You Don't. In D. Mertens and P. Ginsberg (Eds.), *The Handbook of Social Research Ethics* (121-34). London: Sage.

Taylor, S. (1987). Observing Abuse: Professional Ethics and Personal Morality in Field Research. *Qualitative Sociology 10*(3), 288-302.

Thomas, V. (2009). Critical Race Theory: Ethics and Dimensions of Diversity Research. In D. Mertens and P. Ginsberg (Eds.), *The Handbook of Social Research Ethics* (54-68). London: Sage.

Thompson, A. (2002). My Research Friend? My Friend the Researcher? My Friend, My Researcher? Mis/Informed Consent and People with Developmental Disabilities. In W.C. van den Hoonaard (Ed.), *Walking the Tightrope: Ethical Issues for Qualitative Researchers* (95-106). Toronto: University of Toronto Press.

van den Hoonaard, W.C. (2002). Introduction: Ethical Norming and Qualitative Research. In W.C. van den Hoonaard (Ed.), *Walking the Tightrope: Ethical Issues for Qualitative Researchers* (3-16). Toronto: University of Toronto Press.

Waldrop, D. (2004). Ethical Issues in Qualitative Research with High-Risk Populations. In D.K. Padgett (Ed.), *The Qualitative Research Experience* (241-53). Toronto: Nelson.

chapter 10   **Doublespeak and Double Standards: Holding a Rogue University Administration to Account**

John Lowman and Ted Palys

THE TRI-COUNCIL POLICY STATEMENT: *Ethical Conduct for Research Involving Humans* (*TCPS*), published in 1998,[1] (MRC, NSERC, and SSHRC 1998) represented the first harmonized statement of ethical principles for academic research in Canada. Developed under the granting agencies' banner of promoting a "culture of ethics" in Canada's research community, attention during the *TCPS*'s development focused on the need to ensure researcher accountability in the wake of scandalous researcher behaviour, although it appears that such behaviour was largely restricted to the biomedical realm (Tri-Council Working Group 1996, 1-4).[2] Once the policy was implemented, the attention of the research community was on the way research ethics boards were interpreting the *TCPS* and its attendant impact on research (e.g., Fitzgerald 2005; Haggerty 2004; SSHWC 2004; van den Hoonaard 2011). Case studies that shed light on the practices of university administrations in relation to their responsibilities under the *TCPS* were rare.[3]

This chapter presents one such case study by recounting a situation at Kwantlen University College (Kwantlen) in 2007 where two sets of researchers were being dealt with so inequitably that some kind of external intervention was warranted – in this instance, a formal complaint about the university's maladministration of its ethics policy – which in turn generated a sequence of events that spoke volumes about the double standards that Kwantlen's administration employed and the institutional conflicts of interest it engaged.[4] The experience at Kwantlen highlights the lack of effective mechanisms to hold to account rogue administrations that promise policy adherence but fail to live up to that standard.

This chapter thus speaks directly to issues the Canadian Association of University Teachers (CAUT 2011b) raised in its submission to the granting agency presidents urging them to ensure that the revised *Tri-Council Policy Statement on Integrity in Research and Scholarship* would require universities to "uphold academic freedom and act in a manner consistent with collective agreements" and broaden its provisions on conflict of interest "to include potential institutional conflicts, not just those of individual researchers." It was not the first time the problem of institutional conflict of interest and the threat that university administrations may pose to academic freedom have been raised. However, CAUT's concerns have gone unheeded. The *Tri-Agency Framework: Responsible Conduct of Research* (CIHR, NSERC, and SSHRC 2011), which replaced the *Tri-Council Policy Statement on Integrity in Research and Scholarship*, did not adopt CAUT's recommendations. This chapter demonstrates the folly of the agencies' resistance to a more comprehensive set of mechanisms for holding universities accountable than exists in the current memorandum of understanding, which is restricted to the basic requirements for universities to obtain and administer research funds.

The chapter begins by describing concerns about institutional conflict of interest – the elephant in the room – that were voiced in the process of writing the first *TCPS*, and which CAUT repeated with its suggestion that the new framework for *Responsible Conduct of Research* include provisions to deal with institutional conflict of interest and protect academic freedom. We then turn to events at Kwantlen, the academic poster child for institutional conflict of interest and research maladministration. We describe Kwantlen's transition from small university college to aspiring research institution to polytechnic university, and then document the ways that Kwantlen consistently violated its memorandum of agreement with the Social Sciences and Humanities Research Council, became the first university we know of in Canada to stop research ethics board–approved research, and the first university to conduct highly sensitive human research without submitting it for research ethics board (REB) review and oversight. The main part of the chapter describes the Kwantlen administration's reaction to two complaints about the research that was conducted without REB review. The experience highlights some of the reasons that institutional conflict of interest and protection of academic freedom should be built into the new *Tri-Council Policy Statement on Integrity in Research and Scholarship*. The chapter concludes with comments about how Canada's regulatory structure might be revised to better balance proportional and effective regulation of research ethics and research ethics administration with appropriate respect for academic freedom.

The Elephant in the Room

According to Michael McDonald (1998), a member of the Tri-Council Working Group (TCWG) that authored the draft reports that led to the *TCPS,* concern regarding institutional conflict of interest was high on the TCWG's agenda for what at that time was envisioned as a prospective code of ethics:

In constructing the *Code,* our concern was to address central features of Canadian research involving humans, including:

- Increasing private sector dollars pouring particularly into medical research, much of this in the private sector
- Attendant pressures on REBs to issue quick and favourable verdicts on research proposals.

Although this statement was made with particular reference to biomedical research, McDonald (2001, 11) later spelled out the ways that similar conflicts of interest might arise in social science and humanities research venues as well:

With respect to the conflicts of interest, I think there is a good deal of public awareness of the latent and not so latent conflicts of interest that dog private and public sector health research. In the research community, though, I see major blind spots. In universities, for example, social scientists and humanists are quick to view with suspicion industry-funded research. However, as a community they seem singularly unaware of the conflicts that lie in public sector research funding (research sponsors and institutions have their own agendas) and in the members of their own community who are as much driven by the desire for prestige and power as their colleagues in the natural and applied sciences. Institutionally we have a situation in which university REBs generally report to the offices that promote research.

While McDonald's concerns are well founded, his analysis considered only the pressures that often exist to *permit* research in situations where opportunities for funding and the "power and prestige" that sometimes accompanies them arise. However, cases at Simon Fraser University (Lowman and Palys 2000; Palys and Lowman 2014) and the Kwantlen University College case show that administrators also are sometimes unwilling to support – and may even take steps to *impede* – research that is not generating administrative overhead and/or that offends university administrators' image-management sensibilities.

Kwantlen's Research Mandate

Kwantlen opened in 1981 as a college, delivering first- and second- year undergraduate courses to students who would then move on to a university to complete their bachelor's degrees. In 1988, it became one of five university colleges in BC that was authorized to offer baccalaureate degrees under the aegis of one or more of the three provincial universities that existed at the time. In 1995, the five university colleges were awarded the authority to offer degrees in their own right, but they were still not deemed to be fully fledged universities. In 2005, Kwantlen began to campaign actively for full university status, which saw the administration gradually developing a research mandate to complement its teaching role.

To be eligible to receive funding from any of Canada's three research funding agencies – Canadian Institutes of Health Research (CIHR), Natural Sciences and Engineering Research Council (NSERC), and Social Sciences and Humanities Research Council (SSHRC) – a university must sign a memorandum of understanding, which obliges it to create a research infrastructure that includes a research ethics and a research integrity policy, a research ethics board to authorize and oversee studies of living humans to ensure that the research adheres to the principles laid out in the *TCPS,* and an appeal mechanism for negative REB decisions. Failure to comply with a memorandum of understanding can lead to a university being refused funding and/or having the grants it has already received suspended.

In 2002, Kwantlen signed its first memorandum of understanding with SSHRC, thereby making it eligible to receive SSHRC funding. As part of the conditions of the initial memorandum of understanding, Kwantlen created Policy G27 (*Research Involving Human Participants*), its first research ethics policy, which came into effect on 1 October 2002. The policy's purpose was to "ensure that appropriate standards are followed and to support researchers in their efforts to conduct ethically sound research when research is conducted using human participants ... Unless expressly exempted, all research under the auspices of Kwantlen University College and all research on our campuses that involves living human subjects requires prior review and approval by the REB." If research was conducted "under the auspices of Kwantlen," it was required to receive REB review before it could commence. Policy G27's requirements were not limited to SSHRC research – the memorandum of understanding requires review of all human research conducted under the auspices of the university, regardless of whether it is funded or who funds it. The memorandum of understanding also required Kwantlen to ensure that the REB reviewed a particular study before disbursing any research funds.

Ogden's Research on Assisted Suicide

In keeping with these requirements, faculty member Russel Ogden submitted several proposals to the Kwantlen REB to continue conducting his research on assisted and unassisted suicide.[5] His November 2003 proposal to the Kwantlen REB was to conduct confidential interviews with ten to fifteen "NuTech death providers" – that is, persons who had aided another person's suicide by helping to place a helium-filled bag over his or her head. The REB approved the project. On 6 September 2004, Ogden submitted a second proposal called "Observation and Documentation of a NuTech Deathing," which involved attending at least one assisted suicide. Ogden's proposed research included interviewing the participants and collecting data during the suicide by direct observation. After a lengthy deliberation, the REB approved the protocol on 12 July 2005.

At the time he submitted the proposal, Ogden was well aware that Canadian Criminal Code section 241 prohibits "Counselling or Aiding Suicide."[6] In keeping with *TCPS* admonitions that one should be aware of the law relevant to one's research, he had studied the assisted suicide case law and designed his research protocol in a way that he believed precluded his actions being defined as counselling or aiding or abetting a suicide. However, in December 2006, seventeen months after the REB approved the research, the Kwantlen administration sent Ogden two missives ordering him to stop his approved research.

The first, from Judith McGillivray (provost and vice-president, academic), instructed Ogden that he was "not to engage in any illegal activity including attending at an assisted death or participating in any way in the planning of such an event."[7] To this day, it is not clear what triggered the VP-academic's intervention seventeen months after the research was approved. Nor is it clear on what basis McGillivray asserted that attending a death was a criminal event when, in 1994, MP Svend Robinson had attended the assisted suicide of Sue Rodriguez but had not been charged with an offence.[8]

Three days later, on 15 December 2006, Grant Allan (associate vice-president, Office of Research and Scholarship) wrote,

Having considered your July 2005 research proposal,[9] Kwantlen's position is that if you were to attend at an assisted death in the manner described, you would be engaging in conduct which is either criminal or which carries with it such a high risk that it could so be characterized, with serious consequences to you and to Kwantlen, that it would be contrary to the law and Kwantlen's policies for you to do so in your capacity as a researcher employed by Kwantlen.[10]

As far as we know, this stop-research edict is the first time that a Canadian university has invoked the *TCPS* provision that "Institutions may refuse to allow certain research within its jurisdiction, even though the REB has found it ethically acceptable" (Article 1.2, p. 1.3). Convinced that the administration was misinterpreting the assisted suicide case law, Ogden believed that the order infringed his academic freedom to conduct research. He approached the Kwantlen Faculty Association (KFA) for assistance. A week after he received the stop-research edict, Ogden filed a complaint against the administration for violating his academic freedom, while KFA sought advice from CAUT. On 2 April 2007, CAUT wrote to Kwantlen president Skip Triplett urging him to withdraw the stop-research edict. The Kwantlen administration dug in, and another year passed. Faced with this intransigence, CAUT wrote to Ogden on 24 June 2008 informing him that it had established an ad hoc advisory committee to investigate his situation at Kwantlen and determine, among other things, whether Kwantlen had violated his academic freedom.[11]

When CAUT announced that it was going to conduct an investigation of Kwantlen, Ogden's predicament started to generate international news. In a media statement on 4 July 2008, amidst a flurry of newspaper and magazine articles on Ogden's research (Hutchinson 2008; Jaschik 2008; Jerema 2008; Taylor 2008; Todd 2008), Kwantlen claimed that its decision was based on its due diligence, including a legal opinion by one of Canada's leading criminal attorneys, Leonard Doust, QC. The opinion suggested that by attending an assisted suicide a researcher would likely commit the criminal offence of counselling or aiding or abetting a suicide.

Kwantlen's bold claim that it exercised due diligence before ordering Ogden to stop his research does not stand scrutiny. The media release neglected to mention four important facts. First, Kwantlen stopped the research five months before receiving Doust's opinion. It thus appears the opinion provided an *ex post facto* rationalization of a decision that had already been made. Second, Kwantlen did not provide Doust a copy of Ogden's research proposal and the protocol he would use when planning to attend a suicide. This left Doust considering an abstract scenario rather than Ogden's carefully planned protocol that had been years in the making with the relevant case law in mind. Third, an equally eminent criminal attorney – David

Crossin, QC – funded by the Canadian Association of University Teachers and the Federation of Post-Secondary Educators of BC did not concur with Kwantlen's legal opinion. Upon examining Ogden's protocol in conjunction with case law that the Kwantlen legal opinion did not cite, Crossin's opinion suggested that Ogden's carefully considered research conduct was unlikely to be judged a criminal offence. And finally, the Kwantlen REB obtained a third legal opinion, which it refused to release. However, to the extent that the REB approved Ogden's application to observe suicide and assisted suicide, its legal opinion presumably also concluded that Ogden's research was unlikely to constitute a criminal offence. In sum, Kwantlen stopped the research before seeking a formal legal opinion about Ogden's protocol. When it did consult an attorney after the fact, Kwantlen did not provide him with a copy of the research protocol to review. A cloud now hung over Kwantlen as the CAUT investigation loomed. But worse was to come. Added to the administration's doublespeak were its blatant double standards.

The Aboriginal Youth Justice Project

While one researcher was being held to rigorous standards – and ordered to stop his nonfunded and controversial research notwithstanding its ethical probity – those same standards were not being applied to other researchers. On 17 October 2007, the Kwantlen REB held a panel session titled "Dialogue on Research Ethics." During a question-and-answer period, the REB chair Warren Bourgeois and REB member Stephen Dooley disclosed that Dooley had served as the principal researcher on a study of Aboriginal youth without submitting it for REB review.[12] The study in question – the "Aboriginal Youth Justice Programme" (Dooley, Floyd, and Welsh 2005) – was funded by a $37,000 grant that the Vancouver Police Department (VPD) had obtained from the Department of Justice Canada's Youth Justice Renewal Fund.

   The research focused on people living in Vancouver's Downtown Eastside (DTES). The DTES is one the lowest-income urban neighbourhoods in Canada. Its residents have one of the highest HIV and hepatitis C infection rates in the Western world, and it has a long history of street-level prostitution activity. Among its roughly 16,000 residents in 1992 were 500 mentally ill persons, over 350 Latino refugees, and 480 sex workers (Taylor 1993). It has a substantial Aboriginal population (9 percent in 2001), one of the largest open illicit drug use scenes in North America (Strathdee, Patrick, and Currie 1997; Wood, Kerr, and Spittal 2002), and, in 2006, a 22 percent unemployment rate compared to 8 percent in Vancouver as a whole (City of Vancouver 2006, 12).

   Because it is one of the most marginalized communities in Canada, the DTES has been of considerable interest to academics and others who conduct social and medical community-based research. The opening of Insite, North America's first supervised injection site, in 2003, and the Robert Pickton case have intensified research interest in the neighbourhood. The area gained international notoriety in the early 2000s following the disappearance of more than sixty women involved in the street sex trade, many of whom were Aboriginal. Robert Pickton was convicted of six of their murders, and may be responsible for as many as forty-three more.[13] The police investigation of the disappearances, which was subject to scathing criticism not least because of the time it took for the VPD to mount one or admit that a serial killer may have been responsible for the murders, became the subject of the Missing Women Commission of Inquiry (Oppal 2012).

Needless to say, studying such a highly marginalized and vulnerable population poses numerous ethical challenges, especially in research projects that involve more than a minimal risk to participants. It was in this highly charged political and social milieu that, in 2004, the VPD secured funding from the Department of Justice Canada to conduct the Aboriginal Youth Justice Programme research. The contract gave very little time to get the research underway; it had to begin almost immediately.

If ever there was a social scientific research sample that deserved REB oversight and protection, this was it. The research involved two hundred children from forty-three Aboriginal First Nations. One-third of the participants were under seventeen years of age, with some as young as eleven. All were asked to provide intimate personal information via a fifty-nine-item questionnaire administered by inexperienced "peer researchers" who were paid on a piece rate rather than hourly, an arrangement that could have had the undesirable effect of encouraging short cuts to get interviews completed. Questionnaire topics included participants' criminal involvement and arrest history, their home life and guardianship (more than 50 percent of the respondents aged twelve to seventeen had been or were in care of the Ministry of Children and Family Development), and their experience of "starlight tours" by police officers, that is, the illegal practice whereby police drop a person miles away from where they were picked up. The Aboriginal youth justice program report (Dooley, Floyd, and Welsh 2005) does not say whether research participants were told about the VPD's involvement in the study or how participants' confidentiality was protected. Some participants reported that they were homeless, which also raises questions about how researchers dealt with provincial laws that require the reporting of children in need of protection.[14] As far as we can ascertain, consent for the children to participate in the research was not sought from parents, guardians, Aboriginal band councils, or the Ministry of Children and Family Development. The word *ethics* does not appear anywhere in the 178-page report. A consent form is mentioned (ibid., 35), but a copy is not included in the appendices.

Such research requires great care to accomplish without putting the children and youth research participants at even greater risk than they would have been had they not participated in the research. The inquiry that eventually took place in 2008 (described below) concluded that the research constituted "more-than-a-minimal-risk" to participants according to the *TCPS* definition (1.5), which would require the REB to seek a peer review of the research to ensure that appropriate professional standards were met. The only reference in the report to information provided to interview participants about their ethical rights under the national research ethics policy is in the preamble of the interview schedule (Dooley, Floyd, and Welsh 2005, Appendix 1, 139). This preamble falls far short of the information that ought to have been provided about the research, such as where results could be obtained, the procedure to follow should there be a complaint about the conduct of the researchers, the participant's right to decline to answer certain questions or withdraw from the interview at any time, and so on. As to focus groups, little information is given about how informed consent was achieved and how various ethical issues, particularly confidentiality, were handled.

Passing the Buck and Personalizing a Dispute

On 18 October 2007, Ogden wrote to Kwantlen president Triplett notifying him of what appeared to be a blatant violation of Kwantlen's Research Ethics Policy (G27). Ogden pointed out that "Mr. Dooley's research has been celebrated, repeatedly, as an example of research and scholarship at KUC [Kwantlen], despite the fact that there was no ethical oversight to protect the interests of aboriginal participants." In their roles as REB member and chair, respectively, Dooley and Bourgeois were responsible for ensuring that all research conducted under Kwantlen's auspices was conducted according to institutional policy and the *TCPS*. Both were also members of Kwantlen's REB Task Force, which was charged with recommending revisions to the Kwantlen research ethics policy. Ogden urged the president "to take immediate and public action to demonstrate that Kwantlen University College is committed to professional standards in research ethics and integrity in scholarship."[15]

Instead of recognizing the situation as one that may have placed a vulnerable research population at risk, violated the college's memorandum of understanding, and – if so ethically complex a project could fly under the institution's radar – potentially represented just the tip of an iceberg of research ethics maladministration, Triplett framed the issue as a dispute between individuals. On

19 October 2007, Triplett stated that Ogden should make a complaint against his fellow faculty member using the procedure outlined in Kwantlen Policy C6, "Complaints about Instruction, Services, Employees, or University College Policies."

There were several problems with Triplett suggesting that Ogden resort to the C6 complaint procedure. For example, present at the meeting where the research ethics policy violation was disclosed were several Kwantlen senior administrators and six Kwantlen REB members, to whom Ogden copied his email to Triplett. Did this mean that if Ogden did not make a complaint, the various administrators and REB members who were at the meeting where the policy violation came to light would turn a blind eye to that policy violation? Moreover, although it promises due process to all, C6 gives no time limits for responding to complaints at any of the first four steps of the five-step procedure, in which case the administration could spin its wheels indefinitely. Ogden was already experiencing serious delays in the administration's response to his complaint about the stop-research edict. After a year, that complaint still had not been resolved. Given the nature of the Aboriginal youth justice programme and the serious ethical issues it involved, why would Triplett not seek to establish whether the ethics policy violation was an anomaly or an indication of serious ongoing ethics maladministration? What if there were other active Kwantlen research projects involving similarly serious ethical issues that had not been reviewed? In addition, Kwantlen's memorandum of understanding with SSHRC required it to "release funds to researchers only after an Institutional REB has approved the research." Did the Kwantlen Office of Research Services routinely disburse grant funds to conduct research on humans without checking to see if those projects had REB approval? Was no one in the research administration concerned about such a violation of the memorandum of understanding? And finally, if there was going to be a complaint about researcher integrity, Kwantlen's 2002 memorandum of understanding with SSHRC obliged it to "have in place an integrity policy that is consistent with the Tri-Council Policy Statement." Kwantlen did not have a research integrity policy of any kind, let alone one that was consistent with the *TCPS,* and was thus in violation of the memorandum of understanding. Further, the Kwantlen research ethics policy did not contain an appeal mechanism, another violation of its memorandum of understanding. Although Ogden had brought these memorandum of understanding violations to the administration's attention in 2006, Kwantlen continued to violate its agreement with SSHRC.[16] In view of these problems, Ogden did not make a complaint under Policy C6. In light of the "do as we say, not as we do" approach that Kwantlen appeared to be bringing to its research ethics obligations, the serious threat to academic free-dom that the administration's stop-research edict posed, and concern that other research on vulnerable populations was being conducted at Kwantlen without ethics review and oversight – actions that affect the entire research community – it was time for members of the broader academic community to lend support to Ogden and his colleagues' attempts to hold the Kwantlen administration accountable.

An Opportunity for Kwantlen to Show Ethical Responsibility

On 1 November 2007, the two of us wrote to Triplett explaining that we were raising the matter of what appeared to us to be a serious violation of Canada's national research ethics code and Kwantlen's research ethics policy. We called on him to invoke his powers under Kwantlen Policies 3[17] and 3.2[18] and establish an independent blue ribbon committee to investigate the ethics policy violation that was first reported to him on 17 October 2007. We copied the letter to the Department of Justice Canada as it had funded the research, the VPD, and various other key parties (hereafter, the copy list).[19]

On 5 November 2007, Triplett referred our complaint to the Kwantlen Office of Research and Scholarship to investigate. On 27 November, we again wrote to the president objecting to his decision to refer our complaint to the Office of Research and Scholarship, pointing out that, because it was that very office that should be investigated, it would not be appropriate for it to be involved in the investigation. We pointed out that one of the reasons we had decided to make an external complaint was that, by referring Ogden to the complaint policy (C6), the president reinforced the concern that Kwantlen would like to treat the alleged research ethics breach as a dispute between employees when it was not. We further suggested that it was not the principal researcher who should be the primary subject of an investiga-tion, but the Kwantlen administration itself. While the principal researcher clearly had some explaining to do – particularly given that he was a member of the Kwantlen REB and presumably was familiar with the requirements of both the Kwantlen ethics policy and the *TCPS* – the more important question was whether Kwantlen exercised due diligence when it came to ensuring that all research involving humans conducted under its auspices was REB-approved and that the university was living up to its responsibilities as outlined in its memorandum of understanding with the federal granting agencies. Why did KUC release funds for this project without checking that it had REB approval? How many other projects were conducted at Kwantlen without REB review and oversight while the administration was asleep at the wheel?

Adding Doublespeak to Double Standards

On 10 December 2007, Triplett sent an email to the complainants and the copy list announcing,

> In early November 2007, Professors Lowman and Palys alleged that ethical breaches had taken place with regard to a project undertaken by Kwantlen faculty members in 2005.
>
> Kwantlen took these allegations seriously and is currently working to identify a qualified person (or persons) to investigate their allegations. The researchers who were involved in this project strongly support an open and transparent enquiry. The terms of reference for the enquiry will also include a determination of whether process or policy deficiencies exist that Kwantlen's administration must address.
>
> I will communicate with you again when an appropriate person has been engaged for this enquiry and terms of reference and time-lines have been established.

The same day, Triplett distributed this missive saying that Kwantlen "took these allegations seriously" and the researchers "strongly support an open and transparent enquiry," we received a letter from a lawyer representing the principal researcher threatening to sue us for libel if we did not immediately send him "a draft of a clear and unequivocal apology and retraction to [the principal researcher] to be distributed to all of the recipients of the copy list." That same day, Ogden and two other Kwantlen faculty members also received a letter from the principal researcher's attorney threatening to sue them for libel if they did not do the same with a letter they had written to the president mentioning the Aboriginal youth justice research ethics violation and raising questions about the integrity of the REB Task Force.

We later learned as a result of a series of requests under the BC Freedom of Information and Protection of Privacy Act (FIPPA) that, while the Kwantlen administration was publicly promising an "open and transparent" inquiry, it was simultaneously providing more than $6,000 in funding for the principal researcher in the Aboriginal justice project to engage the attorney who sent the letters on his behalf threatening libel action. It thus appears that an open and transparent inquiry was the last thing on Kwantlen's collective administrative mind.

Another missive – the third within twenty-four hours – arrived the next day, a VPD statement under the heading "Letter regarding Vancouver Police Department 2005 business research contract." It was sent to us and the copy list, which the VPD expanded to include the director of the School of

Criminology and the dean of Arts and Social Sciences at Simon Fraser University (SFU), where we are employed. The VPD also sent the letter under a separate heading to Triplett asking him to distribute it to any other parties at Kwantlen who may have received the allegations about the Aboriginal youth justice research. The VPD statement asserted,

> The referenced study was a piece of business information research put out by the Vancouver Police Department and contracted to consultants [the principal researcher and two others] ... Kwantlen University College neither controlled decisions regarding this project nor owns the resulting intellectual property.
>
> Vancouver Police Department business research performed by retained consultants or otherwise is not subject to review or approval by third party academic institution processes ...
>
> It is crucial that John Lowman and Ted Palys stop their speculative disapprovals before serious harm is done to the Vancouver Police Department's relationships with the urban Vancouver Aboriginal community and, in my opinion, before they damage their own or Simon Fraser University's reputations immeasurably by their actions.

On receipt of the threatened libel suit, we consulted the SFU Faculty Association, which in turn approached the administration to discuss our options. In view of the SFU Framework Agreement provision that provides "legal advice, representation and/or indemnification to members of the [faculty] bargaining unit who encounter problems as a result of carrying out in good faith their responsibilities," SFU approached its insurer, Canadian Universities Reciprocal Insurance Exchange (CURIE), for assistance.[20] CURIE provided us with legal counsel.

One of the first actions our counsel took was to ask for clarification of the principal researcher's position. What exactly did his lawyer mean when he asserted that "there are a number of untrue ... comments" in our letters to Kwantlen concerning the Aboriginal youth justice research? Could he please provide a list of these errors? Although Triplett informed the copy list that he would announce the terms of reference and the person to conduct the inquiry, he provided no time frame for that undertaking. Weeks passed, and then months. We heard nothing more. Nor did we hear anything from the principal researcher's attorney in response to our request that he identify mistakes in our complaint. He did not withdraw the libel suit threat.

Given that the principal researcher – who was included in the VPD's list of recipients – had tacitly endorsed the position in the VPD's letter by remaining silent, and given that four months had passed without any answer to our queries, we decided to challenge that letter. On 11 April 2008, we presented the VPD and the copy list with evidence that three Kwantlen researchers, not three independent consultants, had conducted the Aboriginal youth justice research. The evidence was overwhelming and for emphasis, we use a bulleted list:

- The three authors of the research proposal that won them the contract to conduct the Aboriginal youth justice research in the first place gave "Kwantlen" as their institutional affiliation.
- Kwantlen's name appeared sixteen times in the proposal.
- The budget included an item for $12,000 for "faculty time release," another for training and salaries for five Kwantlen students, and an administration fee of $6,549.51.
- The Department of Justice's youth program contracted the VPD to conduct the Aboriginal youth justice research. The VPD, in turn, subcontracted the research to the three Kwantlen faculty members at their Kwantlen address. A 10 December 2004 letter informing them that they had been awarded the contract was sent to their Kwantlen address, not a private consultants' office.
- The executive assistant of Kwantlen's Office of Research and Scholarship witnessed the principal researcher's signature on the contract returned to the VPD.
- A steering committee comprising police, researchers, a member of the Kwantlen Finance Department, and community representatives oversaw the research.
- Kwantlen's name appeared forty-eight times in the minutes of the twelve steering committee meetings.
- Each set of minutes was titled "Kwantlen Research Project Steering Committee Minutes."
- The minutes mention that invoices for the research were submitted by the Kwantlen Finance Department, not three independent consultants.
- The authors of the final report, *Taking Steps Forward: Development of an Aboriginal Youth Justice Programme* (Dooley, Floyd, and Welsh 2005),[21] gave Kwantlen as their affiliation. On page 37, the report noted: "All of the participants who attended the focus group were given a gift of one form or another including carrying bags and pens. In addition, a special gift was provided at each focus group for the person who did the welcome at the beginning of the meeting. The Office of the President at Kwantlen University College provided the gifts."
- Numerous Kwantlen publications list the Aboriginal youth justice research as a Kwantlen project. For example, the "Summary Report for 2004-2007"

of the Kwantlen "National Institute for Research in Sustainable Community Development" – for which the principal researcher served as director – listed Dooley, Floyd, Welsh, and McCormick as the "Kwantlen Faculty Principal Investigators" for the "Aboriginal Justice Programme" and took credit for $60,000 of funding provided by the Department of Youth Canada Justice Renewal Fund.[22]

- On its website, Kwantlen posted a brief titled "A Strong Case for Becoming a Special Purpose University," which stated: "Kwantlen is seeking to be officially identified as a primarily undergraduate, regionally focused university." In promoting its merits to be elevated to full university status, Kwantlen listed the "Vancouver Police Department Aboriginal Youth Justice Project (Criminology and Sociology)" as one of several "examples of Kwantlen Student and Faculty Research Projects." Kwantlen's presentation to the provincial government similarly listed the "Aboriginal Justice Programme" as Kwantlen research.

- Of the $37,000 budget, Kwantlen was paid $4,756.63 (15 percent of the total) as a fee for administering the funds, and another $12,000 (33 percent of the research budget) to pay for teaching time release for one of the researchers. Kwantlen invoiced the VPD for the funds and handled the payroll; the invoices were on Kwantlen letterhead. The VPD made no direct payment to any of the researchers. If the three faculty members were acting as independent contractors, they would have had to perform all administrative duties themselves, including employee payroll, and be paid directly by the VPD for their time. If the VPD had contracted the three faculty members as independent consultants, Kwantlen policy required that those faculty members disassociate themselves from Kwantlen in the process of conducting the research.[23]

- It appears that Inspector John de Haas, the primary VPD contact for the Aboriginal youth justice research, also regarded it as a Kwantlen project. For example, at a Vancouver Police Board meeting on 16 February 2005, de Haas spoke of "the research project currently underway with Kwantlen University College, which was designed to identify successful strategies to reduce the number of Aboriginal youth involved in the justice system."

- The Kwantlen National Institute for Research in Sustainable Community Development "Summary Report for 2004-2007" included a testimonial from Inspector de Haas that stated: "The work was a collaboration that brought Kwantlen as a true third partner to the table. Your process, involving literature review, forums and the ensuing report were extremely important in furthering endeavours toward these goals. Your data acquisition and processing led to clear understandings of what was occurring in the community and what was to be done."

To deny that the Aboriginal youth justice research was conducted "under the auspices of Kwantlen" thus beggars belief, the academic equivalent of the Monty Python sketch in which pet shop owner Michael Palin insists that the stiff parrot he has sold John Cleese is not dead, just sleeping.

We concluded the letter by providing these documents along with the challenge, "If VPD has evidence that contradicts the information provided ... about the [Aboriginal youth justice] research, please produce it." The VPD did not dispute any of the evidence we presented. Instead, it responded that there is a "divergence of understanding" about the status of the Aboriginal youth justice research and that the various policy violations we alluded to "are issues internal to Kwantlen College" (letter, 17 April 2008).

After our 11 April letter to the VPD, President Triplett announced the panellists and the timeframe for the inquiry – fully four months after he first announced that there would be one.

Like so many other aspects of Kwantlen governance we witnessed, the inquiry procedure was a farce. The call for submissions was distributed before the panel's terms of reference were released. Once the inquiry began, it was obvious that it would be anything but "open and transparent." There are numerous examples of this lack of transparency, which are, again, best presented in a list:

- The panel did not disclose whom it interviewed.
- The panel did not disclose how many submissions were made and who made them. Indeed, the panel may not have known who made some of the written submissions.
- It appears that the panel was in possession of submissions that were not provided to the complainants.
- One of the complainants' three submissions was distributed without the attachments that provided the evidentiary basis for its analysis. Despite Kwantlen's subsequent promise to distribute the missing evidence, it was not distributed to at least some of the parties involved in the inquiry.
- Complainants and respondents were prevented from attending each other's interviews with the panel, thereby being denied the opportunity to respond to any allegations that were made about them during those interviews.
- When we received submissions, we were told that we must keep them confidential. We were not asked ahead of time if we agreed to this arrangement, which was foisted on us just one working day prior to the beginning of the interviews. The 401-page package of submissions should have been distributed well ahead of time to give both complainants and respondents time to prepare.

- Instead of the panel operating at arm's length from the Kwantlen administration, Kwantlen required that all inquiries and submissions be sent to an email address (panel@kwantlen.ca) set up for that purpose. However, Kwantlen refused to disclose who answered inquiries sent to that address and refused to disclose what information was being forwarded to the panel.
- Kwantlen justified its confidentiality clause by asserting that the BC Freedom of Information and Protection of Privacy Act (FIPPA) requires it. That is not quite true. The complainants and respondents can waive their privacy rights under the act. When President Triplett said that the respondents "strongly support an open and transparent inquiry," we assumed that they had waived their FIPPA rights – how else could the inquiry be open and transparent?
- When we asked whether Kwantlen had asked the respondents whether they would waive their rights under FIPPA, we did not receive a reply. Indeed, many of our queries to panel@kwantlen.ca were never answered.
- When we asked for the identity of persons making the various submissions that Kwantlen distributed to participants, the request was denied. It may well be that one or more Kwantlen administrators made submissions to the panel, but then used FIPPA to deny access to information that showed who submitted what.

As a consequence of these problems, we decided to limit our involvement in the inquiry to written submissions only.

In addition to the numerous procedural problems, the Panel of Inquiry was not designed to find fault or hold people accountable. The inquiry thus did not have the power and authority that would have applied under the integrity in research policy that Kwantlen should have had in place as per the requirements of its memorandum of understanding with SSHRC signed in 2002.

Conclusions of the Panel of Inquiry

The Panel of Inquiry (2008, 2-3) concluded that the Aboriginal youth justice research was conducted "under the auspices of Kwantlen" and should have been submitted to the REB for review: "We can see no justification for exempting this project from research ethics review. As such, the lack of REB review was a breach of the existing KUC regulations the TCPS and, more broadly, emerging international scholarly standards." The panel concluded that the breach was not wilful. Rather, it resulted "from a convergence of several factors that existed when the project was undertaken," including "poor research ethics leadership" (ibid., 8). Nevertheless, the panel concluded those factors were "not, in this case, a valid justification for not submitting the protocol for KUC REB review" (ibid., 3).

Do As We Say and Not As We Do

Although Kwantlen promised an open and transparent inquiry, it never published the Panel of Inquiry report. The copy Kwantlen sent to inquiry participants was marked "confidential." However, this proviso did not stop the administration from posting on its website a formal response that selectively quoted the report. Kwantlen did not quote the inquiry's main finding that "We can see no justification for exempting this project from research ethics review ... The lack of REB review was a breach of the existing KUC regulations, the TCPS and, more broadly, emerging international scholarly standards." Consequently, on 24 September 2008, we sent an email to the copy list setting the record straight.

Three weeks later, we received a letter from the law firm Fasken Martineau DuMoulin informing us that Kwantlen had retained it to threaten us with legal action if we released any more of the report and would seek damages if we did. In response, we pointed out that the threat was vexatious because: (a) Kwantlen promised an open and transparent inquiry and then reneged on that undertaking; (b) by citing the report in its website "Response," Kwantlen had already violated its own confidentiality requirement, in which case it was hardly in a position to complain when we followed suit; and (c) in any event, the parts we quoted from the report were not from the ostensibly confidential copy we had been sent as two of the participants, but from an unredacted copy released to us as a result of a FIPPA request, which meant that it was now in the public domain.

Fasken Martineau DuMoulin did not reply.

Unresolved Issues

The Panel of Inquiry conclusions did not address the question of culpability that would have arisen under the "Integrity in Research and Scholarship" Policy (B18) that Kwantlen finally introduced on 21 July 2008 after SSHRC put the institution on probation for violating its memorandum of understanding. Policy B18 contains the following protection for "Good Faith Claims:"

> The university will make every effort to protect from retaliation those making an allegation of misconduct in research or who have provided information to the university in good faith ...

No person(s) to whom this policy applies may retaliate against a person(s) making such allegations or providing such information in good faith.

Policy B18 allows for disciplinary action against persons found to have retaliated against a complainant who acted in good faith. Also, it enables disciplinary action against persons "found to have made an irresponsible or malicious allegation of misconduct." While the Panel of Inquiry concluded that the original ethics breach was not wilful, the principal researcher's threatened libel suit most assuredly was, as was the administration's decision to fund it. Under the new policy, surely the threatened libel suit would have constituted "retaliation."

When the principal researcher approached the Kwantlen administration to fund a lawyer to threaten the complainants with a libel action, he must have been well aware of the abundance of evidence demonstrating that the Aboriginal youth justice research was conducted under the auspices of Kwantlen. Further, the inquiry report revealed that the principal researcher had provided the panel with an email he sent on 15 April 2005 to Warren Bourgeois, the Kwantlen REB chair, saying that, "upon reflection I feel that elements of the [Aboriginal youth justice] project should have gone through ethical review." Did the principal researcher inform the Kwantlen administration of this email when he sought funding for a lawyer to threaten us with a libel action for saying much the same thing? Given the abundance of evidence showing that Kwantlen administered the funds, why did he not set the record straight when the VPD made what he must have known was a false claim about hiring him as an independent contractor?

When Kwantlen funded the threat of a libel suit against the whistleblowers, it became a party to the retaliation. A legal opinion prepared by Leo McGrady, QC, for the Kwantlen Faculty Association suggested that, by funding one faculty member's law suit against three others, the administration violated Section 27 of the British Columbia Labour Relations Code, which gives the KFA the exclusive right to represent its members. Further, by becoming complicit in the retaliation against the complainants the administration could be said to have violated Article 24.01 of the Collective Agreement, which defines personal harassment as "repeated offensive comments and/or actions that, by a reasonable standard, create an abusive or intimidating work environment. Personal harassment may occur as a single incident or over a period of time." McGrady stated,

It is not the initiation of the lawsuit itself by Mr. Dooley that constitutes harassment ... Rather, it is the funding of the lawsuit by the University that constitutes the act of harassment ...

The nature of the harassment is compounded here because the very person charged with ensuring a harassment-free work environment ... was the same person guilty of the misconduct – the employer.

Further, by funding the threat of a lawsuit by one faculty member against another – which could have cost $50,000 to $100,000 if the matter had proceeded to trial – the university could be said to have violated its Collective Agreement with the KFA by providing a significant benefit to one faculty member over another. Kwantlen has since assured the KFA that it will not repeat this act.

Kwantlen also placed itself in the position of funding a lawsuit against three faculty members, and then, when those faculty members approached the institution for legal indemnification, the institution turned to its insurer – the University College and Institute Protection Program (UCIPP) – to finance the defence of the lawsuit that the institution itself was funding. UCIPP insurance is available to faculty members who need to defend themselves "from any legal action arising from the proper performance of their duties for the Employer."[24] That is, the institution was funding an action against employees who were acting properly for the employer.

Given the principal researcher's knowledge of the paper trail connecting Kwantlen to the Aboriginal youth justice research and his 15 April 2005 email to the REB chair acknowledging that the Aboriginal youth justice research "should have gone through ethical review," his threatened libel suit looks vexatious. It cost the complainants a considerable amount of time and cost the two insurers, CURIE and UCIPP, substantial expenditures for legal services. Had the principal researcher produced this email at the time the complaints were made, many of these costs would have been unnecessary. More importantly, simply acknowledging the obvious would have allowed greater focus on the bigger issues that lay behind the complaint – that is, whether the participants in the Aboriginal youth justice project were adequately protected, the extent to which Kwantlen was failing to meet its obligations under the memorandum of understanding, and what needed to be done for the institution to get back on track.

With these arguments in mind – but still not yet having in our possession definitive evidence that Kwantlen had funded the threatened libel suit[25] – we wrote to Kwantlen's new president David Atkinson on 1 December 2009 suggesting that Kwantlen should pay restitution. On 21 December 2009, Atkinson sent each of us a letter that "summarily rejected" our request, characterizing it as "spiteful, vindictive and not worthy of a senior academic." He asserted that, although the Aboriginal youth justice research was ethically challenging, the researchers believed that the project steering committee had "full jurisdiction over those challenges," as if that somehow justified their actions.

While these comments could be taken to imply that the steering committee appropriately dealt with research ethics issues, the documentary record does not support that conclusion. The minutes of the steering committee's twelve meetings mention research ethics issues just once: at its first meeting. At that meeting, the committee decided to postpone discussion of research ethics issues to a later date because several Aboriginal leaders were not in attendance. However, according to the minutes from the eleven subsequent meetings, research ethics issues were not discussed. The *Taking Steps Forward* report mentions ethics considerations but once, and only in passing – a reference to the existence of a consent form (35). When asked to provide a copy of the consent form (on 17 October 2007), the principal researcher did not respond. Numerous questions about the ethical probity of the research have never been answered. And yet the Aboriginal youth justice research report (Dooley, Floyd, and Welsh 2005) is still posted on the Kwantlen website.

Conclusion

While there has been some discussion in Canada of the problems that the *TCPS* regime has created for researchers, and several instances where universities have been cautioned or threatened with sanctions for failing to comply with the *TCPS,* the case described in this chapter appears to be the first during the *TCPS* era where academics have carried out greater-than-minimal-risk research on humans without submitting it for REB review. During this same period, Kwantlen also became the first university in Canada we know of to stop research that its REB had approved.

The Panel of Inquiry ultimately concluded that the failure of the research team to submit the Aboriginal youth research for REB review reflected the growing pains of an academic institution as it added research to its teaching function. Our perception of this and other aspects of Kwantlen's research administration is less sanguine. If the Aboriginal youth justice research ethics policy violation was a mere growing pain, why in 2008 did Kwantlen sign a second memorandum of understanding with SSHRC knowing full well that it was not in compliance because it still did not have a research misconduct policy or appeal procedure for negative REB decisions? Did other postsecondary institutions developing a research function experience these kinds of problems? Or was Kwantlen being run by a delinquent administration that invested more energy in acquiring university status than it did in living up to the level of responsibility that such status entails?

The purpose of the inquiry was to examine complaints about the Aboriginal youth justice research. Its terms of reference did not include one of the primary concerns of the whistleblowers – namely, how many other projects were being conducted by Kwantlen faculty without REB review and oversight? That question aside, Kwantlen clearly failed its ethical obligation to protect Aboriginal research participants at a time when it was in blatant violation of the memorandum of understanding that enabled it to receive government funding in the first place.

There is also the matter of the Kwantlen-funded threat to sue the whistleblowers for libel if they did not swallow their whistles. Martha Stewart did not go to prison for trading shares on the basis of insider information but for her attempt to cover up what she did. By the same token, Kwantlen should have paid for the damage its threatened libel suit caused – restitution that it probably would not have been able to avoid under the research misconduct policy that it should have put in place when it signed its first memorandum of understanding in 2002 but did not introduce until 2008, after the Panel of Inquiry had concluded its deliberations and after Kwantlen signed its second memorandum of understanding with SSHRC.

The *TCPS* set up a regulatory framework that ostensibly requires universities and other research institutions who seek granting agency funding to live up to the requirements of the *TCPS,* and it bestows on REBs the ability to halt research that is not consistent with the standards the *TCPS* requires. But what checks and balances have the presidents of the granting agencies created to deal with rogue administrations that state in their memorandum of understanding that they comply with the *TCPS* – their ticket to funding eligibility – while failing to live up to the principles and level of responsibility that such eligibility requires? What happens when, in the process, a university infringes the academic freedom of a faculty member to conduct research?

A second edition of the *TCPS* released in 2010 addressed many of the difficulties that plagued REB review (CIHR, NSERC, and SSHRC 2010), but failed to create any new checks or balances on REB and university administration power (Palys and Lowman 2010, 2011) to ensure that power is not abused and academic freedom is protected. But there is another forum in which such issues can be addressed. In 2011, Canada's three funding agencies began the process of revising another of its policy statements, the *Tri-Council Policy Statement: Integrity in Research and Scholarship,* and invited the research community to provide input into a consultation document called the *Tri-Agency Framework for Responsible Conduct of Research.* The granting agencies' new policy on responsible conduct in research ignored CAUT's submission (2011b) in response to this invitation. The granting agencies are thus continuing to turn a deaf ear to McDonald's warnings about the need to address institutional conflicts of interest and protect academic freedom. The essence of CAUT's submission was that the consultation draft of the revised policy said nothing about the responsibility of college and university administrations to avoid or manage institutional conflicts of interest, uphold the academic freedom of its researchers, and honour their collective agreements with faculty. CAUT argued these concerns *must* be built into a research integrity policy, and we concur.

The case we have described suggests that *Responsible Conduct of Research* should not only spell out the responsibility of university administrations to uphold academic freedom and manage institutional conflict of interest but should also include a mechanism to hold university administrations accountable. While it is possible to make a complaint to a granting agency when a university violates its memorandum of understanding, as was the case at Kwantlen, the Tri-Agency framework for responsible research still contains no mechanism for holding institutions accountable when they do not manage institutional conflict of interest, threaten academic freedom, and harass and threaten members of the research community who, in good faith, dare to question the way they do business. If the three granting agencies seriously meant to foster a culture of research ethics in Canada, they would not have ignored CAUT's recommendations.

Notes

1 In 2010, a substantially revised edition (*TCPS 2*) replaced the 1998 version. Unless otherwise noted, references to "the *TCPS*" refer to the 1998 version, as it was the one in effect when the events described in this chapter occurred.

2 Formation of the Tri-Council Working Group and its mandate to develop a national ethics code came on the heels of data fraud by Dr. Roger Poisson of Hôpital Saint-Luc in Montreal, which received international press coverage in 1994. Articles within the medical community discussed the erosion of public trust this created and called for more extensive monitoring of medical research. See, for example, Weijer et al. (1995). However, it is noteworthy that, in the end, the *TCPS* says nothing about data fraud. A simpler explanation is that various industrialized countries were formalizing federal codes of research ethics and that Canada was merely following suit to ensure its share of the growing number of international multisite studies, particularly in the realm of pharmaceutical clinical trials.

3 Exceptions here would include our recounting of the Simon Fraser University administration's assault on research confidentiality that began with the Ogden case (see Lowman and Palys 2000; Palys and Lowman 2014) and the extensive review that was done of Nancy Olivieri's dispute with Apotex, the University of Toronto, and the Hospital for Sick Children (see Thompson, Baird, and Downie 2001).

4 Kwantlen University College (KUC) became Kwantlen Polytechnic University (KPU) in 2008.

5 Ogden began this research in 1992 at SFU for his master's degree thesis, which he completed in 1994.

6 Section 241 reads, "Every one who (a) counsels a person to commit suicide, or (b) aids or abets a person to commit suicide, whether a suicide ensues or not, is guilty of an indictable offence and liable to imprisonment for a term not exceeding fourteen years."

7 Russel Ogden supplied us with a copy of McGillivray's letter, which was dated 13 December 2006.

8 Rodriguez had unsuccessfully petitioned the attorney general of British Columbia to secure the legal right to assisted suicide. In a five to four decision, the Supreme Court of Canada upheld the decision that denied her request.

9 On 20 April 2007, the REB approved a second study that involved Ogden attending an unassisted suicide, which presumably would be subject to the same stop-research directive.

10 Russel Ogden supplied us with a copy of this letter.

11 CAUT never did complete an investigation as the administration reached a confidential agreement with Ogden that allowed him to continue the research. On 19 November 2008, president David Atkinson sent an email to sociology and criminology faculty – the two departments where Ogden was teaching at the time – informing them that "Kwantlen Polytechnic University, the Kwantlen Faculty Association and Russel Ogden have reached a settlement agreement on the issue of Russel's Academic Freedom as it relates to his research." To the extent that the email stated that "the parties to the agreement are pleased with the resolution" and that Ogden commenced a two-year research leave on 1 January 2009, during which time he carried out the research, it appears that the administration withdrew the stop-research edict, an inference that CAUT subsequently confirmed (CAUT 2009).

12 Professor Bourgeois served as REB chair from 2002 to 2007 and was chair of the interim REB at the time of this meeting.

13 Pickton told a police undercover operative the first night after he was arrested and detained that he was responsible for forty-nine murders. He was charged with a further twenty murders on the basis of DNA and other evidence found on his farm, but in light of the expense of the year-long search of his property and trial for the first six murders the Crown stayed the charges.

14 On learning that some of the children were homeless, the researchers presumably had a legal obligation under the Child, Family and Community Service Act to report the matter to a child protection worker. The report provides no information about what protocol was used to handle such information.

15 Russel Ogden supplied us with a copy of the letter.

16 On 26 March 2008, Kwantlen signed a second memorandum of understanding with SSHRC knowing that it was in violation of that agreement at the time it entered into it. Ogden's subsequent complaint to SSHRC on 28 May 2008 resulted in SSHRC ordering Kwantlen to achieve full compliance by 31 March 2009. If it had not complied by that time, a hold would be placed on the grants it was already administering and it would become ineligible to apply for further grants.

17 Global Executive Constraint: "The President shall not cause or allow any practice, activity, decision, or organizational circumstance which is … in violation of … professional ethics of public bodies and of the post-secondary environment."

18 Treatment of Employees: "The President may not cause or allow conditions that are unfair, disrespectful, undignified, disorganized, improperly discriminatory, or unclear."

19 Judith McGillivray (Kwantlen Provost), Grant Allan (Kwantlen AVP Research, outgoing), Rob Adamoski (Kwantlen AVP Research, incoming), Gordon Lee (Kwantlen VP), Farhad

Dastur (REB Chair), Jan Storch (REB member), Peter Graff (REB member), Sam Migliore (REB member), Warren Bourgeois (REB member and former chair), Arleigh Reichl (REB member), Stephen Dooley (REB member), Kathleen Casprowitz (Chair, Kwantlen Board of Governors), Terri A. Van Steinburg (President, Kwantlen Faculty Association), Claire Morris (President, Association of Universities and Colleges of Canada), Jim Turk (CAUT Executive Director), Chief Constable Chu (VPD), Chief Shawn A-in-chut Atleo (BC Assembly of First Nations), David Johnnson (Executive Director, United Native Nations), Robert Nicholson (Minister of Justice), Tom Christensen (Minister for Children and Family Development), and Mary Ellen Turpel-Lafond (BC Representative for Children and Youth).

20 Our thanks to SFU for approving this request.

21 A curious aspect of this report is that it appeared in three different incarnations that appear to differ only by the number of authors listed. On all three versions Dooley, Floyd, and Welsh's names appear. However, on one version of the report, they are the only authors. On the second version, the name S. MacDonald also appears. On the third version, T. Fenning's name appears as well as MacDonald's. It is thus unclear whether the report had three, four, or five authors, in which case the variation in authorship may itself represent a form of academic misconduct.

22 It is not clear why there is a discrepancy between this claim and Kwantlen financial records, which indicate that the budget was $37,000, not $60,000.

23 Kwantlen Policy H2 prohibits the use of Kwantlen's name and logo for anything but official university business. Policy G1 dealing with conflict of interest holds that, among other things, a conflict arises in a situation where "an employee uses his/her status for the employee's private advantage, whether personal or professional." In other words, Kwantlen faculty should not use Kwantlen's name when they sign contracts as "independent consultants"; nor should they represent their independent research as Kwantlen research.

24 Article 18.06 (a), KPU Collective Agreement.

25 President Atkinson initially refused to provide any records in response to our FIPPA request for records pertaining to the libel suit. We appealed his decision and, on 15 October 2010, following mediation as per the procedure under FIPPA, received records, which, although large sections were redacted, confirmed that Kwantlen did indeed fund the threatened libel suit.

References

CAUT (Canadian Association of University Teachers). (2009). Ogden Case Settled, CAUT Ends Inquiry. *CAUT/ACPPU Bulletin,* March, A5. http://www.cautbulletin.ca/ .

—. (2011a). CAUT Concerned about Proposed Research Misconduct Policy Changes. *CAUT/ACPPU Bulletin 58*(8), October. http://www.cautbulletin.ca/.

—. (2011b). Response from the Canadian Association of University Teachers. Unpublished submission to granting councils.

CIHR, NSERC, and SSHRC (Canadian Institutes of Health Research, Natural Sciences and Engineering Research Council, and Social Sciences and Humanities Research Council). (2010). *Tri-Council Policy Statement: Ethical Conduct for Research Involving Humans.* Ottawa: Department of Supply and Services. http://www.pre.ethics.gc.ca/eng/policy-politique/initiatives/tcps2-eptc2/Default/.

—. (2011). *Tri-Agency Framework: Responsible Conduct of Research.* Ottawa: Panel on Responsible Conduct of Research. http://www.rcr.ethics.gc.ca/eng/policy-politique/framework-cadre/.

City of Vancouver. (2006). *2005/2006 Downtown Eastside Community Monitoring Report.* http://vancouver.ca/commsvcs/planning/dtes/pdf/2006MR.pdf.

Dooley, S., Floyd, R., and Welsh, A. (2005). Taking Steps Forward: Development of an Aboriginal Youth Justice Programme. Unpublished paper, Kwantlen University College, Richmond, BC. http://www.kwantlen.ca/_shared/assets/ayj_report_may2005_0001251.pdf.

Fitzgerald, M.H. (2005). Punctuated Equilibrium, Moral Panics and the Ethics Review Process. *Journal of Academic Ethics* 2(4), 1-24.

Haggerty, K.D. (2004). Ethics Creep: Governing Social Science Research in the Name of Ethics. *Qualitative Sociology* 27(4), 391-414.

Hutchinson, B. (2008). College Orders Professor to Stop Euthanasia Research. *National Post,* 3 July.

Jaschik, S. (2008). When a University Kills Suicide Research. *Inside Higher Education,* 7 July. http://www.insidehighered.com/news/.

Jerema, C. (2008). Kwantlen Shuts Down Controversial Research. *Maclean's,* 7 July. http://oncampus.macleans.ca/education/.

Lowman, J., and Palys, T. (2000). Ethics and Institutional Conflict of Interest: The Research Confidentiality Controversy at Simon Fraser University. *Sociological Practice* 2(4), 245-55.

McDonald, M. (1998). The Tri-Council Policy Statement on Ethical Conduct for Research Involving Humans. *Canadian Bioethics Society Newsletter* 3(3).

—. (2001). Canadian Governance of Health Research Involving Human Subjects: Is Anybody Minding the Store? *Health Law Journal* 9, 1-21.

MRC, NSERC, and SSHRC (Medical Research Council, Natural Sciences and Engineering Research Council, Social Sciences and Humanities Research Council). (1998). *Tri-Council Policy Statement: Ethical Conduct for Research Involving Humans.* Ottawa: Department of Supply and Services. http://www.pre.ethics.gc.ca/eng/archives/tcps-eptc/Default/.

Ogden, R. (1994). Euthanasia and Assisted Suicide in Persons with Acquired Immunodeficiency Syndrome (AIDS) or Human Immunodeficiency Virus (HIV). MA thesis, Simon Fraser University. http://summit.sfu.ca/item/5038.

Oppal, W.T. (2012). *Forsaken: The Report of the Missing Women Commission of Inquiry.* Victoria: Province of British Columbia. http://www.missingwomeninquiry.ca/obtain-report/.

Palys, T., and Lowman, J. (2010). TCPS-2's Enduring Challenge: How to Provide Ethics Governance While Respecting Academic Freedom. http://www.sfu.ca/~palys/PalysLowman CommentsOnTCPS2-2011.pdf.

—. (2011). What's Been Did and What's Been Hid: Reflections on TCPS2. http://www.sfu. ca/~palys/PalysLowmanCommentsReTCPS2Draft2-final.pdf.

—. (2014). Protecting Research Confidentiality: What Happens When Ethics and Law Collide? Manuscript submitted for publication.

Panel of Inquiry. (2008). Panel Report: Kwantlen University College Research Ethics Inquiry. Unpublished Report.

SSHWC (Social Science and Humanities Research Ethics Special Working Committee). (2004). *Giving Voice to the Spectrum: Report of the Social Science and Humanities Research Ethics Special Working Committee to the Interagency Advisory Panel on Research Ethics.* June. Ottawa: Interagency Advisory Panel and Secretariat on Research Ethics. http://www.sfu.ca/~palys/SSHWC -GivingVoice-2004.pdf.

Strathdee, S.A., Patrick, D.M., and Currie, S.L. (1997). Needle Exchange Is Not Enough: Lessons from the Vancouver Injecting Drug Use Study. *AIDS* 11(8), F59-F65.

Taylor, R. (1993). Street Prostitution and Community Action. Vancouver Police Department report.

Taylor, T. (2008). The Ethics of Witnessing Suicides. *Globe and Mail,* 14 July. http://www. theglobeandmail.com/.

Thompson, J., Baird, P., and Downie, J. (2001). *Report of the Committee of Inquiry on the Case Involving Dr. Nancy Olivieri, the Hospital for Sick Children, the University of Toronto, and Apotex, Inc.* Ottawa: Canadian Association of University Teachers. http://www.caut.ca/.

Todd, D. (2008). Academics Fight for Prof's Right to View Assisted Suicides. *Vancouver Sun,* 2 July. http://www.canada.com/vancouversun/news/.

Tri-Council Working Group. (1996). *Code of Conduct for Research Involving Humans* (Draft document). Ottawa: Medical Research Council, Natural Sciences and Engineering Research Council, and Social Sciences and Humanities Research Council.

van den Hoonaard, W. (2011). *The Seduction of Ethics: Transforming the Social Sciences.* Toronto: University of Toronto Press.

Weijer, C., Shapiro, S., Fuks, A., Glass, K.C., and Skrutkowska, M. (1995). Monitoring Clinical Research: An Obligation Unfulfilled. *Canadian Medical Association Journal 152*(12), 1973–80.

Wood, E., Kerr, M.W., and Spittal, P.M. (2002). Factors Associated with Persistent High-Risk Syringe Sharing in the Presence of an Established Needle Exchange Programme. *AIDS 16*(1), 401–36.

part 3   Emotion Work and Identity:
Self-Examination and Self-Awareness

chapter 11

Reconciling the Irreconcilable:
Resolving Emotionality and
Research Responsibility When
Working for the Traumatizer

Sheryl C. Fabian

THE GOVERNMENT OF CANADA's historical efforts to impose Eurocentric cultural ideals on Native peoples were guised in rhetoric that suggested residential schools would remove the "Native" from Aboriginal peoples, to protect "them" from "themselves" (See Churchill 2004; Haig-Brown 2006; Milloy 1999, among others). The earliest Canadian residential schools opened in the nineteenth century; by the 1930s, there were more than eighty schools in operation across the country, with the last school closing in 1996. Government policies encouraged the aggressive assimilation of all Aboriginal peoples (Indian, Inuit, and Metis). Aboriginal children were removed from their families (often with force), housed in residential schools and, under the pretext of education, stripped of their culture, language, and way of life, often made worse by rife physical, sexual, and psychological abuse and neglect. Following years of negotiation, on 11 June 2008, the Canadian government made history when it issued a public apology to Aboriginal peoples and acknowledged the destructive assimilation practices that the federal government had engaged in for almost 150 years. Surrounded by the political leaders of the opposition parties and representatives of First Nation, Metis, and Inuit communities, Prime Minister Stephen Harper delivered a poignant apology. The atrocities that occurred in Indian residential schools (IRS) are well documented, undeniable, and seemingly unforgivable, and although the apology has its critics, many viewed it as a first step in acknowledging a horrendous legacy and an effort to begin the healing processes.

The government apology came on the heels of the implementation of the Indian Residential Schools Settlement Agreement (IRSSA), which came into effect on 19 September 2007, following more than a decade of litigation against the government and churches responsible for residential schools. The settlement agreement, endorsed by government, churches, and survivors, acknowledges Canada's historical efforts to assimilate Aboriginal peoples and provides monetary compensation to survivors of the residential school program. More importantly, it focuses on "healing, reconciliation, and resolution" that is respectful of Aboriginal peoples and their traditions and speaks of a concerted effort to restore community to the multiple generations subjected to these historical atrocities. The settlement agreement, in combination with the apology, aims to build new relationships with Aboriginal groups. To accomplish this, the Indian Residential Schools Truth and Reconciliation Commission (TRC) was created and tasked with educating Canadians about these aspects of Canada's history and building a new era of understanding that acknowledges the value of all cultures. Somewhat ironically, on 25 September 2009 – little more than a year after the historic apology was issued, at the G20 Summit in Pittsburgh, Pennsylvania – Prime Minister Harper seemed to forget this historic moment, stating that Canada has "no history of colonialism" and announcing that we are the envy of the world (Junggren 2009).

As I complete this chapter, after more than ten years of experience conducting residential school research for the Government of Canada, the need for this research and thus the role of contract researchers is ending, as the 19 September 2012 deadline for submitting claims has passed. Accordingly, this chapter is a reflection on my decade-long work as a research consultant and the many changes and challenges I have faced in researching the claims of those subjected to the residential school experience in Canada. It also includes some anecdotal research experiences of some of my colleagues. More specifically, I explore the issue of emotionality in archival research, which can be problematic and debilitating not only for participants but also for researchers. Government of Canada researchers who investigate the claims of residential school survivors review claimant and application materials and use historical records to validate attendance and residence at the schools. Our efforts to verify claims follow traditional requirements of systematic and rigorous research, similar to research conducted in an academic environment. The process involves reading firsthand accounts of the horrors of survivor claims and their descriptions of residential school experiences. Doing this work for prolonged periods is challenging, heart-wrenching, and often unsatisfying, so much so that it is not uncommon for researchers to experience what has been termed *vicarious trauma* (Lerias and Byrne 2003; McCann and Pearlman 1990; Schauben and Frazier 1995; Way et al. 2004). It is impossible to ignore the suffering of claimants, which can be particularly overwhelming when reviewing handwritten accounts. Personal stories seem to be amplified when provided in the claimant's own hand rather than in a more formal and less personal typewritten format. The impact on researchers reviewing such claims is as undeniable as the experiences of the survivors. I do not intend to minimize the traumatic experiences of those in residential schools; rather, I emphasize the fact that simply reading survivor accounts takes an emotional toll on researchers. In turn, this makes us even more aware of the extent and the emotional impact of those experiences on survivors, which further highlights the importance of our work. This chapter is my personal account of experiencing methodology.

I began working on residential school claims in 2002,[1] and although I now have a permanent, full-time faculty position at Simon Fraser University, teaching in the criminology program, I continue to work part-time for what is currently Aboriginal Affairs and Northern Development Canada (AANDC).[2] People often ask why I carry on doing this work. It is much more than a source of income. The work reflects my commitment to those affected by residential schools and, on some level, my attempts, at least internally, to make some kind of amends for past wrongs – as absurd as this might sound. Obviously, Government of Canada research consultants cannot make up for the atrocities of residential schools, nor did we play any role in the policies and practices that persisted for more than a century. And yet it seems many of us feel a personal responsibility to validate the claims of residential school survivors, albeit within the parameters set out by the very group that traumatized these individuals in the first place – meaning, we are bound by the Eurocentric notions of evidence and truth. This chapter begins with a brief summary of the evolution of Government of Canada responses to claims with IRS survivors, including a history of some of the many changes in the processes. I then discuss some of the specific challenges in conducting archival document research by chronicling how policy decisions regarding protocols do not always reflect a complete understanding of the materials available to researchers. I then explore some of the emotional responses researchers have in doing this work, including the experience of vicarious trauma. I conclude with a discussion of the conflict of conscience researchers face in their efforts to reconcile the irreconcilable: the conflict between those to whom we are accountable and those personally affected by the research process and outcomes.

The Evolution of Government of Canada Responses to Residential School Claims

The first residential school claims were filed in the 1990s and have since shifted from this initial litigious process to that of alternative dispute resolution (ADR) and, finally, to the current processes set out in the settlement agreement. The processes in the agreement are specifically designed to meet the more immediate needs of survivors and to be more in keeping with, and respectful of, Aboriginal cultures. While the settlement agreement aims to honour the applicants and survivors, decisions made by those in power (i.e., government policymakers and lawyers) do not always seem consistent with the spirit of the apology, and survivors do not always understand the limits of the agreement. Further, the historical documents used to assess claims are often incomplete, and errors and omissions in records are typical. In conducting research *for* the federal government in relation to Canada's legacy of Indian residential schools, researchers must resolve the conflict that emerges when the employer (i.e., the owner of the data; in this case, the Government of Canada) requires reports regarding the applicants with whom they are trying to make amends. For example, school attendance records can be incomplete or ambiguous in terms of validating an applicant's tenure at a residential school, and researchers are required to follow established protocols when making decisions about confirming or denying an applicant's claim. At the same time, these protocols can effectively bind our ability to honour the claimant's voice because available documents do not meet the burden of proof of residency set by the employer, even though the information provided by the claimant supports residence in the absence of documents that confirm the claim. Consistent with some types of academic research, positivist understandings of truth influence these protocols, leaving no room for interpretation or contextualization. When I started working in 2002, researcher expertise was valued, and documents were read in context; now, we simply "report" information as it appears on the documents. This shift appears to reflect a similar shift regarding what is happening to qualitative work in Canada – minimizing its value and focusing solely on the facts rather than on the grander narrative and the broader context.

The first lawsuits regarding abuses experienced in residential school were filed in the 1990s. The litigious nature of the process meant resolution took many years, and great financial expenditures were required to resolve lawsuits. By 2007, the Government of Canada had spent more than "$200 million processing and defending itself from claims – in contrast to the $38 million ... dispensed for compensation" (Funk-Unrau and Snyder 2007, 285-86). Further, litigation claims involved only the most serious cases of physical and sexual abuse, and the courts did not consider loss of culture, language, way of life, and psychological impact compensable. Finally, the process was critiqued by "some Survivors as exclusionary, time-intensive, financially and emotionally draining, and often unrewarding" (Reimer et al. 2010, 5).[3]

In response to the numerous problems associated with the litigation process, the alternative dispute resolution process was implemented as a "less formal, less complicated, and faster alternative to the courts" (Reimer et al. 2010, 5). As was the case with litigation, ADR dealt solely with physical and sexual abuse claims; the impact of residential schools on the loss of culture and language was not compensable. Although the process was intended to be less complicated than formal legal actions, those opting for the ADR process were still required to prove their claims, and participants report that the process was "arduous and emotionally difficult" (ibid.). As with most government processes, the ADR's was open to critique, so much so that some have referred to it as both a form of social control and one of cooptation (Funk-Unrau and Snyder 2007).

The IRSSA was announced on 10 May 2006 and was approved by all parties involved in the process, including the Government of Canada, legal counsel for former students, churches,[4] the Assembly of First Nations, and Inuit representatives.[5] Initially, 130 institutions were recognized under the IRSSA. Although the list was developed in consultation with the above parties, those affected could apply to have additional schools added. As of January 2014, only nine schools have been added to the original list, for a total of 139 eligible schools.[6] And even thogh the approved IRS list was developed in consultation with the most relevant parties, critics continue to express concerns regarding the criteria for inclusion. As Reimer and colleagues (2010, 5) explain, "Differences in how residential schools are defined for inclusion of the official list depend on whether or not there was federal government involvement and/or whether or not records exist to verify institutions as residential schools." For example, Aboriginal organizations, such as the Aboriginal Healing Foundation, argue that many institutions defined as residential schools by Aboriginal peoples, including industrial schools, home-boarding programs, hostels, and billeting, are excluded from the list (ibid.).

In addition, concerns have been repeatedly expressed that the IRSSA list of eligible schools excludes those who attended as day pupils and did not stay in residence overnight. In fact, in July 2009, a class action lawsuit seeking compensation for day pupils who were affected in the same way as those who lived in residential school system was filed (Walls 2010, 362).[7] This is especially important because the common experience payment (CEP) process (discussed below) only compensates those students who spent the night in an officially recognized residential school. It is agonizing for researchers who must declare students ineligible, even though their narratives show that they were part of the residential school experience. An article in Regina's *Leader Post* recounts the words of one survivor who was deemed ineligible for CEP: "'How is my misery worthless in comparison? ... Molestation doesn't just happen at night,' said [Marjorie] Quewezance, who says she was beaten, sexually molested and emotionally abused while she was a student at St. Phillip's

[Saskatchewan]" (Smith 2007, A3). This is but one example of the many former students who have been excluded from the settlement agreement solely because they returned home in the evenings.

Following the acceptance of the IRSSA, the CEP process began on 19 September 2007, and applications were received until 19 September 2011. Unlike the previous litigation and ADR processes, as part of the settlement agreement, the Government of Canada acknowledged "the general loss of culture and language" that occurred when children were forcibly removed from their home communities and families under the residential school policies (Reimer et al. 2010, 5). Former IRS students who were alive as of 30 May 2005 are eligible for compensation of "\$10,000 for the first year (or part thereof) of attendance at a residential school and an additional \$3,000 for each subsequent year (or part thereof)" (ibid.). The implementation of the CEP finally acknowledged the assimilationist polices of residential schools and government efforts to strip indigenous peoples of their culture, conceding that those affected were entitled to compensation for these losses. The process includes an initial assessment of the case, conducted by the less-than-accurate computer-assisted research system (discussed below), and applicants have the right to first request reconsideration of their claim and then to appeal those results if unsatisfied.[8] These cases involve transcripts of calls to Service Canada that frequently describe the emotions of claimants who recount the abuses they experienced. The person who responds to the calls both transcribes their words and documents their "state of mind";[9] it is not uncommon to see notations like "sobbing loudly," "broke down into tears," or "extremely upset."

In addition to the CEP process, the IRSSA established the independent assessment process (IAP) for those who experienced physical and sexual abuse and other wrongdoing that resulted in serious psychological consequences (Reimer et al. 2010, 6). The IAP process was intended to replace the ADR process, although claimants could elect to remain in ADR. The time frame allotted for the processing of IAP applications is nine months, considerably faster than the previous litigation and ADR claims. Adjudicators conduct hearings, and applicants are eligible for emotional and wellness support through the Indian Residential Schools Resolution Health Support Program provided by Health Canada (ibid.).

In the past, survivors' attempts to claim abuse perpetrated by other residential students were denied; however, under IAP, for the first time, compensation was not restricted to those actions that occurred at the hands of residential school staff and was expanded to include student-on-student abuse. As discussed below, our work repeatedly tells us that many of the named student perpetrators were themselves victims of abuse at residential schools as indicated by their own IAP claims. This is but one example of the cycle of abuse perpetuated by Indian residential schools. Further, we frequently work on claims that emphasize the intergenerational nature of IRS abuses. We often receive research requests and find that we have previously completed abuse claims for the grandparents, parents, and/or children or grandchildren of the applicant. There is little doubt that the residential school experiences of those forced into these institutions explain, at least in part, the high rates of physical and sexual abuse within Aboriginal communities, as well as issues with addiction and substance use (Ing 1991; Smith, Varcoe, and Edwards 2005; Trocmé, Knoke, and Blackstock 2004).

Researching Residential School Claims

Researchers are involved in the collection of archival documents related to residential schools;[10] this can include policy documents, descriptions of the schools and conditions, and those documents that identify students who attended the schools and individuals who worked at the schools or who came into contact with residential students. One of the primary challenges to the work is that the IRSSA identified eligible schools, yet numerous CEP applications were for schools that are not on the list for a variety of reasons. Some schools were excluded because they were not under the jurisdiction of the federal government at the time of operation. This means that if a student attended a residential school "too late," that is, after the government ceased to be formally responsible for the school, as is the case for some of the northern institutions, students are denied compensation and the schools are deemed ineligible, even though the Government of Canada was involved in creating and operating these institutions.[11] Researchers face personal challenges in reconciling the work they do when legal and policy decisions appear to undermine the intent of the settlement agreement. For some researchers, the ability to reconcile the work eventually becomes too much. In fact, one of my former colleagues, after working on more than one hundred appeal cases over several years and never being able to verify a claim, finally terminated her contract. Although this was not the only reason she gave up the work, she found that continuing to review survivors' accounts of the abuse they had endured for such a prolonged period without a successful case was too much of a burden. She explained that she was dismayed by the fact that claimants were encouraged to appeal, even when there was no chance an appeal would succeed because it was clear the claimant did not meet the criteria set out in the IRSSA. This researcher felt the appeal process gave applicants a false sense of hope that previous decisions would be reversed.

The work is further complicated by distinctions between schools in Northwest Territories and Nunavut and the residential school systems that operated in southern Canada and Yukon.[12] Until the mid-1950s, there were four primary residential schools operating in the North: St. Joseph's at Fort Resolution, Sacred Heart at Fort Providence, and two schools at Aklavik – All Saints RS and Immaculate Conception RS.[13] As these schools were closed, a new system of providing education in the North emerged. Rather than students living in a residential school per se, hostels were built in conjunction with associated day schools in close proximity to the hostel. Students would attend school during the day and reside at the hostel overnight. Of even greater interest is the way in which government and churches responded. For example, the initial residential schools at Aklavik (All Saints and Immaculate Conception) were run by the Anglican and Roman Catholic churches, respectively. When new hostels were built in Inuvik to replace the aging residential schools at Aklavik, two separate hostels replaced the two schools – the Roman Catholic Church operated Grollier Hall and the Anglican Church oversaw Stringer Hall. All students at both hostels attended a "'combined school' ... composed of a single administrative facility and 'two instructional wings,' one being Catholic and the other Anglican or non-sectarian" (Milloy 1999, 244).[14] The two hostels were located on the same grounds, with the school situated in the middle of the two facilities; both residential and day pupils attended the school. However, schools that operated to educate all hostel residents are not on the IRSSA official school lists, despite repeated requests to include them. In short, unless students were also residents of an affiliated hostel, they are not considered eligible for CEP, regardless of the fact that they would have been in regular contact with residential staff and pupils. In addition, institutions that opened post-1969 are also excluded from the official schools list.[15]

The magnitude of claims provides some insight into the number of men and women affected by residential schools and, at the same time, demonstrates the exclusion of those deemed ineligible. As of 30 September 2013, 105,548 CEP applications had been received and 102,919 had been processed. A total of 79,111 applicants were deemed eligible for payment, while 23,808 were deemed ineligible (through their initial application or through reconsideration or appeal).[16] As of 30 September 2013, 37,874 IAP claims had been received, of which 23,661 have been resolved. A total of 3,893 claims were deemed ineligible or were withdrawn.[17]

The Emotions of the Work

Researchers in various disciplines, from human geography to health sciences, argue that we must acknowledge our emotions as they allow us to produce better work (see, for example, Rager 2005; Rowling 1999; Widdowfield 2000; Yuen 2011). This certainly holds true for those of us researching IRS claims. Anthropologist Colleen McLaughlin articulates the connection between research processes, cultural perceptions, and individual emotional responses:

> If we look at the processes involved in research – looking and thinking, viewing the familiar differently, making judgements, suspending judgements, being creative, drawing conclusions, taking action and working with others – then we see how inter- and intra-personal these processes are and how connected to the processes of perception. We know that the processes of perception are deeply rooted in emotions about the self, about the external world and in cultural ways of seeing the world. (McLaughlin 2003, 67)

As Government of Canada research consultants, we face unique challenges, as we are bound by protocols and legal decisions over which we have no control. I, and many of my colleagues, have found the need to express the emotional impacts of our work, discussing and processing how it makes us feel, rather than ignoring it. Residential school survivors are not simply applicants or claimants – they are victims of systemic racism and horrific abuses that we cannot ignore. In fact, neglecting to appreciate the people making the claims leads to mistakes in our work as well as problems in relation to vicarious trauma. My colleagues and I feel an overwhelming burden of guilt for what our ancestors have done. The emotional weight of more than one hundred years of historical facts, supported by the narratives of survivors, takes a personal toll. While we are not responsible for the atrocities that occurred, as researchers we are responsible for ensuring that we conduct thorough, meticulous, and accurate research that exhausts all possibilities before failing to confirm an applicant.

Although the work is outside of an academic setting, the research is no less stringent and requires a methodical approach with great attention to detail, and, as in academe, findings must be supported by evidence. Moreover, as is the case in other research settings, we cannot infer findings; instead, we must construct arguments based on archival documents and the interpretation of available documents; in the absence of primary records, ancillary documents may be used but only in certain circumstances and for certain schools. Like academics, we face deadlines, which can be unrealistic and may actually sacrifice the quality of research. For example, when the CEP process was implemented, then Indian Residential School Resolution Canada employees and contractors were under tremendous pressure to meet government-imposed quotas regarding the number of cases to be processed each month. As noted above, northern-school documents are more complicated than southern-school records and actually provide considerably more information when compared with other locations, which means that our work frequently involves greater challenges in confirming residence in northern schools and that the research can be more laborious and difficult to complete in a timely manner.

In preparation for the receipt of CEP claims, the Government of Canada developed and implemented a computer-assisted research system, commonly known as CARS, which was expected to reduce the research burden. Initially, all CEP claims were processed through CARS, and researchers were tasked with verifying the results. Researchers quickly discovered the magnitude of CARS errors was substantial, and especially true for northern cases, in part because of the large number of Inuit claimants whose names involve an especially high incidence of name and spelling variations (including consonants used interchangeably that are not intuitive to English, such as q's and k's, or t's and s's).[18] Initially, CARS ran names only against primary documents, when the gaps in collections in the North typically required a review of ancillary documents to validate claims. Our concerns were quickly echoed by Aboriginal groups, including the National Residential School Survivors' Society, which produced a damning report that articulated the problems (NRSSS 2007). While this report may be linked to increased pressure on staff and consultants to "power through" cases, this may not have been in the best interests of the survivors: hurried research likely resulted in increases in the number of reconsideration and appeal claims, thereby extending the delay in payments. In fact, in my role as the primary person responsible for quality control of North and Nunavut claims, I have seen many errors in CEP and IAP results from both the CARS system and from researchers. The only positive aspect is that the majority of errors are actually in favour of the CEP applicant. When this occurs, the initial settlement awarded stands.

The same cannot be said for IAP cases. Although the frequency of errors is reduced in IAP, the work often requires manual research when errors are found; typically, errors appear to be the result of rushed work, where documents that confirm attendance and/or residence were missed because database searches and document reviews were incomplete. My family would tell you there are evenings when I yell at my computer or emerge from my office to complain about shoddy research or careless errors. While my frustration is real, the blame is better placed on the system and the deadlines rather than on the researchers themselves. Unreasonable quotas and deadlines sacrifice quality. When trying to reconcile my feelings of obligation to right the wrongs of my ancestors, knowing that I play a role in validating claims that might have gone unsubstantiated without going through quality control helps me sleep at night. That said, there are nights when cases keep me awake, or wake me up in the middle of the night, with concerns that I may have missed something or neglected to run a particular search that might produce results favouring claimants. These additional examples speak to what it means to experience methodology when our hands are tied.

In 2001, a unique issue of the *British Journal of Criminology* specifically explored the roles of emotion and research, especially when looking at violence (see Bosworth 2001; Burman, Batchelor, and Brown 2001; Liebling and Stanko 2001; Pickering 2001; Winlow et al. 2001, among others). Although considerations of the emotional impact researchers experience are often applied to those who speak directly with those who experienced or perpetrated violence (see Munn, this volume; Hannem, this volume), our experience as research consultants shows that simply reading claimant accounts, especially over a prolonged period of time, has a substantial impact on those who conduct the research. While little has been written about the emotional byproducts of archival research,[19] the personalized handwritten narratives provided by applicants can be painstakingly difficult to read, but they must be carefully reviewed, especially when research does not lead to an immediate identification of the claimant or the identified persons of interest.[20] Moreover, not surprisingly, many claimants are elderly, and detailed accounts of their past are not always provided. Incomplete memories lead to additional challenges for researchers. For example, it is not uncommon for applicants to name an incorrect school, and alleged dates of attendance are often partial or inaccurate. Accordingly, researchers must search the entire national database (of more than one million records) to ensure claimants are located at all eligible schools, and not only those schools specifically identified in the claims. When we have comprehensive records for the period during which a claimant was at an IRS, the process is relatively straightforward, but frequently this is not the case. School records are often incomplete and erroneous; there are ongoing issues of selective deposit and survival,[21] and there is little doubt that the specific recorders of the information make a great difference to the substantiation of a claim. In the North, the Grey Nuns were quite meticulous and detailed in the recording of information, but the recording practices of various individuals are certainly unique. For some records, a common challenge is to try to decipher handwriting or poor-quality copies. Other records may be sparse, portions of documents may be cut off, and language and spelling differences result in difficulties locating evidence. Furthermore, there is considerable evidence that some government records were deliberately destroyed, especially between the 1930s and the 1950s (Sadowski 2006).

In survivor narratives, there is often an authenticity that is both heart-wrenching and unnerving to the researcher. The details provided, especially when accounts of the abuse mirror those of others who express allegations against the same individuals, not only lead to sleepless nights but to an over-whelming determination, perhaps even an obligation, to substantiate the survivor's claims. Despite our best efforts, however, we cannot always achieve this. One particular case haunts me. The level of detail in the applicant's narrative left me without doubt that the student was in fact a residential school survivor. The survivor had gone by a variety of names throughout her life, and, even with a list of aliases, it was impossible to verify her presence at any school using the available documents. In addition, her first name (likely one assigned to her by the nuns at the school she attended) was extremely common, and there were at least eight others with a similar name during her alleged attendance dates. Despite hours of effort and having multiple researchers review the claim, we were unable to validate her presence at an IRS. More than two years later, there are still nights when I wake up thinking about this case. Furthermore, her attendance dates were from an era where recordkeeping was not as meticulous as it was in later years, and details such as birth dates were inconsistently recorded on documents (frequently the date of birth is a key means to locating an individual, especially when documents have poor legibility or when portions of names are missing). Even then, research frequently demonstrates that dates of birth are recorded incorrectly.

In fact, in a recent case the claimant's IAP application explicitly stated that a priest at the residential school she attended had altered her date of birth during her first year in residence, changing it from January in one year to December of the previous year. It is unclear why this occurred but it may reflect the need to assign the student to a specific grade and demonstrate that she was old enough to attend classes so the church could be compensated. Regardless, the impact of arbitrarily changing an individual's name – either to a French version, as many of the Catholic institutions in the NWT were overseen by the Grey Nuns, a French-speaking religious order, or to eliminate the student's indigenous name – is not only an example of loss of culture; it also influences our ability to confirm a case. It is hard to imagine how such actions are not a form of cultural genocide – or at least a concerted effort on the part of those in charge to strip indigenous children of both their culture and their language.

Similarly, multiple colleagues recount stories related to reviewing documents that consistently show problems with deplorable conditions of residential schools, including overcrowding, insufficient diets, deficient accommodations, and inadequate medical attention provided to residential students. In addition, documents chronicle the inhumane punishments many students endured.

Records show that children were forced to view dead bodies as a punishment for "bad" behaviour (failing to obey the nuns). Other documents record the bullying of a particular student by the nuns and similar behaviours from the other students. Children learn from those around them; staff at residential schools were far too often inappropriate role models. Even worse, we frequently see claims of student-on-student abuse that extends far beyond bullying to include physical, sexual, and psychological abuse from other students. The IAP is the first process that recognizes student-on-student abuse, which means that researchers are increasingly reading files of this nature. It is emotionally taxing to bear witness to a key contributing factor to the intergenerational abuse and trauma that many Aboriginal peoples continue to experience.

Despite the frustrations experienced when a survivor's claim cannot be validated, there are some very rewarding moments in this work. Many of us approach the work a bit like putting together a puzzle, searching for clues that help us locate the evidence of an individual's attendance at these schools. In one instance, with some extra digging and considerable persistence, I was able to build on a researcher's previous work and ultimately validate an IAP claim for a woman who was a resident at a northern school in the early 1920s. One of the most delightful aspects of this case was the fact that the claimant was located based on a photograph that showed her standing in front of the residential school at the age of six. Although this was not a full documents claim,[22] our senior research analyst was made aware of the photos, and they were provided to the resolution manager so that they could be shared with the claimant at her hearing. Similarly, in another case, I was unable to locate documentary evidence of the claimant's presence at an IRS, but my gut told me she was an IRS survivor. I asked permission to refer the case to another researcher, and, although it took her some time, the claimant was finally found on documents under an alias that was not provided in the application.

In other cases, research locates a proverbial smoking gun that substantiates a case. I recall one case in which the claimant discussed abuse that occurred during an overnight outing away from the school. Documents corroborated the specific details of the outing in the presence of the named POI provided by the claimant. In a more recent case, documents supported the applicant's abuse claim, showing that the events were reported to authorities who then determined there was not enough legal evidence to pursue the case. Although the outcomes can be less than satisfactory, locating documentary evidence to validate details of the claimant's narratives is rewarding. Research successes like these represent those rare moments when researchers are satisfied with their work because they feel that they actually play a role in validating survivor experiences, affirming their voices, acknowledging historical wrongs, and holding the Government of Canada accountable.

Exploiting the Exploited

Some might argue that elements of our work exploit those who have been exploited for centuries. We work for the traumatizer, are bound by Government of Canada decisions, and are well compensated for our efforts. This conflict of conscience provides a foundation for our obligation to conduct thorough research, free from errors, that does everything possible to validate claims within the parameters imposed. However, we also witnessed, and continue to see, exploitation at an even more appalling level. When CEP was first implemented, billboards appeared in areas with large indigenous populations encouraging CEP recipients to spend their "windfalls." The fact that there were individuals attempting to take advantage of survivors caused the Aboriginal Healing Foundation to commission a special report to document this as a modern form of atrocity against Aboriginal peoples (Stout and Harp 2007). The stories of survivor exploitation include offering loans with outrageous interest rates while simultaneously encouraging "recipients to spend their money 'in advance' before the LSPs [lump sum payments] are handed out so 'the money is spent before it arrives'" (ibid., 37). Those preying on vulnerable CEP applicants, who are often suffering from trauma and facing addictions, included car sales people coming into their communities to encourage unnecessary purchases (ibid.). Stout and Harp's (ibid.) report is filled with similar examples of the "vultures descend[ing] on the community because they knew people were getting advance payments" in the absence of any financial planning assistance that might aid recipients in managing their payments.

In an even more despicable example, on 31 October 2011, BC Supreme Court Justice Brenda Brown ordered a Calgary law firm that represents more than three thousand IAP claimants to suspend contact with its clients (Barnsley and Martens 2011). Blott and Company was alleged to have offered its residential school IAP claimants "loans at around 30 per cent interest and the option of buying electronic equipment like televisions, sound systems and computers" (Martens 2011). Third-party loans are expressly forbidden under the settlement agreement; furthermore, firms are not permitted to take more than 15 percent from a settlement, except in rare circumstances (Barnsley and Martens 2011).[23] In June 2012, in *Fontaine v. Canada (Attorney General)*,[24] Justice Brown accepted the court-appointed monitor's finding that David Blott had provided residential school IAP claimants with high-interest loans and had failed to adequately represent claimants. A retired BC Supreme Court judge was brought in to oversee the reassignment of IAP cases to new counsel. As Widdowson and Howard (2008, 33) note, "for many lawyers, aboriginal marginalization and dependent legal status is a lucrative opportunity." In June 2014, the Law Society of Alberta imposed the "most serious sanction" available: Blott was disbarred upon acceptance of his resignation (*Law Society of Alberta (Resignation Committee) v. Blott*).[25]

Silencing the Survivors

One of the most interesting aspects of this work relates to Eurocentric understandings of truth and authenticity. Oral history is an important part of indigenous cultures in Canada. However, Government of Canada expectations require that narratives be substantiated to verify claims through documentary evidence. While Dell, Fillmore, and Kilty (this volume) work to ensure indigenous voices are heard and valued, my Government of Canada work appears to do the opposite. Anthropologist Bruce Miller (2011) asserts that oral history is currently on trial in the courts. Although not related directly to our work, as CEP and IAP are not technically legal processes, the role of law in determining what constitutes evidence to support a claim is more than apparent. Miller constructs a compelling argument for the inclusion of oral history as an accepted form of evidence for Aboriginal peoples. He emphasizes chief justice of the Supreme Court Beverley McLachlin's examination of the role of oral history as evidence: "Aboriginal right claims give rise to unique and inherent evidentiary difficulties. Claimants are called upon to demonstrate features of their pre-contact society, across a gulf of centuries and without the aid of written records."[26] However, McLachlin went on to caution,

In determining the usefulness and reliability of oral histories, judges must resist facile assumptions based on Eurocentric traditions of gathering and passing on historical facts and traditions. Oral histories reflect the distinctive perspectives and cultures of the communities from which they originate and should not be discounted simply because they do not conform to the expectations of the non-aboriginal perspective. Thus, *Delgamuukw* cautions against facilely rejecting oral histories simply because they do not convey "historical" truth, contain elements that may be classified as mythology, lack precise detail, embody material tangential to the judicial process, or are confined to the community whose history is being recounted.[27]

Although the narratives that appear in CEP and IAP applications are not oral history per se, it seems that claimants are being held to similar Eurocentric standards that may actually silence survivors because they fail to meet these expectations. Miller (2011, 7) argues that, despite advances and warnings such as those offered by McLachlin, the courts are not the best venue for examining the challenges associated with evaluations of the credibility of oral history traditions. The adversarial nature of courtroom processes serves to further undermine the acceptability of non-Eurocentric evidentiary types and the role of expert witnesses in establishing the validity and credibility of such evidence (ibid.). Government of Canada decisions made in relation to the IAP processes reflect some of these conflicts and concerns. The IAP process is designed to be nonadversarial and nonlitigious, but the burdens of proof and the policy decisions made by Department of Justice Canada continue to be grounded in Eurocentric ideals and notions of legal evidence. The links to positivist understandings of truth are also apparent, especially when documents cannot be interpreted in context with other materials. Decisions regarding compensable schools on the IRSSA apply a Eurocentric legal lens rather than considering what it meant to be a student at a school associated with a student residence, regardless of whether the student attended the school only during the day. Such decisions are further complicated by the fact that, even though the Government of Canada remained a part of the residential school system in Northwest Territories and Nunavut post-1969, student residences that opened after this date are not considered part of the IRSSA and have not been added to the official list of eligible schools.

Tensions also exist among those less familiar with residential school experiences, and public ignorance is quite profound. In several of my classes, I discuss the legacy of residential schools and their role in the overrepresentation of Aboriginal peoples in the Canadian criminal justice system. I frequently ask my students when the last residential school in Canada closed. The guesses usually range from the 1930s to 1950s. Most appear stunned when I tell them it was 1996. Only once has a student known the answer; not surprisingly, she was an Aboriginal student whose band had recently honoured those who had lost their lives in residential schools as part of its participation in the Truth and Reconciliation Commission. An important component of the TRC is to resolve some of the public tensions between resolution for residential school survivors and arguments that "they" need to move on or, worse, "get over it." Nothing makes me angrier than hearing this from friends and family. The result is a mini-lecture that explains what really went on in these schools and the intergenerational abuses that occurred. How can we expect people who experienced such violence "to just get over it" when it is all their family knew for decades? Some seem to understand, others may pretend, while others continue to assert that we should not have to pay for the errors of our ancestors. One of my colleagues actually lost a long-time friend because of her work with residential schools. She came to a place where she could no longer handle the "get over it" attitude and actually stopped talking to her friend. It may be that people simply refuse to understand what went on because it is easier than accepting responsibility for what occurred.

The Role of Vicarious Trauma

Vicarious trauma, a term first coined by McCann and Pearlman (1990), describes the emotional experiences of those working with trauma survivors, typically in a therapeutic role (Vrklevski and Franklin 2008, 106).[27] Although the work I describe is archival, it is clear that I and many of my colleagues have experienced forms of vicarious trauma over the course of our residential school research careers. I am not sure that any of us would have predicted that reviewing documents could lead to the level of emotion we feel or the sleepless nights spent thinking about what we might be able to do to verify a claim.

When first implemented, the CEP workload and accompanying pressures to close cases were extreme and overwhelming. For the first time, we were permitted to work as many hours as possible, whereas earlier in the process there were restrictions on the number of hours we were permitted to work per month. (Such restrictions are even more stringent now.) Although many contractors work from home, the intranet that computer network researchers log into is more efficient in the office. Also for the first time, researchers were permitted to remain in the office in the evening and on weekends. Not only were contractors pressured to produce; similar pressures were placed on staff, who accrued much overtime at substantial rates, working well into the evenings and on weekends. I recall email exchanges over many weekends with the CEP senior research analyst, notifying her when I had completed a series of cases so she could assign me another batch. Even the Government of Canada was aware of the potential impact on researchers through intense workloads and the reading of traumatic narratives. In fact, it provided researchers with access to a First Nations elder who was available to meet with us to discuss our feelings about the impact of reading the countless narratives that described the horrors of residential school life for so many students. Plenty of researchers took advantage of this opportunity and spoke of the importance of sharing their grief with someone who understood it from a place of experience. One researcher shared her experiences after seeing the elder. She talked about catharsis in that he shared his appreciation for the work she was doing as a small step toward reconciliation for the wrongs his peoples endured. She spoke to me about the tears she shed and the solace she took in knowing that, in some small way, validating survivor experiences was symbolically and politically meaningful not only to the specific individuals but also to indigenous peoples on a much broader scale. Unfortunately, the Government of Canada no longer offers such services to contractors.

In preparing this chapter and reflecting upon my own coping mechanisms in conducting this emotional work, I also spoke with current and former colleagues regarding their techniques for dealing with the grief and guilt they experienced. I found myself surprised by some of the responses. Almost everyone mentioned tears or extreme venting sessions to their families or partners (although venting can be difficult as we are restricted in what we can say by privacy and confidentiality agreements). Some researchers explained that they stopped working at home and instead went into the office regularly in order to share their frustrations and sadness with others who could relate to and understand their grief. The office became a place of unity where the day often began with a round of discussing the horrors of the most recent cases people were working on as a means of rationalizing the work and letting go of the guilt experienced about the actions and behaviours of others. And some left the work, at least in part, because giving false hope to claimants was too disheartening.

Conclusion

The truth of our common experiences will help set our spirits free and pave the way to reconciliation.
– Truth and Reconciliation Commission of Canada

Where do we go from here? The IRSSA included the establishment of the Truth and Reconciliation Commission with a complex mandate aimed at "put[ting] the events of the past behind us so that we can work towards a stronger and healthier future" (Castellano, Archibald, and DeGagné 2008, 413). While many are critical of the role and value of truth commissions, I remain optimistic that good will come out of the evils that occurred in residential schools through a better-informed public and because the process emphasizes meaningful healing. The TRC involves a "sincere acknowledgement of the injustices and harms experienced by Aboriginal people and the need for continued healing."[29] However, this involves a multifaceted and intricate approach to the healing process. Paulette Regan, director of research for the Truth and Reconciliation Commission of Canada, provides a persuasive account of how these seemingly impossible goals might be achieved in her *Unsettling the Settler Within: Indian Residential Schools, Truth Telling, and Reconciliation in Canada* (2010), a scholarly text that includes personal accounts. Regan argues that we must move beyond a place for indigenous peoples to "air" their experiences at residential schools in a public venue. We must encourage non-Aboriginal Canadians to relinquish their naive view of Canadian history and take the time and responsibility to engage in a process that ensures that "colonial forms of denial, guilt, and empathy [do not] act as barriers to transformative socio-political change" (Regan 2010, 11). Only if we stop rationalizing the events of the past as something for which we should not be held accountable and resist common "get over it" attitudes will we truly reach a place of healing and reconciliation.

Acknowledgments

I would like to thank Louis Bazinet, Juliana Gee, Michelle Glen, and Susan Kim for sharing their insights and experiences as researchers, my co-editors Maritza Felices-Luna and Jennifer Kilty for their patience, support, and encouragement, and the anonymous reviewers for their contributions to this chapter. Finally, I want to acknowledge all who have been affected by the residential school experience.

Notes

1 Although I have worked on schools in the Alberta, British Columbia, and Yukon regions, the majority of my work at AANDC has involved research for Northwest Territories and Nunavut schools. The focus of my workload for the past four years has been quality control, meaning that, in addition to the occasional initial research assignment, I primarily review the work of other researchers, finalize reports, and deliver research products. Consequently, I see many more cases from a greater variety of schools than other researchers whose main role is to conduct original research for claims.

2 The name of the department has changed numerous times. Since 2002, I have worked for Indian Residential School Resolution Canada, Indian and Northern Affairs Canada, and Indian Affairs and Northern Development, among others.

3 Reimer et al. (2010) provide an excellent comprehensive qualitative study of the impact of the various processes on survivors.

4 The Catholic, Anglican, United, and Presbyterian Churches were involved in both the administration of residential schools in Canada and the IRSSA.

5 AANDC, "Frequently Asked Questions, Settlement Agreement," *Indian Residential Schools,* 15 September 2010, http://www.aandc-aandc.gc.ca.

6 See AANDC's "Statistics on the Implementation of the Indian Residential Schools Settlement Agreement," http://www.aadnc-aandc.gc.ca/eng/1315320539682.

7 Walls (2010) also makes a compelling argument that for those day pupils attending on-reserve day schools rather than classes at residential schools, "federal support of residential schools undermined day schools" (362).

8 See AANDC's "Reconsideration of Common Experience Payments," http://www.aadnc-aandc.gc.ca/eng/1100100015619.

9 The CEP process included opportunities for applicants to contact Service Canada to inquire about the status of their application. During the reconsideration process, researchers could ask Service Canada representatives to contact the applicant to request additional information that might help to confirm a claim. Service Canada's "Contact Us" portion of its website states, "The call-centre staff members have been trained to handle inquiries about the CEP process, applications, and payments" (http://www.servicecanada.gc.ca/).

10 Documents have been collected and scanned into a massive electronic database that holds more than a million records from a variety of repositories, including government archives, church documents, and, in some instances, documents provided by survivors of residential schools.

11 As of 1969, the responsibility for education was transferred to Northwest Territories government. Notably, the territories are not provinces and do not have sovereign status (Milloy 1999, 245-46).

12 Beginning in 1954, the system operating in Northwest Territories, Nunavut, and parts of northern Quebec was distinct from residential schools operating in the rest of Canada. By 1960, all northern residential schools were actually hostels attached to a day school.

13 There were other schools that operated in the North, such as Hay River, NWT. Circa 1930, students at Hay River were transferred to the Anglican School, All Saints at Aklavik, NWT.

14 Prior to 1968, residents of the hostels in Inuvik attended the Inuvik Day School, which came to be known as Sir Alexander Mackenzie School in 1961. In 1968, Samuel Hearne Secondary School opened and high school students attended this facility while elementary students remained at Sir Alexander Mackenzie School.

15 The Federal Hostel at Frobisher Bay (Ukkivik), Iqaluit, Nunavut, is one exception.

16 See AANDC's "Statistics on the Implementation of the Indian Residential Schools Settlement Agreement," http://www.aandc-aandc.gc.ca/eng/1315320539682.

17 See AANDC's "Reconsideration of Common Experience Payments," http://www.aandc -aandc.gc.ca/eng/1315320539682.

18 Applicants frequently provided multiple names by which they were known during their stays at residential schools. It is not uncommon to list three or more aliases in an application.

19 A notable exception is Bosworth's (2001) discussion of emotion and historical research.

20 Frequently, persons of interest (POIs) are not identified by name, and, when provided, name spellings are sometimes phonetic and researchers are frequently required to engage in creative research processes to "decode" the identity of the POI. In addition, persons of interest may be identified only by description markers such as position, language, or appearance, among others (for example, "French-speaking priest with beard"). This involves reviewing the application for additional "clues" that assist us in determining if there is enough information to identify a POI match based on the information provided by the claimant. In the course of this process, we are frequently required to read, often in explicit detail, about the abuses the claimant experienced at the hands of the alleged perpetrator. While we are told that we can ask our senior research analyst to review the application details for us, it is far more efficient for us to look for additional clues ourselves.

21 The phrase *selective deposit* refers to the notion "that some people, groups, and processes have a higher likelihood than others of having their views, lives and so on made a part of the historical record" (Palys and Atchison 2014, 430). The term *selective survival* "reminds us that among those things that are initially put into the historical record ... some have a better chance of surviving the ravages of time than others" (ibid.).

22 Some cases are referred to as *full document requests* as the lawyers representing the claimants have asked that all documents be produced.

23 A comprehensive detailed report of this story was produced by the Aboriginal Peoples Television Network (Barnsley and Martens 2011).

24 See *Fontaine v. Canada (Attorney General),* [2012], B.C.J. no. 1154, 2012 BCSC 839.

25 *Law Society of Alberta (Resignation Committee) v. Blott* (June 17, 2014), http://www.law society.ab.ca/Files/hearing_reports/David_Blott%20_ResignationCommitteeReport_ 30Jun_2014.docx.pdf.

26 *Mitchell v. M.N.R.,* [2001] 1 S.C.R. 911, 2001 SCC 33.

27 Ibid., para. 34.

28 Other similar terms, specific to therapists, include *compassion fatigue* or *secondary traumatic stress, countertransference,* and *burnout* (Vrklevski and Franklin 2008, 106). See also Lerias and Byrne 2003; McCann and Pearlman 1990; Schauben and Frazier 1995; Vrklevski and Franklin 2008; Way et al. 2004.

29 Indian Residential School Settlement Agreement, 2006, s. 1(d), http://www.residential-schoolsettlement.ca/settlement.html.

References

Barnsley, P., and Martens, K. (2011). Residential School Students Say They've Been Hurt by Law Firm. *APTN National News*, 29 November. http://aptn.ca/news/.

Bosworth, M. (2001). The Past as a Foreign Country? Some Methodological Implications of Doing Historical Criminology. *British Journal of Criminology 41*(3), 431-42.

Burman, M.J., Batchelor, S.A., and Brown, J.A. (2001). Researching Girls and Violence: Facing the Dilemmas of Fieldwork. *British Journal of Criminology 41*(3), 443-59.

Castellano, M.B., Archibald, L., and DeGagné, M. (Eds.). (2008). *From Truth to Reconciliation: Transforming the Legacy of Residential Schools*. Ottawa: Dollco Printing.

Churchill, W. (2004). *Kill the Indian, Save the Man: The Genocidal Impact of American Indian Residential Schools*. San Francisco: City Lights.

Funk-Unrau, N., and Snyder, A. (2007). Indian Residential School Survivors and State-Designed ADR: A Strategy for Co-Optation? *Conflict Resolution Quarterly 24*(3), 285-304. doi:10.1002/crq.175.

Haig-Brown, C. (2006). *Resistance and Renewal: Surviving the Residential School*. Vancouver: Arsenal Pulp Press.

Ing, R.N. (1991). The Effects of Residential Schools on Native Child-Rearing Practices. *Canadian Journal of Native Education 18*, 65-118.

Junggren, D.L. (2009). Every G20 Nation Wants to Be Canada, Stephen Harper Insists. *Calgary Herald*, 29 September.

Lerias, D., and Byrne, M.K. (2003). Vicarious Traumatization: Symptoms and Predictors. *Stress and Health 19*, 129-38. doi:10.1002/smi.969.

Liebling, A., and Stanko, B. (2001). Allegiance and Ambivalence: Some Dilemmas in Researching Disorder and Violence. *British Journal of Criminology 41*(3), 421-30. doi:10.1093/bjc/41.3.421.

Martens, K. (2011). Residential School Students Say Law Firm Offered Loans at 30 Per Cent Interest. *APTN National News*, 22 November. http://aptn.ca/news/.

McCann, L., and Pearlman, L.A. (1990). Vicarious Traumatization: A Framework for Understanding the Psychological Effects of Working with Victims. *Journal of Traumatic Stress 3*(1), 131-49.

McLaughlin, C. (2003). The Feeling of Finding Out: The Role of Emotions in Research. *Educational Action Research 11*(1), 65-78. doi:10.1080/09650790300200205.

Miller, B.G. (2011). *Oral History on Trial: Recognizing Aboriginal Narratives in the Courts*. Vancouver: UBC Press.

Milloy, J.S. (1999). *A National Crime: The Canadian Government and the Residential School System, 1879-1986*. Winnipeg: University of Manitoba Press.

NRSSS (National Residential School Survivors' Society). (2007). *A Preliminary Report Regarding the Implementation of the Indian Residential Schools Settlement Agreement*. National Residential School Survivors' Society.

Palys, T., and Atchison, C. (2014). *Research Decisions: Quantitative and Qualitative Perspectives* (5th ed.). Toronto: Thomson Nelson.

Pickering, S. (2001). Undermining the Sanitized Account: Violence and Emotionality in the Field in Northern Ireland. *British Journal of Criminology 41*(3), 485-501. doi:10.1093/bjc/41.3.485.

Rager, K.B. (2005). Self-Care and the Qualitative Researcher: When Collecting Data Can Break Your Heart. *Educational Researcher 34*(4), 23-27.

Regan, P. (2010). *Unsettling the Settler Within: Indian Residential Schools, Truth Telling, and Reconciliation in Canada*. Vancouver: UBC Press.

Reimer, G., Bombay, A., Ellsworth, L., Fryer, S., and Logan, T. (2010). *The Indian Residential Schools Settlement Agreement's Common Experience Payment and Healing: A Qualitative Study Exploring Impacts on Recipients*. Ottawa: Aboriginal Healing Foundation.

Rowling, L. (1999). Being In, Being Out, Being With: Affect and the Role of the Qualitative Researcher in Loss and Grief Research. *Mortality* 4(2), 167-81. doi:dx.doi.org/10.1080/713685968.

Sadowski, E.G. (2006). *Preliminary Report on the Investigation into Missing School Files for the Shingwauk Indian Residential School*. Residential School Archive, Research, and Visitor Centre, Algoma University College, Sault Ste. Marie, ON/Robinson-Huron Treaty (1850) Territory.

Schauben, L.J., and Frazier, P.A. (1995). Vicarious Trauma: The Effects on Female Counselors of Working with Sexual Violence Survivors. *Psychology of Women Quarterly 19*, 49-64.

Smith, D., Varcoe, C., and Edwards, N. (2005). Turning around the Intergenerational Impact of Residential Schools on Aboriginal People: Implications for Health Policy and Practice. *Canadian Journal of Nursing Research 37*(4), 38-60.

Smith, J. (2007). Some Students Left Out of Payments. *Regina Leader Post,* 21 November.

Stout, M.D., and Harp, R. (2007). Lump Sum Compensation Payments Research Project: The Circle Rechecks Itself. Ottawa: Aboriginal Healing Foundation.

Trocmé, N., Knoke, D., and Blackstock, C. (2004). Pathways to the Overrepresentation of Aboriginal Children in Canada's Child Welfare System. *Social Service Review* (December), 577-600.

Vrklevski, L.P., and Franklin, J. (2008). Vicarious Trauma: The Impact on Solicitors of Exposure to Traumatic Material. *Traumatology* 14(1), 106-18. doi:10.1177/1534765607309961.

Walls, M. (2010). Part of That Whole System: Maritime Day and Residential Schooling and Federal Culpability. *Canadian Journal of Native Studies 20*(2), 361-85.

Way, I., Vandeusen, K.M., Martin, G., Applegate, B., and Jandle, D. (2004). Vicarious Trauma: A Comparison of Clinicians Who Treat Survivors of Sexual Abuse and Sexual Offenders. *Journal of Interpersonal Violence 19*(1), 49-71. doi:10.1177/0886260503259050.

Widdowfield, R. (2000). The Place of Emotions in Academic Research. *Royal Geographical Society (with the Institute of British Geographers) 32*(2), 199-208.

Widdowson, F., and Howard, A. (2008). *Disrobing the Aboriginal Industry: The Deception behind Indigenous Cultural Preservation*. Montreal and Kingston: McGill-Queen's University Press.

Winlow, S., Hobbs, D., Lister, S., and Hadfield, P. (2001). Get Ready to Duck: Bouncers and the Realities of Ethnographic Research on Violent Groups. *British Journal of Criminology 41*(3), 536-48.

Yuen, F. (2011). Embracing Emotionality: Clothing My "Naked Truths." *Critical Criminology 19*, 75-88. doi:10.1007/s10612-010-9123-7.

chapter 12   **Grappling with Reflexivity and the Role of Emotion in Criminological Analysis**

Stacey Hannem

*We didn't know until later, and we wondered why Karl was so angry ...
so angry when he came home [from the youth detention centre]. What they
told him was we didn't want him ... and this is a kid! So he started
using drugs, and we couldn't figure out why ... and he was abused there!*
– Francine, the mother of a Canadian prisoner

*Well, yeah ... If I see a pretty woman and there's an opportunity,
I will probably try to look up her skirt ... but if she doesn't even notice
I'm not really hurting anyone.*
– An individual convicted of sexual offences

*I like legs ... so I had this kid in my apartment ... I gave him a beer,
and then he was sleeping on my couch ... I didn't hurt him. I touched
and rubbed his bare legs ... and I masturbated.*
– An individual convicted of sexual offences

THESE ARE REAL NARRATIVE accounts, relayed by research participants to social science researchers. How do you feel when you hear these statements?
What emotional reactions do you have as a parent, a woman, a man, a human
being? The process of listening to and analyzing stories of trauma, victimization, and victimizing others draws an emotional response from the listener –
even if that listener is a social researcher, trained in research methods and

critical analysis. To acknowledge and glean value from the emotional side of research, one must recognize that we enter the field first as human beings with an emotional nature; that is, we must be willing to acknowledge and accept that we cannot stop ourselves from *feeling* in the research moment.

In this chapter, I use examples from my own ethnographic research with released sexual offenders and with the family members of prisoners to examine the experience of emotion work in the research setting. I position the emotional dissonance sometimes experienced by researchers as the product of competing *emotion cultures* (Gordon 1981) – the value-laden emotion culture of origin and the supposedly rational, objective (non)emotion culture of the academy. I begin by first exploring the significance of emotion culture and situating this discussion within the broader epistemological debates.

Emotion Cultures and Fractured Identities: Researchers Are People Too

The qualitative criminologist, as a person, is just as much a product of his or her cultural surroundings, experiences, and place in the social structure as any other individual. Much space and thought has been devoted to understanding the integral role of culture in shaping normative expectations of appropriate emotional experiences and expressions in specific circumstances (Peterson 2006; Gordon 1981; Hochschild 1979). What Gordon (1981) describes as "emotion culture" can be seen as composed of framing rules, feeling rules, and display rules (Hochschild 1979). Framing rules first dictate the meanings that individuals should assign to a particular situation or context – that is, how they should interpret various social situations and what emotion vocabularies would be appropriate responses. These "frames" are provided by societal organizations and institutions and are incorporated as a part of the collective conscience.

Feeling rules "are standards used in emotional conversation to determine what is rightly owed and owing in the currency of feeling. Through them we tell what is 'due' in each relation" (Hochschild 1983, 18). These feeling rules govern the intensity (strength or weakness) of the response, the direction of the emotion (whether it is a positive or negative response), and the duration (whether the response will be fleeting or last over time) of the emotional response (Hochschild 1979). Finally, the display rules provide a normative context for the expression or nonexpression of emotion. In what contexts is it appropriate to display emotion openly, and when is it appropriate to hide one's emotions? What degree of emotion display is suitable (ibid.)? These emotion rules are dependent not only on situation but on one's culture, gender, age, sexuality, and social position. For example, the North American adage that "boys don't cry" speaks to the emotion rules that are established for males, reflecting dominant cultural constructions of masculinity. This type of analysis has been applied to the study of particular emotions and their various expressive displays across cultures.[1]

The social researcher is the product of at least two different emotion cultures: the first, instilled through socialization since birth, is the dominant social and political culture that one is raised in, the *emotion culture of origin*. The second is the supposedly value-neutral, rational, and nonaffective *emotion culture of the academy*, in which one is trained. The normative emotion culture of the world of social science is constructed in opposition to affective, unscientific ways of being in the world, emphasizing the importance of objectivity, rationality, and unbiased analysis. Each of these emotion cultures translates into an identity; the emotion culture of origin shapes one's personal worldview and identity as a sociohistorically embedded human actor, while the emotion culture of the academy seemingly requires that one take on the detached identity of a scientific researcher. The inherent conflict between the (non) emotional norms of the academy and one's emotion culture of origin creates tension in the researcher who is juggling these competing identities.[2] Indeed, as Bloch (2002, 113) tellingly reveals,

> When I tell my colleagues that I am researching emotions in Academia, they smile and some even laugh ... My colleagues laugh because they experience emotions and Academia as incompatible entities ... This cultural incompatibility is not merely expressed in laughter but also in the philosophy and sociology of science where, as a rule, emotions are classified and evaluated as disturbing, subjective elements that impede scientific cognition.

The ability to invoke critical analyses of these emotion cultures does not automatically free one from their hold on our thought patterns and behaviour. Similarly, indoctrination into the second emotion culture of the academy does not erase the first emotion culture of origin, but compounds layers of meaning and expectation, resulting in uncertainty and sometimes crisis. For example, despite her privileged positioning and understanding of the broader sociocultural context of criminality and victimization, the sociologist or criminologist who studies crime is not immune to the moral judgment and condemnation that society places on violent acts of victimization and sexual offending. Yet the emotion culture of the academy seems to prescribe that one must be objective and emotionally detached, and present a balanced, unbiased analysis of the subject. To do otherwise, and to take a position that is overtly ideological or politically situated, risks engendering public criticism and fracturing the notion of the academy as a source of dispassionate knowledge.[3] When it comes to issues of crime, this may be difficult.

Even the most open-minded and humanistic researcher would have difficulty understanding and identifying with the attitudes and behaviours described at the outset of this chapter. When that same researcher is a woman, in a culture where women are the most frequent victims of sexually violent victimization and are taught to fear the possibility of sexual assault (Stanko 1997), her reaction to such accounts will be further complicated. This poses a difficult challenge for the field researcher who, like me, who wishes to engage in the ethnographic study of deviant or criminalized populations to comprehend the lived experience of an individual who sexually victimizes others and to see the world through his eyes. While one might, on the basis of researched and reasoned opinions, argue that even sex offenders have the right to be treated with dignity and not to be exiled from the community, to truly identify with and understand participants in qualitative research on sexual offending is a difficult, if not impossible, task.

Sensitive research is defined as "research which potentially poses a substantial threat to those who are or have been involved in it" (Lee 1993, 4). Given that the term *substantial threat* carries a weighted and restrictive connotation, a broader, more appropriate definition would include topics to which one's emotion culture of origin prescribes intensively negative reactions. These topics are often difficult for participants to speak of and may be difficult for researchers to listen to without displaying emotion. We need to consider the emotional processes and "emotion work" that is carried out when a qualitative researcher is engaged in sensitive research (Gilbert 2001; Dickson-Swift et al. 2009).

It is important to note here that emotional responses are not always predictable; it is unlikely that a researcher would choose to study a subject so abhorrent to her that she could not rationalize and come to terms with it enough to feel that it warranted further investigation. However, emotions are not predicated on our rational, theoretical understanding of a subject. They are reflexive and emerge in the moment; as Kleinman and Copp (1993, 31) suggest, "our feelings about those we study are situational; they depend on what participants say or do." Thus, a researcher may enter the field expecting to be able to understand and accept her informants and be surprised by the experience of negative emotion. One may be able to dispassionately consider and discuss the proclivities of those who experience sexual attraction to children and yet feel very differently when faced with a real person providing sincerely intended justifications for his use and abuse of others. Given academic expectations of openness and objectivity and a feeling of personal preparedness for the task of fieldwork, a qualitative researcher who has negative feelings toward his or her participants may begin to question her competency as a researcher or her social and political beliefs.

How does a researcher manage negative feelings rooted in one's emotion culture of origin toward her participants and still maintain her competing personal identities? I am interested in two aspects of negative emotional responses to sensitive research – first, the struggle to acknowledge and accept the impact of these feelings on one's research, in light of the history of emotional censorship in academia; and second, the implications of acknowledging these feelings and managing them through emotion work on the researcher's understanding of her own moral and cultural positioning.

Research as Emotion Work

Hochschild (1983) first drew attention to the place of emotions in paid labour and the commoditization of emotion management with her study of flight attendants and their experiences of managing their emotions in order to do their job. She coined the term *emotional labour* to describe the efforts of the flight attendants and others in similar fields of customer service. The concept of emotional labour has since been further refined by Steinberg and Figart (1999), who identified two defining characteristics. Emotional labour, first, "[requires] contact with other people external to or within the organization, usually involving face-to-face or voice-to-voice interaction," and second, "requires a worker to produce an emotional state in another person while at the same time managing one's own emotions" (Steinberg and Figart 1999, 13). Social researchers have used the concept of emotional labour as a framework to study many different types of occupational categories, such as secretaries (Wichroski 1994), exotic dancers (Bruckert 2002), nurses (Henderson 2001), and professors (Bellas 1999).[4] However, rarely have they traded their lens of inquiry for a mirror to examine the emotional labour that is performed in academic research as a result of competing emotion cultures. In *Emotions and Fieldwork* (1993, 28), however, Kleinman and Copp note that "intimate relationships usually evoke wide-ranging emotions, from sympathy to hatred. But in our close relations with [research] participants we only expect good will." They also point to the role of the (non)emotion culture of the academy in researchers' emotional labour, highlighting that "as members of a larger discipline, fieldworkers share a culture dominated by the ideology of professionalism or, more specifically, the ideology of science. According to that ideology, emotions are suspect. They contaminate research by impeding objectivity, hence they should be removed … [F]ieldworkers, then, do emotion work (Hochschild 1983) moulding their feelings to meet others' expectations" (ibid., 2).

It is important to first recognize that negative emotional responses to research participants are not only experienced as visceral reactions to such extreme and abhorrent behaviours as rape or child abuse. Emotion work in relation to research participants may take place around conflicts of values, class biases, ethnicities, or interpersonal tensions. There are any number of possible situations that may result in a researcher actively managing his or her emotions toward participants.

In her discussion of researching women's roles in traditionally male academic disciplines, Ramsay (1996) paints a vivid portrait of a researcher's internal conflict between voicing her negative feelings about the subject matter and the need to get "good data." She recounts feeling angered at hearing her subjects' sexist language and negative portrayals of female students in engineering and yet, paradoxically, considering it "good data." Like a good field researcher, she does not vocally question her participants' assumptions or motives, and leaves the field in disgust, feeling that she has somehow colluded with, or at least failed to challenge, these antiquated notions (ibid., 138). While she does not belabour the point, Ramsay's "confessions" are important as they are a rare published example of the disjuncture that may exist between one's identity as an individual and as a researcher. Far too few researchers are comfortable enough to admit to such an unscientific process at work in their research. The many qualitative studies of sexual victimization and perpetration that make no mention of the researcher's personal views on the subject stand as testimony to this unfortunate reality. Kleinman and Copp (1993, 28) suggest that the absence of emotion work in published research should not be taken as an indication that it is not happening; rather, lack of self-reflexivity and the failure to address emotion work as a part of the research process obscures its importance.

In the interests of furthering emotional transparency, I too have a "confession." In my own research with men who have offended sexually, I have encountered numerous stories and situations that I found personally abhorrent. Like Ramsay (1996), I found myself loath to alienate my participants by revealing my true feelings about the activities in which they engaged. I can identify aspects of both *surface acting* and *deep acting* in my emotion work. Surface acting is defined by Hochschild (1983) as the putting on of an outward appearance that is consistent with others' expectations of one's response in that situation. For example, when informants are answering a researcher's questions about their personal experiences and feelings, they expect, at minimum, that the researcher will respond to them with professional, nonjudgmental interest and will certainly not react with disgust, anger, hostility, or other overtly negative emotions. In some cases, they may actually expect or wish to receive an empathetic or supportive response. The context of the research interview, then, creates situational constraints on the types of emotions that one might freely experience and display without disrupting participants' expectations of the interaction.

I have used surface acting to disguise negative emotional responses to participants that, were they revealed, would have shut down the interaction and caused the participant to end his disclosure and thus my access to the "data." For example, the individual mentioned at the outset of this chapter who was convicted of sexually molesting young boys disclosed to me some disturbing exploitive behaviours but justified them with the argument that he "never hurt anyone; like, never actually had sex with them." He was the first participant in a research study that I was conducting on reintegrating released, high-risk sex offenders. Prior to this interview, I had not anticipated hearing such vivid and candid accounts of deviant behaviours and therefore was not prepared for my response to them. In order to stay "in the field" with this individual, I had to stifle my natural inclination to respond with incredulity and to challenge his argument that no harm was done or that penetration had to occur for harm to be done. I could not allow the expression on my face to reveal my inner response to his disclosure. An excerpt from my field notes explains:

The man sitting before me was about 5'10", in his mid-fifties; a large man, around 250 pounds, slightly balding, with a thick beard ... In response to my question about his offences, he began to describe how he had befriended young boys in his neighbourhood, invited them to his apartment and allowed them to try beer and alcohol. He told me that he "liked legs" and would use the boys' legs as a means of stimulation for his masturbatory fantasies. As he described the way that he fondled the boys' legs as they slept, my stomach began to feel queasy. I felt uneasy, anxious and didn't quite know what to say. I had an idea when I had decided to pursue this project that it might be difficult at times, but I hadn't really known how hard it might be not to react to these kinds of stories. Part of me thought that the participants would not want to answer that question, anyway! I felt as though my face were a mask; my "professionally interested" expression of concern pasted over my growing discomfort. I consciously tried not to narrow my eyes or purse my lips to reveal my scepticism at his minimisation of the harm. When he reassured me that he had "never hurt anyone or actually had sex with them" I found myself nodding in understanding and responding "Right. Sure." I didn't know what else to say. I felt torn in ways I had not imagined. I didn't exactly revile this man; I recognized his humanity; that he is a person and not just a "sex offender," but I was fundamentally sickened by his ability to justify and minimise what he had done in exploiting these boys. I wondered at the damage done to his victims and whether they would agree that he had "never hurt anyone"? (April 2003)

Sitting in this interview, I demonstrated surface acting in my conscious efforts to portray a facade that was different from my inner dialogue and feelings. As anyone who has ever tried to disguise a deeply felt emotion in an interpersonal interaction knows, this type of emotion work is difficult, draining, and requires constant cognitive vigilance to pull off successfully. Engaging in surface acting alone means that the actor experiences an emotional dissonance – "the discrepancy between expressions and inner feelings" (Grandey 2003, 89). As a naturally open person whose emotions are often writ large in my expression, I found the effort of surface acting in this encounter and in others like it to be physically and mentally exhausting. To try to mitigate and reduce the strain of this ongoing surface acting, I also engaged in a certain amount of deep acting.

Deep acting, or what Hochschild (1979, 561) has variably referred to as "emotion work," refers to "the act of evoking or shaping, as well as suppressing, feelings in oneself" and requires an "active stance vis-à-vis feeling." That is, the actor does not passively experience her feelings in response to the situation but actively identifies the feeling that she believes to be appropriate, that she *wishes* to feel, or believes herself *obligated* to feel, and engages in rationalizations and emotion management to evoke the desired response. In this way, the actor is able to make her internal emotions and dialogue match the surface expressions presented to others in the situation. Research has found that prolonged surface acting is associated with stress and job burnout, whereas successful deep acting allows the individual to minimize emotional dissonance, to more easily convey the required surface expressions, and thereby reduce feelings of stress in the interaction (Grandey 2003).

The earlier excerpt from my field notes alludes to the presence of deep acting, referring to my recognition of the respondent's humanity, that "he is a person and not just a 'sex offender.'" My notes went on to flesh out this experience and to delineate the cognitive processes that took place during that interview:

I tried to keep in mind that he, too, had been a victim of sexual exploitation. I reminded myself that the proclivity to be sexually attracted to children and pre-pubescent adolescents does not emerge in a social and emotional vacuum. I tried to imagine this man as a boy who had been scared and taken advantage of; I pictured him young, and small, and innocent; as a woman's son. I shut down the images of his victims that came to mind. I tried to feel pity, rather than anger that he had chosen to perpetuate this vicious cycle of trauma. And when I got into my car at the end of the meeting, I prayed that his victims would overcome the abuse that they had experienced, and that they would not go on to inflict suffering on others. (April 2003)

Engaging emotion work in the research moment is not always successful. In this interview, I was able to effectively convey a form of sympathy evoked by my choice to foreground the participant's victimization and fundamental humanity, rather than his victimizing behaviour. The participant and I both left the interview feeling that it had been a positive experience.

In addition to striving to meet others' expectations of them as professional criminologists and academics, qualitative researchers are also grappling with their expectations of their own professional and political ethic as it collides with the worlds of their research subjects. When the spectre of emotion is addressed in qualitative analysis, it has most often arisen in a context where the researchers' own identity and understanding of the world are shaken by their empathy for the pain that their subjects have endured. Take, for example, Campbell's (2002) study of the impact of researching rape. When strangers share heart-wrenching stories of personal tragedy and suffering, an empathic response is only to be expected. Our cultural expectations of a display of empathy are naturally contradicted by professional expectations of objectivity and emotional distance, requiring researchers to perform emotion work. They are expected to display just enough empathy to convey understanding or interest and keep the subject talking, while maintaining a face of professional decorum that will not "taint" the data or skew the results of the interview. While tacit acknowledgment of this ongoing struggle is rare enough, it is even more taboo to speak of an emotional reaction to one's subjects that is less than empathic. In other instances, researchers may struggle to engage emotion work when their emotional reaction to a participant's account does not match how they "should" feel, according to their emotion culture. When one cannot muster an "appropriate" sympathy or feels detached from an emotion-laden story, surface acting is required to maintain the appropriate demeanour.

In some circumstances, an emotional response may catch a researcher off guard, and attempts to engage in surface acting may not be successful in portraying the response that the research participant wants to hear. For example, I interviewed a woman whose husband was convicted of sexually molesting their daughter and several other (nonrelated) children. During the interview, she subtly revealed to me that she knew about sexual abuse in her husband's family of origin that many of the family members were unaware of; she said that she did not know whether to tell them and asked me if I had any suggestions. Attempting to be diplomatic in the face of this ethically difficult situation, I asked her, "Do you think it's something they would want to know?"

> *Isobel:* Oh *hell* no. Do you think what I was told was something *I* wanna know?
>
> *Stacey: [hesitantly and slowly responds]* No.
>
> *I:* No. I didn't wanna know *[long awkward pause]*
>
> *S:* Do you think it would make a difference if you told them?
>
> *I: [sharply responds]* To who?
>
> *S:* To them. Would it change anything about *[Isobel interrupts]*
>
> *I:* Maybe not. But it'd sure change *me.*
>
> *S:* Well then *[Isobel interrupts]*
>
> *I:* It would sure help me.
>
> *S:* If it would help you, that might be helpful then.
>
> *I:* That's why I keep saying, to *who?* It's like I'm nobody. Even some of the ways *you* ask the questions, Stacey, is that *I'm* the ogre.
>
> *S:* Really? You feel that way? *[surprised tone, raised octave]*
>
> *I:* Yeah. Like the questions you were just asking.
>
> *S:* Well, you asked my opinion as to whether you thought I *[Isobel interrupts]*
>
> *I:* But that's your opinion.
>
> *S:* But then I don't know what it is you want to tell them, so I'm kind of, you know ... between a rock and a hard place there. *[nervous laughter]*
>
> *I:* But you *know [the word is drawn out for emphasis]* ... you're a tracker ... I know, we *both* know what I'm gonna tell them. And like I said, their family's screwed up. Thirty years ago I coulda been told some stuff *(Sure)* and I wasn't ... and uh ... you know, all of those clues, I mean, that's *totally* enough for you to know.
>
> *S:* I can guess yeah.
>
> *I:* Yes. Damn good guess too ... and ... but the way that you ask the questions, and I'm not at all in any way criticizing you ... that's society. And you belong to society, as do I. So you will say what society has taught you. And I now am angry at what society's taught you because ... I think I probably knew all along, but because of all the reasons ... but ... I was angry that society has taught people that, because it's not right. But that's the way it is. That's just exactly the way it is. *Oh, poor them.* What about *me?*

In this exchange, my original intent was in fact to obliquely suggest that Isobel *should* share the information so that the family members might pursue counselling or self-care to address the traumatic effects of familial sexual abuse. When I asked her if she thought they would want to know, I expected her to say "yes," and I expected her to suggest that this knowledge might make a difference for this family in coming to terms with their past. However, entering this situation as an outsider and failing to realize that Isobel's motivations were more individualistic meant that I did not give the answer that she wanted to hear. It became clear from her tone and her response that she was looking at this disclosure as a form of revenge for her in-laws' failure to warn her upon marrying her husband that their family was "screwed up." My response ("well then") to her assertion that this revelation could change things for her tacitly revealed my disgust at her desire to use this painful information to further hurt and "get even" with the people that she believed had wronged her. I attempted to recover my more objective status but was not entirely successful, and Isobel responded with feelings of outrage and accused me of judging her and not considering her feelings.

Negotiating the conflict between my personal, moral beliefs around sexual victimization and my professional, "open-minded researcher" identity has required not only continual emotion management but also self-care. When I am engaged in the research moment, my work requires that I appear nonjudgmental, open, and accepting, regardless of the accounts that may be revealed to me. As shown above, an emotional conflict cannot always be predicted or avoided. Even when one feels genuine empathy and concern for the population that one is studying (as I do for prisoners' families), moments of conflict may arise when an individual participant says something that the researcher disagrees with and she is put in a position where emotion work is required.

The writing of field notes is an integral part of not only recording the effect of emotions and emotion work on the research interaction but of debriefing and grappling with what it means to do this emotion work that effectively silences one's gut or true feelings. Acknowledging this emotion work in writing field notes is cathartic as it recognizes the emotional struggles that sometimes take place and reassures the researcher that her emotion work does not disauthenticate her deeply held feelings. I am often asked how I can work and do research with individuals convicted of terrible sexual crimes, particularly against children. The implication of this question is that there must be something wrong with me given that I can stomach sitting in a room with a child molester and listen objectively to his story. When I read my field notes, I am reassured that there is nothing wrong with me; I am human, and I have deep feelings of pain and sympathy for victims. I engage in emotion work because I believe that my research with these individuals can make a difference in our understanding of sexual offending. The aforementioned prayer that I offered up in the aftermath of my first interview with an individual convicted of sexual offences was as much a prayer of absolution for myself as it was a gesture of sympathy for his victims. It was an affirmation that, despite my ability to manage my emotions and to appear objective, I was still in touch with my core values that emphasized the "wrongness" of his actions. In addition to the usual tools of stress-management, self-care in these types of sensitive contexts includes consciously reaffirming one's humanity and identity and recognizing that it is okay to feel these deep emotions and to be conflicted about one's work.

Estranged Bedfellows: Challenging the Divorce of Emotion from Rational Thought

In the fields of criminology and the sociology of deviance, the emotional responses evoked by stories of perpetration and victimization are noticeably absent from analysis, and young researchers are seldom armed with techniques of self-care; nor are they prepared for their own emotional response to such sensitive topics. This is particularly problematic because the phenomenon of crime is an inherently emotional subject that tends to evoke intensely visceral responses and immediate reactions from those who hear of tragic or horrific criminal acts. This emotionality is acutely discernible in the language that citizens, political figures, and the media use to describe the ways that we individually and collectively imagine crime and victimization (Young 1996). Consider the statement of Canadian MP Rona Ambrose, who was in charge of the status of women portfolio under Prime Minister Stephen Harper:

> I am proud that our government has done more than any other government in the history of this country to keep women safe ... We have introduced new laws to make sure that we keep rapists and murders off the street and to make sure that we protect children from sexual predators. That is what women want. (Parliament of Canada, Debates, 4 May 2010)

Raising the spectre of sexual violence against women and children invokes a sense of outrage and seemingly dares political opponents to disagree with the government's priorities. Appealing to the fear and anger that citizens experience when they hear about incidents of violent victimization is a politically useful tool to legitimate "tough on crime" agendas and ensure the support of many voters. Another excerpt taken from a debate on "crime" in the British

House of Commons is even more explicit in its attempt to elicit an emotional response:

> *The Minister of State, Home Office (Mr. Michael Jack):* In starting this debate we should reflect for a moment on the word "crime." It is a neat word to describe a complex problem. Crime itself is a battle and a battleground. It is like a virus. It is not seen and it is difficult to treat but its effects blight the lives of all too many of our fellow citizens. The language that we use to deal with it is powerful. Words like "punishment," "victim," "murder" and "arrest" stir deep emotions and powerful feelings in all of us. Crime is frustrating. Crime is frightening. Crime is complicated. (qtd. in Young 1996, 3)

In this short text, the minister of state managed to sum up three of the very real and powerful emotions associated with crime and victimization: frustration, fear, and bafflement (Young 1996). The minister's description of the impact of crime on the community is clearly not an objective or statistical analysis of the impacts of crime but rather an emotional appeal to a citizenry that is profoundly affected and driven by these feelings, among others, in response to (mis)information about crime. The manipulation of an individual's emotional responses to crime can be used to make ideological criminal justice policies appear "rational" or "common-sense," even in the face of contradictory data.

Given the wide range of emotions evoked by the mere discussion of crime in our society, criminology's unquestioning neglect of feeling and emotion is, at first glance, surprising. However, consideration of the competing ideological traditions of rational positivism and interpretive schools in criminology and the sociology of deviance sheds light on this ironic omission. Historically, in philosophy and the sciences, emotion and reason were portrayed as diametrically opposed; emotion was associated with irrationality, while reason represented measured and rationally calculated thought (Turner and Stets 2005; Kleinman and Copp 1993; Ramsay 1996; Barbalet 2002). As such, the use of emotion is generally not considered a valid approach for scientific analysis.

Rooted in fallible modernist debates, the schism between emotionality and rational thought has more recently been called into question. Neurological research has now demonstrated that severing the links between the cerebral cortex (centre of rational thought) and the subcortical emotion centre of the brain results in difficulty in making decisions and leads individuals to make seemingly irrational or less than ideal choices (Turner and Stets 2005, 22). This finding has led researchers to conclude that human decision making depends on emotions; the emotional context is necessary for human beings to attach meaning or "utilities" to alternatives in order to make "rational" choices (ibid., 22). Existentialist philosophers have long believed that so-called rational decisions are made on the basis of one's emotional response to the likely outcomes of alternative forms of action; more recently, neurological science has shown this to be true. If the concepts of "positive" and "negative" outcomes are not objective, stable categories, how then can one, on the basis of pure reason, determine which is the best option to pursue? Ironically, theorists of rationality rarely consider what processes are at work in determining the difference between positive and negative or good and bad outcomes. It is emotional sensibilities that enable human beings to make these kinds of judgments to maximize pleasure and minimize pain (ibid.).

Given that the functions of emotion and reason appear to be inseparable parts of the decision-making and analytical process, researchers must be prepared to acknowledge that emotion does indeed play a role in the development of knowledge. Sometimes described as "starting from where you are" (Lofland and Lofland 1995, 11), many feminist scholars (see, for example, Reinharz 1992; Hesse-Biber 2005) and other interpretive and phenomenological sociologists (Van Manen 1990; Kleinman and Copp 1993) suggest that emotion can impact the topics that we determine to be worthy of research, the sociological questions that we ask, and the political and cultural approach that we take to our research.[5] However, there is little willingness to admit that, in addition to shaping our research agendas, subjectivity and emotion may also factor into the analysis of data and the conclusions that we draw. To openly acknowledge the role of emotions in constructing social knowledges is to admit that our studies are less than entirely controlled and objective and come up short on the modernist yardstick of scientific method, thereby calling into question the "validity" and value of our claims. Thus, the emotional experience of research is maligned and ignored by many social scientists in hopes that its implications are less obvious to our readers.

Kleinman and Copp (1993) note that when ethnographers and qualitative researchers do acknowledge the emotional aspect of their work, they have a tendency to place these "confessions" in appendices to their research or in chapters written for completely separate works on research methodologies. This careful separation of the emotional from the empirical serves to reinforce the prevailing myth that fieldwork and qualitative research is objective and value-neutral and that data analysis can be separated from the subjectivity of the researcher. Not only is it impossible to entirely separate one's emotional response from the sociological analysis of sensitive topics, but in attempting to do so a researcher may in fact blind herself to important information and cripple the utility of her research. It is counterproductive to perpetuate the false dichotomy between emotion and reason in the area of methodology, and researchers must be willing to admit that we are emotional creatures and not objective instruments of data collection and analysis. By this, I do not mean that one's emotions should be permitted to guide analysis, but rather that it is imperative that the researcher is deliberate and self-aware in making her emotions available for analysis. If the researcher's emotions and emotion work are incorporated in field notes and presented as a part of the research interaction, then they become a layer of data, implicated in analytic insights. Thus, the researcher can subject her own emotional responses to analysis and attempt to identify how those feelings might manifest themselves in the research findings. In this way, through a rigorous process of recording and scrutinizing one's emotions, it may be possible to separate one's emotions about the research experience from the outcomes of the analysis.

Many young researchers enter the field believing that they can carry their critical, analytical approach to the topic as a primary identity, unaware that one's emotion culture of origin may complicate one's response to these issues. Until the role of emotions is openly discussed and accepted in social science research, we are doing a disservice in failing to instruct new qualitative researchers in the art of emotion management and techniques of self-care. This dilemma of emotional reflexivity among researchers is beginning to be recognized in the more traditionally "sensitive" disciplines, such as health research, but criminologists are lagging far behind, clinging to the myth of the emotionality/rationality dichotomy and replicating the censorship of emotions in the next generation of criminologists.

The Emotional Lens and Qualitative Analysis

A final, unfortunate, outcome of the absence of emotional reflexivity in qualitative research is the elimination of an important source of data and analysis. According to Harris and Huntington (2001, 133), "production of reliable knowledge does not rest on the exclusion of the emotional dimension of human existence. In fact, to the contrary, inclusion of a focus on emotions can enrich the process of producing knowledge." Kleinman and Copp (1993) also suggest that qualitative researchers should identify the emotions they experience throughout the research process and use them as data. However, they provide no practical insight as to how one might accomplish this, beyond a suggestion that negative feelings may serve as cues to the researcher's recognition of some injustice, inequality, or problematic situation (Kleinman and Copp 1993). Hochschild (1983, 17) notes that "feeling ... is a sense, like the sense of hearing or sight. In a general way, we experience it when bodily sensations are joined with what we see or imagine. Like the sense of hearing, emotion communicates information ... from feeling, we discover our own viewpoint on the world."

Much research into sensitive topics is undertaken with a suspected social problem in mind, and researchers often choose to focus their studies on issues where they believe social change is required. Thus, recognizing one's own emotional response to a sensitive topic may provide a valuable means of assessing the potential policy implications of our work. For example, in researching the use of community-based initiatives to reintegrate men convicted of sexual offences deemed "high risk" to reoffend, my aim is to gain insight to make these initiatives as successful as possible in order to reduce incidents of sexual victimization in these communities. Recognizing and acknowledging my own emotional response to these men and their accounts of victimizing others raised an important issue; individuals who wish to work with these men must be able to set aside their own negative feelings about the sexual offences that were committed and validate and respond to the men as complex human beings with feelings, needs, and desires. Much as I would be unable to engage these men in dialogue if I focused only on their status as "sex offenders," a potential volunteer would be unable to effectively work with these men if he or she saw them only as a threat to others' safety and a "risk" to be managed.[6]

If a researcher approaches the study with an awareness of his or her emotion culture of origin and dual identity as both citizen and social researcher, then he or she is in a better position to carefully note any emotional reaction to the topic of study and the participants (whether positive or negative) and to analyze this reaction as a possible reflection of dominant framing rules or feeling rules. In situations that evoke negative emotions, such as with men who offend sexually, understanding how society is likely to react to the participants in one's study may help to identify not only potential sites of inequality or injustice but also potential resistances to proposed solutions. An awareness of the feeling rules that govern social reactions to the participants will aid the investigator to accurately situate the research within its social context. Initiatives that attempt to engage a "restorative justice" approach to working with men who offend sexually might be expected to (and do) encounter significant resistance and backlash from a public that is not educated about the benefits and success rate of such endeavours. This insight allows me to consider public education as the key to gaining acceptance for these types of initiatives, which, at first glance, may seem repugnant or foolish.

On the other hand, if the researcher experiences positive or empathic emotions in response to her participants, particularly if they contradict an expectation of negative emotions, then there is space to interrogate one's preconceptions and to question prevailing societal assumptions about the re-search subject. If the researcher experiences unexpected or surprisingly posi-tive emotions, then he or she must question the role of the knowledge gained through the research in shaping this emotional response and consider whether the public dissemination of research findings may have a positive social effect for the participants. For example, I found myself experiencing genuine em-pathy for a man who had been convicted of sexually molesting young children when he said to me, "I just want to be normal! I know that people hate me. I want to live a normal life; I don't want to hurt other people. I know it's wrong! Sometimes it seems like I just can't stop." Putting a human face on this modern-day pariah allowed me to consider the possibility that he sin-cerely wished to change and needed assistance to find a place in the commun-ity. It is possible that sharing these types of accounts might help others to see these men as more than just sex offenders and open their minds to the idea that, as a society, we have a responsibility to help these individuals to change and reintegrate. This view problematizes vigilante responses that would hound released sex offenders out of communities and isolate them and challenges the idea that they are "monsters" that should never be released from prison. This knowledge, gleaned from my emotional response to my participants, requires that, in seeking to act ethically toward my subjects, I must share the insights that I have gained with the public in an effort to begin to break down the stigma that is faced by men who have offended sexually and to improve re-integrative responses in the community.

Given that emotions are inevitable throughout the research process, we need to improve our understanding of their role in criminological analysis. Emotions in research are best utilized through conscious and careful reflec-tion, and recognition of the researcher's emotional response(s) can provide valuable cues for situating social discourse and contextualizing the research findings. To validate researcher emotions and the insight that they provide, we must continue to deconstruct the emotion/rationality dichotomy and to recognize our emotion work and the necessity of self-care. Careful attention to the emotional aspects of qualitative research can only serve to improve the quality of criminological analyses and better equip the next generation of researchers to balance their professional and personal identities.

Notes

1 See Lofland (1985) for an analysis of the emotion culture of grief and Clark (1997) for a cross-cultural study of sympathy.
2 The waters of the emotion culture may be further muddied for researchers who are immi-grants, working within an emotional culture that is foreign to them and that may contradict

their emotion culture of origin, or for those who are the product of a multicultural heritage and simultaneously draw on two or more emotional and cultural scripts.

3   However, even a quick read of recent public comments on academic experts' criticisms of the Canadian government's "tough on crime" agenda calls into question the idea that the academy is seen as an unbiased source of knowledge. Frequently, citizens criticize criminologists as "left-wing" and construct their criticisms of the criminal justice system as rooted in "bleeding heart" ideology.

4   Notice that the study of emotional labour is most often directed at work traditionally done by women, with the exception of professors. However, even the study of emotional labour in academia tends to focus on teaching relations, which is a more "feminized" aspect of the profession.

5   McLaughlin (2003) provides an analysis of the role of emotions in educational research and situates the emotion/reason debate.

6   See Hannem and Petrunik (2007) for more information on the Circles of Support and Accountability initiative to work with released, high-risk sexual offenders.

References

Barbalet, J. (Ed.) (2002). *Emotions and Sociology*. Oxford: Blackwell Publishing.

Bellas, M.L. (1999). Emotional Labour in Academia: The Case of Professors. *Annals of the American Academy of Political and Social Science 561*(1), 96-110.

Bloch, C. (2002). Managing the Emotions of Competition and Recognition in Academia. In J. Barbalet (Ed.), *Emotions and Sociology* (113-31). Oxford: Blackwell Publishing.

Bruckert, C. (2002). *Taking It Off and Putting It On: Women in the Strip Trade*. Toronto: Women's Press.

Campbell, R. (2002). *Emotionally Involved: The Impact of Researching Rape*. New York: Routledge.

Clark, C. (1997). *Misery and Company: Sympathy in Everyday Life*. Chicago: University of Chicago Press.

Dickson-Swift, V., James, E.L., Kippen, S., and Liamputtong, P. (2009). Researching Sensitive Topics: Qualitative Research as Emotion Work. *Qualitative Research 9*(1), 61-70.

Gilbert, K.R.(Ed.) (2001). *The Emotional Nature of Qualitative Research*. Boca Raton, FL: CRC Press.

Gordon, S.L. (1981). The Sociology of Sentiments and Emotion. In M. Rosenberg and R.H. Turner (Eds.), *Social Psychology: Sociological Perspectives* (180-203). New York: Basic Books.

Grandey, A.A. (2003). When "The Show Must Go On": Surface Action and Deep Acting as Determinants of Emotional Exhaustion and Peer-Rated Service Delivery. *Academy of Management Journal 46*(1), 86-96.

Hannem, S., and Petrunik, M. (2007). Circles of Support and Accountability: A Community Justice Initiative for the Reintegration of High-Risk Sex Offenders. *Contemporary Justice Review 10*(2), 153-71.

Harris, J. (1997). Surviving Ethnography: Coping with Isolation, Violence and Anger. *Qualitative Report 3*(1). http://www.nova.edu/ssss/QR/QR3-1/harris.html.

Harris, J., and Huntington, A. (2001). Emotions as Analytic Tools: Qualitative Research, Feelings and Psychotherapeutic Insight. In K.R. Gilbert (Ed.), *The Emotional Nature of Qualitative Research* (129-46). Boca Raton, FL: CRC Press.

Henderson, A. (2001). Emotional Labor and Nursing: An Under-Appreciated Aspect of Caring Work. *Nursing Inquiry 8*(2), 130-38.

Hesse-Biber, S. (2005). *Handbook of Feminist Research*. Thousand Oaks, CA: Sage.

Hochschild, A.R. (1979). Emotion Work, Feeling Rules, and Social Structure. *American Journal of Sociology 85*, 551-75.

–. (1983). *The Managed Heart: Commercialization of Human Feeling*. Berkeley: University of California Press.

Kleinman, S., and Copp, M.A. (1993). *Emotions and Fieldwork*. Newbury Park, CA: Sage.

Lee, R.M. (1993). *Doing Research on Sensitive Topics*. Thousand Oaks, CA: Sage.

Lofland, L.H. (1985). The Social Shaping of Emotions: The Case of Grief. *Symbolic Interaction 8*, 171-90.

Lofland, J., and Lofland, L.H. (1995). *Analyzing Social Settings: A Guide to Qualitative Observation and Analysis*. Belmont, CA: Wadsworth.

McLaughlin, C. (2003). The Feeling of Finding Out: The Role of Emotions in Research. *Educational Action Research 11*(1), 65-77.

Peterson, G. (2006). Cultural Theory and Emotions. In J.E. Stets and J.H. Turner (Eds.), *Handbook of the Sociology of Emotions* (114-34). New York: Springer.

Ramsay, K. (1996). Emotional Labour and Qualitative Research: How I Learned Not to Laugh or Cry in the Field. In E. Stina Lyon and J. Busfield (Eds.), *Methodological Imaginations* (131-46). London: Macmillan.

Reinharz, S. (1992). *Feminist Methods in Social Research*. New York: Oxford University Press.

Stanko, E. (1997). Safety Talk: Conceptualizing Women's Risk Assessment as a Technology of the Soul. *Theoretical Criminology 1*(4), 479-99.

Steinberg, R.J., and Figart, D.M. (1999). Emotional Labour since "The Managed Heart." *Annals of the American Academy of Political and Social Science 561*, 8-26.

Stets, J.E., and Turner, J.H., (Eds.) (2006). *Handbook of the Sociology of Emotions*. New York: Springer.

Turner, J.H., and Stets, J.E. (2005). *The Sociology of Emotions*. New York: Cambridge University Press.

Van Manen, M. (1990). *Researching Lived Experience: Human Science for an Action-Sensitive Pedagogy*. New York: SUNY Press.

Wichroski, M.A. (1994). The Secretary: Invisible Labour in the Workworld of Women. *Human Organization 53*, 33-41.

Young, A. (1996). *Imagining Crime*. Thousand Oaks, CA: Sage.

chapter 13   **Epistemological Violence, Psychological Whips, and Other Moments of Angst: Reflections on PhD Research**

Melissa Munn

I WAS AN UNDERGRADUATE student at university when, in 1989, Rick (a life-sentenced man) was released from prison. I met him while volunteering in a federal penitentiary, and when I discovered he was planning to attend the same school as me while on day parole, I offered to show him around campus and to teach him how to use my roommate's computer. From there, we began a long-term friendship. Over the next few years, I sat in class learning about recidivism and career criminals while seeing something else with Rick and with other ex-prisoners. I watched them "making good" (Maruna 1993, 3) in their transitions to freedom, and this made me realize that the academy was not painting a full picture of life after prison. The exclusion of tales of ex-prisoner successes niggled at me for nearly two decades and ultimately became the foundation for the research I would find myself doing a few decades later as a doctoral student. Instead of looking at failure, I set out to look at those who succeeded after prison. Documenting their struggles and exposing the techniques they used to overcome the challenges seemed like a worthwhile task.

I expected that doing research on prisoner resettlement would be uncomplicated. Most of my academic cohort worried about gathering data, but because I regularly communicated with former long-term prisoners and had their contact information, I knew that I could generate a sample with minimal effort. Becoming re-familiarized with theories after my long absence from the academy seemed like more of an issue but still a surmountable task if I "just applied myself." I was naive. Quite quickly, I realized that the rather binary division I made between method and theory was just one of the simplistic assumptions I would have to challenge in the process of completing a dissertation. More significantly, I was unprepared for the dilemmas that accompanied my vacillation between activism and academia, between being an ally and a "respected" researcher. I thought I could simply integrate both roles and accompanying goals into the process of completing a PhD; instead, I discovered structural, emotional, ethical, and psychological barriers to both. In short, the tasks required to explore prisoner release, re-entry, and resettlement in a way that was acceptable to the academy sometimes grated against my personal ethics and my desire to affect social change. Ultimately, it left me questioning whether one can really be an activist-academic or one must trump the other.

In this chapter, I revisit the research journal I kept throughout the process of writing my dissertation and reflect back on the tensions, the dis-ease, and the angst I felt moving between formal and informal roles as I sought to shift the dominant state-imposed and academically reinforced discourses about ex-prisoners. To give you a sense of how the research unfolded, I begin with my general thoughts on knowledge before moving on to discuss the methodological approach taken, the six major dilemmas encountered, and the resolutions (or lack thereof) to these challenges. Throughout, I address the stress of having a dual role, the tension of being an insider/outsider, the ethics of story appropriation, and the partial resolutions I found in doing committed scholarship and in being part of a research team.

An Academic Exercise?

Prior to beginning my doctoral program, I had been teaching courses at my local community college and always began my semester by posting Peter Berger's (1963) first law of sociology on the screen – "things are not what they seem." I cautioned my students that the search for sociological knowledge is complicated and we must constantly question what seems obvious. In a classic case of "do as I say, not as I do," when I returned to graduate school, I did not immediately apply Berger's law to the process of research. I was at ease because I had read countless accounts of doing research, studied the guidebooks, and knew the formulas and frameworks. The task seemed straightforward enough but, with Berger's words now echoing in my head, I realize that the research process is, to some degree, taken for granted – certainly, it is far more complicated than the presentation in most methods articles and texts. Rather than the messiness that now seems obvious to me, academic texts (even those dedicated to methodology) often ignore or gloss over the methodological contradictions and compromises in favour of formulaic processes and polished finished products.

This is clear to me now, but was not in 2004 when I set out to examine prisoner resettlement in Canada. I generated nicely defined research questions and as a serious student (and as a result of my early course readings) situated myself ontologically by rejecting the positivist tradition of a singular truth or sense of being all-knowing, all-seeing, and objective. I had no interest in performing what Donna Haraway (1988, 584) refers to as a "god-trick," wherein knowledge is presented as emanating from an omnipotent and disembodied source.

Instead, I held the belief that there is no "real" world waiting to be discovered and explained in terms of causation or fixed principles. As David Demeritt writes, "the phenomenon of reality depends on how it is represented to be ... Truth is whatever we agree to call it, there is no Archimedean point from which to observe the world that is independent of it" (qtd. in Hoggart, Lees, and Davies 2002, 2). In accepting this premise, I acknowledged that human action and behaviour are much too complex and nuanced to ever be fully understood or explained; therefore, I recognized the partial nature of knowledge, and I made no claims to be conducting *the* definitive study of resettlement. In the beginning, this position seemed like an academic theoretical exercise, but, as the research process unfolded, it became a fundamental issue with which I struggled.

The First Dilemma: Emancipating/Producing Knowledge

Having done my "ontological due diligence," I was ready to begin *doing* the research. I was gravitating toward "active-subject socially-oriented theories" (Bottoms 2000, 29) which "study the conscious and meaningful actions of people who change in response to their own understanding of how they are understood" (Hoggart, Lees, and Davies 2002, 26), and needed a methodology that could run parallel to this approach.

Ethnography seemed like an excellent way to get at these situated knowledges and experience.[1] For me, ethnography requires participant observation *in situ* to consider the individual/group's experience holistically. Clearly, this was not a viable option because I was not a former long-term prisoner, nor had I been immersed in their postcarceral release, re-entry, or resettlement. At the most, I was a witness to some moments but peripheral to the ex-convicts' experiences. Even at the times when I was involved in their experiences, I was certainly not a particularly methodical observer, and, thus, this method was unavailable to me.

The fact that I was joining a team of researchers who were already working on this project also affected my consideration of a research method. Chris Bruckert and Sylvie Frigon developed an interview guide and had already conducted a few semi-structured interviews. Certainly, I could have rejected this approach and the data they collected but, with some modifications to the questions, an interview approach seemed appropriate. Talking with individuals would allow me to employ an ethnomethodological approach, which Bottoms (2000, 30) argues has three major premises: a focus on nuanced understandings; a rejection of the scientific; and an "emphasis ... on the meaning of social actions to actors and on their detailed understandings of particular contexts."

At the time, I wrote that, in order to appreciate the context of interpersonal interaction, a researcher must recognize and understand that the research process is embedded within the power/knowledge construct (Foucault 1980). I thought that by placing the voices of the ex-prisoner against the dominating discourses, tensions could be explored and I could attempt, as Foucault (ibid., 85) states, to "emancipate historical knowledges from that subjection, to render them, that is, capable of opposition and of struggle against the coercion of a theoretical, unitary, formal and scientific discourse." As an activist, these words resonated with me; they seemed like a call to action. But I felt some dis-ease that I had not yet fully articulated to myself. Part of the problem was that I considered myself a critical scholar and wanted to make sure I was not replicating the studies I so often critiqued for being exploitative or unreflective of the lived experiences of those on the less influential side of extreme relationships of power. The bigger problem to confront was deeper and more personal.

Emancipating knowledge seemed a very lofty objective to me at the time, and I found it difficult to justify what right I had to take on this task. I still very much saw myself as a working-class woman involved with grassroots organizations, and so I began a long process of introspection and reflection on my new role in the academy. On the one hand, I felt unsuited to the task; on the other hand, I felt that I had "earned my merit" through my years of activism, and I did not want to leave research activities to those who never worked on the front lines or shared a cup of coffee with an ex-prisoner. I felt more connection with the research subjects than I did with my academic cohort, but mostly I felt like an outsider knocking on the doors of both groups. I spent weeks and months considering and obsessing about my role as a researcher, and this reflexivity seemed an essential part of the process because, as Hannah Avis (2002, 205) argues, it links the "idea of self to the process of knowledge construction."

The First Resolution: Committing to Committed Scholarship

Discovering the idea of "committed scholarship" (Kobayashi 2001, 58), which requires that research be conducted using qualitative methods, from a critical perspective, and that it be linked to activism, brought me some comfort. Audrey Kobayashi argues that it is morally imperative that a qualitative approach be used "to recognize that subjects' lives are multifaceted, interconnected, contextually situated and deeply meaningful, in ways that cannot be conveyed easily by simple descriptions such as those achieved quantitatively" (ibid.), and interviews helped achieve this goal. The second component, critical research, is "scholarship that conveys the social consequences of the situations that we study, and that attempts to uncover the tensions and contradictions faced by people in those situations" (ibid., 55). In a time of growing responsibilization of individuals and the emergence of particular risk management rationalities, successful negotiation of reintegration is clearly an area that needs consideration. Finally, I had long been a fan of Paulo Freire's *Pedagogy of the Oppressed* (1971, 77) and so made a link between his words, "there is no true word that is not at the same time praxis. Thus, to speak a true word is to transform the world," and the idea of activism. And while I preferred the term *truths*, the sentiment encapsulated the activist principle of conducting committed scholarship.

The Second Dilemma: Being "In" and "Out" of the Know

As a feminist, I did not see a separation between my day-to-day life, my work, or my political activities – all were fully entangled. Certainly, my thoughts on this are not new or unique; indeed, in 1949, Claudia Jones (1995, 117) (in her work on African American women in the United States) stated, "to place the question as a 'personal' and not a political matter, when such questions arise, is to be guilty of the worst kind of Social-Democratic, bourgeois-liberal thinking." Like the work of activist scholars who precede me, this research emerged from a political place and was meant to have a political end. To my surprise, not everyone in the academy supported my attempt to blend my scholarly and personal roles, and members of my committee wanted further reflection. Of course, as I was already insecure about my role as an academic, I took the liberty of wallowing further in my angst.

As part of this process (and probably to my cohort's boredom and my committee's annoyance), I took great pains to discuss my impact on the research with anyone who would let me. I recognized that I both deliberately and unintentionally shaped this research in ways that made it unique. Some of the interviews were conducted with the friends who inspired the work, while the majority were direct referrals from this core group. In a few cases, the stories they told, and the experiences they had during their re-entry and resettlement, included me; not only did my presence influence the research in the present, but, in some instances, it shaped part of their past experiences.

Laurence McKeown (2001, 5), a former IRA prisoner who does ethnographic research on "similar others," speaks to the benefits of this "insiderness":

> From the starting point of a researcher, being knowledgeable about the prison and its history, put me in an advantageous position as I could easily identify the main people I wanted to speak to. I knew most of them on a personal basis, and some were close friends. Those I did not know so well or not at all were at least aware of my history. This meant that no time was lost in getting to know one another and where we were coming from ... We could all share in the same conceptual framework, speak a familiar language and be aware of the particular nuances that an "outsider" might miss.

My role was not as clear as McKeown's (2001) as I was neither an insider (I was not a man who had served a long prison term and been released) nor, truly, an outsider. I had participated in a few releases and resettlement processes and so had some insider knowledge of what it was like to navigate the bureaucracy of the correctional system to achieve conditional release. I had helped to organize temporary absence passes for the men to come out into the community and had waited nervously to see if they would emerge from behind the prison wall to participate in the event we had planned. I would take them shopping to get rid of the dated clothes they brought with them from prison. We would talk about ordering food, taking public transit, dating etiquette, and so on. While these moments may have ensured some familiarity and common language to help nuance what may have otherwise been missed, I could never be fully sure what information these men chose not to communicate to me because of being known – they may have wanted to protect themselves or, conversely, to shield me from parts of their experiences.[2]

The Second Resolution: Accepting Fractionality of Knowledge

From early in the doctoral program and through to my dissertation defence, my committee members challenged my "insiderness." Now, with more confidence in my academic-self, I see this as part of their "research angst" (the dilemmas of doing "good" research and my work reflecting poorly or well on them as mentors), but it was a very minor source of mine. They were concerned over major issues (such as my influence on the direction of the research and my ability to be "objective") and mundane issues (such as the fact that I had interviewed some participants in my home and others in theirs rather than in a "neutral location"). They worried that I would not present the roundness of the narratives because I would want to protect the men – a point to which I will return later. While I acknowledged their apprehensions and sought ways to mediate their worries (e.g., careful design of research and rigour in analysis), I became comfortable with the possible limitations of my dual roles.

I frequently repeated to my committee and cohort that no matter who collected the data, they would only represent a fraction of the stories, and each interview necessarily leads to "different phenomenological realities" (Tewksbury and Gagne 1996, 80). In addition to being known already, various other factors (location, gender, appearance) can influence the content of the interview and shape how the interviewer is perceived. Sometimes even the presence of another person, extraneous to the intended interview, can influence the interview's course and the view held of the interviewer.[3] One particularly clear example occurred during an interview with a man I had not previously met. During our discussion, another former prisoner called to invite me to dinner and then the tone of the interview changed dramatically; the respondent became much more forthright and collegial. It would appear that my relationship with another ex-prisoner gave me an insider-type status that altered his participation in the process. The discussion then proceeded differently; he used more "jailhouse speak," assumed a more relaxed physical position, and adopted a seemingly more frank approach to the narrative.

Given my position that knowledge is always only partial, I accepted that the information given to me was mediated in ways that will, in part, remain unknown and that I could only work with the stories as they were shared. I felt that it would be both arrogant and naive to assume that the stories shared during our interview were *the* stories, but they did provide glimpses into experience. Concurrently, the stories revealed the active agency of the men and me in the knowledge-creation process. Fractionality of knowledge and reactivity are important points to acknowledge, but they are not issues that make the findings dismissible. On the contrary, throughout the analytical and interpretive process, I recognized that I was getting distinct information in a distinct setting, and I valued the uniqueness of the approach and the data.

Despite all the planning and my own reflexive exercises, I needed to remind myself that interviewees always retain the power to decide which stories to tell. Indeed, their control of the narrative reflects both Goffman's (1959) ideas around the presentation of self and the psychological literature that indicates that people may withhold information in order to protect others (DePaulo et al. 1996; Lippard 1988). Thus, the transmission of information operates in a place between protecting the self and protecting others, which linked to another dilemma – did I have an obligation to protect the stories of the men I interviewed or not?

The Third Dilemma: Negotiating the Ethics of Receiving Stories

It was on this point of sharing and honouring stories that an important ethical dilemma emerged. As the following excerpt from my research journal shows, I struggled:

That initial sensation has not left me. Am I "whoring" my friends, and friends of friends, and men previously unknown to me, for my own gratification ... for some letters after my name. In the moments after, when I am just Melissa, and not "The Researcher," they assure me that they trust me, that the work is important, that it's good to be asked about something positive for a change. I guess that I'll cling to those assurances because I know, at least at an academic and political level, that their stories need to be put on the record. (November 2005)

Who was I to ask for or to take the men's stories, to code and decode them, to structure and theorize and present them – to conduct an act that Sarawati Raju (2002, 174) referred to as "epistemological violence"? I was raised by a storyteller and mentored to be one, and so the idea of hearing another's story was in some ways comforting. Appropriating stories for my own ends, however, felt wrong in my bones. I tried to reason that they had agreed to share their stories, as I do likewise. Still, the obligation to "do right" by them (whatever that meant) weighed on me.

The violence also seemed rooted in asking the men to recall their success because in so doing, they needed to revisit their struggles; I worried that this would have a negative impact on them after I left.[4] I silently rebuked myself during the interviews for being excited about a particularly graphic or profound description; my desire to have "good quotes" seemed salacious and sometimes came at the men's psychological expense. Because struggle often precedes success, hearing this part of the journey was, I felt, a necessary part of capturing "authentic voices." I reasoned that my feminism committed me to create space for "neglected voices," even if it was a temporarily uncomfortable place to be. I was also keenly aware that prisoners and ex-prisoners are rarely given a venue to share their stories and, even more rarely, to have them published.[5] Still, I experienced a quandary of conscience (Clark and Sharf 2007) as I questioned whether I was the person who should be presenting the men's stories from my own place of privilege.

The Third Resolution: Exercising Privilege

To partially resolve this dilemma,[6] I revisited the question posed by Raju

(2002, 174): "Do the privileged remain silent even if their speaking, however tinted and biased their voices might be (assuming that they would be), makes a difference?" My answer was "no." I attempted to employ a research process that was respectful of the men and that would allow their own truths to emerge while still critically engaging with their stories. Aihwa Ong's (1995, 354) work supports this choice:

> Given our [researchers'] privileges, there is greater betrayal in allowing our personal doubts to stand in the way of representing their claims, interests and perspectives. The greater betrayal lies in refusing to recognize informants as active cultural producers in their own right, whose voices insist upon being heard and can make a difference in the way we think about their lives.

I knew that ultimately my dissertation was an interpretation of their stories, but I decided to rely on my years of activism, friendship with (ex)prisoners, and my academic training to be reflective of the men's experiences while still engaging in critical analysis. It felt a little like walking a balance beam on tippy-toes with the future letters after my name (and the privilege they provided) acting as a safety harness.

The Fourth (and Still Unresolved) Dilemma: Being Human First?

All of this anxiety centred on trying to reconcile my influence on the research, but I was also now confronting another source of angst: the effect of the research on me. Conducting the interviews had a profound impact on me, and I was unprepared for this possibility. In many cases, I felt the men's pain, not in a detached, therapeutic-relationship type of way, but as a friend. I experienced guilt as they told of painful memories and struggles; I wished that I was more aware and helpful to the individuals I knew during the times they experienced these struggles. I felt shame for exploiting these men for their experiences, which I would then use to form my dissertation. Had I prostituted them and left a fifty-dollar honorarium for their time? As I write this chapter, I am acutely aware that while I am using the past tense to discuss these sensations during the research, I could just as easily use the present tense as the emotions still linger.

In an attempt to maintain some semblance of an official researcher/ interviewee dichotomy, and minimize influence on the research process, I had resisted the urge to cry with them, even though I knew that to do so might have been the more human and appropriate thing to do. While I experience some regret over my lack of visible emotion during the interviews, my previous training as a counsellor helped me recognize that reacting to the sadness of the stories can also lead to the sharing individual "shutting down" in order to not overwhelm the listener. On a more philosophical level, I knew that for a multitude of reasons (including already being known to a few), I was not going to be a blank canvas onto which they projected their story, but I tried to de-centre myself and allow the focus to be on them; I didn't want my tears or outrage to overpower their experience. I also wanted the moment of the interview to be distinct from the other nonresearch times we had shared or would coexperience in the future. I was, as Avis (2002, 198) notes, trying to create "a 'researcher self' that is discrete from any other subject position."

Catherine Kirkwood acknowledged that this splitting of the self might be a dilemma when she wrote that divesting the researcher of emotion in the interview setting is to render the experience less human. She argues against the detached stance that I strived for: "by becoming a responsive, interactive part of the interview, in treating experience as human, non-mechanical inter-action, we must invest the very skills women have learnt so well: receptivity and sensitivity to emotions and personal response" (1993, 22). At this point, I have no resolution as to what "should" have transpired; but, were I to do interview research again, I likely would try to find a place "in-between" where I could share in the respondent's sadness while retaining the focus on him.

Most often my dis-ease centred on a contradiction I felt; despite Ong's (1995) words, I still believe that I was not *giving voice*, as is so often the rhetoric, but rather, that I was *taking it*. This existential dilemma was captured well by one of the participants who said to me during one of the interviews, "and here comes the work that you are going to have to invest in your dissertation and your reward is your PhD and then you'll move on and there'll be another incarnation" (Bobby).

These issues affected me profoundly and, at the time of this writing, are still lingering and nagging, despite my intellectualization of the merits of doing this research and my knowledge that all the men freely consented to participate. My anxiety was somewhat mitigated by the fact that over the years it took to complete this research, some of the men would inquire about my progress and the research findings, and they often provided encourage-ment and spoke to the usefulness of the work. Ultimately, I believe my ex-perience of dis-ease is part of activist scholarship – at some level, adopting this methodological approach is about recognizing injustice and therefore *should* be unsettling. Ultimately, the greater good (getting successes "on the record" and earning my degree) slightly edged out my existential angst. I went ahead with the analysis but confronted my own uneasiness with my new identity as a researcher on a daily basis.

The Fifth Dilemma: Playing Broken Telephone

Having partially reconciled my angst over doing the research, I then faced other ethical dilemmas when I set out to make sense of the data. All interviews were transcribed by a research assistant, a professional transcription service, or me. As if it would mitigate the "taking of voice," I was meticulous about the transcription – comparing the taped interview against the written text to ensure accuracy and to hear the flow of the interviews. At times, it felt as though I was playing a childhood game of "broken telephone," wherein the words that are heard are not the ones that were spoken. Unlike that game, however, I could backtrack and repeatedly re-listen to the men's voices and narratives. When there was discrepancy or where the voice was unclear, my supervisor and I both reviewed the audio recordings. To avoid affecting the "credibility, transferability, and trustworthiness" (Golafshani 2003, 600) of the data, if the words or intention behind the words remained unclear (because of things like poor audio quality or interspersed tangential thoughts), we did not use these excerpts in the analysis.

Rejecting text whose meaning was ambiguous was critical since, as Steinar Kvale (1995) argues, the process of validation in qualitative research does not occur simply in developing the interview instrument or as an inspection at the end of the project; rather, it is about quality control throughout the project's various stages. I know that for knowledge claims to be defensible, rigour must be attended to at every point, and so we were constantly performing "inquiry audits" (Lincoln and Guba 1985) to ensure consistency in our process and adherence to the parameters established in the coding manual. While some scholars may reflect on the above as being fundamentally positivistic concerns, which hold no place in the constructivist research conventions, I disagree. Indeed, I concur with the work of Andrew Abbott (1997, 358):

> Proclamations against positivism often mask an arbitrary unwillingness to think formally about the social world. One asserts that the world is constructed of ambiguous networks of meaning, argues for the complexity of interpretations and representations and then simply assumes that formal discussion of the ensuing complexity is impossible. But this is obviously untrue. Many people have thought formally about ambiguity representation and interpretation. Nothing in those phenomena militates against thinking in a rigorous, even disciplined fashion.

In doing this work, I rejected the positivist tradition of attempting to discover "social laws analogous to the law-like regularities discovered by natural sciences; and an absolute insistence on the separation of facts and values" (Scott and Marshall 2009) but not the need for logico-empirical approaches. I tried to code their words in the context of the story they were sharing so that a measure of confidence in the findings could be achieved. Obviously, another researcher could impose his or her own interpretations on the data, but I wanted to be able to have a reviewer of the same transcripts say, "I would analyze it differently but I can understand why you coded as you did."

I conducted a first-level reading of each transcript to get a sense of the individual's narrative (Hoggart, Lees, and Davies 2002) and, most importantly, to understand how he made sense of his experiences (Chase 1995). This broad-level reading helped me to get a sense of the "verstehen" (Hoggart, Lees, and Davies 2002, 155) and of how the individuals saw themselves and constructed their world.[7] The general narratives were essential to understand context and to get at the "feeling" of the interview, but I wanted to make sure I attended to every word that they had chosen to speak. I needed to be sure that I was not acting as a "casual listener," that I was, instead, attentive to the minutiae; this goal was accomplished through a process of line-by-line tandem coding.

A Complicated Resolution: Team Coding

My doctoral supervisor (Chris Bruckert) and I sat together to code every line of text. In so doing, we were using a type of "investigator triangulation [that] consider[s] the ideas and explanations generated by additional research-ers studying the research participants" (Johnson 1997, 284). This process, while time-consuming and at times emotionally draining, ensured that the more subtle and nuanced stories were likely to be spotted by one or the other re-searcher. Engaging in this activity requires that both researchers have deep and profound respect for each other because disagreements can be frequent, and resolution is often dependent on subject positions and willingness to concede an interpretation. These debates and differences of opinion were not about one of us being "right"; instead, they were a reflection of our desire to let the data speak rather than imposing our preconceived ideas and con-venient theoretical frameworks on the respondent's words. Too often, I wor-ried we might find what we were looking for rather than attending to what the research participants wanted to convey. We were not exceptions to this, and so, if one could not demonstrate to the other that the participant con-veyed the sentiment in a way that was congruent with our lens, we were forced to discard that particular coding. Of course, there was certainly arro-gance in assuming *we* knew what *they* wanted to convey but I found I needed to accept this limit to avoid the analytic paralysis that was sometimes com-forting to me but that was ultimately unproductive.

Despite the times when it would have been much easier to code the material by myself (or by herself), we were committed to working together. We both subscribed to Margaret LeCompte and Jean Schensul's (1999, 67) idea that the words in transcripts are "fat," which means that there can be ambiguities and multiple meanings in the text. The debate, and sometimes tense discussion, over these texts generated valuable insights and connections and resolved and reconciled some of the contradictions that emerged from just looking at or reading the narratives independently.

Further, a team coding approach had the advantage of providing a way of binding the data generated during interviews with friends. Specifically, even though I knew more details than were shared by some of the men, I could only consider what was on the page and what was obvious to my fellow coder. In this way, the men I knew personally were given the same privilege as the other respondents to share or withhold information and to have their words (rather than personal narratives shared in a different and nonresearch-centred venue or context) analyzed. As my committee feared, in some cases, I worried that my friends "looked bad" in the interview, and I hesitated in my acknowledgment of what seemed so obvious to my fellow coder. Sometimes my friends contradicted themselves or appeared instrumental and manipulative to a reader who did not "know" them; I might have "read over" these negative aspects because I knew a bigger picture. Ultimately, team coding kept me honest to the way the respondents presented their story and with a feeling of achieving a high ethical standard as a researcher. It also left me profoundly ambivalent about myself as a human being who might disappoint a friend.

In order to be respectful to the storyteller, when Chris and I disagreed on the meaning, intent, or implications of a particular statement, we would return to the recorded interview and re-listen to the way the individual iterated the phrase and contextualized it by examining the words and phrases and ideas spoken around it. Usually, this auditory clue resolved the issue around interpretation, either by one (or both) of us abandoning our initial reading or in discarding the particular piece of text rather than misinterpreting it. Again, it was not about either of us getting "our way" but trying to reflect the narrative the interviewee wanted to express. The broken telephone seemed to be repaired in the process. While I constantly reminded myself that I was not trying to get at a "truth," I was deeply troubled by the idea of misrepresenting the data and seeing what I wanted to see because of convenience or because it fit neatly with my theoretical framework. I believe that my supervisor shared this concern and, as a result, our coding process became elaborate and, in retrospect, perhaps a bit overly detailed.

Using our codes as "interpretive tags" (Cope 2003, 445), we marked each interview for both "in vivo" codes (terms used by informants) and "constructed codes" (more abstract and drawn out by the researcher) (Jackson 2001, 202). These two types of codes were essential because the men described experiences in ways that were not always the way that a researcher might understand them. For example, a man may describe his body during particular periods (in vivo) and this description might be more abstractly understood in terms of geographic placement or identity (constructed). The result was that items often appeared in multiple nodes and would be cross-referenced during the analysis.

The categorization process began with a few (n < 10) anticipated codes that we had generated from our initial read of the interviews. In keeping with adaptive theory, additions were made as new items and patterns emerged. In some cases, this action meant revisiting earlier interviews to code for something that only became visible in later readings of transcripts. Often a node would have a variety of subnodes within it and this resulted in the development of 293 distinct codes. The amount of coding per document varied dramatically as some men spoke at length and in great depth about their experiences while others were more succinct. In addition, in some instances placement of a paragraph into multiple nodes occurred as the excerpt covered several themes concurrently. The following statistics provide a sense of the magnitude of the coding done and the degree to which I tried to mitigate my research trepidations with rigour. The transcript with the fewest passages coded had 121 items, while the transcript with the most passages coded had 301.[8] Each transcript spoke to a multiplicity of themes, with the least variety occurring in one where there were fifty-three different nodes addressed and the greatest variety occurring in one where ninety-five different nodes were marked.[9] I was desperate for the research findings not to be discountable by other academics or by the participants because of poorly executed method; I felt that if this occurred it would mean that I had wasted the interviewees' time and been a poor activist/scholar.

The Final Dilemma: Creating My Story from Their Stories

Once the interviews were completely coded, I needed to make sense of the data. LeCompte and Schensul (1999, 214) argue that the job of the researcher is to "attribute meanings and importance to patterns and regularities that people otherwise take for granted in everyday life ... to pinpoint the significance or implications of such knowledge for future practice or program innovations ... to set the work in the context of other research on the same topic." I resisted doing this. I recognized that, once on paper in transcript form, the words of the speaker became contestable. As Susan Smith (2001, 29) states, "we are accessing a representation (a vision, an image, an experience) of a text (the world of lived experience) through a text (the interview transcript) that is itself open to interpretation." It is no longer about the individual's intentions but about the reader's rendition, and it is important to consider and situate both the analysis and the analyst. These stories were constructed within a particular format (the interview), which meant that I became the first audience for the narrative (and thus shaped it in some way). I then needed to create a "second level narrative" (Borland 1991, 63) that would inform the way the first narrative was understood. It scared me and made me again question what right I had to impose *my* meaning on *their* words. At the first level, *they* had the power to create the story and now, the power was *mine*. In short, I was back to my earlier existential dilemma – one that I thought I had (partially) resolved.

I kept looking back to the methods literature and tried to cling to Dan McAdams, Ruthellen Josselson, and Amia Lieblich's (2001, xii) work wherein they argue that "meaning is generated by the linkages the participant makes between aspects of the life he or she is living and his or her understandings of these aspects. The role of the researcher is then to connect this understanding with some form of conceptual interpretation, which is meaning constructed at another level of analysis." Throughout this process, I simply wanted to categorize participant experiences but my dutiful supervisor kept telling me I needed to "make sense of it." She would frequently give me draft pages covered in comments that directed me to answer "why is this phenomenon happening?" It was a psychological whip she used to push me to be a "quality" academic. Full of worry over "psychologizing" these men or getting it wrong, I would resist. My ontological position about no singular truth was not really helping. I was ready to quit and reject the acquisition of new letters after my name.

An Unsatisfactory Resolution: Playing the Game

Many times I considered what I would say in my letter of withdrawal from the program. I never wrote it because my friend and former colleague Jake Muller offered some sage advice to me. After discussing my analytic trepidations with him, he told me, and I paraphrase here, "You never need to do this again. Just prove that you can do it and then you can get on with the work that really matters to you." It was the message I needed to hear at that moment. While I was busy writing a chapter on prisoners resisting relations of power by "playing the game," I realized I was doing the same and I felt a solidarity with the men – a solidarity that had been waning since I added the role of researcher to my CV. Ultimately, I accepted that the words in the transcript were completely open to my interpretation, and, at some level, it was no longer about the individual speaker's intentions – they trusted me to "get it," and I needed to trust myself.

As a researcher, I brought preconceived notions about the area of interest and the subjects into the analytic field, and I was sometimes frustrated that my sense of what should be happening did not meet with the experiences of the men. I relied on a hermeneutic approach that recognized that, in trying to find meaning and make (not discover) interpretations, it was essential to move between preconceived notions and the text – to move between the parts and the whole – to engage in the hermeneutic circle or double hermeneutic (Hoggart, Lees, and Davies 2002). Not surprisingly, I struggled with the reality that the hermeneutic approach privileged my role of expert as interpreter of data. My uneasy acceptance of my "expertise" only slightly mitigated my trepidation about how the interviewees would read my words about them. Jake helped me to "just do it," but what if these men, some of whom I had been friends with for decades, resented my analysis of their experiences? I considered sending the text to each of the men for their feedback but ultimately decided not to when my supervisor asked if I was willing to give veto to the respondents. Would I not say something because someone else didn't like it? That question rocked me to my core identity as a feminist activist, wherein I say unpopular things on a regular basis because I believe in them. While I agonized over my right to *take* the men's voices, I was readily denying my own right to voice. Ultimately, I applied what I came to call the "Bruckert Principle," which poses the question, "Could I, the researcher, defend this analysis to the participants?" (Bruckert 2000). This postulate of adequacy is premised on the notion that my analysis would make sense to the participants though they may not agree with it. By adopting this principle, I believe that the work was positioned as engaging the sociological imagination (Mills 1959) by not simply examining biography or retelling the stories but by considering how they intersect with history and social structures.

The Aftermath

A few years after the interviews, I submitted the dissertation to the department of graduate studies. In a true test of the postulate of adequacy, the day before my defence (with knees knocking nervously), I presented some of the findings to a group of Lifeline In-Reach workers.[10] For about an hour, these ex-prisoners listened as I spoke about the experiences of former long-term prisoners. At the end of the presentation, one of the men looked me in the eye and said, "you got it perfect!" and the others nodded or smiled an acknowledgment. I knew I had *not,* but I understood the sentiment – the men in the research had been heard and their experiences understood. Again, I wanted to cry (with relief) but maintained the professional facade of my "researcher self" and just said, "thank you."

I knew that the next day I would face a panel of "experts," but the meeting with the ex-prisoners was the real test of my work, and I subsequently felt the angst leave me – almost. I realized that uneasiness was a necessary part of the process and that my dissertation and subsequent work could not have manifested without this struggle. In writing this chapter, I realize that while all the reflexivity during the process seemed tedious, self-indulgent, and perhaps a way to justify doing the research, it was essential in helping ground myself in my core values and ethics.

Ultimately, the issues I confronted and resolved during the doctoral process illuminated the path beyond graduate school and anchored my subsequent research. Now, in the years after grad school, my main concern is not with tenure and peer-reviewed article publication but with activism – getting the information to prisoners and parolees.[11] I do research in other subject areas too, but my previous exercises in reflexivity showed me that I can be comfortable with this activity only if my commitment to the issue predates my academic interest and will continue beyond the collection and analysis of data. Without this engagement, all the previous and current reflexivity would be about justifying research that *I* wanted to do because *I* was interested. Back in my activist skin, but with letters after my name, the years of angst have ended, and, finally, I am at comfort within/without the academy.

Acknowledgments

The author wishes to acknowledge the Social Sciences and Humanities Research Council for its financial support. Perhaps more importantly, she wishes to thank (again) her supervisor, Prof. Chris Bruckert, for her unfailing support though the "trials and tribulations" of this former PhD student.

Notes

1   The term *ethnography* has been used in a multitude of ways in research. Some research claims to be ethnographic because interviews are used; other research employs the term to indicate that the research was done by an outsider with an insider when, in fact, the outsider is just recounting the field experiences of the other.

2   I recognize that there are many other reasons that certain things are communicated and others are not (presentation of self, legalities, previous interactions on the day of interview, etc.). A detailed discussion of all of these factors is beyond the scope of this chapter.

3   One interviewee asked that his wife be present, and on occasion she would intervene to "correct" some factual detail of his narrative, which, at least temporarily, altered the narrative.

4   In order to mediate this potential risk to the subjects, I tried to be very attentive not just to the words the men used but to their body language and other cues of possible distress. I reminded them that we could stop the interview at any time and turned off the tape recorder at my and their request or when I felt we needed an "off-the-record" break. I tried to make sure that I could stay and chat after the interviews to ease the transition out of the interview. Also, because I believe in committed scholarship, I followed up with the men in the days after the interview and when their transcript was sent to them.

5   For notable exceptions to this statement, see, for example, the *Journal of Prisoners on Prisons, Prison Legal News,* various penal press publications (www.penalpress.com), and the work in convict criminology.

6   I use the term *partially* because I still struggle with this issue.

7   Maruna (1997, 62) writes, "the modern adult defines him or herself in society by fashioning an internalized and dynamic life story, or personal myth, that provides life with unity, purpose, and meaning," and this is an important point to remember in any qualitative analysis.

8   The mean number of passages coded per transcript was 168.

9   The mean number of nodes appearing per transcript was seventy-three.

10 The Correctional Service of Canada (2009) has noted that "[i]n-reach workers make contact, motivate, and assist lifers to achieve the maximum benefits from existing correctional programs in an institution. Through their experience and knowledge of what long-term inmates require, in-reach workers also contribute toward the introduction of additional programs inside the institution. They also provide support to the lifer in processes such as parole board hearings, temporary absences, and judicial review hearings."

11 Chris and I self-published a booklet of some of our main findings for these men so that it would be available at no cost (Munn and Bruckert 2010). I travel to prisons and halfway houses to present the words of these men, and the *PhD* after my name dramatically facilitates my access to these sites and locations.

References

Abbott, A. (1997). Seven Types of Ambiguity. *Theory and Society 26*(2-3), 357-91.

Avis, H. (2002). Whose Voice Is That? *Making Space for Subjectivities in Interviews.* In L. Bondi, H. Avis, and R. Bankey (Eds.), *Subjectivities, Knowledges, and Feminist Geographies: The Subjects and Ethics of Social Research* (191-207). Lanham, MD: Rowman and Littlefield.

Berger, P.L. (1963). *Invitation to Sociology: A Humanistic Perspective.* New York: Anchor Books.

Borland, K. (1991). "That's Not What I Said": Interpretive Conflict in Oral Narrative Research. In S. Gluck and D. Patai (Eds.), *Women's Words* (63-75). New York: Routledge.

Bottoms, A. (2000). The Relationship between Theory and Research in Criminology. In R. King and E. Wincup (Eds.), *Doing Research on Crime and Justice* (15-41). Oxford: Oxford University Press.

Bruckert, C. (2000). Stigmatized Labour: An Ethnographic Study of Strip Clubs in the 1990s. PhD diss., Carleton University.

Chase, S.E. (1995). Taking Narrative Seriously. In R. Josselson and A. Lieblich (Eds.), *Interpreting Experience: The Narrative Study of Lives* (1-26). Thousand Oaks, CA: Sage Publications.

Clark, M.C., and Sharf, B.F. (2007). The Dark Side of Truth(s): Ethical Dilemmas in Researching the Personal. *Qualitative Inquiry 13*(3), 399-416.

Cope, M. (2003). Coding Transcripts and Diaries. In N.J. Clifford and G. Valentine (Eds.), *Key Methods in Geography* (445-59). Thousand Oaks, CA: Sage Publications.

Correctional Services Canada. (2009). *Lifeline In-Reach Workers.* http://www.csc-scc.gc.ca/text/prgrm/lifeline/2-eng.shtml.

DePaulo, B.M., Kashy, D.A., Kirkendol, S.E., Wyer, M.M., and Epstein, J.A. (1996). Lying in Everyday Life. *Journal of Personality and Social Psychology 70*(5), 979-95. doi:10.1037//0022-3514.70.5.979.

Foucault, M. (1980). Two Lectures – Lecture One: 7 January 1976. In C. Gordon (Ed.), *Power/Knowledge: Selected Interviews and Other Writings, 1972-1977* (78-92). New York: Pantheon Books.

Freire, P. (1971). *Pedagogy of the Oppressed* (Trans. M.B. Ramos). New York: Herder and Herder.

Goffman, E. (1959). *The Presentation of Self in Everyday Life.* New York: Anchor.

Golafshani, N. (2003). Understanding Reliability and Validity in Qualitative Research. *Qualitative Report 8*(4), 597-607.

Haraway, D. (1988). Situated Knowledges: The Science Question in Feminism and the Privilege of Partial Perspective. *Feminist Studies 14*(3), 575-99.

Hoggart, M., Lees, L., and Davies, A. (2002). *Researching Human Geography.* New York: Oxford University Press.

Jackson, P. (2001). Making Sense of Qualitative Data. In M. Limb and C. Dwyer (Eds.), *Qualitative Methodologies for Geographers: Issues and Debates* (199-214). New York: Oxford University Press.

Johnson, B.R. (1997). Examining the Validity Structure of Qualitative Research. *Education 118*(3), 282-92.

Jones, C. (1995). "An End to the Neglect of the Problems of the Negro Woman!" In B. Guy-Sheftall (Ed.), *Words of Fire: An Anthology of African American Feminist Thought* (107-24). New York: New Press.

Kirkwood, C. (1993). Investing Ourselves: Use of Researcher Personal Response in Feminist Methodology. In J. de Groot and M. Maynard (Eds.), *Women's Studies in the 1990s: Doing Things Differently?* (18-39). New York: St. Martin's Press.

Kobayashi, A. (2001). Negotiating the Personal and the Political in Critical Qualitative Research. In M. Limb and C. Dwyer (Eds.), *Qualitative Methodologies for Geographers: Issues and Debates* (55-70). New York: Oxford University Press.

Kvale, S. (1995). The Social Construction of Validity. *Qualitative Inquiry 1*(1), 19-40.

LeCompte, M.D., and Schensul, J.J. (1999). *Analyzing and Interpreting Ethnographic Data.* Walnut Creek, CA: AltaMira Press.

Lincoln, Y.S., and Guba, E.G. (1985). *Naturalistic Inquiry.* Beverly Hills, CA: Sage Publications.

Lippard, P.V. (1988). "Ask Me No Questions, I'll Tell You No Lies": Situational Exigencies for Interpersonal Deception. *Western Journal of Speech Communication 52,* 91-103.

Maruna, S. (1993). *Making Good: How Ex-Convicts Reform and Rebuild Their Lives.* Washington, DC: American Psychological Association Books.

–. (1997). Going Straight: Desistance from Crime and Life Narratives of Reform. In A. Lieblich and R. Josselson (Eds.), *The Narrative Study of Lives* (59-94). Thousand Oaks, CA: Sage Publications.

McAdams, D.P., Josselson, R., and Leiblich, A. (2001). *Turns in the Road: Narrative Studies of Lives in Transition.* Washington, DC: American Psychological Association.

McKeown, L. (2001). *Out of Time: Irish Republican Prisoners Long Kesh 1972-2000.* Belfast: BTP Publications.

Mills, C.W. (1959). *The Sociological Imagination.* New York: Oxford University Press.

Munn, M., and Bruckert, C. (2010). *Getting Out. Staying Out.* Self-published booklet.

Ong, A. (1995). Women Out of China: Traveling Tales and Traveling Theories in Postcolonial Feminism. In R. Behar and D. Gordon (Eds.), *Women Writing Culture* (350-72). Berkeley: University of California Press.

Raju, S. (2002). We Are Different, but Can We Talk? *Gender, Place and Culture* 9(2), 173-77.

Scott, J., and Marshall, G. (Eds.). (2009). Positivism. In *A Dictionary of Sociology. Oxford Reference Online*. Oxford University Press.

Smith, S. (2001). Doing Qualitative Research: From Interpretation to Action. In M. Limb and C. Dwyer (Eds.), *Qualitative Methodologies for Geographers: Issues and Debates* (23-40). New York: Oxford University Press.

Tewksbury, R., and Gagne, P. (1996). Assumed and Presumed Identities: Problems of Self-Presentation in Field Research. In J. Miller and R. Tewksbury (Eds.), *Extreme Methods: Innovative Approaches to Social Science Research* (72-93). Boston: Allyn and Bacon.

chapter 14   **Activist Academic Whore:**
                 Negotiating the Fractured
                 Otherness Abyss

                 Chris Bruckert

I AM A WHORE, an academic, and sometimes (I suspect) an academic whore.
In this chapter, I reflect on the challenges and tensions I experience as a
university-embedded, unrepentant retired sex worker and current activist doing
research on the sex industry. Drawing on my own experiences, I seek to destabilize neat categorizations and self-congratulatory platitudes by drawing on
Foucault, Goffman, and feminist theory to explore questions of politics (and
power): the politics of identity, stigma, and legitimacy; the politics of voice
(who speaks, in whose voice, whose truth, and to what end); and the politics
of research, of poking and prying, of coding and of "making sense." It is these
interwoven themes that structure this chapter. Resurrecting a slogan from
the days when feminism was called "women's lib" – the "personal is political"
– I start by positioning the discussion within my personal and professional
journey.

My Journey

During the late 1970s and early 1980s, between dropping out of high school
and attending university, I was a feminist, a single mother, and a sex worker. I
worked as a street-based (and periodically truck stop–based) sex worker, an
in-call worker in a brothelette, an erotic dancer in strip clubs, and a peep
show attendant. While I was not a particularly good, or skilful, or successful
sex worker,[1] I certainly did not feel exploited or dirty; nor was I, much to the
dismay of the journalists who eagerly probe for titillating stories of violence,
abuse, and sexual degradation,[2] ever raped at work or "pimped." I did not
hate (or love) the work. Indeed, my experience was above all banal – sex

work was simply a good way to earn much-needed money to support my son and myself. Of course, perception is contextually conditioned; surrounded by supportive nonjudgmental people who were endeavouring to work and live ethically without attending overmuch to dominant definitions of morality, I did not feel subversive, outrageous, or immoral.

I had no problem reconciling my job with my feminist consciousness; after all, I was committed to women's equality, believed in our right to choose, and was confident in my right, as a modern 1970s woman, to decide what I would do with my body – I could choose to have a baby or not; I could choose to have sex for fun or for money.[3]

My "naive" interpretation of liberation and my confident assurance was destabilized the night I joined a group of like-minded feminist strippers to view the antipornography film *Not a Love Story* (Klein 1981).[4] In that theatre, I was surprised to learn that I was not only a victim (something I had not hitherto realized) but also, like Lindalee Tracey, complicit in patriarchal oppression, "a part of it ... serv[ing] the whole thing." *That* experience was disturbing, and I left the theatre feeling dirty and objectified by a discourse that appropriated and transformed my experience. Indeed, I left that theatre with a new identity thrust upon my consciousness.

In the years that followed, I found myself experiencing that feeling of dis-*ease* and frustration when I spent many hours in university lecture halls where highly educated academics confidently asserted that women like me were either exploited and abused victims, or maladjusted, deviant, and hypersexual. I also "learnt" that in criminology-speak my supportive community was a criminogenic subculture! Long before I had ever heard of Michel Foucault, I, well-indoctrinated into the hierarchy of knowledge, "got" power-knowledge (Foucault 1980) and obligingly struggled to reconcile these authoritative discourses with my own experiences. I squirmed with discomfort as I worked to squeeze my consciousness into a discursive suit that did not fit, no matter how much I tried. I grappled in silence and shame and said nothing. I was silenced by my lack of academic language and legitimacy; by the absence of a space for my experience within feminist, criminological, and sociological discourses; and by the discourses themselves, which delegitimized me and denied my agency. Most importantly, I was silenced by my fear of stigma, of judgment, of being identified as the outsider that I "knew" I was.

Ironically, or perhaps inevitably, the same disciplines that transformed me into an "*object* of sociological inquiry" (Smith 1987, 117; emphasis added) also (eventually) furnished the tools to resist and assert my subjectivity.[5] In the 1990s, when I was doing my doctoral work, we were in the throes of the postmodern debate, and a space was opening up to bring my political/ personal agenda into the academy. I was fortunate enough to benefit from the convergence of the firmly entrenched (though periodically maligned) "sociology of the underdog" (Polsky 1969); the emergent (though yet unnamed) "convict criminology" that affirmed the significance of the "insider" (Jones 1995); the scholarship of (often racialized) academic pioneers that confirmed the imperative of integrating "outsiders" not just as witnesses and informants but as the producers of knowledge (Davis 1981, 1989); cultural feminists writing on "situated knowledges" (Haraway 1988); and feminists' more general increasing valorization of the experiential voice (DeVault 1990). None of this immunized me from feelings of being an outsider in the unselfconsciously conventional academy, an institution that reflects and reaffirms class stratification and where the know/known dichotomy is not only entrenched but is a foundational principle. It did, however, afford me an affirming point of entry – a solid, *ethical,* even *trendy* space.[6] Indeed, if I am to be honest, it gave me more than that. It gave, and continues to give, me a certain cache, a privileged status and legitimacy among a select group of critical academics who believe profoundly in the significance of experiential, reflective analysis and who value the outsider–within.

Somewhat atypical, mine was not a particularly remarkable journey. It is, however, one that resulted in the accumulation of a mismatched set of political, academic, and personal baggage, a bicultural sensitivity, a rather ambiguous identity location, and a disconcerting, fractured otherness. In the coming section, I explore how these intersections play out in my research. I start by attending to the question of stigma.

Negotiating Normative and Inverse Stigmas: Too Much of a Whore for the Academy, Too Academic for the Whores[7]

In *Stigma: Notes on the Management of Spoiled Identity,* Goffman (1963, 3) defines stigma as "an attribute that is deeply discrediting," that transforms a person (in the minds of others) "from a whole and usual person to a tainted, discounted one." More to the point, Goffman draws our attention to the significance of the "relationship between attribute and stereotype" (ibid., 4). In other words, an individual possesses a particular attribute to which a cluster of stereotypes cling. Dominant sex worker stereotypes include assumptions of victimization, disease, drug addiction, and lack of agency (Jeffrey and MacDonald 2006). The whore stigma is so insidious that it "spoils" the identity of the marked, and, unlike other "tainted" jobs such as mortician, custodian, and used car salesman, the occupational stigma is constructed as a personal attribute so that the implications extend beyond the sphere of work; the label becomes a "master status" (Hughes 1945) that has permanence across social *space.* It also adheres across *time* – even being an *ex*-sex worker is an identity marker that can be ascribed definitive value. Indeed, today, almost thirty years after my short-lived sex work "career," the media regularly identifies me as a "former sex worker and University of Ottawa professor," leaving little doubt as to which identity is the most significant.

My personal journey may have been political, but that does not mean that I did not endeavour to protect myself by carefully editing my biography. For many years, I omitted this specific part of my journey – at least until I was secure in my audience. For many years, I lived not only the lie of omission but also a conceptual disconnect: after all, I did not "buy into" the discourse that I should be either traumatized by, or ashamed of, my work in the sex industry. More importantly, I had a nagging suspicion that by allowing myself to be invisible I was implicitly supporting what I perceived to be the exploitative prohibitionist rhetoric.[8] I justified the decision to myself: What business is my past? What is the point? Did I really want to hurt my aging parents? These convenient truths masked a deeper reality: I was profoundly afraid of the consequences of "coming out." I was afraid of real material consequences – of being fired from my job, of not getting into graduate school, of being dismissed, of being (mis)appropriated by feminist scholars. Perhaps even more, I, a budding "serious" scholar, feared that on the basis of my past experiences I would become a token, a novelty, the embodiment of the liberal academy. Feeling dirty and dishonest, I was an *ambivalent* passer (Goffman 1963) – and, perhaps, for that reason I was not a particularly *good* one. Over and over again, I let the mask slip. I spoke too passionately, or used too many insider examples, or employed the "wrong" pronoun. Far too often, I heard the sharp intake of breath, the perplexed look, and then observed the reflection in someone's eyes as they stripped away my veneer and reassessed me in light of this new (and apparently significant) identity. At the end of this private status degradation *moment,*[9] I found myself standing exposed as esteem was replaced by pity, contempt, dismissal, or titillation. Sometimes the experience was different. With those who either directly or indirectly shared my "spoiled identity" (Goffman 1963), I saw suspicion replaced by connection. Such is the power of shared stigma that our differences slipped away (at least for the moment), our bodies relaxed, our vocabulary shifted, and our conversation deepened.

Ultimately, I knew I had to "come out," not only because the duplicity of championing sex worker rights while continuing to conceal my own experience was disconcertingly hypocritical, but also because I felt compelled to put myself on the line to demonstrate "the kind of woman who is/was a whore." Of course, my ability to out myself speaks powerfully to the tremendous privilege of my specific location. Nonetheless, mindful of potential consequences, I eased, rather than walked, out of the proverbial closet. More specifically, I disclosed that I was a retired erotic dancer when I got my probationary (tenure-stream) university position and spoke publicly of my more "disreputable" past as a prostitute only when I had the security of tenure. Today, I still worry what my uncle will think, and I still sometimes hear the sharp intake of breath. And I still see the perplexed reassessment as my audience seeks to reconcile what they (wrongly) presume to be contradictory identities. And I still sometimes hear annoyingly patronizing congratulations – "Good girl," "You have done really well for yourself!" For the most part, however, being a tenured professor is a privileged space that goes a long way to mediating (albeit not erasing) the whore stigma. Cocooned in a circle of amazing nonjudgmental and supportive colleagues, and buffered by the markers of respectability (promotion, research funding, publications), I am firmly "inside" the normative order and enjoy the many advantages of that location. I have increasingly found that being a *retired* whore (who has by definition abandoned the behaviour even if the identity is not so easily discarded) can be (more or less) accepted. Indeed, sometimes it is even lauded in an education industry interested in marketing itself to youthful consumers.

Ironically, being an activist appears to render me a suspect scholar whose commitment to research rigour is open to question. It is in relation to my activism, perhaps not incidentally where my lack of repentance is most evident, that I am most likely to be accused of bias, that my past is most readily employed as a tool to discount, and that the slipperiness of the discrediting and delegitimizing "whore stigma" (Pheterson 1989) is rendered painfully obvious. For example, upon the release of a community-based research report,[10] a local media outlet article started with the assertion that "a report *created* by a University of Ottawa prof *claims* that city police routinely harass workers" (Jackson 2010, 3; emphasis added). Similarly, in response to a newspaper article in which I publicly defended sex workers' right to advertise their services on a popular Internet site, one reader was inspired to comment, "Bruckert a former stripper turned university professor. So much for being impartial. Can we have studies that aren't done by the self-interested?" (*Ottawa Citizen* 2010). Finally, less personal and hurtful, though more significantly speaking to the structural impact of stigma slippage and the entrenched power-knowledge dialectic, is institutional delegitimation. In her 2010 decision, Justice Himel of the Superior Court of Ontario carefully ascribed greater credibility to those academic expert witnesses who are not activists (and are therefore presumably more objective).[11]

If I have found a safe, if occasionally marginal and periodically suspect, space within the middle-class workplace, I find that I inhabit a somewhat ambivalent location in the sex worker community.[12] Here, I am not only stripped of the status and privilege that I wear with disconcerting ease, but the veracity of Foucault's (1982) power relations (as opposed to monolithic power over) is undeniable.[13] Since we can hardly argue that power relations are dynamic and constitutive (Foucault 1982) without recognizing the potency of inverse stigma, it is perhaps not surprising that I am also confronted with the fact that stigmatization is not a one-way street. In this "other" space where intragroup common-knowledge is scripted into the "the hidden transcript" (Scott 1990), being an academic is potentially a deeply discrediting attribute. Some of the stigmatic assumptions speak to a more general (class-cultural) inverse (or reverse) stigma[14] in the identity ascribed to *over*educated academics who are characterized as ivory tower theoreticians far removed from the *real* world. Academic "accents" continue to be read as arrogant or elitist in spite of the fact that the line between the academy and sex work has become rather porous since the early 2000s, when we began to see convergences that speak to complex intersections.[15] On the one hand, technological innovations, third-wave feminism, and students turning to sex work to pay rapidly rising student fees/expenses have made sectors of the sex industry decidedly middle-class (Bernstein 2007). On the other hand, out sex workers are going to graduate from school and claim academic space/authority with increasing frequency.

In the sex worker community, there is a further cluster of (discredited) characteristics that cling to this more general stigma. On occasion, it is engendered by the mistaken assumption that academics profit directly from research funds. Upon reflection, this is hardly surprising; the costs of research are invisible to most people (not just sex workers) who are unfamiliar with the process. While this particular stigma can be resolved through transparency regarding expenses, there is a more profound issue based on scholars' historic exploitation and (mis)appropriation of sex workers' lives and realities. For years, sex workers (and poor people, and prisoners, and the homeless, and the list goes on) have seen their words and their experiences transformed into data, appropriated, and used to advance the careers of academics. Far too often, "a story or statement that, in its oral form, is 'by' the speaker, very often reaches the public in the form of a text 'by' the scholar" (Gluck and Patai 1991, 2); insights from the community are transformed into an academic's "findings." Small wonder members of marginalized communities feel used. In sex worker spaces, academics are "marked" as potentially exploitative – they are *whores* – but not in a good way.[16] Indeed, while some groups endorse collaborative research, I have also sat at numerous meetings and been told that under no circumstances should research be supported. Academics exploit sex workers – they earn degrees, promotions, and status on the backs of sex workers. Period. End of discussion. Conscious of the irony, I nonetheless find it disconcerting and remarkably unpleasant to be the object of a discourse I myself have frequently made and the target of the very resistance I am usually so anxious to celebrate (Bruckert 2000, 2002, 2004, 2012).

How to respond? Instinctively, I want to counter and defend the academy I so often critique. I want to say that while some academics have clearly exploited sex workers to further their own careers, others have taken an extremely principled approach to the issues and actively championed sex workers' rights. I want to say that tarring all academics with the same brush is not only unfair, it is exactly the sort of sweeping stereotypical assessments that sex workers are mobilizing against. I want to say that research can be useful to sex workers. I want to say that while we must problematize the power optics, the reality is that the academy is the first point of contact for policymakers and, as such, sex worker and researcher communities need to strategize. I want to defend myself and find myself shamelessly rehearsing my own intragroup stigmatizing tropes.[17] I also want to say that it would be easier not to put myself on the line, find a "safe" topic, and insolate myself from the subject-object tension and my discredited identity. I want to say that I feel compelled to work in this area precisely for the reasons they enunciate. I *want* to say all that but I rarely *do.* Once again I am silenced by my fear – my fear of being judged, of being stigmatized, of being recognized as the outsider I fear I am. I am also silenced by a nagging fear that they are right.

As my disjointed stigmatized identities converge, I find myself seeking to resolve the questions that bubble up: Who is *the* expert? Certainly marginalized people are the experts of their own lives; however, are they the only experts? Are they the experts of others' lives? Is a sex worker necessarily the expert of the industry? Is there a hierarchy of experiential expertise, and if so what is it based on? Fearful of being pulled into a postmodern vortex, I struggle to reconcile my political commitment to the sex worker rights movement and the nagging academic in my head who chants, "research *is* important – an *authentic* voice is not a *representative* voice."[18] But of course, this pushes me relentlessly to another set of tensions: to what purpose do we undertake research? How do we acknowledge experiential expertise, make research useful to marginalized communities while at the same time undertaking rigorous research in keeping with the demands of the academy? In the remainder of the chapter, I engage with these questions before presenting my modest model of ethical academic whoredom.

Negotiating the Tensions: Academic? Whore? Academic Whore?

Why do we social scientists undertake research? The answers come easily – to make sense, to shed light, to render the invisible visible. Some of us would add, to influence policy and for social change. If we were to be completely honest, we would also have to say that we do research because it is our job, to gain promotion, for prestige, for self-validation, and for professional status. In other words, we do research in our own interests, in society's interests, and in the interests of knowledge. Of course, there is something profoundly contradictory in these goals. There is also a destabilizing acceptance of the normative social order (not to mention arrogance) in our justifications for "poking and prying" (Hurston 1942, 143) into the lives of others. Outside the safety of the hallowed halls of the academy, in rooms filled with sex workers, that arrogance is rendered visible and the contradictions brought into sharp relief. Here, I find my defence of *"good* intentions" rings hollow and claims of *good* (i.e., respectful and ethical) research have little resonance. Here, my complicity in the relations of power-knowledge cannot be wiped away with carefully constructed academic prose. Here, I must engage with these issues of research and expertise that traverse broader issues of ethics and of power.

The first issue is relevance. As an academic, I firmly believe that challenging modernist hegemonic truth claims (reflected in the dominant discourse) by putting all those other truths "on the record" and then developing respectful inclusionary conceptual frameworks is a useful undertaking. It allows us to unpack some of the most detrimental ideas about marginalized communities. I also firmly believe that the theoretical tools of my discipline can catalogue social processes and practices that "have no name" and reveal individual issues to be social problems. For example, drawing on labour theory illuminates the skills and competencies of sex workers; stigma theory focuses our attention on the interconnections between prejudice, interpersonal struggles, and self-esteem; structural stigma alerts us to the embedded stigmatic assumptions of policy. All of this, if it is accessible (which of course it is not if it is tucked away in peer-reviewed articles and/or expensive books and/or written in academese), can be very affirming and helpful to sex workers and their organizations. Many community members would likely agree. It is, however, a question of priority; these investigations simply do not have the same urgency to a sex worker who is preoccupied with much more immediate issues. Research imposes expectations (which at times feels suspiciously like the off-loading of academic work onto the community), and sex worker groups all too often find themselves burdened by demands on their resources but without their timelines, priorities, and questions taken into account.[19] To add salt to the wound, while sex worker organizations are struggling on shoestring budgets and volunteering their time, privileged university-based researchers are receiving hundreds of thousands of dollars to study *them.*[20]

The challenge engendered by being desirable, trendy, or exotic objects of inquiry speaks to another issue – the academy has become increasingly product-oriented, with ever-expanding expectations for academic output. Since academics have to have *something* to write in all those carefully counted peer-reviewed articles, and since the existence of sex worker rights groups has rendered indoor workers accessible objects of knowledge,[21] it is perhaps not surprising that these organizations are inundated with requests from research "tourists"[22] – undergraduate and graduate students and professors – as well as the media, all of whom want to "talk to a *real* sex worker" and feel entitled to take workers' time with their unending personal questions before disappearing from sight, presumably to go off and write all those articles/theses/term papers.[23]

The third concern is more focused on duplicity. Sex workers are incensed with the many academics (some no doubt well intentioned) who have not only twisted and manipulated their stories to fit their own preconceptions (*theoretical frameworks,* in academe-speak) but have been so committed to a theoretical or ideological position that the very questions they ask have restricted rather than illuminated (Weldon 2010). For sex workers, the implications of this academic imperialism are *real:* "Sex work texts portray sex workers as living troubled, conflicted, torturous lives; disrupting social norms facing the consequences of social exclusion and victimhood. The biggest stigmas I face in my life stem from academic writing about my work" (E. Jeffreys 2010, 14).

That said, there is an issue more elusive than the subjectivity of the researcher and whether or not the particular conceptual framework is the "right" one. Of course, we need to be conscientious and respectful and *listen* to what participants are saying, but these important measures do not solve the problem. Duplicity is built into the research process. There are always some areas of the research agenda that are not fully revealed. At the very least, the extent of analysis and abstraction is unlikely to be shared at the onset of data collection. This problem is exacerbated in grounded research, where, by definition, the researcher herself does not know where the research is *going.* Perhaps the term *consent* itself is misleading, suggesting that informants are acquiescing to a process when in fact they cannot, our best efforts notwithstanding, be fully aware of its implications.

Duplicity is arguably embedded in the research process. However, in community-based research the potential is layered. To be clear, genuine community-based research that begins with the community has incredible potential to redress power relations and "foster new knowledge, tools and methods to develop the best strategies for diverse aspects of intervention, action research, program delivery and policy development" (SSHRC n.d.). When such partnerships become a prerequisite for funding, however, we have a new research orthodoxy valorizing instrumental collaborations that potentially (somewhat perversely) cement the expertise of academics on the basis of their rhetorical acceptance/inclusion of community knowledge.[24] More troubling is the disconcerting potential of well-intentioned community-based research to "reinscribe and retrench unjust relations" (de Leeuw, Cameron, and Greenwood 2012, 185). For example, when funds disproportionally support the privileged academics (student stipends, professor's release from teaching, travel to academic conferences) and not the (much) less privileged community "partners" who are expected to provide (often for token or no compensation) their time and expertise, access to the community, and the (all important) gloss of authenticity; when this happens, social stratifications, the very things community-based researchers are (ostensibly) challenging (both methodologically and empirically), are reproduced. It is simple – when academics own data and when community members are *consulted* on a research protocol designed by academics, then knowledge is not being coproduced and the partnership is, at best, a euphemism. Funding bodies may be fooled by such faux partnerships – sex workers see right through it.

This brings us to the fourth issue – the presumptuousness of the research endeavour: research necessitates that we read *across* lives in order "tease out" themes. Indeed, embedded in the research process is a claim to the right, the ability, and indeed the *authority* to make sense of another person's story and to give form and therefore meaning to another's life (Hampsten 1989). The researcher collects, edits, and analyzes to produce a text in which the experiences are transformed into data – data that were extracted, decontextualized, deconstructed, and then temporally or thematically organized. In light of this, it is amazing that researchers will, without any conscious sense of irony, refuse to speak to the media about the social issues they investigate for fear of having their words taken out of context. It is even more amazing that we demonstrate our cleverness by sprinkling our texts with the gems we have mined (Connors 1986) – quotes that have been abstracted from the contexts of the interviews and the lives out of which they emerged, and then carefully presented in the different context of an analytic piece – and then assume a moral high ground by asserting that we are "giving voice" to marginalized people. Indeed, this brings us to my last point.

Sex workers have mobilized and organized into rights groups since the 1970s, and there are for-and-by groups in most major centres in Canada as well as in locations around the world. Since the 1980s, these politicized groups have developed an impressive body of knowledge and are actively seeking to insert their voice in a conversation that has for too long been "about them, without them."[25] Of course, it is not so simple. Sex workers do not speak in one voice, and while their organizations reflect the positions of many workers, they do not (even if it was logistically possible, which it is not) speak for all sex workers. Undeniably, sex worker organizations, like neighbourhood associations, civil rights leagues, feminist anti-abortion groups, or, indeed, any affiliated collective, have their own intellectually worked-up perspectives that are reflected in their agendas. That said, since none of this is unique to sex workers – the same things are most certainly true of researchers and the academic community – it should not in any way delegitimize sex workers' authority to speak. Indeed, when we recognize that social actors are the real "experts of their own lives," we have to wonder why the media, parliamentary subcommittees, and scholars turn to the (research) expert and draw on the experiential knowledge of sex workers to illustrate – implicitly positioning lived truths as second-rate.

Why this is the case is a significant question that speaks to the virility of "hierarchies of credibility" (Becker 1967, 241), affirms the enduring power-knowledge dialectic, and neatly demonstrates the entrenchment of modernist notions of Truth. We also see the insidious nature of stigma: those people who have the most profound knowledge are silenced by a discourse that discredits them as either victims to be pitied and saved or immoral, deviant, or dirty. In either case, their words can be blissfully ignored or appropriated or transformed by those who have the educational, cultural, and class capital to speak authoritatively in their stead. Evidently, knowledge does not exist outside of power – it is woven into its very fabric. Appreciating this dynamic sheds a harsh light on academic privilege and the need to take an ethical position.

Being an Ethical Academic Whore

In my doctoral dissertation, I confidently wrote of "integrating a much-needed voice into the discourse" and asserted that "giving voice to marginalized populations was one of the better uses of academic privilege." I imagined myself as an academic warrior who would undertake meaningful research with sex workers. After all, I came from a good, solid, and deeply committed place. Now, more than a decade later, I continue to struggle. My initial optimism that I could simply participate with the community, take direction from the community, and do research that is useful – in other words, participatory action research (Barnsley and Ellis 1992) – was more complicated and ethically challenging than the warm and fuzzy descriptions would have us believe.[26]

Ultimately, though the path was characterized by self-doubt and missteps, I am absolutely convinced that negotiating the insider–outsider tensions is a worthwhile endeavour. In the process, I have had to look long and hard at myself, my way of being in the world, my ambition, and just how much of a whore I am prepared to be. It has forced me to recognize that the status I, a white, highly educated, well-paid, middle-class woman, enjoy is not an entitlement, something I have earned and therefore deserve, but a privilege; and with privilege comes responsibility. In the end, however, there are a couple of very simple intersecting rules that are no less valid by virtue of the quaint moralistic echo of a bygone era: be respectful, be honest, share, speak up, and know your place!

Appreciating that members of researched communities are the experts immediately engenders respect – respect for knowledge, for insights, and for people's ability to make sense of their own lives (see Dell, Fillmore, and Kilty, this volume). This does not mean we abandon concepts and theories. Rather, it serves as a powerful antidote to reading over our informants and imposing alien and alienating meanings. Evidently, this results in an ongoing, somewhat schizophrenic, internal dialogue. I resolve the tension between interpreting and analyzing and remaining true to the voice (or perhaps more accurately and problematically, the understanding) of informants through rigorous coding[27] and by applying my own personal "acid test": Can I defend this analysis, not to an academic audience but to my interviewees who may not like my findings that, for example, erotic dancers draw on, and thereby legitimate, racialized scripts (Bruckert 2012).[28] Their disapproval cannot muzzle the researcher: being respectful also necessitates that we respect our participants' ability to be self-reflective and to engage critically – anything less is offensively patronizing.

Marginalized people are savvy; they are not particularly impressed with our academic credentials (indeed, does anyone except academics know, much less care, about the difference between a full and assistant professor?) or our CVs. Like all social actors, however, they desire honest engagement. As researchers, it is imperative that we are as forthright and as transparent as possible – about our research, our goals, our intentions, and what we can realistically give back to the community. This necessitates that we do not inflate the significance of our project or make false claims regarding the genesis of our research.[29] Nor should we carefully wordsmith academic research into *community* partnership, tacking on carefully crafted letters of support from community groups to bolster our funding applications.[30]

The third principle of sharing speaks to the imperative that all our human-subject research must meaningfully "give back" to the particular community according to the needs it identifies. Writing academic articles and presenting at international conferences in exotic locales does little to improve the lives of the individuals who entrusted us with their stories. Sharing means not hoarding data and saving them for those all-important peer-reviewed articles – not only are they largely inaccessible to community members who do not have access to university databanks but they take a long time to be released. If we really do have useful information, then we have the obligation to write a report, post online, create information sheets, hold a forum, do a press release, or any other of the myriad ways that we can share the information we have extracted with and from the community. That these forms of dissemination do not count in the academy is a pity – it is not an excuse.

That said, sharing is not a one-size-fits-all endeavour and necessitates creativity and community collaboration to envision substantive (e.g., providing educational materials, writing articles for grassroots organizations, editing a funding application) and less tangible strategies (e.g., advocating when called to do so, supporting individuals in the community, providing access to educational capital, showing up at a rally). At other times, sharing means sharing skills, knowledge, and access. Knowledge transference is not a rhetorical device to ensure one's funding application looks good; nor is it code for telling people what to do. It is about sharing. Sometimes sharing entails exploiting our privilege, status, and all the markers one holds so dear in the interests of others, even at our own (or our career's) expense. Marginalized people do not need us to give them voice: they have their own. They do, however, need us to get off the proverbial soapbox – or at least share it.

The fourth principle, speaking up, is about walking the walk. Talking is easy – waxing eloquently and critically in university lecture halls to students who carefully transcribe and subsequently reproduce our words and ideas at the end of the semester is as risk-free as it is ego-affirming. Conferences and academic papers are similarly insular – evoking at most a lively (and generally respectful) exchange of ideas.[31] By contrast, speaking out publicly, standing up, and/or taking action for the rhetorical ideals we spout with such assurance can have real negative repercussions – to our carefully massaged reputation, to our careers, and/or to our freedom. Speaking truth to power is, of course, personal (and therefore difficult) for those of us in the academy when the power in question is our institutions (who can deny tenure/promotion or, in the case of students, degrees), other academics (who review or evaluate our work), or funding agencies. We need to take our lead from the bravery of those academics who refuse to relegate justice to a disciplinary regime. Russel Ogden, who, as a master's student researching assisted suicide (see Chapter 1, this volume), risked contempt of court to be ethical and protect his research participants and then sued Simon Fraser University (SFU) for failing to support his principled stand comes to mind immediately.[32] Others, such as John Lowman and Ted Palys, have not only taken on SFU (their own institution) for its failure to support Ogden but have also risked the ire of other academics and the threat of a libel suit in order to expose questionable research protocols at Kwantlen University College.[33] Their chapter in this volume, documenting the shocking lack of ethical oversight and the jaw-dropping double standard (and doublespeak) of the institution's administrators, is academic activism at its finest.

Finally, one has to know one's place. Clearly, I have struggled with how to position myself, how to conceptualize my identity, and especially how to negotiate the fragile insider-outsider terrain. Sometimes, however, knowing one's place is straightforward though not easy – it is simply a matter of checking one's ego and inflated sense of importance at the door and being prepared to invest countless precious hours doing tedious (and decidedly unglamorous) tasks: photocopying, editing funding applications, counting condoms, making red ribbons, designing and posting flyers, or standing outside at yet another rally, vigil, or protest held on a cold Canadian winter evening. All of these contributions are important for the community; none of them is recognized or rewarded by the academy. I am reminded of my good friend and former colleague Professor Robert Gaucher, who spurned publishing in his own name and instead started the *Journal of Prisoners on Prisons* (see also Gaucher 2002). He invests his time and remarkable intellect in ensuring prisoners' voices have a forum to be heard. He does not aspire to mediate and give voice (in fact, he would say it was not his to give and a mediated voice is a questionable voice at best) but to facilitate and amplify the voices that he respects and acknowledges as the experts.[34] He knows his place.

Whose Side Are We On?

In 1967, American sociologist Howard Becker famously asked, "Whose side are we on?" (239). Today, almost fifty years after this seminal *Social Problems* article was published, the question still resonates. In this chapter, I have come out about my conflicted identities and (metaphorically speaking) disrobed – shamelessly displaying myself (warts and all) and inviting inspection.[35] To what end? Because, quite simply, I believe that we must, on occasion, put ourselves "on the line" and "get naked." And because, while cognizant of tensions and contradictions, I nonetheless firmly believe that rendering the invisible visible is not restricted to exposing the underbelly of the "other." I am confident that what academics do (or do not do) matters (a bit). I am convinced that when we hyper-privileged "talking heads" blindly reproduce academic conventions as gospel, when we fail to render visible the advantage we derive from the normative order, when we neglect to investigate our own complicity in social structures that delegitimize our research subjects, when we do not challenge power relations through our research, when we hide behind sanitized pseudoscientific paragraphs in our peer-reviewed articles, when we unthinkingly reproduce and reinscribe power relations in our research practices, and when we mask our careerist ambition behind empty rhetorical phrases of "giving voice," then (in)actions have spoken loudly, and Becker's rhetorical question has been answered.

Acknowledgments

I would like to thank Jennifer Clamen, Sheri Fabian, Maritza Felices-Luna, Jennifer Kilty, and Dominique Robert for their invaluable comments on earlier drafts of this chapter.

Notes

1 Indeed, I am a clumsy dancer and then, as now, remarkably inept at casual social chit-chat. This was a significant disadvantage in an industry where finely tuned interpersonal skills are essential.
2 Elena Jeffreys (2011) refers to this as "tragedy porn."
3 For me, sex work is fully consistent with the feminist focus on women's choice. I was to find out that this put me in conflict with feminist orthodoxy of the time. Indeed, even the excellent 1987 text *Good Girls, Bad Girls* is subtitled *Sex Trade Workers and Feminists Face to Face*, which suggests two populations. In the intervening thirty years, as a result of sex workers claiming feminism as their own and third-wave feminists' engagement with sexuality (see, for example, Johnson 2002), things have changed. That said, the bifurcation of feminism and sex worker rights continues to echo in prohibitionists' accusation of complicity in the violence experienced by sex workers. For example, the following comment appeared in response to a media article in which I was quoted as defending the rights of sex workers: "Bruckert – how dare you – when women are being sold and trafficked as 'sex trade workers' in your 'industry'" (*Ottawa Citizen* 2010).
4 This film, which includes interviews with such noted antipornography feminists as Robin Morgan, Susan Griffin, and Kathleen Barry, argues that pornography degrades and objectifies women and therefore is harmful to all women, most especially the sex workers themselves. The plot line revolves around the journey of Lindalee Tracey, a proud and defiant erotic dancer, and director Bonnie Klein's exploration of the genre – what Tracey (1997, 202) later referred to as "Madonna and the Whore Do Pornland." Notably, Tracey, who went on to become a documentary filmmaker, felt betrayed: "I felt exploited, the same way the filmmakers say pornography exploits other women" (ibid., 203).
5 Here, I am referring to Foucault's oft-quoted assertion that "where there is power there is resistance" (1978, 95).
6 This is a tricky location. The convergence of the academic fashion that gave rise to a valorization of the experiential voice conflicts with the conventions of the academy that marginalize. In the case of sex work specifically, the subject has become increasingly researched.
7 The title is an intentional reference to Monica Russel y Rodriguez's (2002, 347) excellent article "Confronting Anthropology's Silencing Praxis," in which she addresses the binaries in her identity as "the Chicano among feminists ... the newcomer in academe, the overeducated at home."
8 Prostitution prohibitionists seek to abolish the sex industry. For those from the "righteous right," this prohibition is based on moral arguments. For feminist prohibitionists, it is based on the profound belief that sex work undermines all women's equality by positioning men to buy "one representative member" (S. Jeffreys 2004; Barry 1995).

9   The language here is intentional. The evaluations appear to be almost instantaneous and the process lacks the public element so important in Garfinkel's (1956) conceptualization. For all that, the experience (and repercussions) is profound.

10 The report, *Challenges: Ottawa Area Sex Workers Speak Out* (2010), coauthored by Frédérique Chabot, was based on forty-three interviews with sex workers (twenty-seven of which were street-based). The sampling, data collection, and analysis were careful and rigorous, meeting and exceeding disciplinary standards.

11 *Bedford v. Canada,* 2010, ONSC 4264 (CanLII). This is not to negate the contribution of the expert witnesses, whose empirical evidence was invaluable to Justice Himel in reaching her decision. Moreover, I firmly believe the pioneering work of Fran Shaver and John Lowman opened the door for a generation of researchers who have had an important impact on the discursive framing of sex work issues.

12 This is not to say that my background (and activism) does not mediate this stigma. More important, however, is my public identity location.

13 While there appears to be a contradiction in Foucault's assertions regarding power relations and power knowledge; in fact, Foucault (1988, 1) does not discount issues of authority: "Relations of power are not in themselves forms of repression. But what happens is that, in society, in most societies, organizations are created to freeze the relations of power, hold those relations in a state of asymmetry, so that a certain number of persons get an advantage, socially, economically, politically, institutionally, etc. And this totally freezes the situation. That's what one calls power in the strict sense of the term: it's a specific type of power relation that has been institutionalized, frozen, immobilized, to the profit of some and to the detriment of others."

14 Reverse stigmas are stigmatic assumptions that invert social stratifications – "bottom up" as opposed to "top down." Goffman (1963, 3) explains that "a language of relationships, not attributes, is really needed. An attribute that stigmatizes one type of possessor can confirm the usualness of another, and therefore is neither credible, nor discreditable as a thing in itself." For example, high educational attainment may be seen as indicating intelligence, a solid work ethic, and laudable ambitions by the middle class but self-indulgent, pretentious, and reflecting a disinclination to do "real" work by working-class audiences. The existence of these reverse or inverse stigmas does not, however, negate the realities of social stratifications, and, while inverse stigmas may be interpersonally significant, they are not embedded and affirmed structurally (Hannem and Bruckert 2012b). Moreover, operating within existing power-knowledge dynamics, they are not afforded the status of "truth" in dominant discourse.

15 I am intentionally drawing a distinction between students who do sex work and sex workers who are students – a distinction that has experiential, ideological, and perceptional significance. Indeed, the two groups have different standpoints. While the former can assume a relational identity location (Trautner and Collett 2010), sex workers who become students negotiate a much more complex and layered identity location.

16 According to the *Oxford English Dictionary,* there are two meanings of *whore:* a prostitute; and to debase oneself by doing something for unworthy, often monetary, motives.

17 For more on intragroup stigmatization, see Hannem and Bruckert (2012a).

18 Of course, the irony is that there is no way of realizing the positivist dream of a "representative sample" in a hidden criminalized, stigmatized, and marginalized sector such as sex work. The same is true for many other populations, including the victims and perpetrators of domestic violence. All of which merely confirms that the positivist ideal of representativeness does not apply to all research. Representativeness does not, indeed it should not, be equated with rigour.

19 See de Leeuw, Cameron, and Greenwood (2012) for critical reflection on the demands that participatory community-based research places on Indigenous communities.

20 Some sex worker rights groups, such as SPOC (Sex Professionals of Canada) and POWER (Prostitutes of Ottawa-Gatineau Work, Educate and Resist), restrict their activities to advocacy and/or public education only while others, such as Maggies and Stella, also provide services. The former are largely unfunded while the latter find themselves perpetually applying for funding to provide services such as bad-date lists, hepatitis A and B vaccines, information guides, and self-defence classes (for more on this, see Clamen 2009).

21 There is a significant irony in this. Historically, conventional wisdom held that research on sex workers focused on the most marginal street-based workers who could be accessed in prison or through social service providers (Weitzer 2005). Today, the existence of sex worker rights organizations has rendered indoor workers assessable. In short, sex workers' resistance may have created the conditions of possibility for their over-research; as we know from Foucault's work on the emergence of the "disciplines" (Foucault 1977), a "captive" population is a potential object of "knowledge."

22 Credit to the late Liz Elliott, who drew my attention to the difference between research travellers who immerse themselves and research tourists who slip in and out of geographic, social, and/or cultural spaces and (somewhat voyeuristically) "see" the exotic highlights.

23 There is, of course, a profound irony (perhaps hypocrisy) here. This chapter will be carefully catalogued on my resumé to justify my own academic production.

24 Instrumentality is not to be confused with exploitation. Critical and feminist social science researchers have long struggled with the tension between friend and participant as they endeavor to navigate the research relationship in a non-exploitative manner (see, for example, Sjoberg and Nett 1968).

25 I, for one, have received far too much of my education from workers who have patiently taken the time to explain their reality to me and to challenge, sometimes disconcertingly, my normative assumptions.

26 For example, as Fine and Weis (2002, 293), "a couple of White women, a well-paid Thelma and Louise with laptops," remind us, "piercing fractures define life within communities" (271). Sex work is an occupational category, not a job description or an identity; not surprisingly, this "community" is no more immune than any other to the intra-stigmatization that reproduces hierarchical stratifications. These fractures can play out in research done collaboratively with a particular labour sector (e.g., dancers).

27 Of course, there is no claim that this is an objective process. Like all researchers, what I can see (and therefore code) is necessarily restricted by the conceptual channels to which I am attuned (see also Kirkwood 1993).

28 I have struggled with this conundrum. For example, the analysis of the interviews collected in the course of a community-based project with Dancers Equal Rights Association revealed that some dancers do not wish to be paid a salary and appreciate the autonomy engendered by the "freelancing" system – a result that was in direct conflict with the association's fight for erotic dancers to be salaried employees.

29 To illustrate the difference, I do much community-based research; however, I am also involved in a large SSHRC-funded project on sex work management. While I am confident that the findings will prove useful to sex worker communities, I am highly cognizant that this project emerges from the academy and will first and foremost benefit the academics and students involved. I share this with the advisory committee composed of community representatives.

30 At POWER (Prostitutes of Ottawa-Gatineau Work, Educate and Resist), university-based researchers regularly approach us requesting letters of support for this or that funding application. Recently, one such offer came with the specification that we do not have to do anything else – leaving little doubt as to the purpose of the partnership.

31 Writing articles, except for the sting of a critical rebuttal that, let's be honest, opens up the possibility of more peer-reviewed articles, is also insular.

32 Ogden's fight to protect participant confidentiality did not end with SFU and has plagued his career. He continues to pay the price for his principled stance (see Lowman and Palys 2000).

33 The libel suit, described by Lowman and Palys as a "Kwantlen-funded threat to sue the whistleblowers for libel if they did not swallow their whistles" (this volume), is a significant and destabilizing threat with potential financial, professional, and personal consequences. Their tenacity and courage in the face of this are noteworthy.

34 Melissa Munn (this volume) is another academic who endeavours to use her privileged position to amplify the voices of those who are, far too often, silenced or disregarded. A long-time advocate for prisoner rights, Munn launched an open-access electronic Penal Press Archive in 2010 in order to disseminate this "primary source of prison history from within" (www.penalpress.com).

35 This process makes me uncomfortably aware of an internal tension. Shamelessly inviting judgment, I am fearful of rejection and exposure. I have been inspired by the lessons I have learned from the brave researchers who have come before me and remember the enthusiasm of my students about hearing the real stories of research and researchers (see, for example, Ceglowski 2002; Russel y Rodriguez 2002; Adams 2000; Hoyle 2000; Borland 1991; Patai 1991; Fine and Weis 2002).

References

Adams, C. (2000). Suspect Data: Arresting Research. In R. King and E. Wincup (Eds.), *Doing Research on Crime and Justice* (385-94). Oxford: Oxford University Press.

Barnsley, J., and Ellis, D. (1992). *Research for Change: Participatory Action Research for Community Groups*. Ottawa: Women's Research Centre.

Barry, K. (1995). *The Prostitution of Sexuality: The Global Exploitation of Women*. New York: New York University Press.

Becker, H. (1967). Whose Side Are We On? *Social Problems* 14(3), 239-47.

Bell, L. (Ed.). (1987). *Good Girls, Bad Girls: Sex Trade Workers and Feminists Face to Face*. Toronto: Women's Press.

Bernstein, E. (2007). Sex Work for the Middle Classes. *Sexualities* 10(4), 473-77.

Borland, K. (1991). "That's Not What I Said": Interpretive Conflict in Oral Narrative Research. In S. Gluck and D. Patai (Eds.), *Women's Words* (63-75). New York: Routledge.

Bruckert, C. (2000). Stigmatized Labour: An Ethnographic Study of Strip Clubs in the 1990s. PhD diss., Carleton University.

–. (2002). *Taking It Off, Putting It On: Women in the Strip Trade*. Toronto: Women's Press.

–. (2004). Resistance. In M.F. Bosworth (Ed.), *Encyclopedia of Prisons and Correctional Facilities*. Thousand Oaks, CA: Sage.

–. (2012). Workin' It: Sex Workers Negotiate Stigma. In S. Hannem and C. Bruckert (Eds.), *Stigma Revisited: Implications of the Mark* (55-78). Ottawa: University of Ottawa Press.

Bruckert, C., and Chabot, F. (2010). *Challenges: Ottawa Area Sex Workers Speak Out*. Ottawa: POWER.

Ceglowski, D. (2002). Research as Relationship. In N. Denzin and Y. Lincoln (Eds.), *The Qualitative Inquiry Reader* (5-24). Thousand Oaks, CA: Sage.

Clamen, J. (2009). *Taking Action: Canadian Sex Worker Organizing*. Ottawa: POWER.

Connors, D. (1986). I've Always Had Everything I Want, but I Have Never Wanted Much. PhD diss., Brandeis University.

Davis, A. (1981). *Women, Race and Class*. London: Women's Press.

–. (1989). *Women, Culture and Politics*. New York: Vintage.

de Leeuw, S., Cameron, E., and Greenwood, M. (2012). Participatory, Community-Based Research, Indigenous Geographies, and the Spaces of Friendship: A Critical Engagement. In *Participatory Research and Indigenous Geographies*. Special issue, *Canadian Geographer 56*(2), 180-94.

DeVault, M. (1990). Talking and Listening from Women's Standpoint: Feminist Strategies for Interviewing and Analysis. *Social Problems 37*(1), 96-116.

Garfinkel, H. (1956). Conditions of Successful Degradation Ceremonies. *American Journal of Sociology 61*(5), 420-24.

Gaucher, R. (Ed.). (2002). *Writing as Resistance: Journal of Prisoners on Prison Anthology (1988-2002)*. Toronto: Scholar's Press.

Gluck, S., and Patai, D. (1991). Introduction. In S. Gluck and D. Patai (Eds.), *Women's Words* (1-6) New York: Routledge.

Goffman, E. (1963). *Stigma: Notes on the Management of a Spoiled Identity*. New Jersey: Prentice-Hall.

Fine, M., and Weis, L. (2002). Writing the 'Wrongs' of Fieldwork. In N. Denzin and Y. Lincoln (Eds.), *The Qualitative Inquiry Reader* (267-97). Thousand Oaks, CA: Sage.

Foucault, M. (1977). *Discipline and Punish: The Birth of the Prison*. New York: Vintage.

—. (1978). *The History of Sexuality, Vol. 1*. New York: Pantheon Books.

—. (1980). Two Lectures – Lecture One: 7 January 1976. In Gordon C. (Ed.), *Power/Knowledge: Selected Interviews and Other* Writings, *1972-1977*. (Trans. C. Gordon). (78-92) New York: Pantheon Books.

—. (1982). The Subject and Power. *Critical Inquiry 8*(4), 777-95.

Hampsten, E. (1989). Considering More Than a Single Reader. In Personal Narratives Group (Eds.), *Interpreting Women's Lives: Feminist Theory and Personal Narratives* (129-38). Bloomington: Indiana University Press.

Hannem, S. (2011). Theorizing Stigma and the Politics of Resistance: Symbolic and Structural Stigma in Everyday Life. In S. Hannem and C. Bruckert (Eds.), *Stigma Revisited: Negotiations, Resistance and Implications of the Mark* (10-28). Ottawa: University of Ottawa Press.

Hannem, S., and Bruckert, C. (2012a). Concluding Thoughts: Academic Activists, a Call to Action. In S. Hannem and C. Bruckert (Eds.), *Stigma Revisited: Negotiations, Resistance and Implications of the Mark* (176-82). Ottawa: University of Ottawa Press.

—. (2012b). Theorizing Stigma and the Politics of Resistance. In S. Hannem and C. Bruckert (Eds.), *Stigma Revisited: The Implications of the Mark* (10-28). Ottawa: University of Ottawa Press.

Haraway, D. (1988). Situated Knowledges: The Science Question in Feminism and the Privilege of Partial Perspective. *Feminist Studies 14*(3), 575-99.

Hoyle, C. (2000). Being a "Nosy Bloody Cow": Ethical and Methodological Issues in Researching Domestic Violence. In R. King and E. Wincup (Eds.), *Doing Research on Crime and Justice* (395-406). New York: Oxford University Press.

Hughes, E.C. (1945). Dilemmas and Contradictions of Status. *American Journal of Sociology 50*, 353-59.

Hurston, Z.N. (1942). *Dust Tracks on a Road*. Philadelphia: J.B. Lippincott.

Jackson, K. (2010). Sex Workers Claim Police Harassment. *24 Hours: Ottawa News*, 2 December.

Jeffrey, L., and MacDonald, G. (2006). *Sex Workers in the Maritimes Talk Back*. Vancouver: UBC Press.

Jeffreys, E. (2010). Sex Work, Migration and Trafficking Matters: Non-Sex Workers Writing about Sex Work. *Intersections: Gender and Sexuality in Asia and the Pacific 23*, 14-19.

—. (2011). Why Feminists Should Listen to Sex Workers. *Scavenger*, 11 June.

Jeffreys, S. (2004). Prostitution as a Harmful Cultural Practice. In C. Stark and R. Whisnant (Eds.), *Not for Sale: Feminists Resisting Prostitution and Pornography* (386-99). North Melbourne: Spinifex.

Johnson, M.L. (Ed.) (2002). *True Confessions of Feminist Desire*. New York: Thunder's Mouth Press.

Jones, R.S. (1995). Uncovering the Hidden Social World: Insider Research in Prison. *Journal of Contemporary Criminal Justice 11*, 106-18.

Kirkwood, C. (1993). Investing Ourselves. In J. de Groot and J.M. Maynard (Eds.), *Women's Studies in the 1990s: Doing Things Differently?* (18-39) New York: St. Martin's Press.

Klein, Bonnie Sherr. (Dir.) (1981). *Not a Love Story: A Film about Pornography*. Ottawa: National Film Board.

Lowman, J., and Palys, T. (2000). Ethics and Institutional Conflict of Interest: The Research Confidentiality Controversy at Simon Fraser University. *Sociological Practice 2*(4), 245-55.

Ottawa Citizen. (2010). Online Classified Ads Give Sex Workers Safe Avenue to Work: Criminologist [Article comments], 19 October.

Patai, D. (1991). U.S. Academics and Third World Women: Is Ethical Research Possible? In S. Gluck and D. Patai (Eds.), *Women's Words* (137-53). New York: Routledge.

Pheterson, G. (1989). *A Vindication of the Rights of Whores*. Seattle: Seal Press.

Polsky, N. (1969). *Hustlers, Beats and Others*. Garden City, NY: Anchor Press.

Russel y Rodriguez, M. (2002). Confronting Anthropology's Silencing Praxis. In N. Denzin and Y. Lincoln (Eds.), *The Qualitative Inquiry Reader* (347-75). Thousand Oaks, CA: Sage.

Scott, J. (1990). *Domination and the Arts of Resistance*. New Haven: Yale University Press.

Sjoberg, G., and Nett, R. (1968). *A Methodology for Social Research*. New York: Harper and Row.

Smith, D. (1987). *The Everyday World as Problematic*. Boston: Northeastern University Press.

SSHRC. (N.d.). *Community University Research Alliances*. http://www.sshrc-crsh.gc.ca/funding -financement/programs-programmes/cura-aruc-eng.aspx.

Trautner, N., and Collett, J. (2010). Students Who Strip: The Benefits of Alternate Identities for Managing Stigma. *Symbolic Interaction 33*(2), 257-79.

Tracey, L. (1997). *Growing Up Naked*. Vancouver: Douglas and McIntyre.

Weitzer, R. (2005). New Directions in Research on Prostitution. *Crime, Law and Social Change 43*(4-5), 211-35.

Weldon, J. (2010). Show Me the Money: A Sex Worker Reflects on Research into the Sex Industry. In M. Ditmore, A. Levy, and A. Willman (Eds.), *Sex Work Matters: Exploring Money, Power and Intimacy in the Sex Industry* (12-15). London: Zed Books.

Concluding Thoughts

Maritza Felices-Luna, Jennifer M. Kilty, and Sheryl C. Fabian

THIS BOOK EXPLORES SOME of the research practices that critical social scientists from law, criminology, sociology, and nursing invoke in their work with qualitative methodologies and constructivist, critical, postmodern, and postcolonial paradigms. While some chapters focus solely on the author's specific and often personal experiences in doing critical social research, others draw from the author's career-long observations of the field, although most are a combination of both. Throughout the chapters, the authors not only discuss the methods they use, but they also reflect on the concerns, problems, and resistances they confront in their work. These challenges emerge from a variety of sources, including within themselves, the broader academic research community, their institution of affiliation, the participants, and the community or site where the research takes place. The contributors discuss a number of different issues — from the role and practices of the researcher and the research process itself to the political and institutional contexts in which their research is produced. Despite the diversity of topics and questions that the authors address, there are five interconnected and, in some instances, interdependent axes that run through the contributions. These axes are intended as a point of reference for the reader to reflect on the interconnectedness of the chapters, and we hope that they will initiate some important conversations; however, these points are not presented as definitive conclusions to the many issues and questions the authors raise in the text.

Consideration of the Role of the Researcher in Knowledge Production

All of the contributors challenge the idea that research can be wholly neutral and objective or disconnected from the material realities and, in some instances, the politics of the researcher and the research process. Instead, the authors begin from the position that research is shaped by the sociopolitical, cultural, and economic contexts in which it takes place, as well as by the scholars, participants, and communities involved in the project. In order to take these forces into account in the planning and execution of their research and in the interpretation of their findings, contributors noted the importance of practising reflexivity, documenting how the theories and methodologies they draw upon allowed them to see and make sense of a phenomenon in a particular way. Further, they demonstrate the need to be reflexive about their own persona (their identity, history, values, and politics); the relationships they establish with co-researchers, participants, and the community in which their research is conducted; and the ways these relationships affect the research process and thus knowledge production. Although scholars who engage in reflexivity face the risk of what Bourdieu (2004, 89) calls a narcissistic reflexivity, which is "often limited to a complacent looking-back by the researcher on his own experience," it is essential to conduct a "reflexive critique capable of giving it [social science] a higher degree of freedom with respect to the social constraints and necessities that bear on it as they do on all human activity" (ibid., 90). Through these reflexive processes, the contributors were able to use different theoretical and methodological frameworks in creative ways to produce innovative interpretations of the phenomenon being researched.

Contributors also highlight the need to challenge traditional conceptions of science that can preclude researchers from drawing on political activism, personal experience, emotion, and other alternative ways of knowing. In particular, van den Hoonaard reminds us that we must be wary of blindly adopting cultural signals, symbols, and norms and values of positivist research, especially given its potential impact on qualitative methodologies. Rather than clinging to unrealistic claims of objectivity perpetuated by traditional science, this text provides a forum that embraces the new understandings offered by these less conventional discussions. In fact, we suggest that these are indeed indispensable sources of insight because they help the researcher dialogue with different conceptual and methodological tools. Utilizing emotion and personal experience to carry out and make sense of research represents a significant challenge given the prevalence of certain positivistic values that continue to influence how the scientific community thinks about, frames, and shapes the knowledge production and dissemination processes. Ultimately, the contributors demonstrate that the processes of experiencing methodologies are as important to consider as the findings and results of the study.

Power Relations in, through, and as a Consequence of Research

Qualitative methodologies and constructivist, critical, postmodern, post-colonial, and participatory epistemologies acknowledge the impossibility of producing "pure" spaces of research free of power relations. In fact, the contributors acknowledge that power relations might never be neutralized or settled, that they are continually negotiated throughout the research process, and, therefore, that researchers need to be aware of where power resides and how its relations shape and affect the research project. Chunn and Menzies's contribution specifically acknowledges the inequality often faced by academics who apply a critical lens. To begin, researchers must recognize their privilege and the possibilities it grants them (e.g., access to resources and information and influence on policy) as well as the limitations it imposes on them (e.g., the need to "play the academic game" and sustain a certain type and level of "productivity" to maintain status and privilege in academe). Understanding power relations also means recognizing that participants and collaborators are not powerless when facing the researcher and that they do have some means of manoeuvring through situations shaped by power differentials (e.g., utilizing the researcher's need for participants to destabilize the traditional researcher–participant power relationship).

Moreover, within certain environments, the prestige commonly attributed to the researcher can be a source of mistrust and even disdain for the researched. While researchers have a long history of exploiting participants, as Felices-Luna describes, the extent to which some research ethics review boards now focus so intently on the researcher's potential for exploiting participants can actually perpetuate the very power imbalances the researcher is attempting to challenge by constructing participants as lacking agency. Researchers must think beyond the researcher-participant dyad to have a more complete picture of the power relations affecting the project, so as to be aware of other social actors that directly or indirectly influence the research process and to whom the researcher might be in a dominant or subordinate position (either socially in terms of status or pragmatically in terms of need and dependence). Finally, the power dynamics produced by the research process (e.g., recognizing a marginalized population as a legitimate and equal partner) and the knowledge that can come from collaboration have the potential to disrupt or subvert power differentials and may help to produce lasting social change (for example, Bellot, Sylvestre, and St-Jacques and Dell, Fillmore, and Kilty, this volume).

Producing Ethically Grounded Research

In efforts to prevent harm and risk, the creation of research ethics review boards (REBs) opened the door to the growing institutional regulation of research and the researcher by universities, government agencies, public and private institutions (for example, schools, prisons, and corporations) as well as funding councils. In this vein, research ethics review boards similarly exhibit one of the cornerstones of contemporary neoliberal societies – namely, the prediction and management of real and potential risks (Haggerty 2004; Lupton 1999). This sociopolitical shift affects critical social research on two fronts. The first is the progression toward the corporate university, whose use of a business model approach to structure and govern places of higher learning contributes to the remaking of students as consumers of an "academic product" (Cheyfitz 2009). A key feature of the corporate university's agenda is expansion, which requires limiting the prospective riskiness of academic endeavours that may be perceived as discrediting to the public's perception of the university (ibid.). Research ethics review boards, as the bodies primarily responsible for assessing and evaluating research involving human participants, determine the levels of acceptable and unacceptable risk that proposed research projects present. REBs consider not only the potential harms to the individual researcher and the participant but also the university's potential liability or responsibility should harm emerge from a proposed study and the damage such harm could do to the university's branding, marketing, and student and professorial recruitment.

A key feature of this collection is the growing discussion of the ways in which institutional research ethics review boards direct and control the execution of research so as to minimize institutional and administrative liability. As several contributors describe, REBs have increasingly adopted positivist and risk logic to evaluate qualitative, exploratory, and participatory action research applications. Van den Hoonaard's chapter in particular identifies the broader signs and symbols that together reveal the changing nature, or what he refers to as the colonization, of qualitative research. REBs often use language that differs discursively and in practice from qualitative approaches; for example, applying a positivist understanding of rigour increasingly requires qualitative researchers to generate audit trails – a nearly impossible task for an ethnographer. Such ethics requests correspond with the decreasing use of ethnography – once a staple of qualitative research, particularly prison sociology. These criticisms lie not with the boards themselves but with the mechanisms used to determine the potential for "research risk" that remake the qualitative researcher as an (un)ethical subject. Haggerty (2004) convincingly argues that the academy's interpretation of ethics has shifted from assuming the competence of the researcher to one based on institutionalized distrust of the researcher's ability to negotiate herself and her research ethically while in the field. Regardless of a researcher's years of experience and training, REBs require the individual applicant to demonstrate – often through the adoption of more structured and predetermined research designs – that she is, in fact, an ethical researcher.

This fact, in conjunction with institutional efforts to use standardized methods to assess and predict potential risks in social research (questionnaires, surveys, dichotomous yes/no questions) – what Guillemin and Gillam (2004) refer to as procedural ethics – has created a normative approach to how research itself is conceived and conducted, but which is ill suited to some qualitative research methodologies. For example, the evaluation criteria used to determine the ethicality of a project often require certain information be established and decided upon in advance. However, many of the responses to standard REB questions emerge from ongoing decisions that can be made only while in the field. Many qualitative projects evolve through the relationships established during the research and are based on the trust and rapport that develop between researchers and the participants. An ethnographer, for example, cannot possibly predetermine all of the topics of discussion, questions asked, information revealed, sites of observation and interaction, and duration of conversations to be had with participants. Similarly, demands for informed and written consent from participants can be problematic for social researchers doing work on sensitive topics and where participants are unwilling to sign their names (and may be at risk of harm for doing so). There are many individuals and groups (rebel groups, resistance organizations, activists, and former prisoners, to name but a few) that may be uncomfortable or legitimately skeptical of signing their name for research purposes due to socio-economic or political positioning, language, or cultural barriers.

Contributors keenly identified that one of the consequences of primarily focusing on procedural ethics (Guillemen and Gillam 2004) is that post-ethics application research design adaptation and on-the-ground field research decisions are interpreted as risky and thus bureaucratically problematic. While procedural ethics contribute to ethical thinking about research, they cannot respond to all of the questions, dilemmas, or problematics that emerge in those "'ethically important moments' in doing research – the difficult, often subtle, and usually unpredictable situations that arise in the practice of doing research" (Guillemin and Guillemin 2004, 262). Thinking of ethics as a procedural framework fails to acknowledge the "messy actualities" (Barry, Osbourne, and Rose 1993) of doing research, largely because it presupposes a linear and straightforward process that begins with a research design that is approved and carried out as designed. In addition to procedural ethics considerations, we need to reflect upon those questions, moments, and happenings that expose us as potentially ethically vulnerable. There is no set of predetermined responses or courses of action that researchers have to draw upon to respond to the dynamic, fluid, and thus shifting nature of doing research (particularly field research) (Ezzy 2005; Felices-Luna, this volume; Hesse-Biber and Leavy 2011); these responses are ethically important moments because they mark a point at which a wrong may be done (Guillemin and Gillam 2004). In these moments, procedural ethics are of little help in determining the most ethical course of action. Much like anything else, we typically perform better with time and experience, meaning the more seasoned researcher will have a greater number of experiences to draw from in these moments. This suggests the value of REBs becoming more flexible, acting instead as a sounding board for researchers as they traverse through the research journey and not solely as a board that primarily serves to vet research designs before the researcher conducts research.

Resistance and Hurdles

Not surprisingly, given that the focus of much of their research is on sensitive topics and injustice, many of the contributors are inspired by the works of Michel Foucault and his writings on resistance, which emphasize the importance of listening to marginalized and subjugated knowledges – or those "voices from below" (Chunn and Menzies, this volume). Much of Foucault's work examines power in its diverse and diffuse forms, and his later work in particular stresses the need not only to let "those most affected by power" guide and incite local action against it but also to learn from them (Pickett 1996, 455). With this theoretical position as a point of entry and framework to structure their research, contributors all exemplified the importance of acknowledging, examining, and coming to understand how resistance forms, its functions, and its potential value for contributing to social evolution, advancement, and change. While the book's authors all study resistance in some form – be it the ways in which prisoners (and other incarcerated populations) resist correctional brutality; challenges to judicial and systemic injustices; the effects of madness and its governance; sociopolitical activism; or culture as a form of resistance and empowerment – we must also consider resistance as a mechanism scholars use to produce critical social research. Particularly important for the book, and as several of the chapters explore, critical scholars engage alternative interpretations and/or use qualitative research methodologies as a form of resistance to the normative order of academic positivism.

In this sense, this book as a whole provides an interesting lens through which to think about the value of engaging with resistance – either as a topic for study in and of itself or as a mechanism through which to structure and produce critical social research. For example, as social scientists doing qualitative research on difficult-to-access populations and communities, the contributing authors all noted that they make an effort to showcase and learn from the subjugated knowledges of the participants and communities upon and with whom they do their research. In fact, there are repeated references throughout the chapters to the notion of doing research *with* participants and the community rather than *on* them or *for* them. Challenging traditional social science fieldwork research designs by incorporating participants in the design and execution of the project is a useful way to gain entry into the community research site and to build rapport with potential participants. This is particularly important given the sensitive nature of some research and of the historical sociopolitical relations between researchers and the community. Take, for example, research that examines Aboriginal participants and communities. Given the history of white researchers entering and exploiting Aboriginal communities in the name of research, ensuring participants that they have some control and ownership over the data is an important development that challenges traditional research paradigms. The growing use of community-based and participatory action research methodologies by qualitative researchers also demonstrates the value of challenging and resisting traditional institutional discourses that conceptualize the researcher as expert and objective neutrality as essential for the production of "good" research. This theoretical and methodological framework emerged across a number of disciplines with the development and evolution of feminist, antiracist, postcolonial, and Marxist paradigms (to name but a few) . In terms of the disciplinary affiliations of the book's contributors – namely, criminology, law, and the sociology of deviance – nowhere is the focus on privileging voice more salient than in ethnographic prison sociology, feminist criminology, and what Taylor, Walton, and Young (1973) name convict criminology.

Finally, in addition to considering resistance as a topic of research and engaging it as a methodological tool, the contributors also discuss at length their experiences of institutional resistance (from structures such as research ethics review boards, university administrations, and the academy) to some of their qualitative research projects and designs. Examples of institutional resistance include, but are not limited to, strict ethics requests for participants to sign their name as proof of informed consent, the growing problematization of snowball sampling, demands to know all the interview and research questions and locations in advance, REB approval of a project followed by failure to support the researcher when the research experiences media scrutiny (as in

Ogden's case), and even the corporate university agenda that provides greater financial support for research that fits its business model for expansion. However, as a number of the chapters elucidate, research is rarely purely linear or methodologically and ethically predetermined. Resistance may come from any number of sources and can both challenge and facilitate critical social research; what is key and what the contributors to this volume attest to is that it is important to consider resistance – to analyze and think about it in all its incarnations so as to understand how it shapes and contributes to the production of our work.

Commitment to Social Change

Contributing authors write of the need for praxis in research and are committed to generating or supporting social, political, or economic change through different strategies. This is not an easy task given the preeminent antagonisms that sometimes exist between the activist and the academic worlds. Such issues are highlighted in both Bruckert's and Munn's contributions in particular. The discordancy of these two worlds is based partly on the pragmatic concern with the concrete realities and experiences of those in vulnerable situations and the intellectual (and therefore oftentimes the abstract) endeavour of the latter. Those contributors who actively engaged in some form of activist-academia testify to the difficult task of juggling these two worlds, but they also demonstrate that it is possible to reconcile them and that it is feasible to simultaneously produce knowledge and social change (see Bellot, Sylvestre, and St-Jacques; Perron, Holmes, and Jacob; and Dell, Fillmore, and Kilty, among others). On the part of the scholar, this often requires sacrifice in terms of time, resources, and even academic advancement and recognition, a willingness to negotiate contradictory demands and expectations from both worlds, as well as the readiness to participate in activities that on the surface appear to be unrelated to the academic enterprise. On the part of those in the field working alongside the scholar, it requires an openness to engage with concepts, methods, and the constraints of the academy despite being overburdened by their sometimes precarious material realities. Due to the toil such a collaboration can present, it can only be achieved through establishing and maintaining trust and respect between all those involved in the research process and by recognizing the value and expertise each party holds.

Final Thoughts

It is our hope that this volume will serve as a starting point for greater academic discussion of the issues presented across these five axes. However, if we are to identify a long view of the ways in which this volume contributes to the more abstract thought on qualitative method, we must return to and re-iterate our incipient focus on the ways in which we *experience* methods and methodologies. The conception of this book was borne out of the editors' collective experiences and observations that a staggering majority of methods literature fails to offer these kinds of reflexive and often personal discussions. Similarly, in our mutual attempts as young scholars trying to publish our work, we found most journals we considered for submission had different (and often poorly explained) requirements regarding the discussion of method. Some journals required pages of description and more finite details, while others required reducing these discussions to but a paragraph in which to note the methods of data collection and analysis. This is understandable, of course, given the number of journals now available and the growing interdisciplinarity in much academic research.

Together, these two trends signalled to us the need for greater reflexive transparency in academic discussions about methodological decision making. To the benefit of students and those new to a particular method, most methods texts act as "how-tos"; while important, this approach does not allow for the space required to outline the tensions, challenges, debates, or questions raised while in the field or in "the thick" of a research project. As the title of this book suggests, it is important to demarginalize the voices of participants as well as those of committed researchers who embrace emotion and action in knowledge production. Research decisions do not end with selecting the method of data collection or the analytic strategy. They flourish in the field and continue to affect us as we make sense of our data and think back to and through particular happenings, conversations, and moments in our research journeys. It is our hope that critical social researchers take up this agenda in the future in their published works so as to engender greater dialogical exchange among authors. While it is clear that the ways in which we *experience methods* are contextually situated and subjective to the individual and the research project, noting similarities and divergences between experiences will only serve to foster a more well-informed methods consciousness in critical social researchers.

References

Barry, A., Osbourne, T., and Rose, N. (1993). Liberalism, Neoliberalism, and Governmentality: An Introduction. *Economy and Society 22*(3), 265-66.
Bourdieu, P. (2004). *Science of Science and Reflexivity.* Oxford: Polity Press.
Cheyfitz, E. (2009). The Corporate University, Academic Freedom and American Exceptionalism. *South Atlantic Quarterly 108*(4), 701-22.
Ezzy, D. (2005). *Qualitative Research Methods.* New York: Oxford University Press.

Guillemin, M., and Gillam, L. (2004). Ethics, Reflexivity, and "Ethically Important Moments" in Research. *Qualitative Inquiry* *10*(2), 261-80. doi:10.1177/1077800403262360.

Haggerty, K.D. (2004). Ethics Creep: Governing Social Science Research in the Name of Ethics. *Qualitative Sociology* *27*(4), 391-414.

Hesse-Biber, S.N., and Leavy, P. (2011). *The Practice of Qualitative Research* (2nd ed.). Los Angeles, CA: Sage Publications.

Lupton, D. (1999). *Risk*. New York: Routledge.

Pickett, B.L. (1996). Foucault and the Politics of Resistance. *Polity* *28*(4), 445-66.

Taylor, I., Walton, P., and Young, J. (1973). *The New Criminology: For a Social Theory of Deviance*. London: Routledge.

Contributors

CÉLINE BELLOT is an associate professor at the School of Social Work at the Université de Montréal. She works on homelessness policies and practices, with a particular focus on the ways they affect street youth, and on the relationships between social and penal policies. Céline also carries out evaluations of innovative interventions for marginalized populations that endorse their social participation and professional integration. Her projects are often carried out in partnership with different community groups.

CHRIS BRUCKERT is a full professor in the Department of Criminology at the University of Ottawa. Over the past twenty years, she has devoted much of her energy to examining diverse sectors of the sex industry. She has undertaken qualitative research into street-based sex work, erotic dance, in-call and out-call sex work, clients, male sex workers, and management of the sex industry. She endeavors to put the principles of committed scholarship into practice and is active in the sex worker rights movement.

DOROTHY E. CHUNN is a professor emerita of sociology at Simon Fraser University. She has collaborated on a number of SSHRC-funded research projects, including a study on the impact of (un)safe housing on the health of women in Vancouver's Downtown Eastside and a current study of the history of autonomous, unmarried motherhood in Canada. She is also co-leader of a team working in the thematic area "Criminal Justice System, Mental Health, and Substance Use" at the SFU Centre for the Study of

Gender, Social Disparities and Mental Health. Her publications include several coedited collections: *The Legal Tender of Gender: Welfare, Law, and the Regulation of Women's Poverty* (2010); *Reaction and Resistance: Feminism, Law, and Social Change* (2007); and *Women, Madness and the Law: A Feminist Reader* (2005).

COLLEEN ANNE DELL is a professor and research chair in substance abuse at the University of Saskatchewan in the Department of Sociology and School of Public Health. She is also a senior research associate with the Canadian Centre on Substance Abuse. Her research program is grounded in an empowering, community-based participatory approach and draws upon her extensive frontline work experience.

SHERYL C. FABIAN is a senior lecturer in the School of Criminology at Simon Fraser University. Her research interests include intimate partner violence, criminal harassment, the Canadian Indian Residential School system, and academic integrity. She regularly teaches courses in minorities and criminal justice, women and criminal justice, and qualitative research methods, as well as introductory criminology classes. She is actively involved in ongoing discussions and research with her Faculty of Arts and Social Sciences colleagues regarding the scholarship of teaching and learning and is a faculty mentor for the graduate student Certificate Program for University Teaching and Learning.

MARITZA FELICES-LUNA is an associate professor in the Department of Criminology at the University of Ottawa. Her research and teaching areas of interest are political violence, armed conflict, and qualitative methodology. She publishes in national and international journals in English, French, and Spanish. Her work has appeared in *Qualitative Sociology Review, Champ Pénal, Criminologie, Déviance et Société,* and the *Canadian Journal of Criminology and Criminal Justice.*

CATHERINE FILLMORE is a senior scholar and former associate professor in the Sociology Department at the University of Winnipeg. Her research practices involve participatory, community-based projects that focus on social justice issues. Her areas of study include self-harm among marginalized women and girls, healing approaches for addictions among First Nations women, and the potential of art mentorship projects as agents of change for disenfranchised youth.

SYLVIE FRIGON holds a PhD from the Institute of Criminology at the University of Cambridge. She is a professor in the Department of Criminology at the University of Ottawa where she has taught since 1993. In 2000, she coedited *Du corps des femmes: Contrôles, surveillances et résistances* (2000) and a special issue on women and confinement in Canada for the journal *Criminologie* titled "Femmes, enfermemement au Canada: Une décennie de réformes. Her books include *L'homicide conjugal au féminin: D'hier à aujourd'hui* (2003), *Écorchées* (2006), *Chairs incarcérées* (2009), and a children's novel, *Ariane et son secret* (2010), which was a finalist for the literary prize Le Droit and the Trillium Book Award. She edited a collection called *Corps suspect, corps déviant* (2012), and her new book, *De l'enfermement à l'envol: Rencontres littéraires,* was published in 2014.

STACEY HANNEM is an associate professor in the Department of Criminology at Wilfrid Laurier University in Brantford, Ontario. Her research interests focus on the effects of crime and incarceration on families and systemic inequalities in the justice system. She is coeditor (with Chris Bruckert) of *Stigma Revisited,* a collection of empirical research on stigma (2012), and has recently published in *Feminist Criminology, Canadian Journal of Law and Society, International Journal of Offender Therapy and Comparative Criminology,* and *Canadian Sociological Review.*

DAVE HOLMES is professor and university research chair in forensic nursing. He is also director of the School of Nursing and associate dean of the Faculty of Health Sciences at the University of Ottawa. Based on his CIHR- and SSHRC-funded research on risk management in the fields of public health and forensic nursing, Holmes has published over one hundred articles in peer-reviewed journals and thirty-two book chapters. He is coeditor of *Critical Interventions in the Ethics of Health Care* (2009), *Abjectly Boundless: Boundaries, Bodies and Health Care* (2010), and *(Re)Thinking Violence in Health Care Settings: A Critical Approach* (2011). He was appointed honorary visiting professor in Australia, the United States, and the United Kingdom.

JEAN DANIEL JACOB is associate professor at the School of Nursing, Faculty of Health Sciences, at the University of Ottawa. His SSHRC-funded doctoral research explored nursing practice in forensic psychiatry and, more precisely, how fear influences nurse-patient interactions in this environment. His research interests are situated within psychiatry/forensic psychiatry and include topics such as the violence, risk, ethics, and sociopolitical aspects of nursing practice. As a researcher, Jean Daniel is a member of the University Chair in

Forensic Nursing (2009-14). As a registered nurse, his professional practice is grounded in psychiatric emergency services as well as acute psychiatry.

JENNIFER M. KILTY is an associate professor in the Department of Criminology and the Social Science of Health at the University of Ottawa. Much of her research centres on the intersection between health and law, including analyses of self-harm, substance use, and, most recently, the criminalization of HIV nondisclosure. She has also examined the social construction of dangerous girls and women, feminist theory and method, and the gendered nature of incarceration. In addition to a number of book chapters, her research has been published in *Canadian Journal of Law and Society, Prison Journal, Feminism and Psychology, Qualitative Sociology Review,* the *International Review of Victimology, Criminologie, Contemporary Justice Review, Criminology and Public Policy,* and *Women and Criminal Justice.*

JOHN LOWMAN is a professor in the School of Criminology at Simon Fraser University. Since 1977, he has studied prostitution, prostitution law, and prostitution law enforcement in Canada. His publications include the *Vancouver Field Study of Prostitution* (1984), *Street Prostitution: Assessing the Impact of the Law, Vancouver* (1989), *Violence against Persons Who Prostitute in British Columbia* (with Laura Fraser, 1996), *Men Who Buy Sex* (with Chris Atchison and Laura Fraser, 1997), and *Beyond Decriminalization* (with Pivot Legal Society, 2006). He has given testimony before various parliamentary committees and public inquiries and appeared as an expert witness in *Bedford v. Canada.* Following a lengthy controversy over research confidentiality and a successful grievance against SFU for attempting to stop his research because he said he would refuse to become an informer if courts or police attempted to force him to reveal research participant identities, Lowman developed a keen interest in the ethics and law of research confidentiality. With colleague Ted Palys, he continues to criticize colleges, universities, and funding agencies that do not walk their talk when it comes to protecting research participants.

ROBERT MENZIES is a professor of sociology at Simon Fraser University. Since the 1980s, he has written extensively on the relationship between mental health and criminal justice, the history of madness and legal order, the sociology of criminology, and the psychiatric survivor movement. His book publications include *Survival of the Sanest: Order and Disorder in a Pre-Trial Psychiatric Clinic* (1989), *Regulating Lives: Historical Essays on the State, Society, the Individual, and the Law* (2002), *Contesting Canadian Citizenship: Historical Readings* (2002), *Women, Madness and the Law: A Feminist Reader* (2005), and *Mad Matters: A*

Critical Reader in Canadian Mad Studies (2013). Among other projects, he is currently preparing a book on "criminal insanity" in British Columbia history; and with colleagues across the country, he is involved in the "After the Asylum" project – a study of the deinstitutionalization movement and its legacy – along with the development of a research and education website called "historyofmadness" that documents past and present experiences of madness in Canada.

MELISSA MUNN is a professor at Okanagan College, where she teaches sociology and women's studies. She continues to prioritize her activism; in so doing, she relies heavily on the words shared with her during her PhD research to give men and women behind bars hope for the future. Her current research focuses on the history of the penal press in Canada, and she is finding the dilemmas of doing archival research easier to resolve than the ones she encountered while writing her dissertation.

RUSSEL D. OGDEN holds full-time faculty appointments in both the Department of Sociology and Department of Criminology at Kwantlen Polytechnic University in BC. He was a visiting professor in the Department of Criminology at the University of Ottawa in Winter 2014. Assisted death and ethical conduct in research are among Russel's primary academic interests, and his research has been published in a number of journals, including *Death Studies* and *Health Law in Canada*.

TED PALYS is a professor in the School of Criminology at Simon Fraser University. His areas of research and teaching include qualitative, quantitative, and mixed methods research; research ethics and especially the ethics and law of research confidentiality; and relations between Indigenous and non-Indigenous peoples in Canada and internationally. He is coauthor of *Research Decisions: Quantitative, Qualitative and Mixed Methods Approaches,* a research methods text used in universities and colleges across the country. Ted was one of six academics from across the country to be appointed to the Social Science and Humanities Working Committee on Research Ethics that advised the presidents of the granting agencies on ways the *Tri-Council Policy Statement* could better speak to the diversity of social science and humanities research – and especially more qualitative research. He is currently completing a manuscript with colleague John Lowman titled "Going the Distance: The Ethics and Law of Research Confidentiality," which considers the debate over confidentiality policy that began when a graduate student in his department became the first researcher in the country to be subpoenaed and asked to surrender confidential research information to a court.

AMÉLIE PERRON is an associate professor at the School of Nursing, Faculty of Health Sciences, University of Ottawa. Besides her doctoral research on psychiatric nursing care in a correctional setting, she has worked on many research projects in the fields of psychiatry and forensic psychiatry in Canada, France, and Australia. She received financial support from the Canadian Institutes of Health Research for her doctoral work. Her fields of interest include nursing care provided to captive and marginalized populations, psychiatric nursing, forensic psychiatry, power relationships between health care professionals and patients, as well as issues of discourse, subjectivity, risk, gender, and ethics. She also writes on issues relating to the sociopolitical aspects of nursing education, knowledge, and epistemology. Her clinical practice is grounded in community psychiatry and crisis intervention. She has published numerous articles in peer-reviewed journals and is the receiving editor for *Aporia*.

LAURA SHANTZ obtained a doctorate in criminology from the University of Ottawa in 2012. Her research interests include marginalized and criminalized older women, nonprofit organizations, and labour market information. Laura's research has been published in the *Canadian Journal of Law and Society, Aporia,* and the *International Journal of Prisoner Health.*

BERNARD ST-JACQUES has acted as a community organizer for the Network of Help to the Homeless and Indigent of Montreal (le Réseau d'aide aux personnes seules et itinérantes de Montréal, or RAPSIM) since 2002. RAPSIM coordinates communication between a number of different organizations that work to assist those with precarious and transient living situations in Montreal. He is responsible for files related to public space, social profiling, and justice. In 2003, he put in place an initiative to defend the individual and collective rights of marginalized people, l'Opération Droits Devant. In 2006, he co-founded the Rights First Clinic (Clinique Droits Devant), which provides information and accompaniment to transient people confronted with the judiciary.

MARIE-ÈVE SYLVESTRE is an associate professor at the Faculty of Law of the University of Ottawa, where she teaches criminal law, punishment theory, and legal theory from a critical and multidisciplinary perspective. Her research focuses on the punitive regulation of poverty and social conflicts related to the occupation of public spaces in Canada (including conflicts related to homelessness, sex work, drugs, and public protests). She has published extensively in international and Canadian journals in law, criminology, and geography. She received the 2011 Canadian Association of Law Teachers' Scholarly Paper Award for an article titled "Rethinking Criminal Responsibility for

Poor Offenders," published in the *McGill Law Journal,* as well as the 2011 Quebec Bar Foundation Award for best legal manuscript for an article on the penalization of homelessness in Canada, published in the *Canadian Journal of Law and Society.* In 2012, she was granted the Young Researcher of the Year Award for the arts, humanities, and social sciences at the University of Ottawa.

WILL C. VAN DEN HOONAARD is a long-standing field researcher whose current areas of teaching and research cover qualitative and ethnographic research, research ethics, the Baha'i community, and the world of mapmakers. He has served on the (Canadian) Interagency Advisory Panel on Research Ethics, SSHRC Standard Grants Committees, the Aid to Scholarly Publications Programme, and as book review editor of several journals. Before coming to the University of New Brunswick, he represented an international NGO at the United Nations in New York and conducted fieldwork in Iceland. His book *The Seduction of Ethics* was listed by *Hill Times* as one of the top one hundred Canadian nonfiction books in 2011. It also received honorable mention by the Charles H. Cooley Award Committee of the Society for the Study of Symbolic Interaction, 2012.

Index

Note: CAUT stands for Canadian Association of University Teachers; CSC, for Correctional Service of Canada; DTES, for the Downtown Eastside neighbourhood of Vancouver; IRSSA, for the Indian Residential Schools Settlement Agreement; "Kwantlen," for Kwantlen University College; "memo of understanding," for "memorandum of understanding"; OCAP, for ownership, control, access, possession (ethical principles); SFU, for Simon Fraser University; and *TCPS*, for the *Tri-Council Policy Statement: Ethical Conduct for Research Involving Humans.*

Inuvik, residential school hostels in, 252, 264*n*14

Jack, Michael, 278-79
Jenny, Claire: and creation of prison dance productions, 82-83, 88. *See also* Point Virgule (Parisian dance company), productions by, *and entry following*
Joliette Institution for Women (Quebec), Point Virgule/Les Productions C dance production at, 83, 84; participants' experiences of, 92, 98
Jones, Claudia, 290
Jooss, Kurt: *The Green Table* (dance production), 84
Journal of Prisoners on Prisons, 303*n*5, 319

Kingston Prison for Women, 138, 140
Kirby, Sandra, and Kate McKenna, 40; on "conceptual baggage" of feminism, 127, 140*n*3
Kleinman, Sherryl, and Martha A. Copp: *Emotions and Fieldwork*, 270, 271, 272, 279, 280, 281
knowledge/expertise of community members, recognition of, 185; in Aboriginal women's research, 45-47, 51, 52-58, 317; in defence of Montreal's homeless, 64-69; in research on sex workers, 315-16, 317, 319
Kwantlen Faculty Association (KFA): and Aboriginal Youth Justice Programme, 234-35; and Ogden case, 26, 27, 221, 239*n*11
Kwantlen University College (later Kwantlen Polytechnic University), 9, 216-38; and Aboriginal Youth Justice Programme, 222-36, 318-19; and first memo of understanding with SSHRC, 219-20, 225-26, 232, 233; and Ogden's assisted suicide research, 21-23, 35, 141*n*12, 212*n*3, 220-22, 332-33; and Ogden's unassisted suicide research, 7, 25, 29, 33, 222, 239*n*9; research mandate/funding eligibility of, 219-20; and second memo of understanding with SSHRC, 236-37, 239*n*16. *See also entry below;* Aboriginal Youth Justice Programme; suicide, assisted, Ogden's research on; suicide, unassisted, Ogden's observation of
Kwantlen University College ethics board: and Aboriginal Youth Justice Programme, 222-26, 227, 232-33, 234, 235, 236-37; and

Ogden's assisted suicide research, 21-23, 35, 141*n*12, 212*n*3, 220-22, 332-33; and Ogden's unassisted suicide research, 7, 25, 29, 222, 239*n*9

language, of correctional system: and "inmate" as euphemism for "prisoner," 136-37; as pseudofeminist, 134, 136, 138
language, positivist. *See* positivist cultural signals/terminology
Laurendeau, André, 212*n*5
Lee, Raymond M., 153-54, 155, 156, 164; and Claire Renzetti, 152, 153
Ligue des droits et libertés, 69
Lombroso, Cesare, and Guglielmo Ferrero, 118, 141*n*8
Lowman, John, 30, 321*n*11
Lowman, John, and Ted Palys: on institutional doublespeak/double standards, 9, 216-38; and Kwantlen Aboriginal Youth Justice Programme, 222-38, 240*n*25, 318-19, 323*n*33; and Ogden case, 220-22, 318

Mair, George B.: *How to Die with Dignity*, 19
Maison Tanguay (Montreal prison), Point Virgule dance production at, 83, 84; participants' experiences of, 96-97
Maplethorpe, Leena, 31-32
Marcie (woman whose unassisted suicide is observed by Ogden), 15-17, 25-35; and account of death, 16, 23-31; apparatus/procedure used by, 25-26, 27, 30-31; and cause of death, 16; and day of death, 27-31; and death as freedom, 16, 32; and earlier suicide attempt with mother, 25-26; executrix of, 30, 32; and forensic investigation of house, 32-33; health problems of, 16, 28; legal forms read by, 29-30; music chosen by, 30, 31; Ogden's connection/early meetings with, 25-26; and possible police entrapment, 30; suicide research by, 26
marginalized voices, in feminist research/analysis, 8, 104, 105, 113-19, 120, 331; and avoidance of certain issues/topics, 115; as drawn out through visual/performing arts, 120; and evolution from gender difference to sameness/equal treatment, 117-18; in historical/sociocultural context, 112-13, 116-19; historical studies of, 115-16, 117; and inequality of researcher-participant

acceptance of "fractional knowledge," 290-92; and activist/academic dilemma, 10, 286-87, 290, 295, 302, 303n11, 333; as committed scholarship, 288-90, 303n4; and comparison of taped interview to transcript, 296-97; and consideration of withdrawal from doctoral program, 300-1; and defence of analysis/presentation of research to participants, 300-2; and exercise of privilege in receiving/appropriating stories, 293-94; and exploitation of participants, 213n11, 289, 293-95; and insider/ outsider role, 286-87, 290-92; and interview process, 288-89, 290, 291-301, 303n3; and rarity of prison publications, 293, 303n5, 319, 323n34; and rejection of positivist stance, 287-88, 296-97; as story created from participants' stories, 293-94, 299-300; and team coding of text, 297-99; and truth(s), 288, 290, 294, 298, 300; unsuitability of ethnographic approach to, 288

prisons: dance as therapy in, 7-8, 81-100; in-reach workers in, 301-2, 303n10; publications of, 293, 303n5, 319, 323n34; research on nursing in, 8-9, 147-70; and researchers' access to women, 8, 125-40, 154; and resettlement success stories, 10, 286-302

Les Productions C, dance co-productions by, at Joliette Institution for Women (Quebec), 83, 84, 92, 98

Prostitutes of Ottawa-Gatineau Work, Educate and Resist (POWER), 322n20, 322n30; report published by, 310, 321n10

prostitution: Bruckert's former work in, 306-8, 310; in DTES, 222; prohibitionists against, 320n8; rights groups and, 322nn20-21, 322n30. See also Bruckert, Chris, as academic/activist and former sex industry worker, and entries following; sex workers

Public Hospital for the Insane (New Westminster, BC), 110

qualitative research, critical approaches to. See critical qualitative research, in social sciences

Quebec Bar (Barreau du Québec), 70, 71, 72, 74, 75

Quewezance, Marjorie, 249-50

Regan, Paulette: Unsettling the Settler Within: Indian Residential Schools, Truth Telling, and Reconciliation in Canada, 262

research ethics review boards (REBs). See ethics review boards, and entry following

Réseau juridique VIH/SIDA, 69

Réseau Solidarité Itinérance du Québec, 69

residential school claims, review of, 9, 245-62; as archival work, 247, 251, 253-54, 255, 261, 263n10; challenges of, 248, 251-55, 261-62; as emotion work, 252-57; and findings of ineligibility, 249-50, 251, 252; as means of responsibility/making amends, 247, 248, 253-57; positivist influence on, 248, 259-60; as work for traumatizer, 248, 253-54, 258, 259-60, 261. See also entries below; emotion, in reviewing residential school claims

residential school survivors: emotions of, 249-50, 256; government apology to, 245, 246; government responses to, 247-51; as intergenerational, 251, 260; research on claims by, 9, 246-47, 251-62; as told to "get over it," 260, 262; and Truth and Reconciliation Commission, 246, 260, 262

residential school survivors, government responses to, 247-51; alternative dispute resolution, 247, 248-49, 250; common experience payments, 249-50, 251, 252, 253-54, 258, 261, 263n9; and exclusion of certain schools/students, 249-51; independent assessment process, 250-51, 252, 254-57, 258, 259-60; litigation process, 247, 248-49, 250; settlement agreement (IRSSA), 245-46, 247-52, 258, 260, 262. See also specific topics

residential schools, 245; abuses at, 245, 248-51, 253, 256, 257, 260, 264n20; boarding vs day, 249-50, 260; churches and, 246, 249, 252, 255-56, 263n4; conditions/treatment of students in, 256-57; final closure of, 260; hostels as, 252, 263n12; in Northwest Territories/Nunavut, 251-52, 255, 256-57, 260, 263-64nn11-14; as run by Grey Nuns, 255-56

right to die: literature on, 16, 19-20; organizations advocating, 19, 20-23, 25, 28, 35-36

Right to Die Society of Canada, 20

rigour, 141n11, 167, 183-84, 188; in Aboriginal women's project, 52; and audit trail, 184,

Printed and bound in Canada by Friesens

Set in Syntax and Bembo by Artegraphica Design Co. Ltd.

Copy editor: Joanne Muzak

Proofreader: Jillian Soichet Gunn

Indexer: Cheryl Lemmens